COMMUNICATION AND TERRORISM

PUBLIC AND MEDIA RESPONSES TO 9/11

edited by

Bradley S. Greenberg
Michigan State University

HAMPTON PRESS, INC.
CRESSKILL, NEW JERSEY

Printed in the United States of America

Library of Congress Cataloging-in-Publication Data

Communication and terrorism : public and media responses to 9/11 / edited by Bradley S. Greenberg.
    p. cm. -- (The Hampton Press communication series)
  Includes bibliographical references and index.
  ISBN 1-57273-496-5 (c) -- ISBN 1-57273-497-3 (p)
  1. Terrorism and mass media--United States. 2. Terrorism in mass media. 3. September 11 Terrorist Attacks, 2001. I. Greenberg, Bradley S. II. Series.

P96.T472 U63 2003
303.6'25--dc21

2002032879

Hampton Press, Inc.
23 Broadway
Cresskill, NJ 07626

COMMUNICATION AND TERRORISM

PUBLIC AND MEDIA RESPONSES TO 9/11

THE HAMPTON PRESS COMMUNICATION SERIES
Mass Communication and Journalism
Lee B. Becker, supervisory editor

Magazine-Made America
   The Cultural Transformation of the Postwar Periodical
      David Abramhamson

It's Not Only Rock and Roll
   Popular Music in the Lives of Adolescents
      Peter G. Christensen and Donald F. Roberts

Global Media: Menace or Messiah? Revised Edition
      David Demers

American Heroes in the Media Age
      Susan J. Drucker and Robert S. Cathcart (eds.)

The Ultimate Assist
   The Relationship and Broadcast Strategies of the NBA and
   Television Networks,
      John A. Fortunato

Communication and Terrorism
   Public and Media Responses to 9/11
      Bradley S. Greenberg (ed.)

Media, Sex and the Adolescent
      Bradley S. Greenberg, Jane D. Brown, and
      Nancy L. Buerkel-Rothfuss

Community Media in the Information Age
      Nicholas W. Jankowski with Ole Prehn (eds).

China's Window on the World
   TV News, Social Knowledge and International Spectacles
      Tsan-Kuo Chang with Jian Wang and Yanru Chen

forthcoming

Journalism Education in Europe and North America
   An International Comparison   -
      Romy Fröhlich and Christina Holtz-Bacha (eds.)

Newspapers and Social Change
   Community Structure and Coverage of Critical Events
      John C. Pollock

Contents

Preface

In response to 9/11, communication researchers across this country and elsewhere geared up to examine responses to this unique tragedy. At Michigan State University, for example, a team convened on that Tuesday to design a questionnaire, obtain a random sample of telephone numbers, and seek approval from the human subjects board. On Wednesday, it trained interviewers, and interviewing began on Wednesday evening. Elsewhere, the pattern was similar. In yet other venues, ongoing studies offered researchers an opportunity to extend their investigation by adding a component that dealt with 9/11. But how to find out who was doing what, and speedily? That question was answered by the executive leadership of the International Communication Association, the National Communication Association, the Broadcast Education Association, and the Association for Education in Mass Communication and Journalism. They all authorized and facilitated an inquiry from me to their memberships, in which I volunteered to coordinate and share information about research in progress or planned. More than 100 responses led first to a mailing among all those who responded, identifying who was doing what, and then to a specially convened program on 9/11 research at the NCA Convention in Atlanta in November 2001.

Next, the plan for a coordinated volume of research emerged and this is the product of that plan. Seemingly, bringing together quality research on a single topic—especially this topic—makes similarities and differences more apparent. In addition, the structure of this volume is designed to encompass the full range of social communication issues relevant to the 9/11 events. To have them together in a single unit, rather than spread across a cornucopia of journals, should be useful for scholars who wish to continue to study such issues as news diffusion, media and interpersonal communication, and emotional, cognitive, and behavioral responses in times of crisis. Presumably, as well, this enhances our understanding of these phenomena in noncrisis periods.

The first set of chapters looks at the communication behaviors—mass and interpersonal—of varying segments of the public. The second set examines content dimensions of the news coverage, as well as non-news content symbols that played a role in our understanding and reactions to that day's events. Studies in the third section then deal with the nature and range of public responses, how children, young people and adults coped.

Studies done hurriedly may suffer from that haste. Although any study can be improved by giving more time to its development, not to have studied this news phenomenon for that reason would seem foolish. Furthermore, this volume has been selective in its presentation of research. The 20-plus studies represent the best of the research made known to us, and none declined the opportunity to participate. Additional, high-quality studies will become available, for it is unlikely that we captured all that was being done. New content analyses of the news coverage probably will emerge, for that is a unit of study that is not time-bound. In addition, many of the chapters should be considered an initial report, for some authors have much yet to do with their data; more definitive pieces will be forthcoming.

The goal was to have this collection available by 9/11/02. As I write this note in June 2002, it appears we will be close to that goal. If so, I have the authors to thank for producing readable and editable manuscripts and for responding to queries and critiques in short time frames. In addition, Lee Becker offered concise and useful suggestions as the book series editor. Moreover, Linda Hofschire edited a set of the manuscripts, proofed chapters and galleys, and contributed in other ways to this volume's development. However, without the efforts of Phyllis Kacos, this volume would not yet be completed. She reformatted all manuscripts to a common standard, compiled, checked and rechecked a master set of references, corresponded with every author to clarify questions from me, from her and from the publisher, and inserted all editing changes in all parts of the book.

All royalties from this volume have been designated for UNICEF. This book is dedicated to the men and women of the press who provided us with news and information on and about 9/11, and to all those people who permitted researchers to question them about their reactions to these events. It also is dedicated to my principal supporter, my wife Dee.

Bradley S. Greenberg

June, 2002

Introduction: Reflection on Media in Times of Crisis

Jack Wakshlag

It seems that every generation has its own example of the critical role of media during crises. For those older than me, it might have been Pearl Harbor. For me it was, "Where were you when you heard JFK was shot?" More recently it was the Challenger explosion or the assassinations of John Lennon or Bobby Kennedy. The World Trade Center disaster and the thousands of lives that were lost once again required the full resources of a "free press" to communicate the event and the enormity of its impact on those in this country and around the world. We all knew what happened within hours. A new name, Osama bin Laden, was added to the rogues' gallery of infamous leaders whose motivations seem incomprehensible. The media brought his image into our homes.

It was not all that long ago that communication research focused on the "hypodermic needle" effect. It was all about how media cause the masses to conform, or how media produce innumerable social ills. When there is an abundance of media sources, however, it is clearly more about what people do with media than what media do to people. And if anything distinguishes today's media environment from that of the past it is the abundance of choice, and not only in the United States. Newspapers, magazines, radio, television, and the latest communication innovation, the Internet, combine with interpersonal sources to create a huge matrix of communication options. As this volume goes to press, the typical American home has almost 100 channels of television to choose from. 24/7 news sources like CNN, Headline News, Fox News Channel, MSNBC and CNBC are relatively recent additions to the media scene, made possible by technological innovations leading to cable television and now DBS. Since the events of 9/11, people in the United States are watching more news from these news sources than from the three traditional broadcast networks. Technological innovation inevitably leads to ever-increasing choice by driving down the cost of entry.

Well over half the U.S. population can access the Internet from home. Perhaps most surprising is the relatively small amount of time people spent with the Internet during the crisis and its aftermath, and how television remained dominant—at least in terms of time spent. Every new medium has generated predictions of the demise of existing older forms. But radio did not make print obsolete, television did not make radio or movies obsolete, and the Internet has not driven down the use of television, even among the young. Actual measurement of time spent with television under normal circumstances has shown no decrease in viewing as a result of the Internet. The present volume indicates repeatedly and strongly that the same holds true under particularly extraordinary circumstances as well.

The needs served by media during this crisis do not appear to me to have changed from those observed in earlier crises—surveillance, correlation, cultural transmission seem as critical and real for a free society today as they did when they were first discussed more than half a century ago by Harold Lasswell (1948). But the abundance of choice has reinforced a paradigm shift in media effects research and that shift is strongly evidenced in this volume. Researchers who focus on media use and the resultant effects of selective exposure embark on a more difficult and complex journey than those who investigated media under the simple effects models prevalent not so long ago. But simple effects, simple explanations, and simple solutions, although appealing and often popular, can lead us down tragically distorted paths. It was the simplicity of conviction and righteousness, if anything, that generated the shockingly tragic events of 9/11.

The crucial role of media in world events today is seemingly taken for granted. It is amazing, that news organizations have the resources in place to do the kinds of things they do, as quickly as they do. The financial demands are immense and media companies do not bat an eye when it comes to spending what it takes to fulfill their critical roles in times of crisis. In these times it becomes apparent that news organizations and the media companies that support them are far more than what cynics call "businesses capturing eyeballs to sell to advertisers." Thousands of dedicated people working at news organizations around the world take their roles and responsibilities seriously, often putting themselves in harm's way, and some, unfortunately, lose their lives doing so. These organizations and the professionals who work there believe in what they do. The results of their efforts are what this book is about.

THE CHRONOLOGY OF 9/11

8:45 a.m. A highjacked passenger jet, American Airlines Flight 11 from Boston, crashes into the north tower of the World Trade Center.

9:03 a.m. A second hijacked airliner, United Airlines Flight 175 from Boston, crashes into the south tower of the World Trade Center.

9:30 a.m. President Bush, speaking in Sarasota, Florida, says the country has suffered an "apparent terrorist attack."

9:43 a.m. American Airlines Flight 77 crashes into the Pentagon.

10:05 a.m. The south tower of the World Trade Center collapses.

10:10 a.m. A portion of the Pentagon collapses.

10:10 a.m. United Airlines Flight 93, also hijacked, crashes southeast of Pittsburgh.

10:28 a.m. The World Trade Center's north tower collapses.

1:04 p.m. Bush says, "Make no mistake, the United States will hunt down and punish those responsible for these cowardly acts."

4:00 p.m. CNN reports that U.S. officials say there are "good indications" that Saudi militant Osama bin Laden is involved in the attacks.

4:10 p.m. Building 7 of the World Trade Center complex is reported on fire.

5:20 p.m. The 47-story Building 7 of the World Trade Center collapses.

5:30 p.m. CNN reports that U.S. officials say the plane that crashed in Pennsylvania could have been headed for one of three possible targets: Camp David, the White House, or the U.S. Capitol building.

7:45 p.m. The New York Police Department says that at least 78 officers are missing. The city also says that as many as half of the first 400 firefighters on the scene were killed.

8:30 p.m. President Bush addresses the nation, saying the U.S. government will make no distinction between the terrorists who committed the acts and those who harbor them.

10:49 p.m. CNN reports that Attorney General Ashcroft told members of Congress that there were three to five hijackers on each plane armed only with knives.

THE CHRONOLOGY AFTER 9/11

Sept. 20   Tom Ridge is appointed Homeland Security Director.

Sept. 22-30   Five individuals become ill or find lesions, later attributed to anthrax.

Oct. 4   Authorities confirm that photo editor of *The Sun* has inhalation anthrax.

Oct. 5   *The Sun* photo editor dies; first U.S. death from inhaled anthrax since 1976.

Oct. 7   The U.S. begins its military strike in Kabul, Kandahar, and Jalalabad.

Oct. 14   Letter with anthrax opened in Sen. Daschle's office.

Oct. 17   House shuts down for testing. Senate stays open two more days.

Oct. 21-22   Two postal workers die from anthrax.

Oct. 23   Anthrax found in White House post room at military base.

Oct. 27   U.S. jets bombard Taliban front line.

Oct. 29   President increases immigration safeguards.

Oct. 31   Anthrax claims fourth victim.

Nov. 12   Alliance moves into abandoned Kabul.

Nov. 16   Positive test for anthrax in letter to U.S. Sen. Leahy.

Nov. 21   94-year-old dies from inhalation anthrax.

Dec. 6   Kandahar, last major Taliban stronghold, falls.

Dec. 21   Interim Afghan government sworn in.

Feb. 5   Funding for bioterrorism increased by 319%.

Mar. 7   Fierce battle for al-Qaeda stronghold in eastern Afghanistan.

Apr. 17   Exiled king returns to Kabul.

May 30   Recovery efforts at World Trade Center are officially ended.

May 31   This book goes to publisher.

Authors

Sandra J. Ball-Rokeach is Professor in the Annenberg School for Communication, University of Southern California

Michael Basil is Associate Professor in the Faculty of Management, University of Lethbridge

Robert Baukus is Associate Professor and Head in the Department of Advertising and Public Relations, Pennsylvania State University

Mike Beardsley is Greer Chair in the Department of Mass Communication at Louisiana State University

Mihai Bocarnea is Assistant Professor in the Center for Leadership Studies, Regent University

Aaron Boyson is a doctoral student in the Department of Communication at Michigan State University

Constance Bridges is a doctoral student in the School of Communication Studies at Bowling Green State University

William J. Brown is Professor and Dean of the College of Communication and The Arts, Regent University

Xiaomei Cai is Assistant Professor in the Department of Communication at the University of Delaware

Scott Caplan is Assistant Professor in the Department of Communication at the University of Delaware

Elisia Cohen is a doctoral candidate in the Annenberg School for Communication, University of Southern California

Steven R. Corman is Professor in the Hugh Downs School of Human Communication at Arizona State University

John Courtright is Professor and Chair in the Department of Communication at the University of Delaware

Bernhard Debatin is Associate Professor in the E.W. Scripps School of Journalism at Ohio University

Kevin Dooley is Professor in the Departments of Management and Industrial Engineering at Arizona State University

Margaret Finucane is Assistant Professor in the Department of Communication at John Carroll University

Colleen Fitzpatrick is Assistant Professor in the Department of Information and Computing Sciences at the University of Wisconsin-Green Bay

Yuki Fujioka is Assistant Professor in the Department of Communication at Georgia State University

Jack Glascock is Assistant Professor in the Department of Communication at Illinois State University

Bradley Greenberg is University Distinguished Professor in the Departments of Telecommunication and Communication at Michigan State University

Thomas Hargrove is a reporter for the Scripps-Howard News Service, Washington, DC

William B. Hart is Assistant Professor in the Department of Communication and Theatre Arts at Old Dominion University

Frances J. Hassencahl is Assistant Professor in the Department of Communication and Theatre Arts at Old Dominion University

Cynthia Hoffner is Associate Professor in the Department of Communication at Georgia State University

Linda Hofschire is a doctoral candidate in the Mass Media Program at Michigan State University

Cary Horvath is Assistant Professor in the Department of Communication at Slippery Rock University

Amal Ibrahim is a doctoral student in the Department of Communication at Georgia State University

Steve Jones is Professor and Head in the Department of Communication, University of Illinois at Chicago

Joo-Young Jung is a doctoral candidate in the Annenberg School for Communication, University of Southern California

Yong-Chan Kim is a doctoral candidate in the Annenberg School for Communication, University of Southern California

Ken Lachlan is a doctoral student in the Department of Communication at Michigan State University

Jennifer Lambe is Assistant Professor in the Department of Communication at the University of Delaware

Xigen Li is Assistant Professor in the Manship School of Mass Communication at Louisiana State University

Laura F. Lindsay is Professor in the Manship School of Mass Communication at Louisiana State University

Kirsten Mogensen is Associate Professor in the Department of Communication, Journalism and Computer Science at Roskilde University, Denmark.

Emily Moyer is a graduate student in the Department of Communication at Michigan State University

Elisabeth Noelle-Neumann is founder and director of the Allensbach Institute for Opinion Research, and Professor Emeritus of Communications Research at the University of Mainz

Crystal L. Park is Assistant Professor in the Department of Psychology at the University of Connecticut

Jay Perkins is Associate Professor in the Department of Mass Communication at Louisiana State University

Elizabeth Perse is Professor in the Department of Communication at the University of Delaware

Katherine Pieper is an undergraduate research assistant in the Department of Communication at Michigan State University

Donnalyn Pompper is Associate Professor in the Department of Communication at Florida State University

Lee Rainie is Director of the Pew Internet & American Life Project

Jutta Roeser is Visiting Professor in the Department of Communication at the University of Bochum

Susan Royer is Vice President, Education and Research, Sesame Workshop

Thomas E. Ruggiero is Assistant Professor in the Department of Communication at the University of Texas at El Paso

Wendy Samter is Associate Professor in the Department of Communication at the University of Delaware

Gudrun Schaefer is junior researcher at the Essen Institute for Gender Studies, University of Essen

Kelly Schmitt is Assistant Director of Sesame Street Research at the Sesame Workshop

Matthew W. Seeger is Associate Professor in the Department of Communication at Wayne State University

Timothy Sellnow is Professor in the Department of Communication at North Dakota State University

Nancy Signorielli is Professor in the Department of Communication at the University of Delaware

Stacy Smith is Assistant Professor in the Department of Communication at Michigan State University

Leslie Snyder is Associate Professor in the Department of Communication Sciences at the University of Connecticut.

Melissa Spirek is Associate Professor in the School of Communication Studies at Bowling Green State University

Guido Stempel is Distinguished Professor Emeritus in the E. W. Scripps School of Journalism, Ohio University

Mary M. Step is Instructor in the Department of Communication Science, Case Western Reserve University

Susan Strohm is Senior Lecturer in the Department of Advertising and Public Relations, Pennsylvania State University

Robert R. Ulmer is Associate Professor in the Department of Speech Communication at the University of Arkansas at Little Rock

Steven Vennette is a doctoral candidate in the Department of Communication at North Dakota State University

Jack Wakshlag is Chief Research Officer, Turner Broadcasting System, Inc.

Jiali Ye is a doctoral student in the Department of Communication at Georgia State University

I

DIFFUSION OF NEWS
OF THE ATTACKS,
COMMUNICATION PATTERNS,
AND RELATED BEHAVIORS

1

Diffusion, Media Use and Interpersonal Communication Behaviors

Bradley S. Greenberg
Linda Hofschire
Ken Lachlan
Michigan State University

Why should one do another news diffusion study? What is different about the dissemination of this news event that hasn't already been documented?

Several answers are available. First, the literature on news diffusion does not yet account for the presence of the Internet (Rogers, 2000). The dominance of television in the diffusion of *major* news events for the past 40 years is attributable to its increasing availability and immediacy (Rosengren, 1987). At the same time, defining a news event as major often stems from a strong television presence. There is difficulty in ascribing the origin of major to some events that may have achieved that distinction because of television coverage (e.g., OJ Simpson and Gary Condit) rather than from other criteria. We could, then, be on the verge of the Internet's presence as a strong news disseminator for major, breaking events. Online newspapers and 24-hour news sites afford new opportunities for competition with traditional television news coverage. Streaming video of live news events has become more available through one's computer and is likely to be more generally accessible. Thus, by examining the role of the Internet in the news dissemination of the 9/11 terrorism incidents in comparison with traditional media, we can provide at least a baseline for the role it may play in the future, if not today.

Second, news diffusion research points to the increasing importance of interpersonal sources of information for initial awareness of catastrophic events, followed by the subsequent inundation of interpersonal channels. In crisis, we try to inform others about what is happening or just want to talk with someone (Gantz & Greenberg, 1993; Greenberg, 1964a, 1964b). At the same time, there are Internet options that parallel more traditional interpersonal channels (e.g., chatrooms, bulletin boards, and e-mail). Are these being used to supplement traditional interpersonal channels or are they primary outlets of interpersonal communication? Furthermore, diffusion research has not yet clarified the relative significance of interpersonal and mass communication channels in informing us or dealing with our anxieties. This chapter attempts to enrich the diffusion paradigm with measures of exposure to both mass media and interpersonal sources in combination with measures of affective and attitudinal responses to a catastrophic news event.

Third, social researchers are not immune to significant news events. We cope in different ways. Some lament, some seek solace with others, some seek solitude. Still others organize research studies of the phenomenon. This fits within a tradition of "firehouse" research (Deutschmann & Danielson, 1960) that has been especially applied to the diffusion of news arena. Unexpected events, most typically associated with the deaths of celebrated individuals or the deaths of large groups of unfamiliar individuals, prime the media pump and create myriad research opportunities (Rogers, 2000). To document the nature of responses to the first significant terrorist successes on our mainland provides, at the least, important historic information. Moreover, given the unprecedented magnitude of the event, one anticipates an especially strong need for information and exceptionally intense responses among respondents.

The rate of diffusion of news of extraordinary events has been shown to be largely a function of two factors—the media emphasis given the event and situational variables, especially the time of day at which the event occurs. In addition, for lesser news events, the salience of the particular event for the individual plays a prominent role (Greenberg, Brinton, & Farr, 1965; Greenberg, Gantz, & Brand, in press). These are not mutually exclusive factors. When the media, notably television, focus all their reporters, cameras, and energy on a single event, its rapid diffusion to the vast majority of the population is a foregone conclusion. Essentially, total coverage by television and radio remove all options to not being made aware. If you've initially missed the direct media experience, someone will tell you in person, by phone or, perhaps by e-mail. But you do have to be awake. Events occurring before 9 a.m. EST will have a different diffusion pattern on the West Coast, as evidenced elsewhere in this volume (Greenberg, Cohen, & Li, 1993). Events occurring after midnight will have a different rate of diffusion on the East Coast. On both coasts, everyone will eventually know (amount), but some sooner than others (rate). Although salience is a critical factor for events of lesser importance, a full-blown media effort overpowers disinterest. Many so-called major news events in which we have little interest become known to us because we cannot avoid media reports.

For these reasons, we are drawn to study the most catastrophic news event to occur on U.S. soil.

METHODS

Sample and Procedure

Due to the time-sensitive nature of the study, interviews were conducted by telephone. A local market research firm produced a set of randomly generated phone numbers for the greater Lansing, Michigan, area. On September 12, 2001 undergraduate students at Michigan State University were trained to conduct interviews. Each received an independent sample of 40 phone numbers and was instructed to complete four interviews, preferably with two men and two women.

Phone interviews were done on the evenings of September 12 and 13. A response rate of 63% yielded 314 interviews with respondents 18 and older. Of the respondents, 48% were in their 30s or younger, 31% in their 40s and 50s, and 21% were over 60. In terms of gender, 43% were male and 57% were female. Respondents included 83% White, 6% Black, 3% Hispanic, 3% Asian, 5% other. Almost all the respondents had completed high school, and 40% completed college. Wednesday interviews yielded 49% of the respondents with the remainder on Thursday. The questionnaire averaged 12 to 15 minutes to complete.

Instrument

A 72-item questionnaire assessed the respondents' media and interpersonal activity, attitudes toward the media, opinions about the attacks, and more general feelings and concerns about the events.

First Response. Several questions pertained to how people initially found out about the attacks and their immediate reactions. These included the specific time they first found out, from what source they found out, which channel (if television) and from whom (if another person), their location, their first emotional reactions, and the first thing they did after finding out.

Media Use. For Tuesday and Wednesday, respondents reported how many hours they watched the news on television, listened to the news on the radio, and visited Web sites for information about the attacks. For a subsequent analysis, the television and radio exposure measures were summed into a media use index. Because only half the sample was asked about Thursday media use, those questions were excluded from that index.

Questions addressed respondents' specific preferences and perceptions of different media and networks. For Tuesday and Wednesday, interviewees were asked what specific TV networks they watched, which network they thought did the best job of covering the attack, and why they thought that network did the best job.

Internet Use. Respondents who visited Web sites for information about the attacks were probed with questions addressing their Web site preferences and opinions (i.e., which Web sites they visited, which one they spent the most time on, and why they chose that site most often). Additional questions about Internet use determined if the respondents had used any chatrooms or bulletin boards for information, whether they had sent or received any e-mail about the attacks, and if they had had any difficulty accessing online sources.

Interpersonal Interactions. Questions about interpersonal communication behaviors after the attacks were a prime focus. Respondents indicated if they told others after they found out about the attacks, if they were the first to inform them, how many people they told, how many people informed them, and how many people they spoke to about the attacks on both Tuesday and Wednesday. The last three of these interaction items were summed into an index to represent their total interpersonal interactions about the attacks on the day of and the day after the attacks.

Responses to Reports of the Attacks. Questions were posed to evaluate citizen reactions to the attacks. Five items determined the extent of worry respondents experienced after their exposure to the news coverage. The content of the items included worrying that someone they know might be a victim, that another major attack would take place soon, that it would personally affect them, that it would affect their family, and worrying about flying on commercial airplanes in the future. A three-point scale, *very worried, somewhat worried,* or *not worried* was used. The items were summed into an aggregate scale of individual worry.

A second set of response questions addressed the physical symptoms respondents experienced after the attacks. They were asked if they felt nervous or tense since the attacks, dazed or numb, if they had cried, had trouble sleeping, or felt like not eating. These five items were summed to create an index of total reported physical symptoms.

How they dealt with their worries and symptoms was examined by asking what they were doing to cope with the events. Nine categorical responses emerged: talking, praying, giving something, keeping informed, living a normal life, thinking, physical activity, nothing, and other.

Media Accuracy. Respondents assessed the accuracy of media information—television reporting on Tuesday and Wednesday, and radio reporting in general—on a three-point scale with these labels, *not very accurate, somewhat accurate,* and *very accurate.* The three items were summed into a scale of perceived media accuracy.

Press Limits. A set of three statements focused on the issue of limiting the amount and content of media information in order to protect national security:

- Television should not show scenes of rejoicing about these attacks from other countries.
- Media in the United States provide too much information that terrorists can use.
- Media criticism of our weaknesses to terrorist attacks makes us even more vulnerable.

Response categories offered were *agree, not sure,* or *disagree.* The three responses were summed into an index of approval of limiting news information.

Impressions. Open-ended items tapped respondent perceptions of two other issues. The first asked what picture of the attacks
on the World Trade Centers (WTCs) stood out strongest in their
minds. The categories developed from responses to this question
included the plane hitting the second tower, the tower falling, debris
or smoke, people jumping, police/firemen, death/bodies, and the
Pentagon. A second item asked who they felt was responsible for the
attacks. The categories that formed were Osama bin Laden, a
terrorist group, Islam/Muslims/Arabs, Palestine, Iraq/Hussein, and
the U.S. government.

RESULTS

Communication Behaviors

Mass Media Use. Fully 50% the respondents reported first
hearing the news from someone else, whereas 33% said they first
heard from television, and 15% from the radio. The information
diffused extremely rapidly: By 9 a.m. on Tuesday, September 11 (15
minutes after the attacks began), 22% said they knew of the attacks;
by 10 a.m., 82% knew; and by 11 a.m., 94% said they knew. It took
barely more than 2 hours for diffusion to be comprehensive.

Television was the most important source of information
across the first 3 days, as stipulated by 88% of the sample and 8%
said the radio was most important. One half watched television for 7
or more hours on Tuesday; this dropped to 19% on Wednesday and to
11% on Thursday. By contrast, radio was ignored by 48% on Tuesday,
and listened to for less than 1 hour by an additional 28%.

The perceived accuracy of television increased with daily
coverage: 58% thought the information they got on Tuesday was *very
accurate*; This percentage rose to 71% on Wednesday and 80% on
Thursday. Initial doubts gave way to strong credence.

Internet Use. Three fourths said they had access to the
Internet. Of these, only 35% visited any Web sites for information
about the attack, and only 2% said the Internet was their most
valuable information source. The CNN Web site was most often
sought. On Tuesday, 56% of those with Internet access spent 30
minutes or less online and 78% spent 1 hour or less. On Wednesday,
the comparative figures were 68% and 83%. No one spent any time in
Internet chatrooms discussing the attack. Only 8% spent any time on
Internet message boards. In contrast, 68% received e-mail and 48%

sent e-mail about the attack. 72% believed the information they received online was *very accurate*.

Interpersonal Communication. Two thirds of the sample tried to tell someone else about the events right after they began. Half of this subset told one or two others, but 14% told nine or more what was happening. Three out of every five talked with at least nine others on Tuesday and nearly half talked with at least nine others on Wednesday.

Reactions to the Attacks

Nearly half the respondents (44%) reported crying in the first day or two after the terrorist attacks on New York and Washington, DC. More than half said they felt more nervous or tense, and more than half felt dazed or numb as they watched the tragedy unfold. At least one in five said they had trouble sleeping and did not feel like eating.

Disbelief and surprise were the first reactions from 66% of the sample. In terms of coping with these events, one in five talked with friends, relatives and others; one in five said they prayed; one in six said they tried to keep informed; and 8% said they did nothing.

One third of the sample was *very worried* about flying on commercial airlines. One fifth each were *very worried* that there would be another major attack in the near future, that it would affect their own life personally, and that it would affect their own family, and 15% believed that someone they knew might be a victim.

Respondents were asked what images from the attacks were strongest in their minds. Three out of five respondents said it was the plane hitting the tower and 15% said it was the towers falling. Sixty-five percent specifically said that Osama bin Laden was responsible for the attacks, 13% said Islam or Arabs, and 8% said a terrorist group. Half the respondents felt that U.S. media provide too much information that terrorists can use.

Demographic Differences

The data were next analyzed to determine whether there were differences in the diffusion pattern and reactions to the attacks based on the gender, education, and age of the sample members.

Gender. More women (66%) than men (53%) said they did not want to watch any more of the WTC coverage ($p < .02$). Women expressed more worry than men about the after effects of the terrorism attacks ($p < .001$). The scale average for women ($M = 9.6$ on the 5–15-point scale) meant they were *somewhat worried*, and the men (M = 8.6) less so. Of five possible stress symptoms, women reported more of them (M = 2.2) after the attacks than the men (M = 1.6), (p < .001). Men and women were equally likely to cope by talking with others and by seeking information. However, the women were much more likely to resort to prayer; 32% of the women and 14% of the men said they used prayer to cope (p < .001).

The women believed there should be more restraints on the press coverage than the men (p < .01). Their average score (M = 2.0) reflected a *not sure* posture as to whether the media provided too much information that might be of use to the terrorists, whereas the average score for men (M = 1.8) was less in favor of such restraints.

More men (42%) than women (30%) visited Web sites (p < .07), and men reported spending more time online on Wednesday (1.7 hours) than women (1.3 hours; p < .06). Tuesday time online was the same for both men and women (1.7 hours), so it was the women who shortened their online time on the second day.

Education. The sample was divided into three groups based on level of education: Those with a high school degree or less (22%), those with some college training (38%), and those with a college degree (40%). There were systematic differences by education in the initial diffusion of information about the WTC tragedy.

Television was cited by 48%, 38%, and 25% of the groups from lowest to highest educational level as the first source of information. Another person as the first source of information was cited by 38%, 48%, and 59% of the groups (p < .03). This pattern is largely a function of variation in where the education groups were located at the time the initial information was made available. More than half of the two lower education groups was at home, as compared with 33% of the college-educated group. One fourth of the high school graduates, 31% of those with some college, and 43% of the college graduates were at work (p < .01). In turn, the college graduates were most likely to learn from a co-worker (49%), as compared to those with some college (31%) and those with high school educations (19%; p < .02).

Coping by talking with others varied by education. Only 12% of high school respondents coped by talking with others compared with 30% in the two higher education categories (p < .02). Additionally, those with the least education were most in favor of greater restraints on the press (p < .03).

Age. Five age groups were created from the sample: under 30 (28%), 30s (21%), 40s (17%), 50s (14%), and older (21%). Initial diffusion of information varied substantially across these age groups.

Those in their 40s and older were more likely to find out about the WTC attacks before 10 a.m. (87%) than those in their 30s (81%) or younger (71%; $p < .04$). Television as a first source of information was more prominent for those in their 50s (41%) and older (55%), whereas other persons were more likely the first source for those in their 40s and younger (60%; $p < .01$). Co-workers (50%) more likely told those in their 30s through 50s; the older learned more so from relatives (44% ; $p < .01$). Those in their 40s and younger more often said that surprise was their first response (37%) as compared with the older groups (15%; $p < .01$).

Tuesday television time was highest in the two oldest age groups at nearly 7 hours ($p < .02$). This same age pattern difference in viewing was reported for Wednesday television time as well, although at a lower level of 4.7 hours for the two oldest age groups ($p < .01$). The least radio listening (less than 1 hour) occurred in the 60s and older group ($p < .01$). The oldest age group talked with the fewest others on Tuesday (5.4 people) and Wednesday (4.3), whereas all other age groups averaged 7.7 conversations with others on Tuesday and 6.6 on Wednesday. Both differences are significant at $p < .01$. When asked if they tried to tell anyone else after they first found out, 70% of those in their 30s or younger said yes, compared with 60% in their 40s and 60+s, and 46% in their 50s ($p < .07$).

The index of worry was highest in the youngest age group (9.9) and lowest among the oldest (8.7; $p < .03$). However, stress symptoms followed a curvilinear pattern. From youngest to oldest, the average number of symptoms reported (of five possible) was 1.8, 2.1, 2.3, 2.0, and 1.5 ($p < .03$). Talking with others as a means of coping with the news also had a curvilinear relationship with age; 26% of those under 40, 42% of those in their 40s, 27% in their 50s, and 9% of those 60 and over said they coped by talking with others ($p < .001$).

Perceived media accuracy and the perceived need for press restraints also tended to increase with age. Both these findings were marginally significant ($p < .10$).

Indices of Media and Interpersonal Activity

An index of total media use was constructed by summing hours spent with television and radio on Tuesday and Wednesday. A parallel index of interpersonal communication activity was constructed by summing how many people they told, how many people informed them, and how many people they spoke to about the attacks on both Tuesday and Wednesday.

The simple correlation between these two indices was trivial and insignificant (.08), suggesting that different subsets emphasize one form of communication more so than the other. In terms of demography, there were no consistent media exposure index differences in terms of gender, age or education. The interpersonal communication index also did not vary by gender or by education, but did so by age. The youngest (30s and younger) had the most interpersonal contacts, averaging 12, and the oldest (60s+) had the fewest, averaging 7, $p < .001$.

More importantly, the relative merits of media exposure and interpersonal communication (IP) were examined as means of dealing with personal concerns and physiological responses to news of the attacks, as well as perceptions about media restraints and media accuracy. A median split across both indices yielded sufficient cases across four conditions; 67 in the high media/high IP group, 108 in the low media/low IP group, 85 in the high media/low IP, and 52 in the low media/high IP group.

Table 1.1 answers these research questions. In the first section, respondents with the highest exposure to media and to interpersonal communication reported the largest number of physiological symptoms, whereas those with the lowest exposure to media and to other people reported the smallest number. Both main effects—for media and for interpersonal activity—were significant ($p < .001$); the interaction was not.

The second section of Table 1.1 demonstrates that interpersonal communication was significantly related to worries about the aftermath of the attacks ($p < .001$), but that media exposure was not.

In the third section, neither index was independently related to stronger requests for press restrictions, but there is a significant interaction ($p < .06$). The locus of the interaction was such that those high in both media exposure and interpersonal contacts were most likely to want additional restrictions on the press. The final section shows that neither media exposure nor interpersonal exposure was related to assessments of media accuracy.

Given the independent effects of media and interpersonal communication on the physiological symptoms and personal concerns of the respondents, we calculated their composite relationship with these outcomes. The multiple correlation of the two indices with symptoms (.272) maintained the significance of both of them; the beta for interpersonal activity was .220 ($p < .001$) and for media activity was .134 ($p < .02$). The multiple correlation with personal worries (.245) was based primarily on the index of interpersonal communication activity, whose beta was .222 ($p < .001$). Multiple

Table 1.1. Correlates of Mass Media and Interpersonal Communication About the Attacks

Physiological Responses to the Attacks					
	Mean	*SD*		*F*	*p<*
High Media/High IP	2.60	1.49	Media	6.78	.01
High Media/Low IP	1.85	1.40	IP	11.96	.001
Low Media/High IP	1.98	1.48	Media X IP	1.44	ns
Low Media/Low IP	1.62	1.19			

Worries About the Aftermath of the Attacks					
	Mean	*SD*		*F*	*p<*
High Media/High IP	10.04	2.88	Media	.88	ns
High Media/Low IP	8.88	2.43	IP	11.31	.001
Low Media/High IP	9.59	2.22	Media X IP	.34	ns
Low Media/Low IP	8.78	2.42			

Support for Press Restrictions					
	Mean	*SD*		*F*	*p<*
High Media/High IP	2.11	.64	Media	1.85	ns
High Media/Low IP	1.90	.64	IP	1.06	ns
Low Media/High IP	1.87	.60	Media X IP	3.46	.06
Low Media/Low IP	1.94	.61			

Perceived Media Accuracy					
	Mean	*SD*		*F*	*p<*
High Media/High IP	2.59	.44	Media	.67	ns
High Media/Low IP	2.64	.41	IP	.03	ns
Low Media/High IP	2.59	.42	Media X IP	.68	ns
Low Media/Low IP	2.56	.47			

correlations for perceived press accuracy and curbs on the press were not significant.

DISCUSSION

Returning to the motives for conducting this research, the Internet was clearly not a significant force in the initial or subsequent diffusion during the first 3 days of this event. Three reasons can be suggested. First, this was a highly visual activity. Much of what we knew and learned occurred from what we could see, and television was bringing it to us live. Until the Internet can do the same and do it as quickly and as well, it cannot compete with the immediacy of television. That technical convergence with video is not yet widely available, but is expected to be. The Internet can better serve as a diffuser of niche news/information that is salient to smaller segments of the population (e.g., the outcomes of national fencing competitions or election results from small nations). Second, the Internet was not prepared to handle this event. In our sample of Internet users, 38% reported serious difficulty accessing the Web sites of interest to them. The sudden inundation of access attempts went well beyond the limits of the receiving sites. That technological limitation has now been fixed at some sites. The third reason is more speculative. Does the Internet have sufficient credibility and does it yet provide the comfort or peace of mind that users now obtain from television in time of crisis?

This was another unique news event whose diffusion was examined. Old habits are difficult to change. Over the past 40 years, the American public has come to rely on television, not only for the news elements, but also for some explanation or closure that comforts them in difficult moments (e.g., the death of Princess Diana, the *Challenger* explosion, a cluster of assassinations). Often, that explanation originates with a recognizable and trusted newsperson. If and when the Internet is judged to provide this more personal element, it may become a larger factor in news diffusion.

At the same time, non-news components of the Internet mesh with our interests in the role of interpersonal communication. There was little use of bulletin boards and chatrooms; perhaps greater activity ensues later in the diffusion sequence. There was large-scale use of e-mail moving both to and from our respondents at the outset of this event. Receiving initial information from others was as strong as has ever been demonstrated. Talking about the event was a dominating activity for the three days examined in this study.

Interpersonal communication was abundant and singularly focused. Yet, the purposes it served are unclear. One of most significant findings here, and the most perplexing, is that the amount of interpersonal activity was *positively* related to greater worry about the personal implications of the terrorist activity and *positively* related to the number of physiological anxiety symptoms. The conundrum of a cross-section survey does not permit us to disentangle which came first, these negative outcomes or the build-up of interpersonal contacts. Perhaps they reciprocate, feeding into each other. What is clear, is that the interpersonal communication did not ease these anxieties, at least within the first three days. There is obvious need for more intensive study of the role(s) played by personal contact in crisis situations that are initiated by mass media coverage of news events.

Linking media use and interpersonal activity also raises new questions. First, they are not associated with each other, as identified both by the correlation analysis and the subdivision of the sample by median splits on both factors. A post hoc analysis of these four groups offers some information as to their demographic differences, but little insight into attitudinal or behavioral differences. Although there are no gender differences among the groups, there are substantial differences in age for each of the two communication components. Those low in interpersonal activity are older than those high in interpersonal communication ($p < .001$), and those high in mass media activity are older than those low ($p < .02$). In addition, there is a tendency for the more educated to be less active with mass media ($p < .08$).

Furthermore, the media use linkage to outcome responses from this news event is weaker than the interpersonal connection. Media use has a weaker, positive relationship to physiological anxiety symptoms and it is unrelated to level of concern or to the perceptions of media accuracy or potential press limitations. The most basic effects of media exposure in this sample are the identification of the chief villain and the omnipotence of the image of the plane(s) crashing into the WTC.

Findings here also demonstrate an interplay between demographic and situational variables that has not been made clear in prior studies. The key situational variable is time of day, which impacts not only on the rate and amount of diffusion, but also on where you are, when you find out, how you find out, and so on. These situational characteristics are tied directly into life-cycle characteristics (e.g., whether you work or not) which in turn are functions of demographics (e.g., age, education). Thus, understanding the rate and amount of diffusion as well as subsequent interpersonal behaviors may be managed better within a paradigm that overlays traditional diffusion of news variables onto the antecedents provided by demography and life cycle.

The third motive in doing this research was as a personal and professional means of coping with the shocks. Designing the study with colleagues, getting input from others, training interviewers, badgering the human subjects committee for overnight approval, and quickly processing the data all furthered the end of "doing something about it."

2

Media Sources of Information and Attitudes About Terrorism

Guido H. Stempel III
E.W. Scripps School of Journalism
Thomas Hargrove
Scripps Howard News Service

Coverage of the terrorist attack of September 11, 2001, was as pervasive as that of such major events as the Kennedy assassination and the *Challenger* disaster. It differed in that it was so long lasting. The Kennedy assassination lasted a long weekend culminating with the funeral. The arrest on Friday and the shooting on Sunday of Lee Harvey Oswald ended that aspect of the story.

The *Challenger* explosion also was followed by investigation of its causes and of the space program, but the coverage lessened. There was no villain to be pursued. However, the terrorist attacks of September 11 gave way to the war on terrorism and the pursuit of bin Laden, and the volume of coverage remained abnormally high even for a major news story long after the attack. Surveys by the Pew Center showed that 74% of respondents said they were following the story closely in mid-September, and 78% said they were following it closely in mid-October (Pew Research Center, 2001). These figures were much higher than figures for other recent major news stories, and this suggests that media use also increased. If so, it reversed recent trends. Studies of media use in 1995 and 1999 by the Scripps Survey Center at Ohio University and the Scripps Howard News Service found significant declines in watching both local and network television news and in newspaper reading (Stempel, Hargrove, & Bernt, 2000).

There is reason then to look at what happened to media use not only immediately after the terrorist attack, but for the weeks that followed as the event remained at a high level of newsworthiness. There is also reason to look at whether this coverage had any impact of the response of Americans to the terrorist attack and the war on terrorism. This study, made in the last 12 days of October 2001, addresses those concerns.

RESEARCH QUESTIONS

We sought to determine the following about media use, attitudes about terrorism, and the relation between the two. Our research questions were as follows:

RQ1: How did people find out about the terrorist attacks?
RQ2: How have the terrorist attacks affected people's lives?
RQ3: How extensive was media use at the time of this survey, some 5 to 6 weeks after the terrorist attack?
RQ4: What sources were helpful in informing people about terrorism?
RQ5: What relation is there between media use and reactions to terrorism?
RQ6: What is the relation between various demographic variables, media use, and response to terrorism?

METHOD

Scripps Howard News Service and the E.W. Scripps School of Journalism at Ohio University conducted a national survey from October 20 to October 31, 2001. Interviewing was conducted by telephone from the Scripps Survey center at Ohio University. Interviewers were trained by one of the authors and by the Center director, using a questionnaire we developed and pretested.

Telephone numbers were selected by computer randomly, and household respondents were selected randomly. In each household, we asked to interview the person (18 or older) who would be the next to celebrate a birthday. We completed 1,131 interviews. Respondents were asked how they had first learned of the terrorist attack, which sources of information about terrorism had been useful, how many days in the previous week they had used television news, radio news, daily newspapers, and the Internet, whether their sense of safety had been lessened, whether they had made changes in their personal lives, and how likely they felt it was that they would be the victim of a terrorist attack.

Of the respondents, 54% were female and 46% male. The median age was 42, and 28% of the respondents were older than 55. The median income was $43,000. Of the respondents, 92% were high school graduates and 37% were college graduates. Seventy-two percent were White, 13% were African American, 10% were Hispanic, 2% were Asian, and 3% gave some other answer. The sample thus reasonably well matched census figures except that our respondents were more highly educated.

RESULTS

About 50% of the respondents found out about the attacks from television, as Table 2.1 shows, but as Table 2.2 indicates, television became the dominant source of information. We cross tabulated by four regions: northeast, New England and mid-Atlantic states; south, everything south of the Mason-Dixon line plus Arkansas and Texas; midwest, states west of Pennsylvania up to and including the tier that runs from North Dakota to Oklahoma; and west, everything

Table 2.1. How People Found out About Terrorist Attacks by Sex, in Percent

		Men	Women	Total
Television		47	52	49
Friends and Co-workers		21	20	21
Radio		19	15	17
Family member		9	9	9
Other, don't know		4	4	4
	N	516	615	1,131

Table 2.2. How People Found Out About Terrorist Attack by Region, in Percent

	Neast	South	Midwest	West
Television	42	55	47	52
Friends and Co-workers	28	20	22	13
Radio	17	12	21	19
Family members	7	9	7	12
Don't know, other	6	4	2	3

Note. Differences 9% or larger are statistically significant.

west of the midwest and Texas. Of the respondents from the Northeast, many of whom were at work when the terrorist attacks occurred, only 42% found out about the attack from television, whereas 28% found out from friends and co-workers (Table 2.2). In the south, 55% found out from television; in the west, 52% found out from television; and in the midwest, 47% found out from television. Of those who were employed full time, only 44% found out from television, whereas 24% found out from friends. Of those not working full time, 59% found out from television and 14% from friends and co-workers. Yet, as Table 2.3 indicates, nearly everybody considered television news a useful source and more than two thirds considered it the most useful source. However, two thirds of the respondents considered family and friends, radio news, and daily newspapers useful sources, which indicates that people were by no means depending on a single source. The average person found more than three sources useful. Women were considerably more likely than men to find TV news most useful. Men were more likely than women to find newspapers, radio news, and Internet most useful. It also is noted that the Internet was considered a useful and/or most useful source by far fewer people, which reflects less use of the Internet.

For radio news and newspapers, the useful figure was about the same as the average daily use figure, and for TV news, the useful figure was higher than the average daily use. Table 2.4 also shows that use of media by men and women was nearly equal except for the Internet, where use by men was substantially higher. Sixty percent had used the Internet at least once in the week before the interview. Given that and the availability in the workplace, the Internet-use figures are surprisingly low. On the other hand, the figures for television use and television reliance are among the highest ever found in any survey. Nearly 68% of the respondents indicated they had watched TV news every day in the previous week. All these

Table 2.3. Useful Sources of Information About Terrorism by Sex, in Percent

	Useful			Most Useful		
	Men	Women	Total	Men	Women	Total
TV news	90	92	91	64	74	69
Family and friends	66	71	69	2	2	2
Radio news	69	67	68	9	8	8
Daily newspapers	64	69	67	12	8	10
Internet	41	33	37	8	5	6
News magazines	28	33	30	3	1	2
Other, don't know				1	2	1

Note. Differences 6% or larger are statistically significant

Table 2.4. Average Daily News Media Use by Sex, in Percent

	Male	Female	Total
TV news	81	84	83
Radio news	60	60	60
Daily newspaper	62	60	61
Internet	44*	33*	38

* $p < .01$

figures are significantly higher than those from the 1999 study, and the television figures are significantly higher than those from the 1995 study (Stempel et al., 2000).

Table 2.5 shows patterns of use by age that are essentially the same as in our 1999 survey (Stempel et al., 2000). For both newspapers and TV news, use increased with age. For radio news, it was the 35- to 54-year-old age group that had highest use, and for the Internet, use was highest for the youngest group. However, the gap between 18- to 34-year-old and 35- to 55-year-old Internet users was much less—only 5% compared to 9% in the 1999 study.

We asked three questions about respondent's reaction to terrorism:

Table 2.5. Average Daily Media Use by Age, in Percent

		18–34	35–54	55+
TV news		74	82	93
Radio news		59	64	55
Daily newspaper		48	57	78
Internet		46	41	24
	N	325	448	324

Note. Differences 7% or larger are statistically significant

1. How much has the September 11th attack altered your sense of safety? Would you say personally you feel much less safe, somewhat less safe, or has it had no effect?
2. Did the terrorist attack cause you to make any changes in your personal life?
3. How likely do you think it is that you personally will be the victim of a terrorist attack—*very likely, somewhat likely* or *not likely*?

Table 2.6 shows that women felt more threatened by terrorism than men did. Nearly two thirds of women respondents felt less safe and slightly more than one third felt they were very likely or somewhat likely to be the victim of a terrorist attack. More women than men also indicated they had made changes in their personal life as a result of the terrorist attacks.

Table 2.6. Reaction to Terrorism by Sex, in Percent

	Men	Women	All
Feel much less or somewhat less safe	47	64	56
Made changes in personal life	26	32	29
Very likely or somewhat likely I'll be victim of terrorist attack	23	36	30

Note. Differences 6% or larger are statistically significant.

Table 2.7 indicates that 18- to 34-year-old respondents felt less safe than older respondents. The difference between the youngest and oldest groups was 17%. Those aged 18 to 34 also were more likely to feel they might be a victim of terrorist attack. Yet it was the respondents aged 35 to 54 who were most likely to have made a change in their life.

It comes as no surprise that, as Table 2.8 indicates, residents of big cities took the terrorism threat more seriously than people elsewhere. However, the margins were small, with 60% of those in big cities feeling less safe compared to 54% of those in rural areas. Most striking, however, is that those who live in suburbs were less likely to feel they were likely to be a victim of attack than those who live in small cities or rural areas. Only 25% of those in suburbs felt in danger of attack. For those who live in big cities, small cities, or rural areas, more than half of those who felt less safe said they were at least somewhat likely to be victims of attack.

Table 2.7. Reaction to Terrorism by Age, in Percent

	18–34	35–54	55+
Feel less safe or somewhat less safe	62	59	45
Made changes in personal life	30	36	18
Very likely or somewhat likely I'll be victim of terrorist attack	34	30	26

Note. Differences 7% or larger are statistically significant.

Table 2.8. Reaction to Terrorism by Where Respondent Lives, in Percent

	Big City	Small City	Suburb	Rural Area
Feel less safe	60	54	57	54
Made changes in personal life	35	27	27	23
Very likely or somewhat likely I'll be victim of terrorist attack	35	29	25	29
N	364	290	230	225

Note. Differences 7% or larger are statistically significant.

Given the concerns people had and given the volume of media coverage, was that media coverage helpful? Table 2.9 shows almost an even three-way split, with 33% saying the media coverage made them feel worse, 31% saying it made them feel better, and 27% saying media coverage had no effect. Note that women were more likely than men to say both that media coverage helped and that it made them feel worse, and much less likely to say media coverage had no effect. Media coverage, therefore, had more perceived impact on women. Given evidence in Table 2.3 that shows media use by men and women nearly equal except for the Internet, the difference in reactions to that coverage is difficult to explain.

Those findings are addressed in Table 2.10. How did the perceived effects of media coverage relate to feelings of being unsafe or vulnerable to attack? Those who said media coverage helped them to cope were slightly less likely to feel unsafe and were much less likely to feel they would be a victim of terrorist attack, by comparison

Table 2.9. Reaction to Media Coverage by Sex, in Percent

		Men	Women	All
Media coverage helped me cope		26	36	31
Media coverage made me feel worse		29	36	33
Media coverage had no effect		37	19	27
Don't know, no answer		9	9	9
	N	516	615	1,131

$\chi^2 = 47.29$ $df = 3$, $p < .001$

Table 2.10. Impact of Media Coverage on Reaction to Terrorism, in Percent

	Feel Less Safe	Made Changes in Life	Feel I Am Likely Victim
Media coverage helped me cope	60	32	32
Media coverage made me feel worse	65	33	43
Media coverage had no effect	45	18	29
Don't know, no answer	28	35	15

Note. Differences 6% or larger are statistically significant.

with those who felt worse from the media coverage. Yet, the most striking result here is that those who said media coverage had no effect were less likely to feel unsafe, make changes, or feel vulnerable to terrorism than both those who said either the media made things worse or that the media helped them.

Table 2.11 addresses whether the impact of media coverage is related to media use. Use of newspapers, television, and radio news was greater for those who said media coverage helped them cope. Those figures indicate a slight positive effect of media use. However, for the Internet the opposite was true. Those who said media coverage made them feel worse were more likely to use the Internet than people who said media coverage made them feel better.

We also looked to see if education and income were related to the impact of media use. On education we found only that those with postgraduate education were more likely to say that media coverage helped them cope. For income, there was one striking difference. Of those with incomes greater than $80,000, 41% said media helped them to cope, which was 10% higher than the overall figure.

DISCUSSION

Television has been the dominant medium in informing the American people about the terrorist attacks and the war on terrorism that followed. Nine out of 10 Americans in our study found TV news coverage useful. Yet, other media played a part. Two thirds of those interviewed found newspapers and radio as useful news sources. The average American obtained useful information from three media sources. Yet, television was considered the most useful source by 69%.

Table 2.11. Impact of Media Coverage by Average Daily Media Use, in Percent

	Newspaper	TV	Radio	Internet
Media coverage helped me cope	64[c]	85	62	35
Media coverage made me feel worse	58[ab]	80	57	40
Media coverage had no effect	47[abc]	82	60	40
Other, don't know	68[ab]	85	63	29

Note. Figures with same superscript are significantly different from each other.

We found a high level of media use in this survey, which was conducted some 5 to 6 weeks after the terrorist attack. Average daily use of television news was 83%, which was slightly more than 20% higher than the daily use of newspapers and radio news. The Internet was far behind at 38%. Americans over age 55 reported even higher use of both television news and newspapers with average daily use of television news at 93% and of newspapers 78%. Only one fourth of those over age 55 used the Internet on the average day.

The terrorist attacks made more than half our respondents feel less safe and made more than one fourth feel they might be victims of terrorist attacks. Women were more concerned than men, and people between 18 and 34 years of age were more concerned than respondents 35 or older. Those who lived in big cities were more concerned than those who lived in small cities, suburbs, or rural areas. Surprisingly, those who lived in suburbs were less likely to feel they might be the victims of attack than those who lived in small cities or rural areas. Despite these concerns, less than half the respondents reported they had made changes in their personal lives.

Media coverage was perceived to be helpful by some people and not by others. There was about an even three-way split among those who said it helped, those who said it made things worse and those who said it had no effect. Media use of those who said media helped them cope was higher than media use of those who said media coverage made them feel worse.

In short, Americans turned to the media in large numbers not only at the time of the terrorist attack, but for weeks later. For many Americans, the media were a help in a time of unprecedented national crisis.

3

Internet Use and the Terror Attacks

Steve Jones
University of Illinois at Chicago
Lee Rainie
Pew Internet & American Life Project

The mission of the Pew Internet and American Life Project is to explore the impact of the Internet on everyday life in the United States. On September 11, 2001, terror attacks changed everyday life for at least the foreseeable future, and the Pew Internet & American Life Project sought to determine what changes, if any, the attacks brought about online.

In the days immediately following the September 11 terror strikes on the World Trade Center (WTC) and the Pentagon, the number of Americans online dropped. But there were signs by the end of September that online activity was returning to the usual levels. At the same time, there were conspicuously more Internet users getting news online after September 11 than in previous periods. More than two thirds of Internet users (69%) have used the Web to get news and information related to the attacks and their aftermath. Half of Internet users—more than 53 million people—

have gotten some kind of news about the attacks online. Many online Americans have used the Internet to stay "on alert" for news developments by subscribing to e-mail news updates and getting newscasts streamed to their desktops. Among those watching developments most carefully online are 33% of Internet users who have gotten information about the financial markets because of their concern about the economic impact of the terror strikes against America.

Perhaps the most significant development online after the attacks has been the outpouring of grief, prayerful communication, information dissemination through e-mail, and political commentary. Nearly three quarters of Internet users (72%) used e-mail in some way related to the events—to display their patriotism, contact family and friends to discuss events, reconnect with long-lost friends, discuss the fate of the victims, and share news.

Other Internet users went to chatrooms, bulletin boards, commemorative sites, and other online communities to describe their anguish, offer consoling words, broadcast their patriotism, and debate, even yell at times, about the meaning of the September 11 events. One third of Internet users read or posted material in chatrooms, bulletin boards, or other online forums and most report that those virtual commons were civil, rational places. Another 12% visited commemorative sites, many of which were created in the wake of the attack.

It is important to stress that for all of the online activity that focused on the terror assaults, this was not a breakthrough moment for use of the Internet compared to other technologies. There was not a flight to new technologies from television as a news source or from the phone as a communications tool. Indeed, there was very heavy reliance on television and the telephone even among the most committed and active Internet users.

METHODOLOGY

The findings presented here come from two periods of phone survey work by Princeton Survey Research Associates for the Pew Internet & American Life Project. Both periods were before the U.S. attacks on the Taliban regime in Afghanistan. The first survey took place from September 12 through September 19, 2001, involving 2,039 adults, some 1,138 of whom were Internet users. In that sample, the margin of error is +/- 2% for the entire sample and +/- 3% for answers based only on responses from Internet users at a 95% confidence level. The second survey took place from September 20 through October 1, 2001, involving 1,029 aged adults 18 and over in the continental United States, 525 of whom were Internet users. The margin of error on the entire sample from this survey is +/- 4% and +/- 6% for Internet users at a 95% confidence level.

The sample for this survey was a random digit sample of telephone numbers selected from telephone exchanges in the continental United States. The random digit aspect of the sample is used to avoid "listing" bias. It also provides representation of both listed and unlisted numbers (including not-yet-listed numbers) by random generation of the last two digits of telephone numbers selected on the basis of their area code, telephone exchange, and bank number.

Nonresponse in telephone interviews produces some known biases in survey-derived estimates because participation tends to vary for different subgroups of the population, and these subgroups are likely to vary also on questions of substantive interest. In order to compensate for these known biases, the sample data are weighted in analysis. The demographic weighting parameters are derived from a special analysis of the most recently available Census Bureau's Current Population Survey (2000). This analysis produces population parameters for the demographic characteristics of adults aged 18 or older, living in households that contain a telephone. These parameters are then compared with the sample characteristics to construct sample weights. The weights are derived using an iterative technique that simultaneously balances the distribution of all weighting parameters.

This chapter also cites Web traffic data from comScore Networks, a research firm in Reston, Virginia, that provides Internet usage intelligence to the public and private sectors based on a sample of 1.5 million global opt-in users. Those data were made available at the request of the Pew Internet & American Life Project. More information about comScore Network's methodology can be found at http://www.comscore.com/about/about_method.htm.

FINDINGS

In the first days after the attacks, the nation was engrossed in the rescue effort, the investigation, and the stories that emerged from the attacks themselves. Many people stayed offline as they watched television, talked to family and friends, and tried to absorb the enormity of what happened. It also meant that much of the "normal" online activity dropped significantly as people flocked to news sites, sent and read e-mail related to the attacks, and visited virtual places where they could discuss the events and their aftermath.

In the days after the attacks the number of people using the Internet fell, as did the number of people sending and reading e-mail

As illustrated in Table 3.1, the overall size of the online population of Americans was down in the days following the attacks. Even the heaviest users of the Internet, the truly "wired" cohort who usually go online every day and have plenty of Internet experience, were not quite as fervid in their use of the Internet in the days just after the attacks. These highly wired Americans were also using e-mail somewhat less than they had. On any given day in February, the survey shows that 82% of the heaviest users of the Internet send or read e-mail. That compares to the 71% who were sending and reading e-mail on an average day during the period from September 12–19.

These survey findings were confirmed by network traffic data shared with us by ComScore Networks (Table 3.2). The traffic data provided additional illustration that although overall Internet usage was down, those using the Internet were using it heavily.

Table 3.1. Internet Use the Week of 9/11/2001

Types of Use	Percent of Internet Users
Went online "yesterday" for any purpose	51%
Send or read e-mail	42%
Get news online	27%
Seeking hobby information	10%
Browsing for fun	13%
Doing work-related research	13%
Seeking medical or health information	3%
Buying products	2%

Table 3.2. ComScore Networks Measures of Internet Traffic (in Billions)

	September 4–5	September 11–12	Change
Number of site visits	1	3.4	240%
Number of page downloads	5.7	21.2	272%
Number of minutes spent online	8.2	28.3	245%

The number of sites visited by those online more than doubled, as did the number of page downloads and the number of minutes spent online by those who had logged on. What were these heaviest Internet users doing online?

THE RISE IN INTERNET USE FOR GETTING NEWS

Many more people than usual were seeking news on the Internet in the days following the attacks. Our surveys showed that on an average day online in the 4 weeks before the terror attacks, 22% of Internet users got some kind of news, often by chancing upon news items while browsing or doing other activities on Web sites. As shown in Table 3.3, on the day of the attacks, 28% of Internet users were getting news online and in the period of September 12-19, 27% were getting news on a typical day.

Overall, 50% of Internet users, or about 53 million people, went online looking for news about the attacks and the aftermath at some point in the first 3 weeks following the attacks. More men than women were news consumers. Some 57% of men with Internet access sought news about the attacks and the aftermath, compared to 43% of women. (By comparison, women were more likely than men to have sent e-mails to family and friends about the assaults.)

Web-based news was not the only news-seeking activity. Some 15% of online Americans got audio or video versions of newscasts streamed to their desktops and 7% of Internet users signed up to get e-mail news alerts about the continuing coverage of

Table 3.3. News Gathering By Internet Users. (September 20–October 1, 2002)

Type of news gathered	% of Internet users
News about the attacks	50%
Information about financial markets	33%
Information about Osama bin Laden	23%
Information about Afghanistan	21%
Download pictures of American flag	19%
Information about victims or survivors of the attack	15%
Check flight status of someone's plane	13%
Information about Islam	13%
Visit commemorative Web site	12%

the attacks and their aftermath. Of Internet users, 25% reported that they were multitasking on 9/11 by having the television or radio on while they were surfing the Web or sending e-mail.

Generally, people went to specific news sites with which they were familiar; 58% of online Americans reporting doing that. But more than 25% of Internet users turned to search engines to dig for information; 23% used search engines to track down the information they wanted; and 6% reported that they went to both search engines and news sites to get material.

News seeking had an international dimension. ComScore Networks reported that there was a huge spike in international traffic to U.S.-based news Web sites in the days immediately following the attacks. The data show that on September 11 and 12 unique visitor traffic to cnn.com grew 680% to 11.7 million, msnbc.com grew 236% to 9.5 million, cbs.com grew 819% to 1.7 million, nytimes.com grew 206% to 1.7 million, washingtonpost.com grew 225% to 1.2 million, and usatoday.com grew 174% to 1.1 million.

MORE NEWS IS GOOD NEWS—BUT NOT RIGHT AWAY

Although there was heavy use of the Internet for news seeking, the Internet has not supplanted traditional news media. Indeed, for most Americans, the Internet was not a primary resource for news, nor for reaching out to others, after the terror attacks, but it was a helpful supplement to television and the telephone and many found it useful for expressing their sorrow and anger at the assault.

Our surveys showed that Americans, including Internet users, relied mostly on television for their news and the phone primarily for their communication needs in the days following the terror attacks. For many online Americans, the Internet played a useful supplemental role as a communications tool—through their use of e-mail and instant messaging—and as a news source.

Asked how they first heard of the attacks, about two thirds of respondents said they heard from traditional electronic news media sources, television and radio, and about one third heard about the assaults in conversation (see Table 3.4). The figure for conversational exchange is remarkably high, possibly because the attacks took place during a time of day when many people were just congregating at their workplaces and probably because of the magnitude of the news. Half of those who heard about the attacks from other people heard it in a telephone call and it is likely the case that those conversations

Table 3.4. How People First Heard of the 9/11 Terror Attacks. (September 12–19, 2002)

How information was learned	Percent of Internet Users	
Television		44%
Network news	20%	
Cable channel	11%	
Local news	9%	
Don't know/no response	4%	
Talking with others		31%
Face to face	16%	
On the telephone	15%	
Radio		22%
Don't know/no response		2%
Internet		1%

were shocked exchanges of the news. It was the kind of story that many people needed to bring to others' attention and needed to discuss with others immediately.

The general picture of many Internet users that emerges in the aftermath of the attacks is that they were aggressively using all the means at their disposal to get information about the unfolding crisis and to make contact with their networks of loved ones and friends. That meant they were anxious consumers of TV news and restless users of the telephone even more than they used online tools.

Eighty-one percent of respondents said they got most of their information from television and about 11% said they got most of their information from radio. There was no statistical difference between Internet users and nonusers in reliance on TV news or radio. Only 3% of Internet users say they got most of their information about the attacks and the aftermath from the Internet.

It can be said that our results are not all "good news" for news on the Internet. In the aftermath of the attacks, there were considerably fewer Internet users going online to do things unrelated to getting news or using e-mail to communicate. Compared to our tracking survey findings from before September 11, 2001, the number of people getting hobby news on a typical day between September 12–19 dropped by 50%; the number buying products online fell by 50%; the number seeking medical information fell by 40%; the number browsing the Web just for fun dropped by 35%; and the number doing work-related research fell by 24%.

There were important distinctions to note among different types of Internet users. Veteran Internet users went online with much higher intensity than newcomers in the aftermath of the terror attacks. Those with 1 year or less experience were the most likely to log on less frequently right after the attacks.

This is part of a larger trend we have observed in tracking surveys. Many newcomers report that they were using the Internet less than they were 6 months before the attacks because of time constraints. In contrast, many veterans reported they were using the Internet more than they did 6 months earlier because they were doing more research, and in all likelihood devoted their time online to gathering news and information about the terror attacks.

DID THE INTERNET "WORK" ON SEPTEMBER 11?

Nearly one third of the respondents (32%) said they had some trouble placing phone calls on September 11 and about one eighth of these respondents turned to the Internet to make contact with loved ones and friends. At the same time, 43% of Internet users said they had at least some trouble accessing the Web sites they wanted to consult for news about the attacks—15% of Internet users said they had a lot of trouble in the first hours of the attacks getting to a Web site. Of those who had difficulty, 40% eventually reached the site they had tried at first and another 39% went to other sites to seek information about the attacks. But one fifth of those who had trouble simply gave up on using the Internet to get news about the attacks.

Most Internet users in this survey reported overall satisfaction with the Internet's performance. Almost half of Internet users (47%) said they got at least some modest benefit from their use of online tools. Some 34% said the Internet helped them learn more about what was going on and 30% said it helped them connect to people they needed to reach. Men were more likely than women to cite the benefits of the Internet for getting news about the terror strikes.

However, most of the people who actually used the Internet to gather news and contact key family and friends had a positive assessment of the role of the Internet in their lives following September 11. For instance, 67% of those who went to news Web sites for material about the attacks said the Internet helped them learn more about what was going on. Similarly, 70% of those who e-mailed family members about the attack and 66% of those who e-mailed friends said the Internet helped them connect with people they needed to reach. And more than three quarters of those who got news online or exchanged e-mail about the assaults gave some kind of positive assessment about the role of the Internet in their communication or information gathering.

THE INTERNET: A PERSON-TO-PERSON MEDIUM IN A TIME OF CRISIS?

The need to talk to others, be they friends or family (or, in some cases, strangers) proved very strong after 9/11. In the 2 days after the terror attack, three quarters of all respondents (74%) reached out to loved ones and friends by phone or via the Internet. Some 82% of Internet users used the phone or e-mail to make contact with people they care about in the first 48 hours after the attacks.

On the day of the attacks, 51% of respondents phoned family members and 40% phoned friends about the crisis. About one quarter (23%) tried to reach someone to try to find out if she or he was safe. Interestingly, Internet users were more likely than non-Internet users to be using the phone to reach out to potential victims. On that same day, 15% of respondents who were Internet users sent e-mail about the crisis to family members and 12% sent e-mail to friends. (More women than men did this.)

Additionally, 6% of Internet users sent instant messages to someone on 9/11, which is about the same level of use of instant messaging that takes place online on any given day judging from previous surveys.

The need to reach out to others was not confined to friends and family. One third of those who use the Internet reported posting or reading comments about the attacks on a Web site bulletin board, in a chatroom, or on an e-mail list. The vast majority reported reading material, rather than contributing to a discussion. Some 28% of Internet users were observers on the virtual commons; 5% of Internet users said they posted to such communities. Men were more likely than women to have written something in such places; and young Internet users (those aged 18–29) were by far the most likely to have read what others had said. In the 48 hours immediately following the attacks, 13% of Internet users "attended" virtual meetings or participated in virtual communities by reading or posting comments in chatrooms, online bulletin boards, or e-mail listservs. That is substantially greater than normal. On a typical day, only 4% of online Americans visit chatrooms.

Asked about the discussions that were unfolding on bulletin boards, in chatrooms, and on e-mail lists, 46% said the postings were mostly about how the United States should respond to the attacks, 22% said they were mostly about consoling those who were sad about the attacks, and 19% said they were mostly about ways people can personally deal with the attacks in their communities.

Asked to judge the nature of the online discussions they observed, most said they were civil rather than angry (57% vs. 37%), rational rather than heated (72% vs. 21%), and focused mostly on people rather than policy (57% vs. 35%).

E-mail exchanges were common, too, and the types of e-mail sent and received as reported by respondents are summarized in Table 3.5.

CONCLUSION: SIGNS OF A RETURN TO NORMALCY ONLINE

In the final week of September, a period before the U.S. retaliatory bombing began against the Taliban regime in Afghanistan, patterns of Internet use were returning to average levels. In the period between September 20 and October 1, 57% of Internet users were online on a typical day. The number of people sending and reading e-mail on any given day had risen, too, as shown in Table 3.6. Between September 20 and October 1, 49% of Internet users were handling e-mail.

The most striking finding from this survey is that more Internet users continued to get news online after 9/11 than had done so before the attacks. It is well possible that the Internet has "proven itself" as a useful medium for supplementary information, particularly as an extension of television news. Whereas television

Table 3.5. E-Mail Use Immediately After 9/11

Type of e-mail Use	Percent of Internet Users
Received or sent patriotic material by e-mail.	46%
Received or sent e-mail prayer requests.	33%
Received or sent e-mail messages of consolation.	25%
Sent e-mails to people they had not spoken to in years.	12%
Received e-mails from people they had not spoken to in several years.	10%
Received or sent accounts of survivors or victims.	9%
Received e-mail with hate material in it.	2%

Table 3.6. Internet Use Before, During and After 9/11

Activity	August 13–September 10	September 12–19	September 20–October 1
Went online "yesterday" for any purpose	56%	51%	57%
Send or read e-mail	51%	42%	49%
Get news online	22%	27%	26%
Seeking hobby information	20%	10%	22%
Browsing for fun	20%	13%	20%
Doing work-related research	17%	13%	15%
Seeking medical or health information	5%	3%	5%
Buying products	4%	2%	2%

tends to provide breadth of information relatively quickly, particularly in times of crisis, the Internet provides a means by which people can "dig deep" for the specifics of the news. Although it is far beyond the scope of this chapter's ability to confirm it, one may speculate that we have witnessed another version of media "convergence" insofar as media users, long savvy now to the strengths and weaknesses of particular media, are using multiple media to meet their information needs.

4

Public Perceptions of Media Functions at the Beginning of the War on Terrorism

Elizabeth Perse
Nancy Signorielli
John Courtright
Wendy Samter
Scott Caplan
Jennifer Lambe
Xiaomei Cai
University of Delaware

Scholars have recognized for more than 50 years that mass communication is a functional activity of a healthy society. Building on Lasswell's (1948) writings, Wright (1986) pointed out that the mass media serve four valuable functions: surveillance, correlation, socialization, and entertainment. *Surveillance* marks the information role of the mass media. Through *surveillance,* mass communication alerts the public and monitors government activities. *Correlation* is the explanation function in the mass media, in which they educate and highlight important issues and events. Socialization connects people to the larger society, increasing social cohesion. *Entertainment* is the rest, relaxation, and tension reduction function of the mass media.

These functions are important in all societies and at all times—in peace and in war. Uses and gratifications research has shown that the functions people believe the media serve direct their choice and use of different media channels and content (e.g., Katz,

Blumler, & Gurevitch, 1974). Moreover, media practitioners factor in an audience's expectations about the functions that media should fulfill in decisions about content, format, and timing of different entertainment and news material.

There is no time, however, in which these functions of the mass media are so apparent as during a crisis. When natural disasters, weather, military, or terrorist activities threaten, the functional importance of the mass media increases. Recognizing their importance, mass media respond by devoting extraordinary resources to coverage. News channels marshal their resources to focus on news gathering and reporting. Entertainment programming is abandoned by other networks to fill the audience's needs and demands for information. Media outlets respond to the audience's heightened needs for information, explanation, solidarity, and tension reduction.

Prior research indicates that people do have greater needs for mass media during crisis situations. In his writings on the media coverage of the Kennedy assassination, Schramm (1965) noted that the public uncertainty about the future of the U.S. government resulted in greater needs for information, explanation, and consolation. During the 1973 Yom Kippur War, Peled and Katz (1974) observed that most Israelis wanted the media to devote most of their time to surveillance and correlation. During the Persian Gulf War, Delaware residents believed that the media functions of surveillance and correlation were vital to their lives (McLeod, Perse, Signorielli, & Courtright, 1993).

In an extension of this stream of research, this chapter reports the results of a study that continues the exploration of the audience's perceptions of the mass media during crisis. The chapter focuses on the audience's perceptions of the importance of the functions of mass communication during the first several weeks following the attacks on the World Trade Center (WTC) towers and the Pentagon, including the week the "War on Terrorism" began in Afghanistan.

SURVEILLANCE AND CORRELATION

Surveillance and correlation are functions of the mass media that are particularly important in democratic societies. The mass media serve as a watchdog, by tracking activities in the environment as well as by monitoring internal and external activities and potential threats. During crisis situations, surveillance and correlation become especially important functions of the media. Due to constraints, however, media are often limited in fulfilling these roles completely. Despite devoting massive resources to covering the crisis, the media often find news gathering to be difficult. During the aftermath of the attacks on the WTC, for example, there was some uncertainty about the cause of the attacks, the reasons behind them, the number of casualties, and the location of elected officials. Confusion and disarray in the area affected news gathering. Moreover, those sources who could best explain the significance and implication of crisis events were often unavailable to the press. The most knowledgeable sources were occupied with government agencies, advising government leaders making critical decisions.

Still, during a time of crisis, surveillance is a heightened need for the audience. Following the WTC attacks, news media use increased dramatically. In the week following September 11, all broadcast and cable television news organizations saw larger audiences (White, 2001). Even the "new" media were seen as sources to fill surveillance and correlation needs. Reuters reported that traffic at U.S. government Web sites increased dramatically in the days following September 11 (White, 2001). Sites operated by the FBI, the White House, and the military ranked second only to Web news sites ("Government Web sites," 2001). There are indications that even news saturation cannot fill the audience's need for surveillance. A major criticism of British television coverage of the Gulf War, for example, was that it was "not informative" enough and "repetitive" (Morrison, 1992).

SOLIDARITY

The solidarity function of the mass media is the socializing function. The mass media serve to bond people to their society by reinforcing social norms and rules. This function is particularly highlighted in times of crisis. McLeod, Eveland, and Signorielli (1994) found that the public reported greater needs for solidarity-building media content during the Persian Gulf War than it did 1 year after the conflict. Content analyses of the Persian Gulf War coverage point out that "yellow ribbon" media coverage was common (Dennis et al., 1991). Stories discussed the patriotic actions of ordinary people. Coverage of the WTC attacks also fostered solidarity. News coverage highlighted the heroes of Flight 93 and the brave acts of the police and firefighters at Ground Zero; stores sold out of flags and symbols of patriotism were seen everywhere.

Solidarity is not only functional, but is also linked to several media effects. The desire to support our country often leads to rally effects, or great increases in approval ratings for our nation's leaders. Since September 11, President Bush has moved from the target of political pundits to a leader enjoying extraordinary public approval.

TENSION REDUCTION

Tension reduction is an important function of the mass media. Although it is not widely studied, people often report that the media help reduce some of the anxiety associated with the uncertainty of the crisis. Peled and Katz (1974) observed that about one third of Israeli citizens expected television to reduce their tension during the Yom Kippur War. Peled and Katz further speculated that television's entertainment programming, especially action-adventure programs and movies, could help distract viewers from their war fears. Tension reduction is often seen in the fast production of patriotic songs and mementoes. Indeed, several songs about September 11 quickly appeared and moved up the Billboard charts.

COMFORT

Comforting activities are those that seek to reduce stress and fears (Burleson, 1994). Although prior writings on the functions of the mass media have not considered how media coverage can serve as a source of comfort, it is clear that media coverage can console upset viewers. Research following the explosion of the space shuttle *Challenger* in 1986 found that people who were more upset were more likely to spend time with television than people who were less emotionally distraught by the event (Kubey & Peluso, 1990; Riffe & Stovall, 1989). Because media coverage includes credible information and sources, the reassurances of journalists, politicians, and relief workers might provide even greater comfort than one's family and friends. A recurrent news frame is the reassurance provided by officials, the strength of the people involved in a tragedy, and the eventual restoration of order (Gans, 1979), all themes that could comfort the audience.

THE SCOPE OF THE STUDY

In any sort of crisis, research has shown that all functions of mass communication are important to audience members (e.g., McLeod et al., 1993; Mindak & Hursh, 1965). The relative importance of each function, however, has varied depending on the nature of the crisis. McLeod and his colleagues suggested that crises, such as assassinations, that trigger feelings of instability among audience members, highlight the importance of solidarity-building and tension-reduction functions. Crises such as wars, on the other hand, are more complex and longer lasting, and thus underscore the need for information. The crisis situation resulting from the attacks of September 11, and the subsequent launch of the War on Terrorism beginning with the military action in Afghanistan create a context that is both uncertain and complex.

Our first research question, built on prior work, asked the following:

RQ1: What are the public's perceptions about the functional roles of the mass media in the weeks following the attack on the World Trade Center and the Pentagon?

Perse (2001) recently summarized literature indicating that in times of crises, demographic differences among people become less important in terms of predicting perceptions about various media functions. However, prior research has found that some demographic characteristics of people affect their perceptions about media's functional roles (McLeod et al., 1993). Children, for example, might have a greater need than adults for tension reduction and comfort (Peled & Katz, 1974). Those who use the media a good deal may be more likely to endorse media's surveillance and correlation functions than those who use the media less frequently (McLeod et al., 1993). Hence, this study sought to answer the following research question:

RQ2: Which demographic, media use, and attitudinal variables are most strongly related to perceptions about the importance of different media functions?

Finally, we also were interested in examining whether public perceptions of the functions media served following the September 11 attacks differed from those observed during the 1991 Gulf War. The final research question asked:

RQ3: Are there differences in the public's perceptions about the functional roles of the mass media between the attacks of September 11, 2001, and those during the 1991 Gulf War?

METHODS

A national random digit dial survey was conducted by a professional research firm during the week of October 8, 2002. This was a notable week in the War on Terrorism. Data collection began the day after the United States began military action in Afghanistan. Moreover, this was the week that Vice President Dick Cheney voiced the belief that the anthrax mailings were linked to the September 11 attacks. In all, 401 completed surveys were obtained, representing a 73% completion rate. The sample was 61% female and 85% White. The sample ranged in age from 18 to 92 ($M = 47.75$, $SD = 17.04$).

Media Roles

Five roles for the media during crisis situations (Providing Information, Explaining Significance, Solidarity Building, Tension Reduction, and Providing Comfort) were derived from prior research on the functions of the media (e.g., Peled & Katz, 1974; McLeod et al., 1993; Schramm, 1965). Respondents rated the importance of each role on a 7-point scale (with a 1 indicating *not at all important* and a 7 indicating *very important*). Table 4.1 reports descriptive statistics of the study's analytical variables.

Media Use

Several measures of media use were obtained. Respondents estimated how much time they spent on a typical day watching television news, listening to radio news, watching cable news, reading newspapers, using online news sources, and watching entertainment television. Respondents also reported how much they relied on the media for information and for escape and distraction from the crisis (with a 1 indicating *not at all* and a 7 indicating *very much*). Descriptive statistics are shown in Table 4.1.

Attitudes about the Media and Feelings Towards The Crisis

Eleven 5-point Likert statements adapted from prior research about the importance of media roles during crisis (McLeod et al., 1993)

Table 4.1. Descriptive Statistics for Variables Used in the Analysis

	Mean $(N = 401)$	SD
Media Role Importance[a]		
Providing information	5.85_a	1.66
Explaining significance	$5.77a$	1.72
Building solidarity	5.78_a	1.63
Reducing tension	5.02_b	2.03
Providing comfort	5.03_b	2.07
Political Orientation		
Liberalism (1)—Conservatism (7)	4.31	1.50
Media Use (in hours)		
TV news	1.85	1.63
Entertainment TV	1.78	1.44
Radio news	1.65	2.27
Cable news	1.23	1.41
Newspaper reading	0.98	0.88
Online news	0.61	0.80
Media Reliance[b]		
Information	6.00	1.52
Escape–distraction	2.90	2.03
Media Approval Index[b]	4.02	0.97
Media Factors[c]		
Fairness	3.27	0.76
Openness	3.44	0.81
Fear	3.64	0.83

[a]1 = *not at all important*, 7 = *very important*
[b]1 = *not at all*, 7 = *very much*
[c]1 = *strongly disagree*, 5 = *strongly agree*

Note. For Media Role Importance, means with different superscripts differ significantly.

were used to assess a range of personal feelings and attitudes about the media. Principal components analysis with varimax rotation identified three factors. The first, *Media Openness* (eigenvalue = 2.43) was comprised of five items reflecting the view that the media should be relatively open in its coverage of events during the aftermath of the attacks on the WTC and the Pentagon. This factor represents an endorsement of showing protests, even anti-U.S. protests, and news that might be critical of the U.S. government. The second, *Media Fairness* (eigenvalue = 2.23) was composed of three items that mark beliefs in media credibility and an item endorsing government trust as a news source. The third factor, *Fear* (eigenvalue = 1.17) included items reflecting people's fear and assessments of personal threat.[1] Factor scores created using the regression method were used in further analyses. Additionally, overall approval of the media was assessed with a single statement: "All in all, the news media are doing a good job covering the recent U.S. military action." Response categories ranged from 1 (*strongly disagree*) to 5 (*strongly agree*).

Demographic Variables

Educational level and income were both measured on 7-point scales with high scores indicating greater income and education. The median education was a technical or 2-year college graduate. The median household income level fell between $25,000 and $45,000 annually. A measure of political orientation was created by averaging two items indexing how liberal or conservative respondents reported themselves to be on social and economic issues (scores ranged from 1 very liberal to 7 very conservative). The two items were positively correlated ($r = .55, p < .001$).

---

[1]The item statements for each factor were: Media Openness: "The news media should cover rallies protesting our government's actions," "The news media should cover anti-American protests that take place in other countries," "The news media should be allowed to report stories freely," "The news media should be able to criticize the U.S. government's actions," and "The news media should have access to the information that the public needs to know." *Media Fairness*: "The news media coverage of the recent U.S. military action is accurate," "The news media coverage of the recent U.S. military action tells the whole story," "The news media coverage of the recent U.S. military action is fair," and "The government can be trusted to decide what the public should hear." *Fear*: "I have become more afraid in my daily life since the terrorist attacks" and "There is a serious threat of terrorism in the United States."

RESULTS

As expected, respondents reported all five media roles to be very important. T-tests revealed, however, that there were some differences in salience of the five roles. Respondents saw the three roles of Providing Information (M = 5.85), Explaining Significance (M = 5.77), and Building Solidarity (M = 5.78) as equally important. But, all three of these were viewed as significantly more important than the roles of Reducing Tension (M = 5.02,) and Providing Comfort (M = 5.03), which did not differ significantly from each other. These results also are shown in Table 4.1.

In order to explore more fully the importance of these media roles after the terrorist attacks, ratings were compared with earlier data collected during the weeks following the start of the January 1991 military action in the Persian Gulf (McLeod et al., 1993). In all, there were few differences in the audience's perceived importance of these roles in the two crises. Respondents were significantly more likely to believe that the media should build solidarity at the beginning of the Afghanistan War on Terrorism than they were during the Persian Gulf War: $t(581) = 1.97$, $p < .05$. Additionally, respondents were marginally more likely to believe that providing information was important during the Persian Gulf War than at the start of the 2001 War on Terrorism: $t(662) = 1.95, p < .06$.

Predictors of Media Roles

The main goal of this study was to explore the factors associated with the importance of the five media roles. Stepwise regression procedures were used to assess which demographic, media use, and media attitude factors were linked to greater beliefs in the importance of the five roles of the media at the beginning the War on Terrorism. All five equations were significant. The results are shown in Table 4.2.

Providing Information. The final equation accounted for 15% of the variance in importance for the media to provide information. Two attitudinal factors, Media Openness and Fear of Terrorism were the only positive, significant predictors. Beliefs in the media's information-providing role are linked to greater endorsement of an open media stance that might even include content critical of U.S. policy along with greater fear of terrorism.

Building Solidarity. The final equation accounted for 15% of the variance in perceptions about the importance of the media's role

Table 4.2. Stepwise Regressions: Regressing Media Roles

Providing Information	β	
Media openness	.22***	Final R^2 = .148
Fear of terrorism	.12*	
Media reliance information	.14*	
Final $F(18, 308) = 2.80, p < .001$		

Building Solidarity	β	
Media fairness	.17*	Final R^2 = .147
Fear of terrorism	.13*	
Conservatism	-.14*	
Media openness	-.13*	
Final $F(18, 308) = 2.77, p < .001$		

Providing Comfort	β	
Educational level	-.20***	Final R^2 = .227
News media approval	.19**	
Media reliance information	.15**	
Final $F(18, 308) = 4.74, p < .001$		

Explaining Significance	β	Final R^2 = .274
Media reliance for information	21***	
Fear of terrorism	.20***	
Conservatism	-.15**	
Media openness	.11*	
Radio news	-.12*	
Final $F(18, 308) = 6.07, p < .001$		

Reducing Tension	β	Final R^2 = .172
Entertainment TV	-.16**	
News media approval	.17**	
Media reliance information	.12*	
Media reliance escape-distraction	.12*	
Final $F(18, 308) = 3.36, p < .001$		

*$p < .05$; **$p < .01$; ***$p < .001$.

in Building Solidarity. Media Fairness and Fear of Terrorism were significant, positive predictors. Conservatism (reflecting more liberal political stances) and Media Openness were significant, negative contributors. More liberal, but fearful respondents, who believe that the media coverage has been fair, but also believe that the media should not present content critical of our country's policies, are more likely to endorse the solidarity-building function of the media.

Providing Comfort. This equation accounted for 23% of the variance in endorsing the media's role in providing comfort and sense of well-being. In all, three variables contributed to the equation. News Media Approval and relying on the media for information were significant, positive predictors. Educational level was a significant, negative predictor. Using online news sources was a marginal, negative predictor. Respondents who are less educated, but approve of media coverage and rely on it, are likely to endorse the media's role in comfort.

Explaining Significance. Seven variables accounted for 27% of the variance and significantly predicted the importance of Explaining Significance. Relying on the media for information, fear of terrorism, News Media Approval, Media Fairness, and Media Openness were all significant, positive contributors to the equation. Conservatism (reflecting more liberal political stances) and radio news listening were significant, negative predictors. More liberal respondents who are somewhat fearful of terrorism, who endorse open media coverage, rely on the media for information, and believe that the media are fair and doing a good job are more likely to believe that the media should explain the significance of news events.

Reducing Tension. Four variables accounted for 17% of the variance and significantly predicted the importance of the media role of Tension Reduction. In all, News Media Approval and reliance on the media for information as well as distraction-escape were significant, positive predictors. On the other hand, watching entertainment television was a significant, negative predictor. Tension reduction by the media is more important for respondents who watch little entertainment television and approve of the media while relying on it for both information and distraction.

DISCUSSION

The results of this study differ somewhat from prior research on the importance of the functional roles of the mass media during times of crisis. Earlier studies of military conflicts (e.g., McLeod et al., 1993; Peled & Katz, 1974) found that providing information was clearly perceived as the most central and important function of the media. Our results, however, revealed that Providing Information was important, but no more important than the Explanation and Solidarity-Building functions. These differences certainly suggest that the nature of the crisis affects the importance that society places on the media at the time. Unlike the Persian Gulf War, where there were few immediate threats of safety because the action was taking place on the other side of the world, the aftermath of the September 11 attacks was marked with a heightened sense of uncertainty and concerns about terrorist attacks on U.S. soil. Moreover, the data were collected at a time of intense concern about the potential for biological terrorist attacks. In the current data, the external attacks, coupled with high levels of uncertainty, seem to be associated with equal needs for the media to provide information, explanation, and solidarity.

The results of the stepwise regressions reinforce prior knowledge about the role of the mass media during crisis situations. Notably, we observed virtually no connection between demographic variables and perceptions about the importance of the five media roles. Crisis situations tend to reduce the differences among people as they become more dependent on the mass media (Ball-Rokeach & DeFleur, 1976; Perse, 2001). Fear of terrorism, however, was significantly and positively linked to the media roles of providing Information, Explaining Significance, and Building Solidarity. Fear has been found to be a motivating force in persuasion (e.g., Boster & Mongeau, 1984); clearly fear also affects perceptions about media roles. This finding is especially notable because the data were collected during the height of the fear about terrorists and anthrax attacks.

Although prior research indicates that restrictive attitudes toward the media can be quite prevalent during times of crisis (McLeod, Perse, Signorielli, & Courtright, 1999), we found that endorsements of more open media coverage were significantly linked to believing that the media should provide information and explanation. Less restrictive news, which includes coverage of protests (in the United States and overseas) as well as criticism of U.S. government policy, is viewed as an important aspect of knowledge about U.S. involvement in the War on Terrorism. This attitude toward open media coverage, however, was significantly and negatively linked to perceptions about the importance of media's Solidarity-Building function. Protests and criticism are clearly viewed as contrary to the kind of support for our government policies that are valued during rally times (e.g., McLeod et al., 1994).

Media use variables did little to explain perceptions about the importance of the five media roles. This may be due to the changes in the media environment that have taken place in the past 10 years. During the Kennedy assassination, viewers were glued to one of the three major networks. During the Persian Gulf War, CNN was the dominant source for cable subscribers (Greenberg, Cohen, & Li, 1993). By the time of the WTC attacks, most cable subscribers had access to three all-news networks, CNN, MSNBC, and Fox. In this media-saturated environment, identifying effects on perceptions about media roles due solely to media use may prove to be more difficult.

For this study, we explored one additional function of the media that has not been included in prior research: a comforting role in which the media help provide a sense of well-being. Although few studies have explored the media's ability to comfort, anecdotal evidence certainly points out that people can gain some sense of relief in knowing that others share their feelings and emotions. During the coverage of the aftermath of the Kennedy assassination, for example, people reported that watching television helped them deal with their grief (Greenberg & Parker, 1965). Our findings point out that people value media's comforting role when they trust the media and when they rely on the media for information. Interestingly, this function is more important for those with lower levels of education. This was the only analysis in which demographic variables were significantly linked to media roles.

Prior research on emotional distress strongly suggests that people's appraisals, or evaluations, of a situation play a significant role in determining the magnitude of their stress response (Lazarus, 1991, 1999; Lazarus & Folkman, 1984). Such appraisals, among other things, involve assessments of whether the distressing event is relevant to important personal goals, whether there are viable coping options, and so on. Moreover, Lazarus (1991, 1999) argued that emotional distress subsides as an individual arrives at less threatening appraisals of a situation.

Results here suggest that, for some people, the information gleaned from the media about the events surrounding September 11 was extremely influential in their initial appraisals of the terrorist attacks and their longer term implications. This appeared to be especially true for individuals with relatively low levels of education. Perhaps one reason for this finding is that, compared to individuals with higher levels of education, those with lower levels have fewer alternative sources from which to garner and/or discuss information. For these individuals, the media serve as the primary source on which appraisals are formed. Thus, in this capacity, the media may serve a comforting function by helping distressed individuals arrive at less threatening appraisals of a crisis situation. Future studies should explore further the relationships among media reliance, education level, and perceptions of importance of the Providing Comfort function of the media. In particular, ascertaining the kinds of media content that are linked to relatively benign appraisals of crisis events would be useful.

Once again, the results of our study point out that the media serve important functions during times of crisis. Their functional roles are valued by society, but differences in perceptions about the media, notably beliefs in media bias and restriction, affect the importance of these roles. Future research should explore how the changing media environment, especially the increase in 24–7 news outlets, influence people's uses of and perceptions about the mass media during times of national crisis.

5

Media Use, Information Seeking, and Reported Needs in Post Crisis Contexts

Matthew W. Seeger
Wayne State University

Steven Vennette
North Dakota State University

Robert R. Ulmer
University of Arkansas–Little Rock

Timothy L. Sellnow
North Dakota State University

Crises are most often described as specific and surprising events that create high levels of uncertainty by disrupting established patterns or expectations and that produce high levels of perceived threat (Quarantelli, 1988; Seeger, Sellnow, & Ulmer, 1998). Uncertainty about the cause, consequences, and level of harm is one of the principal consequences of crisis events (see Gouran, 1982; Hermann, 1963; Weick, 1988). Crisis, then, can be expected to prompt intense searches for information particularly when the event is seen as novel, severe, and when the consequences are more direct or personal. These searches usually involve media channels. Although many efforts have examined the patterns and methods of information diffusion during crisis events, few have specifically identified the types of information sought or detailed the ways in which contextual variables might affect informational needs.

Our purpose in this investigation was to examine what is arguably the most significant crisis event to affect the United States. As such, this and other 9/11 investigations may be viewed as benchmarks for understanding many of the communication dimensions of a national crisis. We were particularly interested in merging efforts to identify pattern of information diffusion from mass media investigations (DeFleur, 1987; Gantz, 1983; Greenberg, Cohen & Li, 1993; Steinfatt, Gantz, Siebold, & Miller, 1973) with notions of uncertainty and uncertainty reduction from organizational crisis and disaster management (Seeger et al., 1998; Weick, 1988). Moreover, the psychological and emotional impact from the 9/11 events can be expected to prompt particularly intense adaptive responses among audiences, including, we expect, intense needs for information. It was our expectation that crisis-induced uncertainty would prompt specific information-seeking behaviors and that audiences would express specific preferences regarding kinds of information. We also believed that other factors, demographic and contextual, would influence these information preferences.

Crisis and Uncertainty

Crises include a wide array of natural and man-made disasters including extreme weather events, economic collapses, extremely violent acts, structural failures, outbreaks of disease, transportation accidents, defective products, work stoppages, serious industrial accidents, and terrorist attacks, among others (Meyers & Holusha, 1986; Mitroff, Pauchant, & Shirvistava, 1988). Crises are increasing in both number and severity concomitant with increased dependence on complex technological systems (Perrow, 1984). The consequences of large, complex systems include "diminished capacity of individuals to comprehend the system, more centralized decision-making, limited public access, growing control by experts, and system rigidity" (Seeger et al., 1998, p. 232). Perrow (1984), in developing his normal accident theory, suggested that large, complex systems create interactiveness and tight coupling such that unanticipated outcomes, including crises, are inherent to the system. Thus, crisis can be said to be a normal feature of such complex systems. Moreover, larger structures and systems, bigger tankers, global companies, longer bridges, wider bodied airplanes, and even higher skyscrapers, mean that failure creates more widespread harm. As Perrow (1984) noted "human made catastrophes appear to have increased with industrialization as we build more devices that could crash, burn or explode" (p. 9).

Crisis is generally recognized as having three primary features: threat, short response time, and surprise (Hermann, 1963).

Threat represents a severe discrepancy between desired and existing states, such that high-priority goals and values are jeopardized (Billings, Thomas, & Schramm, 1980). Loss of human life, destruction of property, disruption of a sense of stability, security, and safety, breakdowns in support structures, systems, and routines are some of the threatening consequences associated with crisis. During crisis, the interval between events and consequences is compressed such that participants and managers must act very quickly to mitigate harm (Gouran, 1982). These responses often must be undertaken without adequate information about cause, consequences and without adequate resources for response (Sellnow & Ulmer, 1995). Finally, crisis is almost always unanticipated and surprising to a majority of participants and observers. By definition, these events are outside the established routines and familiar, predictable patterns and expectations that govern day-to-day life (Billings et al., 1980; Gouran, Hirokawa, & Martz, 1986).

Uncertainty, the degree to which future outcomes can be predicted, is one of the principal conditions of a post crisis environment. Weick (1993), for example, suggested that in some crises, "people suddenly and deeply feel that the universe is no longer a rational, orderly system. What makes such an event so shattering is that both the sense of what is occurring and the means to rebuild that sense collapse together" (p. 633). Crises may involve fundamental loss of understanding regarding both what is happening and what can be done. Several factors contribute to this high uncertainty condition. Established patterns, routines, and structures used to predict outcomes are disrupted (Weick, 1988). Airline disasters disrupt air travel patterns so that it is not possible to predict when flights might leave or arrive (Ray, 1999). Toxic releases may make both air and water unsafe, prompting evacuations and disrupting families (Seeger & Bolz, 1996). New information, then, is necessary to rebuild predictive structures. The inadequacies of basic crisis-related assumptions, beliefs, cognitive frameworks and sensemaking structures are often vividly demonstrated by a crisis (Pauchant & Mitroff, 1992; Turner 1976). Thus, in the absence of additional information, an airline disaster may suggest that assumptions of airline safety no longer hold. Residents are often afraid to return to a toxic spill area not knowing if it is safe. Additionally, basic structures and channels of communication are often disrupted during crisis such that it is not possible to access required information. Natural disasters, floods, hurricanes, and snow storms, may down telephone lines, disrupt travel of news reporters, or stop delivery of papers (Sellnow, Seeger, & Ulmer, in press). Crises are sometimes accompanied by the emergence of novel channels of communication, flyers, community radio broadcasts, signs and posters, so that information can again be disseminated (Sellnow & Seeger, 2001).

Specific kinds of information are needed in a high uncertainty, post crisis environment. These include information about cause of the post crisis and identification of responsible parties, consequences such as scope of harm and instructions for mitigation of harm, and information about corrective actions necessary to reduce risk and re-establish security (Ice, 1991; Seeger et al., 1998). Questions about cause, blame, responsibility, and culpability arise for several reasons. Blame and responsibility, for example, are associated with legal liability. These questions also allow participants and observers to reassess their attitudes toward groups and individuals associated with the crisis. Institutional legitimacy is also associated with questions of blame (Seeger, 1986). Issues regarding consequences and mitigation of harm represent critical post crisis uncertainties. Participants need information about what actions they can take to reduce risk and harm. In the case of toxic gas releases, for example, information about avoiding exposure, protecting skin and eyes, and symptoms of exposure is necessary (Seeger & Bolz, 1996). Information about consequences and scope of harm gives cues as to personal impact, how serious the crisis is, and about what might constitute reasonable levels of concern and attention. Information about corrective actions necessary to reduce risk and re-establish security concerns the normative readjustment to a new post crisis understanding of risk (Turner, 1976). Moreover, questions about presence of legitimate order and structure may arise. Post crisis audiences, therefore, may need to hear that there is a system of authority and control and it is taking appropriate action. These forms of uncertainties about cause, consequences, and corrective actions, then, represent a set of plausible information needs for audiences during post crisis.

Information Diffusion

A significant body of research has developed around the concept of news diffusion. Broadly, this work seeks to understand patterns of diffusion of news regarding critical events (DeFleur, 1987; Gantz & Greenberg, 1993; Greenberg et al., 1993; Pettey, Perloff, Neuendorf, & Pollick, 1986; Quarles, Jeffres, Sanchez-Ilundian, & Neuwirth, 1983). Greenberg (1964a), for example, found that news of events spread quickly and that people turned to the media even if they initially learned from an interpersonal source. Petty et al. (1986) investigated the *Challenger* space shuttle disaster and concluded that 79% of their sample heard of the event within 30 minutes and 88% within 90 minutes. They also examined relationships between emotional responses, news knowledge, and channels of first knowledge. Reported feelings of shame, for example, were associated with lower levels of news knowledge and may have diminished information seeking. Moreover, medium of first knowledge was associated with emotional response, such that "those who learned through mass media were less sad than those through interpersonal channels" (p. 175). They concluded that vividness of the channel and immediacy of knowledge contributes to a more negative emotional affect. Delay in time and moderation through interpersonal channels appeared to mediate negative emotional reactions.

Based on previous investigations of crises and information diffusion, specific expectations regarding responses to the 9/11 tragedies can be proposed. Given the importance of the event, its initial timing, and its vividness, news was likely disseminated quickly through radio or personal contacts initially, followed by information seeking via television. The continuous coverage available from CNN, Fox News, MSNBC as well as the major networks, likely enhanced the impact of television as a preferred channel. In this investigation, we focused on the initial emotional state of audience members and its relation to gender and age. A strong initial response of disbelief or confusion would enhance information-seeking behaviors. Particular kinds of emotional responses, such as fear, might be associated with particular kinds of informational needs, such as hearing about additional threats. Moreover, it also is likely that audience members overall would express preferences for specific kinds of information, such as cause, consequences, blame, and scope of damage.

The loss of life, the destruction of property, the intentionality of the act, and the vivid symbolic loss combine to make the 9/11 disasters at the World Trade Center (WTC), the Pentagon, and in Pennsylvania the worst crisis in modern US history. The morning of September 11, then, was a time of very high levels of emotional turmoil and uncertainty.

METHOD

Data for this study were collected within 5 days of the 9/11 event in three geographic areas: the Detroit, Michigan metropolitan area; Fargo, North Dakota; Little Rock, Arkansas. Survey questionnaires were circulated to generate as broad a convenience sample as possible. Questionnaires were circulated in classes and distributed to graduate students with requests that they distribute them at work sites. Our goal was to build as large and diverse a sample as possible within the 5-day interval following the 9/11 event. The survey questionnaire collected data regarding gender, age, initial emotional response, and the kinds of information respondents wanted to receive immediately following the tragedy. We also asked respondents to describe any personal connection to the events. Initial emotional responses to the crisis and the types of information respondents wished to receive were measured using Likert-type scales.

RESULTS

A total of 1,775 surveys were distributed. Of these, 1,374 were returned for a return rate of 77%. A total of 1,329 questionnaires were sufficiently complete for data analysis. Age of the respondents ranged from 12 to 61 with a mean of 22.5. The sample was almost equally distributed by gender with 686 (52%) women and 641 (48%) men. Respondents reported on average spending 8.34 hours within the first day collecting information about the tragedies and having their daily routines interrupted for an average of 1.09 days. When asked "Did you know anyone or have any friends or family who you thought might be affected by the tragedy?" 39% responded "yes."

The narrative accounts of personal connection to the tragedy were quite diverse. A larger number of respondents indicated that they had friends or relatives in New York or Washington, DC. Many others indicated that they had relatives flying at the time of the attacks. Some reported having lived or worked close to the attack sites, whereas many indicated that they had visited the sites. Other relatively common connections included serving in the military reserves, or having family or who served in the military or military reserves.

Respondent's desires to receive nine types of basic information about the events were assessed with a series of 5-point Likert-type questions, with responses ranging from 1 (*strongly agree* [SA]) to 5 (*strongly disagree* [SD]). Initial emotional response was assessed using an additional seven questions (see Tables 5.1 and 5.2).

Information about cause was the highest reported informational desire followed by information regarding additional threats, scope of damage, and the larger implications. Lowest reported informational desire concerned reassuring information from religious leaders, information about closures and cancellation, and reassuring information from political leaders. Respondents indicated

Table 5.1. Expressed Informational Desires (in %)

	SA	A	N	D	SD	Mean	S.D.
Cause	76	21	2	0	0	4.72	.56
Threats	65	27	5	2	1	4.55	.72
Damage	58	36	5	0	0	4.51	.67
Implications	44	39	13	3	0	4.25	.81
Rescue	43	35	18	3	2	4.13	.94
Who affected	41	40	15	3	1	4.19	.84
Politicians	27	35	28	7	3	3.77	1.02
Closures	19	29	32	14	6	3.41	1.13
Religious	17	24	39	12	7	3.35	1.56

Table 5.2. Initial Emotional Response (in %)

	SA	A	N	D	SD	Mean	S.D.
Sorrowful	47	37	11	2	0	4.26	.88
Sad	44	35	15	3	1	4.16	.94
Angry	39	32	21	6	1	3.98	1.04
Confused	34	39	16	6	16	3.92	1.07
Frightened	24	31	26	13	5	3.58	1.90
Depressed	17	23	34	17	6	3.28	1.58
Calm	14	31	27	16	8	3.21	1.23

strong initial emotional responses to the events. Summing strongly agree and agree responses, the strongest initial emotional responses were sorrow (84%), sadness (79%), confusion (73%), and anger (71%). Smaller proportions were frightened or depressed.

We examined the relationship between initial emotional state, perceived utility of information and respondent gender and age using Pearson's R. These results are in Tables 5.3 and 5.4.

Gender was related to both desire to receive particular kinds of information and initial emotional response. Women were more strongly interested in eight of the nine types of information listed, although several of these correlations were modest, given the large sample size. Only in the case of information regarding cause of the tragedy was gender not significantly related to informational needs. The strongest relationships were between gender and information

about closures and cancellations, assurances from religious leaders, and information about the larger implications. In terms of emotional response, gender was significantly related to all options except anger. The strongest correlations indicate that women were more likely to report being sad, frightened, sorrowful, and confused. Men were significantly more likely than women to report being calm.

Age also was related to initial emotional response and to reported informational needs, although again these correlations were modest. The younger the respondent, the more likely the report of being confused. Older respondents were more likely to report being sad, sorrowful, and depressed. A significant inverse relationship was found between age and utility of information about closures and cancellations while a positive relationship was found between age and utility of information regarding who might be affected.

Correlation coefficients were also calculated for the relationships between the kinds of information desired with the seven initial emotional states (see Table 5.5).

A variety of significant relationships were found between kinds of desired information and initial emotional response, although many were relatively modest given the large sample size. Confusion,

Table 5.5. Relationship of Perceived Desire for Information to Seven Initial Emotional Responses

	Emotions						
	Confused	Angry	Depress	Fright	Sorrow	Sad	Calm
Information Needs							
Damage	.106	.179	.071*	ns	.233	.194	-.077*
Cause	.115	.129	.095	.100	.22	.185	-.083*
Implications	.065*	.195	.11	.09	.226.	.203	-.078*
Threat	.124	.200	.142	.169	.223	.195	-.072*
Closures	.067*	.133	.114	.091	.100	.064*	ns
Politicians	.194	.296	.111	.217	.273	.275	-.154
Religious	.124	.147	.076	.116	.231	.175	-.095
Who affected	.124	.209	.193	.144	.272	.296	-.134
Rescue	.139	.248	.192	.135	.267	.290	-.148

*$p < .01$. All other correlations are $p < .001$.

for example, was most strongly related to hearing from political leaders and hearing about rescue attempts, followed by receiving information from religious leaders, about threats, and about who was affected. Anger was strongly related to hearing from political leaders, receiving information about rescue, and about who was affected. Depression was most strongly correlated to information desired concerning who was affected and rescues. Most strongly related to initial emotional states of fright were hearing from political leaders and information about additional threats. Being sorrowful was significantly related to all nine areas of information desired and had the highest correlations across all nine informational types. It was most strongly related to desired information from political leaders, about who was affected, rescue attempts, damage, and hearing from religious leaders. Sadness was most strongly related to information about who was affected, rescue attempts, hearing from political leaders, and receiving information about implications. Having an initial response of being calm was, as might be expected, negatively related to all nine types of information areas but at a consistently more modest level. The strongest negative correlations concerned hearing from politicians, hearing about who was affected, and information about rescue attempts. Across all seven initial emotional responses, hearing from political leaders consistently generated the highest correlations of all types of information desired.

DISCUSSION

Results from this study should be interpreted cautiously due to the convenience nature of the sample and the interval between the 9/11 events and data collection. These results show that respondents had intense emotional responses and information needs and that these needs were significantly related to both gender and age. Respondents were most interested in basic information about cause, threat, and damage. Cause and damage were the most consistently high informational needs. This may be in part a function of the timing of the events and the initial implication that the first crash was an accident and, for some time after, a suggestion that other threats existed. Hearing from religious leaders and information about closures and cancellations were the most variable, probably due to the more specialized nature of this information. Similarly, initial emotional responses were very intense, particularly sorrow, sadness, anger, and confusion. Sorrow and sadness appear to be the most consistent emotional responses across this group, while being frightened was the most variable. Taken together, these results are broadly consistent with an uncertainty view of crisis, where a surprising and threatening event creates strong emotional arousal leading to high levels of uncertainty and informational needs. These needs concern the basic structure of the event (i.e., cause, threat, and damage). Reported levels of confusion, although high, did not emerge as a dominant emotional response. We had expected higher levels of confusion consistent with crisis literature and the time interval when many news outlets were describing the first crash as an accident. It may be that confusion did not dominate or that feelings of confusion dissipate very rapidly as information becomes available in a manner consistent with Steinfatt et al.'s (1973) attribution or disassociation phenomenon.

Gender was a strong indicator of both emotional response and perceived informational utility. Women had stronger emotional responses. Women also appear to be more interested in information about closures and cancellation and reassurances from religious leader and information about the larger implication of the tragedy, suggesting a gender basis for how these events are viewed. It is possible, for example, that women in this group retain more responsibility for day-to-day family management issues and thus need more information about closures and cancellations and about larger implications of these events. Women may in some ways have greater responsibility for managing the adaptive responses to crisis. Similarly, age affected the way these events are viewed. Younger respondents were significantly more likely to be confused and frightened. Older respondents were more likely to be sad. Younger respondents were more interested in information about closures and cancellations whereas older respondents were interested in information regarding who might be affected. Older individuals may have larger and more extensive networks of friends and family who might have been directly affected by the crisis. Age also adds the perspective of experience to understanding and interpreting crisis events such that older individuals may experience less uncertainty.

The picture that emerges for informational needs in time of crisis is complex. Crisis creates high emotional arousal and high informational needs of diverse types although gender, age, and emotional state all appear to play important roles. Universal needs in this case appeared to concern cause, threat and damage. In this case, there also appeared to be a need to hear from political leaders.

6

Tracking Media Use and Gratifications

Tom Ruggiero
University of Texas–El Paso

Jack Glascock
Illinois State University

FDR's death (Miller, 1945), JFK's assassination (Greenberg, 1964a), Eisenhower's death (O'Keefe & Kissel, 1971), the George Wallace (Schwartz, 1973) and Ronald Reagan shootings (Gantz, 1983), and the *Challenger* explosion (Kubey & Peluso, 1990; Mayer, Gudykunst, Perrill, & Merrill, 1990; Riffe & Stovall, 1989) have each served as a U.S. news event of national prominence with which researchers have investigated the news diffusion and media use process. The primary justification for this may be their sheer authority to capture the collective consciousness of an entire nation.

Similarly, the September 11 terror attacks on New York City's World Trade Center (WTC) and the Pentagon by Islamic fundamentalists provided an extraordinary opportunity for communication scholars to study the news event diffusion process and media uses and gratifications. Although some scholars have called for research that attempts to model the diffusion process on events that receive less than national media coverage (Mayer et al., 1990), we argue that the national event model continues to be extremely useful. Because most individuals can precisely recall specifics, such as time and location, emotional state, and media use associated with their awareness of a tragic historical event, the self-report methodology is apt to be relatively rigorous.

On September 11, and thereafter, as the mass media began disseminating "news," government agencies and individuals relied on different media for information vital to comprehending this national crisis event. Because of its ubiquity, accessibility, and technological ability to broadcast in "real time," television has in contemporary times served as the principal media choice during national crises for most Americans. As time elapsed from the crisis event, other media such as newspapers and the radio were perhaps able to offer opportunities for more detailed information, and for some citizens, more believable, fair, and accurate information. Additionally, the introduction of the Internet into the mass media menu now provides a supplementary and innovative method in the news diffusion process. Individuals are able to select their source input by logging on to a multitude of news-related Web sites and even to participate in electronic discussion groups and listservs. E-mail communication also now allows for the interpersonal diffusion of the news, much as the telephone has functioned in that role for decades.

Whatever medium is selected, it appears that a person's first source of news during a news event is influenced by a range of factors. Basil and Brown (1994) noted that there are chance factors including the person's location (at home, at work, in transit), or the time of day (reading the morning newspaper or watching the evening news broadcast). Other factors include an individual's interpersonal communication networks, and how important the previous person in the diffusion process judges the news to be.

This study attempts to track people's media usage patterns following the September 11 tragedies by combining two methodologies: news diffusion and the uses and gratifications approach, which examines people's media choices and their motivations for those choices. Primarily, we sought to answer the following questions: How did people first learn of the attacks? What were their media usage patterns for 1 week following the September 11 events? What role did media gratifications play in their media choices? Additionally, we explored the role of the Internet in the news diffusion process and we tracked the diffusion process over a 1-week time period. At the same time, this study utilized the uses and gratifications approach to the news event diffusion process. Uses and gratifications is an audience-centered approach that developed as a method of increasing knowledge about mass communication's influence on the audience. This perspective holds that people's selection of and uses for communication channels depend, in part, on their personal goals

(Katz, Blumler, & Gurevitch, 1974). Uses and gratifications perceives individuals as active communicators because they are aware of their communication goals, appraise different communication channels, and choose the channels that they believe will gratify their needs. Accordingly, media choice depends on people's experience with and perceptions about how well different communication channels fill various needs (Katz et al., 1974; Perse & Courtright, 1993).

From theses perspectives, we posed the following research questions:

RQ1: What role did demographic factors play in Internet and e-mail usage during the week following the WTC attack news event diffusion process?

RQ2: What are the relative roles of interpersonal and mass media in the news event diffusion process with the introduction of the Internet and e-mail?

RQ3: What role did the Internet play in how media usage diffused during and after WTC attack over a 1-week period?

RQ4: How did media gratifications contribute to media usage during the WTC attack news event diffusion process?

METHOD

A survey questionnaire was distributed during the first part of October, 2001, among 320 college students at three universities—one in the midwest, one in the southwest, and one on the East Coast. The questionnaire was administered to students in basic communication courses at the three universities. These students were deemed an appropriate sample in the news diffusion process because, as university students, these young adults had access and familiarity with the Internet, as well as television, newspapers, and radio (Tapscott, 1998).

The questionnaire consisted of items designed to measure respondents' media usage and gratifications over a 1-week period immediately following the September 11 attacks. Respondents were first asked how they first heard about the tragedy, then what their "first media choice" was at regular intervals over the 1-week period (*first several hours, that evening, the next day, 1 week later*). After each media choice question, respondents were given a list of 11 items to determine uses and gratifications. Respondents indicated on a five-choice Likert scale (*not at all* to *very much*) their agreement with each item. These gratifications were stated as follows: "Allowed me to get the information that I wanted quickly." "Provided detail I wanted in their news stories." "Out of habit." "Educated me about events going on during the crisis." "Was readily available." "Fit easily into my daily schedule." "Was most believable, fair, accurate." "Provided timely and up-to-date information." "To communicate with friends." "Focused on what was important to me." "Found their coverage dramatic." "Reinforced my sense of the importance of the story." Respondents also were queried about their Internet use during the news event diffusion process (*time spent online, number of Web sources used*). Demographic variables such as the respondents' *age, ethnicity,* and *gender* were also queried.

RESULTS

The average age of the participants was 22.5 years, ranging from 16 to 55 years old. The sample consisted of 112 males (35%) and 206 females (64%). The breakdown for ethnicity was White 58%, Hispanic 25%, African American 7%, Asian American 8%, Other (Native American, Mexican national, no response) 2%.

Participants heard about the tragedies through either interpersonal sources, primarily face to face (33%) and the telephone (15%), or broadcast media (i.e., television, 28%, and radio, 24%, and the Internet, 1%). As can be seen in Figure 6.1, television was the primary source of information during the week following the attacks. However as the week progressed, TV usage decreased, whereas newspaper and Internet usage increased.

No differences were found for media usage and gender for any of the time segments measured in the study. For ethnicity no significant differences were found for first hearing about the attacks, media usage hours after the attack, or the evening of the attack. However, media usage by ethnicity did differ significantly the day following the attacks ($p < .05$). Although all ethnic groups primarily got their news from television (71% on average), differences were found for secondary sources with Hispanics more likely to access radio (20%), Whites, newspapers (12%), and African Americans (17%) and Asian Americans (21%) the Internet. Differences among races 1 week after the tragedies also were insignificant.

During the time period of the study, 62% reported using the Internet. Of the participants who used the Internet, 58% reported using it in their homes, followed by at school (26%) and at work (14%). Most users reported using the Internet less than 1 hour (80%)

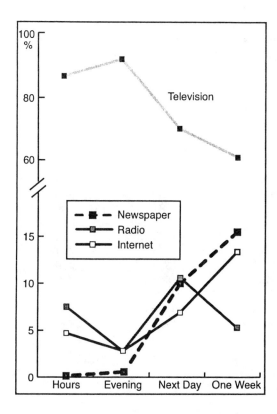

Fig. 6.1. Media usage in percent for respondents during the 1-week period following the attacks on New York and Washington, DC. Television usage declined from a high of 92% the evening of the attacks to 62% 1 week later. Internet and newspaper usage, minimal or negligible at first, rose to 14% and 16% respectively by the end of the week.

and accessing from two to five sites (61%). E-mail usage was reported by 59% of participants during the week following the crisis. Of those who used the Internet, 71% reported also using e-mail. A sizable number of all respondents indicated they used e-mail because it was their normal way of communicating with friends and relatives either locally (20%) or by long distance (33%).

No differences were found between genders or ethnicities for Internet usage. A significant difference was found for e-mail usage by gender, with females (63%) reporting more usage than males (50%; $p < .05$). For e-mail usage, African Americans (38%) reported significantly less use than other ethnicities, which ranged from 57% (Hispanic) to 65% (Asian American; $p < .05$).

The gratifications items were factor analyzed using the principal components method and Varimax rotation. Three factors were extracted: Surveillance, Accessibility, and Socialization (see Table 6.1). For the four time periods studied, the mean for each gratification factor seemed to be relatively consistent throughout (see Figure 6.2).

Table 6.1. Factor Analysis of Uses and Gratifications Items

Item	Factor 1 (Surveillance)	Factor 2 (Accessibility)	Factor 3 (Socialization)
Readily available	.4013	*.7560*	-.0991
Provided detail	*.7996*	.2427	.0164
Dramatic	.5591	.0067	.4176
Educational	*.7316*	.4351	.0518
Out of habit	.0063	*.7536*	.1611
Important	*.7705*	.0296	.3018
Informative	*.7385*	.3257	-.0822
Reinforcement	*.7047*	.2272	.2615
Fit into schedule	.2635	*.7722*	-.0060
Up-to-date, timely	*.8406*	.2329	-.0498
Communication	.0951	.0569	*.8947*
Credible	*.6310*	.0863	.1023

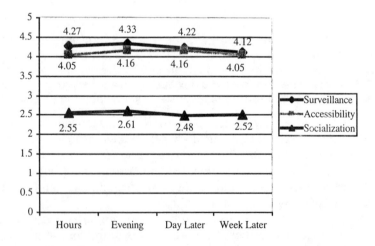

Fig. 6.2. Gratification means for each time segment examined during the WTC crisis. Gratifications were based on a 5-point Likert scale that ranged from 1 *not at all* to 5 *very much*.

For each time segment a multivariate analysis of variance (MANOVA), using the gratification factors as dependent variables, was used to analyze the data. Given a significant multivariate result, significant gratification factors were identified by univariate F tests. Post hoc analyses, using Tukey's test, were then used to detect differences among media usage for each significant gratification variable.

A significant multivariate effect was found for each time segment (see Table 6.2). During the immediate aftermath of the crisis, television met users' surveillance needs more than the Internet. The Internet users scored higher on socialization than TV users. During the evening of the attacks, TV users scored higher on the surveillance

Table 6.2. Overall Media Usage and Gratifications Received During the Week Following the September 11 Tragedies

Media	n	Surveillance	Accessibility	Socialization
			Gratification	
Hours following				
Television	277	4.32[a]	4.06	2.5[b]
Internet	17	3.73[b]	3.84	3.4[a]
Radio	24	4.14	4.06	2.6
Evening of				
Television	294	4.38[a]	4.19	2.61
Internet	15	4.04[b]	4.09	3.20
Radio	9	3.97	3.60	1.77
Day after				
Television	225	4.39[a]	4.25[a]	2.52
Internet	26	3.77[b]	3.86	2.96[a]
Radio	34	3.72[b]	4.14	1.88[b]
Newspapers	34	3.98[b]	3.78[b]	2.39
One week later				
Television	196	4.23[a]	4.12a	2.46
Internet	45	4.10	3.97	3.04
Radio	17	4.99	4.33a	2.76
Newspapers	49	3.84[b]	3.65[b]	2.22
Magazines	8	3.80	3.13[b]	2.13

Note. Different superscripts indicate significant differences ($p < .05$) using Tukey's test.

gratification than Internet users. The next day, TV users scored significantly higher than all other media users on the surveillance factor. Users during this time segment also found watching television more accessible than reading a newspaper. A week later, after all-day TV coverage had ended, TV users scored higher than newspaper users on the surveillance factor, but not significantly higher than Internet or radio users. By this time, users generally found broadcast media more accessible than print media.

DISCUSSION

One of this study's primary goals was to examine the role of the Internet in the news event diffusion process. Results suggest that the Internet was not comparable to television in terms of high media usage. Despite this, in contradiction to a recent study that suggested that the Internet may be underutilized as a mass medium (Stempel, Hargrove, & Bernt, 2000), these data suggest that the Internet competed comparably with other mass media, particularly newspapers.

Study results indicated that television provided the highest media usage for respondents throughout the 1-week period following the attacks. Although television usage declined from a high of 92% the evening of the attacks to 62% one week later, Internet and newspaper usage, minimal or negligible at first, rose to 14% and 16%, respectively by the end of the week. We would argue that the potential of the Internet to play an increasingly significant role in the news event diffusion process exists. During the time period of this study, 62% reported using the Internet. Of the participants who used the Internet, most (58%) reported using it in their homes, followed by at school (26%) then at work (14%). The fact that respondents were able to access Internet news from three separate locations bodes well for its future potential as a news event disseminator.

Several general conclusions are apparent for media gratifications during the week after the attacks. Respondents, during the first part of the week, perceived greater news satisfaction from television than other major media sources such as the Internet, radio, and newspapers. Perhaps because the networks provided full-day coverage for 4 days following the terrorist attacks, this enhanced the news surveillance gratification obtained from television. Respondents also reported, especially toward the end of the week time period, broadcast media more easily fit into their daily routine than print media.

Not surprisingly, respondents seemed to find flipping on a television or radio much easier than finding a newspaper or magazine to read. Because younger adults may be less likely to read a newspaper and more inclined to get their news from television, such usage may be habit.

Overall, the role the Internet seemed to satisfy more than other media was that of socialization. Relative advantages offered by the medium such as interactivity and ability to communicate through e-mail apparently contributed to its usage.

Media gratifications were relatively constant during the aftermath of the tragedies with news surveillance and accessibility comparable and greater than the need for socialization. The finding that media usage changed over this period of time indicates that the audience was active in terms of selecting various media to fill different gratifications, which remained stable. Television was likely the medium of choice because of its extensive coverage and its relative ease of access. Only when TV programming returned to its regular schedule did other media such as the Internet and newspapers make inroads into the respondents' primary news media usage patterns.

The results of this study also add information to the discussion about the relative roles of interpersonal and mass media in the news event diffusion process. Data from this study found, like Hill and Bonjean (1964), that interpersonal means played a larger role in the initial diffusion of the news event than mass media sources. One of the strongest (and oldest) suppositions of news diffusion research is that the higher the salience of the news event, the higher the rate of interpersonal diffusion. The results of the study were comparable to other crisis news diffusion events such as the Kennedy assassination (Greenberg, 1964a).

Finally, some caution should be taken in generalizing the results of this study. Using a convenience sample of college students, the selection was not random. However, for this study and others involving the Internet, the young adult cohort is ideal. More at ease with computers and the World Wide Web than a wider range of respondents might be, college students exist in a technologically advanced information environment. Students have ready access to the Internet through campus computer labs, as well as through home–university linked computers (Tapscott, 1998).

The results of this investigation may have other implications for future news diffusion research. The role of the Internet, along with newspapers, as a source of information, did intensify during the 1-week time period following the WTC attack. Given the relative advantages of the Internet (immediacy, increasing accessibility, and providing detailed information) one might predict that future Internet usage will increase relative to that of more traditional media such as print.

7

*Tracking Media Consumption Among Monitors and Blunters**

Melissa M. Spirek
Colleen Fitzpatrick
Constance R. Bridges
Bowling Green State University

University students in the United States and Canada reported in a recent Web survey that they watched 5 or more hours of television on September 11, 2001. In Brown, Bocarnea, and Basil's (2001) Web survey, 81% of the 852 students surveyed indicated that television was the most important information source for following the news story about the terrorist attacks. Television also was ranked as number 1 by 72% of the respondents when asked to rank the various media sources they plan on using for following that news story. These college students were like millions of others across the United States who turned to television sets for timely information about 9/11, as has been done in prior historic tragedies (Dayan & Katz, 1992) and with other terrorist attacks (Bandura, 1998). What is interesting is how viewers coped with this particular stressful media content. From

*The authors thank Craig Curtis and Edith M. Spirek who made this study possible.

the perspective of many viewers, what was unique about this destruction was that this was not a war or tragedy in another country like the Persian Gulf War (Greenberg & Gantz, 1993; Ross, 2001; Young & Jesser, 1997). Terrorists had hit home.

A great deal of public concern has been expressed about the physical, emotional, and cognitive effects the terrorist attack in the United States has had on the television viewing audience (Toller, 2001). The stress-inducing televised images that led to this concern are many and varied. These broadcast images ranged from morning television news coverage of the World Trade Center (WTC) after the jet crashed into the first tower to live coverage of the second jet's crash into the second tower. Then flames flashing from the Pentagon crash were broadcast before the black imprint left by Flight 93 was shown.

Exposure to tragic and emotionally upsetting media images is not unusual and in fact appears to be increasing (Sparks, 1986b). Two elements could be contributing to this trend: the proliferation of multichannel cable and dish systems that offer literally hundreds of stations (Baruch, 1989; Heeter & Greenberg, 1988) and the live television broadcasts of disasters and tragedies that at times are even uninterrupted by advertising (Bandura, 1998; also see Meyrowitz, 1985, for a general discussion of the implications of live television broadcasts). The prevalence and intensity of mass media-induced fright reactions and even depression has stimulated programmatic research on the ways in which television viewers can effectively cope with these emotional disturbances.

Unlike the studies that examined children's media-induced fear (Strasburger & Wilson, 2002), the relationship of personality or individual differences to mass media reactions has emerged as an increasingly popular theme in the literature on adults' responses to stressful media. Arousability (Sparks, Spirek, & Hodgson, 1993), sensation-seeking, machiavellianism (Tamborini & Stiff, 1987), enjoyment of frightening films (Sparks, 1986) and the desire to see destruction (Tamborini, Stiff, & Zillmann, 1987) are examples of five individual differences examined in relationship to viewing stressful or even frightening media. Of particular interest to the media research proposed here is the work of Miller, who has studied coping styles for dealing with stress.

ADULTS' MONITORING AND BLUNTING DIFFERENCES IN INFORMATION STYLES FOR COPING WITH THREATENING SITUATIONS

S. Miller (1987) observed that individuals differ according to their preferred ways of coping with uncontrollable threatening events. These coping style differences seemed to be related to the individual's willingness to seek out information about threatening situations (S. Miller, 1992a, 1996). In order to systematically examine these information preferences and to test the blunting hypothesis (S. Miller, 1981), Miller developed a scale that differentiates between individuals' preferences for information about an upcoming threatening situation (S. Miller, 1987). The Miller Behavioral Style Scale (MBSS) divides individuals into one of two coping styles on the basis of their responses to four independent stressful scenarios.

Studies have shown the MBSS to be a reliable and valid measure that identifies "monitors" and "blunters" and lends support to the blunting hypothesis (S. Miller, 1981; S. Miller & Grant, 1979). The blunting hypothesis posits that before encountering a stressful situation, monitors experience the greatest anxiety when information is not available. Blunters experience the greatest stress when they are not able to distract themselves. In other words, monitors prefer voluminous information in the face of a negatively stressful event, whereas blunters prefer low amounts of information. A key component to the classification of the monitors and blunters is that the stressful situation be beyond one's control. Anxiety is decreased when facing an uncontrollable stressful situation by either seeking or avoiding additional voluminous information (Fisher, 1986).

MONITORING AND BLUNTING DIFFERENCES FOR COPING WITH STRESSFUL MASS MEDIA

The first published mass media communication study that utilized Miller's coping style distinction was completed by Sparks and Spirek (1988). They investigated the monitoring and blunting coping preferences of adults as a means of studying human activation and arousal systems and their relationship to viewing stressful or frightening media. These researchers argued that the MBSS allows innate differences to be measured within the activation and arousal systems, which in turn influence one's media consumption.

According to Tucker and Williamson (1984), the activation system is associated with left-brain processing and is biased toward internal information flow. These researchers also proposed that the arousal system is associated with right-brain processing and is biased toward external information flow. The activation-arousal framework's relationship with emotion was explained by Sparks and Spirek (1988):

> since the arousal system is primarily associated with emotional expression, individuals with an arousal system bias will tend toward higher degrees of affective intensity. In contrast, individuals with a bias toward activation rather than arousal will tend toward an internal attentional focus and will be more likely to withdraw from the immediate environment. (pp. 198–199)

Sparks and Spirek also noted that the activation bias results in blunted emotional responses, whereas an individual with an arousal bias attends to novel stimuli. They argued that the MBSS is linked to an adult's activation or arousal bias.

Before encountering a stressful situation then, monitors were expected to feel the greatest anxiety when information was not available. Blunters were expected to feel the greatest anxiety when they were not able to distract themselves. It was also hypothesized that those who are monitors will be more likely to expose themselves to information about the uncontrollable stressful event, whereas the blunters would not seek out the additional information. Two studies, one that examined emotional response to *Nightmare on Elm Street* and a second that examined emotional responses to the news broadcasts of the *Challenger*'s explosion, supported both hypotheses.

Mass media monitoring and blunting investigations with adults in a setting with the focus on ecological validity are scarce. The scope of this limitation is more apparent when one considers the practical implications the monitoring and blunting distinction holds at a time when more tragedies and disasters are being broadcast live.

CURRENT INVESTIGATION

In summary, although a variety of studies have linked monitoring and blunting differences to stressful media consumption with children (Hoffner, 1997; Spirek, 1992), with teens (Hoffner, 1995), and with adults in experimental conditions (Sparks, 1989a, 1989b), the number of studies that have investigated adult consumption of mediated content related to an uncontrollable stressful event in the real world is limited. The historical tragedy of 9/11 provided a traumatic and salient situation for responding to that void.

The current investigation tests the activation-arousal framework to determine its ability to predict individual differences in information seeking of the highly negative emotional information of September 11, 2001. It is predicted that monitors will seek voluminous information and therefore increase their consumption of news after the terrorist attack, whereas blunters will decrease their news consumption. The reverse is predicted with television programs where news is not the focus but rather entertainment is highlighted. Monitors' consumption of programs where the main focus is not to inform but is rather to entertain will decrease and blunters' consumption of programs where the main focus is not to inform but is rather to entertain will increase. Television consumption by the monitors and blunters of September 10 will be compared to that of September 12. The following directed hypotheses are advanced.

H1: High monitors/low blunters will increase their consumption of television news after the uncontrollable stressful terrorist events of September 11, 2001.
H2: Low monitors/high blunters will decrease their consumption of television news after the uncontrollable stressful terrorist events of September 11, 2001.
H3: High monitors/low blunters will decrease their consumption of television programs that are entertaining (not news) after the uncontrollable stressful terrorist events of September 11, 2001.
H4: Low monitors/high blunters will increase their consumption of television programs that are entertaining (not news) after the uncontrollable stressful terrorist events of September 11, 2001.

METHOD

Participants

Students enrolled in a Fall 2001 introductory communication class at a large midwestern university were recruited for the study. A media journal activity had been assigned to begin September 10, 2001, and provided a unique opportunity for this investigation. The final sample included all students who volunteered. The overall recruited sample who volunteered consisted of 41 males and 69 females ($N = 110$).

A monitoring score and a blunting score were calculated for each of the participants. The scoring replicated the procedure operationalized with earlier activation-arousal studies that used the MBSS (Sparks, 1989a, 1989b; Sparks & Spirek, 1988). Gender was not related to the scale classifications so data were collapsed across this factor. For the monitoring subscale, the scores ranged from 4 to 16 and for the blunting subscale, the scores ranged form 1 to 11. A median split also was calculated with 11 emerging as the median for the monitoring scale and 4 emerging as the median for the blunting scale.

Participants who scored above the monitoring scale's median and below the blunting scale's median totaled 30. These participants comprised the study's high monitoring/low blunting group (Monitors). The means and standard deviations for the category of the high monitors/low blunters' subscales were calculated: monitoring ($M = 13.33$, $SD = 1.32$) and blunting ($M = 2.37$, $SD = 1.35$). Participants who scored below the monitoring scale's median and above the blunting scale's median also totaled 30. This second group of participants comprised the study's high blunting/low monitoring group (Blunters). The means and standard deviations for the category of the high blunters/low monitors subscales were also calculated: monitoring ($M = 8.70$, $SD = 2.02$) and blunting ($M = 6.87$, $SD = 1.80$).

Materials

The independent variable is personal coping style as measured with the MBSS. Discriminant and convergent validity has been documented within studies (Sparks, 1989a, 1989b) and across a variety of uncontrollable stressful situations (e.g., S. Miller, 1992a, 1992b, 1996; Warburton, Fishman, & Perry, 1997).

The dependent variable of television programs watched was measured according to self-reports of television viewing. At the participants' midwestern university, classes were held and no memorial services were organized until weeks after September 11 so both of these potential influences did not have to be addressed when considering external factors that might have influenced television program consumption.

Each of the 60 students' media diaries was coded for September 10 and this procedure was repeated for September 12. Only broadcast shows were included in the data set. The use of DVDs, VCRs, or video games did not meet the current study's criteria of viewing broadcast TV shows. Each program entry was coded for the television program as being news or entertaining (not news) and the duration of this program was also recorded to the nearest half hour. For a program to be included as "having been viewed," a student needed to indicate that he or she had viewed at least 15 minutes of the program and this show was then rounded up to the nearest half hour. If the participant watched 14 minutes or less, the program was not included in the data.

To be included in the news category, the television program was required to have a hard news segment and the main purpose of the program was to inform as opposed to entertain. The program's news stories were required to meet the traditional characteristics of news: timeliness, importance, prominence, proximity, and oddities (Fedler, Bender, Davenport, & Kostyu, 1997). Timeliness in particular was viewed as key in conveying the information the reporters had to share. News included programs identified as news shows (e.g., nightly network news, *Headline News*), news magazines (e.g., *Dateline, 60 Minutes*) and morning shows (e.g., *Good Morning America*). The main purpose of shows not in the news category was identified as being to entertain. Shows identified as not news included movies, talk shows (e.g., *The View, The Oprah Winfrey Show*), situation comedies (e.g., *Friends*), game shows (e.g., *Hollywood Squares*), cartoons (e.g., *The Simpsons*), shopping network shows (e.g., *QVC*), and dramas (e.g., *Law & Order*).

Procedure

On September 10 and September 12, 2001, participants completed a diary of their media consumption. The students recorded when, what, with whom, where, and the duration of their television viewing. Four weeks after completing the media diaries, students completed a questionnaire that included the MBSS scales.

RESULTS

The four hypotheses were tested with one-tailed paired sample t tests. As shown in Table 7.1, statistically significant results emerged for three of the four hypotheses. The first hypothesis was found to be statistically significant with the monitors' news consumption [$t(29) = -7.71$, $p = .00$, $d = .99$]. Monitors' consumption of television news on September 12 increased when compared with September 10, 2001. In direct contrast, the second hypothesis that predicted that blunters' news consumption would decrease was not supported [$t (29) = -.94$, $p = .18$]. Blunters' television news consumption on September 10 did not significantly decrease on September 12.

Table 7.1. Mean Hours of Daily Television Viewing

	September 10 (N = 30)	September 12 (N = 30)	t	Sig.
News				
High monitors/low blunters	.97	4.13	-7.71	.00
High blunters/low monitors	.95	1.13	-.94	n.s.
Entertaining (Not News)				
High monitors/low blunters	2.67	.45	7.23	.00
High blunters/low monitors	1.62	2.43	-3.37	.00

Note. Cell entries are the number of hours viewed on September 10 and September 12.

The third and fourth hypotheses predicted that monitors' consumption of non-news or entertaining content would significantly decrease whereas the blunters' consumption would increase. Statistically significant findings emerged with the third hypothesis [t (29) = 7.23, p = .00, d = .97] that predicted that monitors would significantly decrease their entertaining or "non-news" viewing of broadcast television. Similarly, statistically significant differences emerged with the blunters' increased consumption of entertaining or "non-news" programs [$t(29)$ = -3.37, p = .00, d = .75] between those two dates.

DISCUSSION

The activation-arousal framework was fruitful for reviewing individual differences for comparing the consumption of television content the day before and the day after the terrorist attack in the United States. This unfortunate tragedy served as a situation that allowed the activation-arousal research to continue beyond its traditional experimental setting.

High monitors/low blunters significantly increased their consumption of news programs after September 11th as predicted in the first hypothesis. This finding is consistent with the activation-arousal framework that argues that individuals identified as monitors would want to consume large amounts of information about an uncontrollable stressful event. This study argues that in order to decrease anxiety, monitors actively sought additional information about September 11 by watching television news programs. It is interesting to note that similar results were not found with the blunters and therefore it is not simply the case that all audience members—both monitors and blunters—increased their consumption of television news. This could have easily been the case since the number of hours of news exponentially increased after the terrorist attacks.

The second hypothesis that predicted that blunters' consumption of television news would significantly decrease was not supported. A potential reason for this could be a floor effect with the number of hours the students view news. If a blunter does not watch many hours of news to start, it is difficult to decrease one's total consumption over time. It could be that blunters do not seek out news in general so an uncontrollable situation being broadcast would not permit him or her to view even less.

The third hypothesis was supported. High monitors/low blunters were more likely to decrease their viewing of television shows that focused on entertaining or were "not news" programs. These monitors decreased their viewing of shows that did not have a news focus over the 3 days is logical because their consumption of news shows could potentially displace entertainment viewing time.

The fourth hypothesis that predicted that blunters would increase their consumption of entertaining shows to allow them to "blunt" or avoid the voluminous information about the attack was supported. This finding is especially impressive because of the large increase in news coverage. These participants had to seek out shows that did not focus on new updates about the terrorist attacks. As one student wrote, "I did not want to hear about a bunch of speculation from reporters who really did not know what was going on."

One weakness of this study is that two different week days of television consumption were compared. Perhaps the students' typical media consumption on Mondays is not comparable to that of Wednesdays. A second weakness is that the television programming formats changed with many stations airing only news coverage of the terrorist attack.

The monitoring and blunting preferred coping differences with uncontrollable stressful television content need to be tested with other media. For example, Wiggins' (2001) research of the effects of September 11 on Google is one example where scholars can determine if it is the monitors who are turning to the web for additional information when faced with an uncontrollable stressful event. Another study could look at how monitors and blunters draw from a variety of media. This additional research will recognize the increasing complexity the current media consumer faces in the "Information Age."

8

Media Use in Germany Around the Attacks in the United States

Jutta Roeser
Gudrun Schaefer
Bochum University

When we planned a study about young adults' perceptions of political TV programs, we were not able to foresee that our topic would be dramatically changed and dominated by the terrible events of September 11. In August 2001 we prepared group discussions with young adults (20-25), students on the one hand and working people on the other. Supported by four examples, we wanted to discuss the interviewees' media use, especially their TV use, their preferences concerning TV programs, their general interest in political questions, and the way they define *politics*.

Then, on September 11, when the twin towers collapsed, our research design had to be revised and changed because we were aware that most Germans were affected by the attacks rather strongly. A close link with the United States, based on historical experience and cultural similarities, was proved by the deep shock that also hit public life in Germany. At many German schools, teachers discussed with their students about the horrible events, and on 9/11 itself, many people stood in train station halls and stared at the big TV screens that were installed there. All these people seemed to forget their daily work and duties while they tried to understand the pictures of the collapsing twin towers, pictures that were repeatedly shown by CNN and all other stations. So, on 9/11 and the days after, the Germans stayed in collective presence in front of their TV sets, abroad or at home, and we decided to integrate this special behavior in our theoretical frame and in our research design. At the beginning of our group discussions, which started on September 25, we discussed with young adults about their way of using media after the attacks and we tried to analyze the reasons for the reported behavior.

We want to introduce some data about media use in Germany at normal times and about some trends concerning young adults. After this, we shortly explain the methods of our study, based on group discussions and the methods of two further surveys. In the third part, we refer to representative data about the change of media use after the terror attacks, and then we enrich this data by the results of our own qualitative study that especially focuses on the view of young adults and on the role of television during this time of crisis. Finally, we want to discuss the audience's shift toward television and draw conclusions about the special role of television.

MEDIA USE IN GERMANY BEFORE THE ATTACKS: SOME BASIC DATA

As recent studies prove, television still is the most important medium for Germans. Nearly 85% of the population (aged 14 years and more) watch television nearly every day and 98% of German households own at least one TV set. Apart from the great appreciation for television, radio and newspaper also get major attention by German media users: 85% listen to their radio every day. Radio accompanies people especially when people get up, when they drive to work, and also during their work time.

Newspapers still get respectable rates: About 79% of Germans read at least one newspaper a day (Ridder et al., 2001). (For more information about the media, the media system, and media research in Germany, see Brosius & Holtz-Bacha, 1999).

An interesting fact may be that the daily media use in Germany increased from 310 minutes in 1970 to 502 minutes in the year 2000. This result is mainly caused by a bigger budget of leisure from 1970 to 2000. But also a central thesis of media use seems to be proved by these data: New media never replace old media, but new media are added to the old ones by the users who spend more and more time with them. There is a third reason that explains how the German population spends 8 hours and more per day using various media. This great amount of time can only be explained by the fact that people listen to the radio while driving and working and that they watch television while doing chores. Besides that, it may be no exception that someone is surfing the Internet while listing to a CD or watching television. The situation of a person who listens to the radio or other audio media while reading a newspaper, a book, or a magazine sounds quite familiar. So we can see that the 502 minutes are cumulative data.

As mentioned previously, television is still the most attractive medium for most Germans. About 45% of the population would miss television most of all if they had no possibility to watch it further (Eimeren & Ridder, 2001). Those users who prefer private TV stations say that television is the most important medium for them. The increasing rates of TV use result from a rising perception of entertainment programs. Media researchers could observe that TV use in Germany tends to become a medium that is used while doing other things. In former times, TV perception in Germany was focused on the viewing situation itself; parallel activities were not a routine as for example in the United States.

In comparison to the United States, TV use in Germany still is focused around prime time. Whereas radio rates are high until 6 p.m., television reaches the highest level between 8 and 10 p.m., when about 60% of the population watch television! It is clear that radio and television are compensating media, in the evening television quickly replaces the radio. This change of use is nearly complete: Between 8 and 10 p.m. only 5% to 10% percent of the population listen to their radio. All these results show that it is justified to call television the "prime medium" of the Germans at the beginning of the 21st century. But it also has to be stressed that newspapers and radio (and recently the World Wide Web, too) are nearly as important as television in "normal" times of media use.

It is noticeable that the young generation in Germany is setting new trends. They don't find daily newspapers as important as the older generation, they like different TV programs and altogether they seem to dissociate themselves more and more from politicians and from political themes in the media. Infotainment programs, tabloid magazines, and other hybrid forms of information and entertainment were added to traditional TV news after the establishment of private TV stations. These new forms were mainly established in commercial programs. Young people especially prefer such programs and tend to turn toward private TV offers and to reject "pure" political information via television.

These trends are the background for our current study about the acceptance of political programs by young adults. Carrying out focus group discussions, we were interested in learning the reasons that lead to TV information abstinence, and we also wanted to know how young adults evaluate different forms of political TV programs. Last but not least, we hoped to give some recommendations as to what type of political program would interest young people between ages 20 and 25.

After the attacks, we asked questions about media use on and after September 11 in six group discussions with young adults. In the next section, we briefly explain the methods and then present the results concerning the detailed arguments about using media in special ways after 9/11. Besides our own research, we refer to some quantitative results of surveys about media use in Germany after 9/11.

METHODS

We refer to three sets of empirical studies. First, we refer to studies published at *Message,* a German journal for journalism. *Message* presented results by surveys of newspaper and online journalists about the rates and contacts of their newspapers and their websites (Holzapfel, 2002; Wiebersiek, 2002). The second study was done by the well-known German institute of public opinion research, Forsa. Commissioned by the TV journal *TV-Today*, this study asked a representative sample of 1,002 persons on September 19 and 20 about their TV use after the attacks and their opinion about the quality of TV reporting (Forsa, 2001, *TV Today*, 2001). Third, we present results of our group discussions with young people aged 20 to 25, that we led in September and October 2001 (Roeser & Schaefer, 2001). We held six focus group discussions between September 25 and October 30, 2001, and each group had four regular members. Four groups consisted of working people and two groups of students. The working people were trainees, young adults, whose practical job training includes 1 day a week at a kind of college. This is where we met the trainees and carried out the discussions. The students were from the University of Bochum. They studied different subjects but not media or communication science. Concerning our general questions, we organized separate groups of women and men because one of our main questions was whether young women and men show different attitudes toward political reporting in the media. Former research results demonstrate that women, more than men, take on a certain distance toward political topics on television and other media, especially when institutional forms of politics are the focus of reporting.

Focus group members were asked how they had heard about the terror attacks. We wanted to know if and how their media use had changed after 9/11. We especially tried to find out the meaning of different types of media in the aftermath of the disaster. Additionally, we asked if social relations became more important in the context of media use at that time, for example the perception and discussion of TV programs together with friends or with the family. Then we did some research concerning the motives of the young people for seeking information about the events. Last but not least, we wanted to know which aspects of the reporting they criticized.

MEDIA USE ON AND AFTER SEPTEMBER 11

Quantitative Data

As representative surveys can prove, television, radio, newspapers, magazines, and Internet information pages were used more intensively after the attacks than before. Concerning print media, especially big newspapers reached higher rates after the attacks (Wiebersiek, 2002). But the numbers decreased on a normal level rather quickly after some weeks. Only three newspapers that are very well known in Germany—*Frankfurter Allgemeine Zeitung (FAZ)*, *Die Tageszeitung (TAZ)*, and *Süddeutsche Zeitung (SZ)*—could gain a higher level of buyers than before the attacks on a long term (Wiebersiek, 2002). Web sites also were used more than at normal times, but it made a difference concerning the sites: Comedy sites were neglected, whereas the sites of big TV stations and journals got respectable rates. So media researchers say that the character of the "original medium," for example, a well-known journal, like *Spiegel* or *Stern,* influences the confidence and the interest of the users for this special type of site in times of crisis (Holzapfel, 2002).

But besides that, television became the leading medium after the attacks. When asked what medium was the most important one after the attacks, more than 80% of the Germans indicated television. Just 8% named radio, 7% the newspaper. The Internet with 2% and journals with 1% fell on the last ranges of importance (Forsa, 2001).

The dominant position of television was explained by several questions and their results. Exactly 40% of the interviewees (especially persons older than 30) said the best reporting about the attacks was published by public television. This means that public television in Germany still has the best image concerning serious information and objective reporting. In addition, 24% named news channels as their favorite source of information. These rates are much higher than normal rates for news channels in Germany and they confirm that people seek serious and quick information in times of crises. But also RTL, Germany's first and most popular private TV channel, was able to gain respectable rates: 17% liked the RTL program best. RTL also was successful in the quality of reporting: 23% named Peter Kloeppel from RTL as most competent journalist, reporting about the attacks, 21% named Ulrich Wickert from the public channel ARD.

The TV users also were asked if they liked the number of special programs that were shown about the attacks. Fifty-eight percent told the interviewers that the number of specials was okay. Only 3% complained that there was too little reporting about the attacks, whereas 42% said that there was too much reporting.

When asked how long the terror attacks would influence the TV programs in the future, a majority answered that the programming would be changed for about 1 month. Twenty-three percent thought there could be different programming for about 6 months, and 16% were of the opinion that TV programming would change for a year, longer than a year, or even forever. These answers show how people are touched by historical events, and consequently they give a historical if not eternal meaning to this experience. In contradiction to that, 16% said that the programming would be influenced by the attacks just for 1 week.

The last question, asked by Forsa for *TV Today*, concerned the canceling of comedy programs after the attacks: 54% agreed with the decision of TV directors to replace comedies with information programs for about 1 or 2 weeks. Of the viewers, 24% had welcomed a comedy break that was longer than 1 week. Only 7% said that there had to be no break. These results show that German viewers seemed to perceive the situation after the attacks as a highly exceptional one, and consequently this state was also mirrored by TV use at this time. In the next section, we present some reasons for changed media use in the time after the attacks. These are the results of our qualitative research.

ANALYSIS OF GROUP DISCUSSIONS:
THE SPECIAL VIEW OF YOUNG ADULTS

Based on six group discussions, we analyzed five questions concerning media use in the context of the terror attack.

RQ1:   How did the young adults hear about the terror attack on September 11 and how did they use the media on this day?

When the attacks began, it was 2:45 p.m. German time and 15 minutes later, TV stations began reporting. In all the groups, participants talked without hesitation about how they had heard about the attack. It became clear that everyone was able to remember this situation exactly. There is a similar trend in Germany concerning the opening of the wall between western and eastern Germany in 1989 and for the older generation, the attack on John F. Kennedy: Everybody is able to remember the place where he or she heard about it. On September 11, there were two variations: either people heard about the attack by chance through the media—because they happened to be listening to the radio at their workplace, using the Internet, or watching television at home; or they heard about the attack because friends or family members phoned them. After hearing the news, they immediately turned to the media for more information. It becomes clear that the attack also had a dramatic effect on people in Germany. Clearly, everyone found it important enough to immediately inform friends or relatives by telephone. Upon arriving home, nearly everyone turned on the television immediately and continued watching for hours.

Many participants spoke about seeing the TV pictures for the first time. The drama of the event was fully conveyed only through a visual context, through the TV pictures. For example, one male trainee described what he imagined when he heard the radio news; a very small plane crashing into the World Trade Center, and he continued describing how he was completely stunned when he watched the actual pictures later on television. The meaning of the event only became really clear through a visual context.

In some groups, the first impression of the TV pictures was compared to scenes from fictional programs. This comparison was often heard in Germany: People said in the first few moments they believed they were watching a film. A male trainee described his thoughts as follows: "Cool, they're showing *Independence Day*"—and shortly afterwards—"It's for real!" Someone else said he had associated the pictures with "science fiction" at first. But we can assume that these young men did not really believe the scenes were from a film—the trainees, for example, already knew about the catastrophe from the radio. Thus, in our opinion, people used this comparison because they wanted to find a way to express the horror and incomprehensibility of the attack: Pictures and stories known as a normal part of fictional programs suddenly happened in the sphere of the news and therefore in the sphere of reality. The pictures were similar, but their meaning differed dramatically.

RQ2: Which role did the different types of media play in the aftermath of September 11? Did differences exist compared to media use in a normal situation?

Television was the most important medium in this international crisis. This was the result of our interviews as well as from the representative survey we mentioned previously. Besides this, the group discussions showed that the relevance of other types of media was dependent on the everyday media preferences of the interviewees. Those who normally read a daily newspaper continued to do so; those who normally got their information from the World Wide Web turned to the Web at least now and again during the crisis. Thus, the importance of each of the media types essentially corresponded with its importance in everyday life.

In particular we found the following trends. The *radio* was very often used at the workplace or while driving the car in order to obtain information on current developments. Generally speaking; the radio was an important medium for keeping up to date only when no other medium was available. Thus, nobody in the groups talked about radio use at home.

Only a few participants named the *newspaper* as an important medium during this time. This must be seen in a general context, daily newspapers are no longer as important for the younger generation in Germany as they are for the older one. Participants who do not usually read a newspaper told us they took a look once in a while at the newspaper of their parents or colleagues, but they didn't buy an edition specially after September 11. One female trainee was an exception: She consciously decided just to use newspapers to keep up to date because she could not tolerate excessively dramatic TV news pictures any longer. Another exception was a female student who argued explicitly against newspapers; she didn't find them current enough. She felt that something new could be happening every hour and this could only be gleaned from television.

We found an interesting result concerning the Web. The Web was sometimes important for the special situation on September 11, but not so much in the aftermath. In this international crisis, the Internet appeared to have taken on a rather secondary role. Even those participants who usually use the Web reported that they used it rather less than usual.

What could be the reason for this? This question leads us directly to one of the advantages of television. In the face of the international crisis, special journalistic performances and strengths were required. In our groups, many participants expressed that they wanted orientation and for the facts to be put in order. They praised background information, soundly investigated facts and different experts offering a wide range of perspectives on the event. This need for such unique journalistic competence may be the reason why the Web was not named as very important. The Web may offer a lot of information, but it is not a guarantee of reliability and credibility.

The young adults turned first to *television* to satisfy their need for information—whereas the data of media use mentioned earlier shows that many of the (older) Germans also chose newspapers. There are two reasons for the great importance of television. First, TV as a visual medium conveys the strongest and most authentic impression of the terrible events. Second, information programs fulfill the need for journalistic competence and background knowledge. Thus, combining visual quality with journalistic competence, television had a special meaning on and after September 11.

Compared with media use in normal situations the Germans invested a lot more time in news and information programs (such as political magazines, talk shows, and documentaries). It is, therefore, no surprise that most people were in agreement with the changes made to the normal program schedule in the week after September 11. Many participants also praised the German music station Viva, which cancelled all its programming for a few days and only broadcast a black screen with the sentence "Out of respect for the victims of the terror attack in the USA we are not broadcasting at the moment." At the same time, some of the interviewees felt that the number of programs about the attack was excessive.

Did young people prefer other channels than the ones they usually watched? In some cases, yes. Many participants used the special news channels more than usual for getting a quick overview—two German stations and also CNN. In addition, some expressed a greater preference for the public service programs because they found them more serious and credible. The big private stations that young Germans watch anyway were also mentioned. Many group members told us that they often switched between stations, selecting the right kind of reporting for their current needs.

RQ3: How important was it to talk about the events and to use media together with other people—friends, family members, or colleagues?

Many participants found family members very important for discussions—especially young adults who still live with their parents. Intensive talks were viewed in a positive light. These talks generally took place independently from shared media use. It is noticeable that conversations with friends about the attack do not appear to play an important role. Perhaps these young adults preferred discussions with older people in such situations because at another point in our group discussions (on another theme) the participants often described the older generation as more politically competent and informed. Another reason could be that it is not common practice for the younger generation to engage in political debates among themselves. *Work colleagues* were also important. There are radios at many workplaces. The trainees reported that in the aftermath of the attack, the use of radio had changed: Music was no longer as important as information. The radio was turned up louder when the news came on. Colleagues listened together and discussed the current situation.

RQ4: Which reasons and motives did the group members name for their interest in seeking out information concerning the attack?

It should have become clear that the Germans were strongly affected by the terror attack, and they used the media very extensively for background information and for keeping up to date. Besides these general reasons for media use, the participants mentioned their motives for interest in more detail. Many felt uncertainty and fear as to how things would continue. In two groups where this fear was an important theme, we found two explanations: one based on a local context and another based on a more global view.

The global view concerned the fear of war. One group with male trainees discussed it intensively. They were afraid "the big bang" could happen. They were not only worried about German security but also of world security, for example, the fact that a nation could set off a nuclear bomb. One female student said she had phoned her friend the night after September 11 to warn her; as her friend didn't have a television she didn't know about the bomb dropped on Kabul. These group members, therefore, wanted to be well informed about current international developments, although they argued at the same time that they as "small fry" had no chance to prevent a war. In this context, some participants strongly expressed sympathy with older Germans who had lived through World War II because of their particularly great fear of war. The local context was important in one group of female trainees. They expressed their fears about the developments in Germany because some of the terrorists had lived there. These group members were particularly concerned by the fact that one of the terrorists had at some point lived nearby, only a few miles away from their town. They felt especially affected because of this proximity and described their fear as resulting from personal involvement.

Altogether, we found three different postures toward the event. First there was described a general need for information ("to know how things will continue," "to keep up to date," "to understand what happened and why"). This was expressed in all our group discussions. Second we found a position of viewing the pictures as spectacular action. This position was expressed in one group with male trainees. They found the reports "extreme" and "interesting because it doesn't happen every day," they praised the visual quality of television and some web pages because you could see "100% of the crash." The group members self-critically analyzed their position and found themselves "a little bit voyeuristic." It became clear that their view was partly influenced by a certain fascination, but they were also interested in other themes. Third there was a position of sympathy for the American people directly affected. This position goes hand in hand with an interest in human interest reports and was held above all by a group of female trainees.

RQ5: Which aspects of media reporting did the participants criticize? In particular, did they feel that the very intensive reporting had been too excessive?

The German media reported the attack very extensively. For the first 3 days, nearly all regular TV programs had been cancelled and in the subsequent weeks there was an abundance of special programs and special written reports in all the media. Thus, all participants took the view that the media reported extensively and some felt this was right, but others felt it was too much. This difference of opinion was apparent in the Forsa survey: Whereas 61% of the young people (14–29 years) agreed with the extensive reporting on television, 32% said that it was too much. In the survey there were more young men than women who felt it was excessive, but in our group discussions it was especially the female trainees who disagreed: Some of them felt it was already too much after 2 days.

Which arguments were mentioned in our group discussions? A lot of participants criticized the continued repetition of the same pictures and information in the news. There was in fact a discrepancy between the wide range of reporting and the small amount of actual exclusive news. The two groups of female trainees were especially critical. They said they "always saw the same pictures" and they complained that the subject was "reported to death."

Through further discussions it became clear that some female trainees in particular made a distinction between the news on the one hand, which they criticized because of the repetition, and some kinds of infotainment programs on the other hand, which they praised. After the first 2 days, they preferred tabloid style reports about human interest themes, which they called "background information." For example they were interested in stories about firefighters, about the fate of individual victims, and about the grief of relatives. Seeing such stories, they felt deep empathy for those directly affected. Perhaps this explains the gendered TV preferences the young adults expressed in the survey. Whereas young men did not have show a special preference, many young women (36%) preferred the private station RTL, a large commercial channel that presented a mix of hard news and human interest stories after the attacks.

The group of male students also took a critical view, but their arguments partly opposed those of the female trainees. The students strongly criticized the infotainment and tabloid style programs. They also criticized the news, because here too they showed very sensational and emotional pictures which sometimes were accompanied by music. They complained that the TV stations tried "to make money with emotions" and "to win viewers by showing tears." This position is probably a special view held by higher educated (male) Germans.

Finally, some groups complained of biased reporting, for example the apparent delight of some Palestinians that was uncritically broadcasted by all TV stations. They argued that they wanted to understand the viewpoint of Western as well as non-Western nations and to see the situation from various different perspectives. Many participants, however, commented positively that the intercultural perspective had been put across very well in the aftermath of September 11.

DISCUSSION

There was great interest and empathy in Germany immediately after the attacks and in the following weeks. The Germans, therefore, agreed with the very intensive reporting by the media during the first days. We suppose that media were used so intensively initially to cope with the sudden shock, TV viewing especially could express the common experience of a whole nation hoping to understand and possibly to get through these terrible events. Therefore, the deep shock led many viewers to foresee a long-lasting change in TV programs for the future (which in fact didn't happen).

In the aftermath, the audience developed a differentiated media use between that of lasting interest and a feeling of too much. In this context our group discussions give some hints that this excess is founded on a critical view of the news, because of the discrepancy between the wide range of reporting and the small amount of actual exclusive news.

In this exceptional situation the strengths of television seem to be what we would like to call a *multifunctional character*: Television gave the audience visual quality *and* actuality *and* journalistic competence and thus became the most important medium. The journalistic quality was guaranteed by the preselection of and commenting on information by the TV stations and this became important, not so much at the beginning but more and more in the following days. The Internet lost acceptance in this situation because people got quick information, but less reliability. In addition, television enabled the viewers to switch quickly between the different programs and stations, for example, German *and* American channels, private *and* public stations and, importantly, a switch between information (news) and narration (tabloid magazines). So television was the multifunctional medium that fitted perfectly to the uses and needs of the German audience during this situation of international crisis.

After 2 weeks, users returned step by step to a more normal media use, and we could observe a wide range of media use patterns, adapted exactly to the viewers' needs during this situation. So, we once more emphasize the competence and flexibility of media users: We should be aware that media users usually follow their everyday routines, but that they are also able to create very special and well-adapted media use patterns, fitting exactly to the special situation in times of exception.

II

The Content of News and Non-News Elements of the Terrorist Attacks

9

How TV News Covered the Crisis: The Content of CNN, CBS, ABC, NBC and Fox*

Kirsten Mogensen
Laura Lindsay
Xigen Li
Jay Perkins
Mike Beardsley
Louisiana State University

Thousands of people had just arrived at work in the World Trade Center (WTC) in New York when American Airlines Flight 11 slammed into the North Tower at 8:45 a.m. EST. Within minutes, CNN televised live pictures from the scene of the disaster. Here is how CNN anchor Carol Lin described the incident at 8:49:50 a.m. on September 11, 2001:

> This is just in. You are looking at obviously a very disturbing live shot there. That is the World Trade Center, and we have unconfirmed reports this morning that a plane has crashed into one

*We are grateful to the management and staff at CNN and FOX for taking time to share their insights with us. We also would like to thank the following students who helped us code the programs: Ashley Guidry, Ying Kong, Xinkun Wang, Stacy Humphries and Jennifer Ali. Finally, we are in debt for ideas and editorial support to our colleagues in the September 11 Research Group at LSU: Ralph Izard, Anne Cunningham, Susan Brown, Craig Freeman, Renita Coleman, Robert McMullen and Denis Wu.

of the towers of the World Trade Center. CNN Center right now is just beginning to work on this story, obviously calling our sources and trying to figure out exactly what happened.

ABC, NBC, CBS, and Fox News also began televising live pictures from the scene. When United Airlines Flight 175 hit the South Tower approximately 18 minutes later, the networks, including CNN and Fox News, covered the crash as it happened. Viewers watched live footage of thousands of people running from the burning towers and the towers collapsing in a plume of ash and debris. Television covered the crash of American Airlines Flight 77 into the Pentagon at 9:45 a.m. and of United Airlines Flight 93 crashing southeast of Pittsburgh. Viewers saw the evacuation of the White House, heard about the closing of the nation's borders and of the air traffic control system, and waited anxiously for word about the president, who was moving between secured air force bases on Air Force One.

The news spread quickly and television was thrust to center stage for its biggest role since the Kennedy assassination. This study sought to answer two basic questions. Did television help Americans cope with the crisis, or did it act as an impartial messenger? What journalistic values lay behind the coverage? To answer these questions, we analyzed the content of CBS, CNN, Fox, NBC and ABC during the first 8 hours of televised coverage after the attack on the WTC and we interviewed decision makers and journalists at CNN and Fox News.

MEDIA COVERAGE OF CRISIS EVENTS

Public crises can be defined as "natural or manmade events that pose an immediate and serious threat to the lives and property or to the peace of mind of large numbers of citizens" (Graber, 1980, p. 225). Among examples of other key crises in U.S. history are the Japanese attack on Pearl Harbor on December 7, 1941 and the assassination of President Kennedy on November 22, 1963. According to Neal (1998):

An extraordinary event becomes a national trauma under circumstances in which the social system is disrupted to such a magnitude that it commands the attention of all major subgroups of the population. . . . The major task, individually and collectively, is that of integrating the traumatic event into the fabric of social life in order to make it less threatening. (pp. 9-12)

When the social order is seriously disrupted, the public usually will desire as much information as the media can provide. Incomplete information at a time of crisis leads to suspicion and rumor (Schaalman, 1965). Violence often erupts when the public is sad and angry at the same time (Neal, 1998). However, if people can easily determine the degree of danger present from television, then there tends to be less extreme behavior (Mindak & Hursh, 1965). During a crisis, television provides not only facts and meanings, but offers a kind of therapy to viewers (Schaalman, 1965), and it functions as a ready medium for government officials who need to address the public (Graber, 1980).

Researchers have identified three stages in crisis coverage (Graber, 1980; Schaalman, 1965):

1. Media concentrate on what has happened and help coordinate the relief work. The chief problem is to get accurate information. It is reassuring to the public to see that authorities are coping properly with the disaster (e.g., that police, firefighters, and ambulances are on the scene and that the mayor and governor are touring the disaster site).
2. Media broadcast reactions from ordinary people and information and comments from officials striving to maintain law and order. The public demands interpretations, reassurance about the social values of society and help in expressing grief.
3. Media support social reintegration.

METHODS

Two methods were used to gather data for this study: content analysis of the first 8 hours of news coverage following the attacks by CNN, Fox News, ABC, NBC and CBS, and interviews with media professionals at CNN and Fox News. This study is a part of an ongoing project by the Reilly Center for Media & Public Affairs at The Manship School of Mass Communication, Louisiana State University, of how the networks covered the September 11 crisis.

Interviews

To understand the factors influencing television networks' content on September 11, 2001, the researchers interviewed 10 CNN and 9 Fox

News staff members including managing editors, producers, anchors, guest bookers, and reporters. These are the people who, in the daily operation of a television network, decide what stories to cover, how to cover them, and which stories make it on the air. The interviews were conducted in the interviewee's own newsrooms, using a flexible, semi-structured questionnaire containing eight open-ended questions. Interviewees were allowed to talk freely about anything that they found important in connection with the 9/11 coverage. The interviews lasted 20–80 minutes. All interviews were recorded, transcribed, and analyzed to identify themes and issues.

Content Analysis

Content analysis was used to identify specific trends and tendencies of the coverage during the first 8 hours of the 9/11 crisis. The content of the network news coverage was examined as a consequence of the news organizations' decision making in a crisis situation. Content analysis offers a foundation for a multidimensional look at the news coverage and for further analysis of the role of television during a national crisis. Based on the literature and previous research, we proposed the following:

1. Media serve as a guiding and consoling source instead of just as an information source in a crisis situation involving national interest.
2. Media demonstrate visible patriotism in a crisis situation involving national interest.
3. Media rely more on government sources than other sources in a crisis situation involving national interest.
4. Media advocate American values (democracy, freedom/liberty, justice, human rights) in a crisis situation involving national interest.
5. Media emphasize human interest in a crisis situation involving tragedy more than other political and economic factors.
6. Media frame the coverage based on moral/religious issues rather than political, economic, criminal, environmental, or human interest issues.
7. Media coverage focus shifts during the different stages of crisis.

The news coverage of five networks—ABC, CBS, NBC, CNN and Fox News—was selected for content analysis. These networks were selected because of their dominant status in television news coverage in the United States. They also include three different types of television media: the established wireless television network, cable television network, and a relatively new, independent television network. The first 8 hours were chosen because they contained the most important stages of the incident, the most intensive coverage of the incident, and changes in coverage due to the rapid development of the incident. The recorded news content of the five television networks was acquired through Vanderbilt University's video library.

The study unit is the news story. The story is defined as a group of studio and field shots that specifically address one topic or issue and run consecutively. The story can start with or without the lead from the anchor or it can be a story solely reported by the anchor or a reporter. The actual news coverage runs consecutively without clear segments of stories. For the purpose of content analysis, the following cues were used to identify a story: (a) a switch from the anchor to the field reporter, or vice versa; or (b) a scene change, and the voice over of a different reporter; or (c) the anchor or reporter changed the topic and started reporting on a different aspect of the event instead of mentioning something briefly, and the coverage of the topic ran for a significant amount of time (at least 30 seconds). The stories identified ran from 30 seconds to 12 minutes. A total of 1,117 stories were identified from the first 8 hours coverage of the five networks, including 303 stories from ABC, 192 stories from CBS, 184 stories from NBC, 232 stories from CNN, and 206 stories for Fox News.

The recording unit of the content analysis includes words, phrases, sentences, and themes identified for measuring attributes in the coverage. The following key variables were coded:

- *Stage of coverage.* The first 8 hours of coverage was divided into three stages: Stage 1: 8:48 a.m. to 11 a.m.; Stage 2: 11 a.m. to 3:00 p.m.; and Stage 3: 3 p.m. to 5 p.m.
- *Content orientation.* Determination of content orientation was based on whether the story consisted primarily of (a) facts describing what is happening; (b) analysis of information, facts, or events; (c) consoling or comforting words to make the audience feel safe and secure; or (d) guidance about what the audience needs to do.
- *Coverage frame.* Following Entman's (1991) definition, the coverage frame is defined as the aspects of a perceived reality identified through a

story that makes these aspects more salient in the news coverage. The frame was identified through the story angle or story focus. For example, if a story dealt with national security, government policy, or international relations, it was considered to have a political frame; a story discussing economic impact had an economic frame; a story reporting about human feeling, human well-being, family, or love was considered to have a human interest frame.

- *Patriotism demonstrated.* Explicit statements about devotion, love, and loyalty to one's country were seen as indications of patriotism. For example, "I will not tolerate an attack on America; I will do whatever it takes to defend America" was coded.
- *Value emphasized.* Coders looked for references to values that are associated with the American society—specifically words or expressions (synonyms) denoting the meaning of democracy, freedom, justice, and human rights—to determine if these values were emphasized.
- *Topics.* A topic was identified as the main focus of the story. The categories included WTC, Pentagon, safety (concerning future attack), government and U.S. president, criminal activity and terrorism, personal story, American public, U.S. Arab community, and past events. When more than one topic was observed, the topic that received the most attention in the story was considered its topic. When multiple topics were addressed in one story, the story was considered an overview.
- *Key issues.* A key issue was defined as a point in question that was of special importance in the news coverage (e.g., the problems, questions, or disputes discussed in the coverage). When more than one issue was addressed, the main focus of the story was considered the key issue. One key issue was the incident itself: what happened, when did it happen, and where? Other categories of key issues included terrorism, U.S. government reactions, severity of disaster, rescue efforts, safety concerns, economic impact, victims of the tragedy, Arab community in the United States, reactions from Muslims or Arabs outside United States and reactions from other parts of the international community.

- *Source.* A source was defined as a name of a person or an organization associated with direct or indirect quotes in a story (e.g., government officials, witnesses, experts, airline officials, or the president).

Seven coders were trained using a unified coding protocol and by following the procedures prescribed by Riffe, Lacy, and Fico. (1998). About 1 hour of the news coverage from two network stations, CNN and ABC, was used for an intercoder reliability check. Scott's Pi was used to test the intercoder reliability for nominal variables; Pearson's correlation coefficient was selected for interval and ratio variables. The results of the test showed that intercoder reliability for the nominal variables ranged from .78 to .96; and for ratio variables ranged from .82 to .92.

INTERVIEW FINDINGS

CNN

Professionalism, not Americanism, appeared to be the guiding force in the early hours of 9/11 at CNN. Top executives said repeatedly that they did not have time to ponder the consequences of their coverage, to think whether they were reassuring their audience, to debate whether they were inflaming anti-Arab prejudice, or even to coordinate the messages being delivered. Instead, they said they did what they always try to do in a breaking situation—stay on top of the news, get official sources on camera, make sure the information is accurate, and keep the coverage balanced and fair. This professionalism led them, almost by instinct, to be careful not to panic the nation.

The professionalism required to handle a story of this magnitude was apparent from the start. On the morning of 9/11, some 40 news executives had gathered at CNN-Atlanta and approximately 40 others were on a conference call from various key bureaus for the day's morning news meeting. They were discussing the top story of the day—the possible return of Michael Jordan to professional basketball—when Edith Chapin, deputy bureau chief in New York, broke in by phone to say a plane had just crashed into the WTC. "Everyone in the room without a word being spoken instantly got to their feet and started running down to the newsroom," said

Keith McAllister, senior vice president and national managing editor for news at CNN. "It was literally all 40 people leapt to their feet and piled out of the room."

There was no master plan to which reporters could refer, no manual for covering disasters. CNN instead operated on instinct and gut reaction. "Over the years, we have had discussions about process," said McAllister. But as for a plan, "we've been doing it for so many years that it's to some degree instinct. And, you know, our business relationships are designed for it as well. Our whole system is designed for breaking news." Because this was a breaking news story with constant updates for an extended period of time, CNN news executives made all decisions on the fly. Previously learned lessons were critical. McAlister noted that CNN does not hire people right out of college and that inexperienced people would not be placed in key positions during a breaking news story. Some of those interviewed cited the lessons from the Oklahoma City bombing as a key factor in helping them shape their coverage of 9/11.

Incoming shots were screened for taste, and on-the-air guests were probed for comments before they were put on the air. But that was not unusual, and it was not done because the journalists were thinking about the consequences of their reporting on the mood of the American public, on foreign relations, or on the world as a whole. It was done because that's what CNN's journalists do on a day-to-day basis. "These things are happening like this," said McAllister, snapping his fingers. "It was chaos and screaming across the room. So when the footage comes in, this is a reflex because we do it a lot." Asked if he thought about the need to reassure his audience at any point, McAllister replied he did not. "My job is not to think those thoughts. My job is to cover the news and to do it with balance and fairness and accuracy and speed," he said.

Liz Mercure, supervising producer for CNN, was in charge of the control room as the critical hours of the drama unfolded. She agreed that the coverage was too chaotic for people to think about what they were doing—they had to react and that is where experience and grounding in basic journalistic values takes over. "We were so in the mode of just covering the story that there wasn't a lot of pre-planning or cognizant thought about it. You just do it as it happens. And it just happened for hours and hours and hours. There's no planning here. You're just following where the story takes you."

Gary Tuchman, a CNN correspondent at Ground Zero, acknowledged, however, that on-camera personnel have to be aware of the impact they have on the audience, and projecting an aura of calmness and reassurance is always a part of the job. "The most important thing is to stay cool," he said. "Don't lose your head. The viewers are counting on you to give them information. It doesn't mean you have to be dispassionate, (it) doesn't mean you can't show anger. But you can't talk like a chicken without your head, because people are relying on you to calm them and inform them at the same time."

Coordination of coverage was a major problem for CNN. Although it has bureaus in New York and Washington, its key executives, and most of its resources, are based in Atlanta, far from the action. Communication between bureaus was established by using a continuously running conference call and through a "super desk" format within the CNN domestic newsroom, where key personnel from the various CNN networks—CNN International, CNN Domestic, CNN Europe, CNN-Latin America, and so on, worked closely together.

Coverage in the first 24 hours was heavily reliant on first-hand sources, on statements and news conferences held by key governmental officials and on analysis delivered by former governmental officials. Joy DiBenedetto, vice president of Network Bookings at CNN, said her department was careful to find experts who were knowledgeable and not prone to over-speculation. The bookings department at CNN is in charge of lining up experts and governmental officials for the CNN anchors and reporters to interview on air. "We don't want to put somebody on the air that says something that's premature or somebody that doesn't have all the facts," DiBenedetto said. "In a time like 9/11, we did discuss who's the right person to put on." Gail Chalef, managing editor of Network Bookings, said journalistic balance played a major role in deciding whom to book for an interview. "You were asking if we would book somebody who's angry at Muslims, well that's . . . that's not balanced, that's not what we do," she said.

The two-source rule that most reporters rely on was not a factor in the first 24 hours of coverage. Events were moving too quickly to insist on double sourcing for all pertinent information. In addition, the pictures themselves were a source of information that collaborated and confirmed what eyewitnesses and governmental officials were saying about the disaster. When CNN did decide to air one-source reports, it was careful to identify the report as being uncorroborated. ◙

Initially, CNN correspondents used caution when describing the first plane crash, although they quickly raised questions about whether it might be intentional. The first eyewitness account aired on CNN came from Sean Murtagh, a CNN producer, only minutes after the disaster. He identified the plane as a twin engine jet, possibly a 737 passenger jet. He informed viewers that the normal flight paths for commercial aircraft would not bring planes near the WTC, letting viewers draw conclusions from that information. CNN interviewed Ira Furman, former National Transportation Safety Board chairman, just minutes after the second plane hit the trade center. He also said there was no reason for planes to be near the WTC and suggested the two crashes were deliberate acts. But it was nearly an hour into the coverage before CNN definitively quoted governmental officials as saying this was an act of terrorism, and even that first mention was couched carefully—CNN quoted an Associated Press (AP) dispatch that said government officials believed the plane crashes were an act of terrorism.

This cautionary approach in terms of sourcing continued throughout the day. CNN reported at one point that the Pentagon and a building on the Mall in Washington, perhaps the Old Executive Office Building, might be on fire. It followed that report with an interview with CNN correspondent Greta Van Susteren, who was in the parking lot at National Airport, less than 1 mile from the Pentagon. Van Susteren was careful to report only what she could see—a huge plume of smoke coming from an area near the Pentagon, and that she had heard a loud noise just before the smoke appeared. Once again, CNN waited until someone else, in this case the AP, reported that the Pentagon had been hit by a plane and then it quoted the AP as reporting this fact.

CNN used a parade of governmental officials to confirm reports or to reveal new details. This had the side effect of showing that the government was still functioning, that officials were still in charge and that the Republic would stand. Mercure, CNN's producer, noted that following the story usually results in putting governmental officials on the air and those officials often will make reassuring remarks. "But again, it's not planned," she said.

Although the men and women of CNN said they weren't trying to be reassuring or to help the country through the trauma, they acknowledged that they sometimes had to weigh conflicting journalistic values. In those cases, some thought was given to the need not to panic the nation. "There were editorial decisions that were made where we were mindful of an obligation to be really sure about what we were saying and keep it in context," said McAllister. "There were a number of things that came through the intelligence community which, if we'd gone on television with them, which would have been acceptable by the normal roles of sourcing and all that, but if we'd gone on TV with it, it would have led to panic."

The journalistic value of fairness and balance guided much of CNN's coverage once Osama bin Laden was identified as a prime suspect. McAlister said CNN took pains to make certain it did not paint the entire Muslim population with a broad brush. "We all felt an obligation to make sure that our reporting was fair in that respect," he said. "There you feel a sense of pro-active obligation. We've been down this road as a society before and seen what happens. All of us as individuals in this organization feel that . . . there are times where you need to be very careful and make sure that you're presenting the full story."

Taste also played a major role in decisions on what should be shown on air. CNN did not show pictures of people jumping from the WTC windows, for example. McAlister said that was a calculated decision. CNN also was careful to limit the human carnage it showed on the air. Although that decision was made easier by the destruction at the scene, there were instances where the network could have shown much more than it chose to do. CNN Correspondent Gary Tuchman recalled walking to a Brooks Brothers store where he used to shop in New York. The store was being used as a morgue and buckets used to collect human remains were interspersed with expensive suits. "There were no bodies there, just buckets for the remains they were recovering," he said. "The destruction was so complete that I . . . never saw one victim. I was careful with my language," he said. "I didn't want to talk about body parts, people, seeing them in buckets."

Tuchman said his decisions on what to show and what to say were based on "our own professional standards. If I had said something that repulsed people here in Atlanta headquarters, they would have called me and told me about it. But I think that's part of what they expect out of us, to have the tact to know what to say, and how to say it and when to say it."

Fox News

Fox News echoed statements by CNN: There was no time to consult a plan or analyze events: You acted on instinct and relied on experience to get the job done. Many of the professionals who were interviewed had covered major events before. Anchor Shepard Smith, for example, had covered the bombing of the Murrah Federal Building in Oklahoma City, and Senior Correspondent Eric Shawn had covered the earlier WTC bombing. The overall feeling of the Fox News staff was that they were dealing with something bigger than anything they had ever dealt with before. Jon Scott anchored Fox

News's coverage that morning: "I wasn't prepared for those buildings to fall down," Scott said. "And it just seemed like shock piled on shock on top of shock." Although everyone in the studio, newsroom, and control room was personally distressed by what was going on, they quickly realized that they had to get as much information out as thoroughly, accurately and as carefully as they could.

Although Fox News has a disaster plan to cover events such as a plane crash, earthquake, or similar catastrophic event, the events of September 11 were overwhelming. It was, as Dennis Murray, executive producer, said, the ". . . biggest story, ever, anywhere, and won't go away." Roger Ailes, Fox News CEO, ran the coverage. Planning meetings, strategically and logistically, were small and spontaneous. To handle the constant demand for coverage, Fox News formed and re-built teams based on early and later coverage. John Stack, vice president of newsgathering, commented on the need for continuous response: "Breaking news usually moves in an orderly path. The second plane changed that. The continuous breaking situation came so quickly you had to get back into the job and did not have time to think." The focus was on accuracy and the process required to bring news to the air.

At Fox News, several stages of coverage emerged during the first 8 hours: instinctive reaction, making sense out of calamity, and addressing emotional responses as the tensions built and viewers became anxious. As the story unfolded, it became clear parts of the overall story were occurring in other locations. The network needed to provide teams at other sites to access information quickly. Getting accurate information to the public and helping make sense of it were two primary values mentioned. According to Stack, "you became reactive, and you just get into doing your job." He followed this comment by describing the steps he followed: checking the accuracy of the information coming in, processing it down from the desk to the show producers, and putting it on the air in a way that made sense to the audience.

Source verification was a prime concern. Bill Shine, network executive producer, described a "brain room" of talented researchers, located in the basement of the Fox News building with the purpose of fulfilling requests for information. An urgent file was used to pull key facts about the WTC, the Pentagon, public officials, key groups, and possible targets or terrorists like Osama bin Laden. The anchor and producer began juggling people who knew the area and who had been consulted previously. Information and/or sources were put on in a manner and order that made sense. Among the options were wire services, the Internet, monitored radio broadcasts, law enforcement, Mayor Rudolph Giuliani's EMS setup, Fox News contacts at the

Pentagon Department of Defense, other key organizations, and correspondents in the field. The assignment desk would verify and get multiple inputs while alerting the executive director in the control room, who informed the talent. The central theme came from the desk. "The main goal was to inform and ensure accuracy, especially in this atmosphere," Stack said. "The goal, encouraged and supported by Ailes, was fair and balanced information on the air."

In an unfolding story, things constantly change, not just in terms of new information coming in, but new information that is different from what was reported earlier. Stack described the information flow from the assignment desk as following a series of steps before it is aired, including identifying a high-level source, verifying the source, and securing multiple reports of the information. Fox News would tell viewers if there was only one source for information and whether the information had been confirmed. If the information wasn't right, it was corrected on air as quickly as possible. Stack emphasized "while we are not in the business of upsetting the audience, we certainly are in the business of informing them. But, we have to make damn well sure it's accurate information, especially in this atmosphere. That's the tone that took over at that point." Fox News was receiving information from the New York Port Authority, the Federal Aviation Authority in Washington, the Department of Defense, and other key sources when the Pentagon was hit. "Even with that information coming in," Stack continued, "we were desperately seeking second and third sources so that we could be as accurate as possible; and when we didn't have a second or a third source, we qualified as best we could as we were announcing it on the air."

Verification did not always happen. In some cases, a decision had to be made about airing information without a second source. Stack noted that cable news must move investigative reporting and vetting of information through an almost instantaneous process because of its around-the-clock coverage.

Providing information that helps the public understand the context of what is happening is another important journalistic value. Shawn summed this value up as follows: "I knew I had a job to do, which was putting it [the plane crashes] in some context and trying to explain what was happening." Because Shawn had previous experience covering terrorist activities, he felt a sense of responsibility to help the viewer understand the broader issues related to the facts that were coming over the wires and from reporters in the field. By providing context for the story, the journalist provides a sense of history and gives background so that viewers understand the nature of the event. The journalist recognizes the needs of people to know what happened, how it could have happened, why it happened, and what or who caused it to happen.

Previous experience was mentioned repeatedly as invaluable in giving context to breaking events. Jon Scott noted that he was given a tour by the director of security at the WTC after the 1993 bombing attack. He drew from this experience when he covered the Oklahoma City bombing and during the WTC attack. These experiences allowed him to talk about why buildings fall down and what they learned after the 1993 WTC attack. He also was aware that 50,000 people worked in the WTC on any given day and that the buildings had been designed to withstand the impact of a jetliner. Shawn echoed the value of experience to provide context for news coverage. Shawn had covered the 1993 WTC bombing and the subsequent trials of the Islamic radical militant groups. When the first plane hit, he began to consider the possible involvement of Osama bin Laden. He made calls to a terrorist expert in Washington who mentioned that one of the defendants tried for the bombing of the WTC in 1993 had gone to flight school in Oklahoma.

Creating an atmosphere that would convey the seriousness of the crisis without creating panic was essential. Several respondents said they were trying to maintain calm and be as dispassionate as they could, realizing that they were there as conduits of information. Scott summarized, "At some point it occurred to me that part of my job that day was just to sort of, as dispassionately as possible, just let people know what was going on, but to let them know that these were, for all the horror of them and the catastrophe involved, they were isolated events and the country wasn't going to come to a grinding halt just because now, the center of the military and two skyscrapers in Manhattan fell down."

Fox News also was careful in its selection of visual coverage. One shot of a person jumping from the towers was aired and none of the maimed or dead. The concern, according to Shine, was whether the information added to the story—could it be just as easily said as shown?

In contrast, coverage of Palestinians cheering in the streets was aired repeatedly—three instances in a very brief period. The key here, said Shine, was that it showed that there were different feelings elsewhere in the world. "The tape gave Americans an understanding that there will be people that don't like us." To balance this tape, the president's message to the public about avoiding repercussions to Muslims was aired immediately.

Content Analysis

During the first 8 hours, the networks focused on the following major topics: WTC (29%), president and government activity (18%), terrorism and criminal activity (10%), the Pentagon (8%), and air traffic and safety (9%; see Table 9.1). However, NBC, CNN, and Fox News had considerably more coverage of the two points of attack—the WTC and the Pentagon—than the other two networks. NBC and Fox News both had 42% and CNN 41% on those two topics, compared to 32% for CBS and 29% for ABC. Key issues identified from the stories were description of the incident (18%), severity of disaster (18%), terrorism (15.%), U.S. government reaction (14%), and safety concerns (13%; see Table 9.2). But although terrorism and severity of disaster were the most covered issues overall, the amount of coverage varied considerably among the networks. As can be seen in Table 9.2, CBS (21%) and Fox News (21%) had almost twice as much coverage of terrorism as the other three networks and CBS (22%), and NBC (20%) had considerably more coverage of the severity than the other three networks.

Table 9.1. Percentage of Topics in Networks' First 8 Hours of coverage ✕
(N = 1,117 stories)

Topic	Network					Total
	ABC	CBS	NBC	CNN	Fox	
World Trade Center	23	28	34	31	32	29
President and government	18	16	9	19	25	18
Criminal and terrorism	7	10	10	10	15	10
Overview	11	11	17	4	8	10
Pentagon	6	4	8	10	10	8
Air traffic	8	4	7	5	4	6
Safety	4	3	6	0	1	3
Middle East	4	3	3	3	0	3
Enemy	3	4	1	5	3	3
Business	2	2	1	1	1	2
Personal story	1	5	0	4	0	2
American public	3	3	0	0	0	2
Past events	3	2	1	2	0	2
International	1	1	2	0	0	1
U.S. Arab community	1	0	0	0	0	0
Other	5	5	2	4	0	3

Table 9.2. Percentage of Key Issues

Key Issues	Network					Total
	ABC	CBS	NBC	CNN	Fox	
Description of incident	15	13	27	25	14	18
Severity of disaster	18	22	20	14	18	18
Terrorism	13	21	12	12	21	15
U.S. Government reaction	14	8	11	15	18	14
Safety concerns	15	15	16	10	9	13
Rescue effort	7	6	6	9	9	7
Victim of the tragedy	1	3	1	6	2	3
Muslim or Arab	5	1	4	2	1	3
Economic impact	1	3	1	1	2	1
International reaction	1	1	1	2	0	1
Arab community in the U.S.	0	0	0	0	0	0
Other	9	8	1	5	4	6

The proposition that media serves as a guiding and consoling source instead of just an information source in a crisis situation was not supported. In fact, more than 76% of the stories were identified as presentation of facts, whereas 19% of stories were primarily analytical. Fact presentation dominated coverage time at 76%, whereas 19% of coverage time was devoted to analysis. ABC, CBS, NBC, and CNN devoted about 80% of the coverage to present facts. Fox News devoted 65% of their coverage to presenting facts while allocating significantly more coverage than the other four networks to analysis (26%). The coverage devoted to guiding and leading the audience during a crisis (2%) and to consoling or easing stress and anxiety of the audience (3%) was negligible (see Table 9.3).

The proposition that media emphasize human interest stories in crisis situations involving tragedy more than political or economic factors was not supported by the first 8 hours of coverage. Only 4% of the stories were framed from a human interest perspective. Political (22%) and criminal (12%) were two major aspects of the coverage. The amount of stories framed from a human interest perspective was similar among all networks except NBC (1%). CNN (26%) and Fox News (25%) had more stories with political frames than the other three networks. Nearly half of the stories were framed as stories of disaster (44%), with NBC (54%) focusing on disaster the most and ABC (38%) the least. NBC (18%) also framed significantly more stories with safety concerns than the other four networks. While the

Table 9.3. Percentage of Story Primary Orientation

Orientation	Network					Total
	ABC	CBS	NBC	CNN	Fox	
Fact	78	80	82	77	65	76
Analysis	19	16	17	16	26	19
Consolation	3	3	1	3	4	3
Guide	1	2	1	3	3	2
Other	0	1	0	0	2	1

stories framed as disaster and safety concerns may be associated with welfare of people, human interest was not found to be an evident competing frame of the stories (see Table 9.4).

The proposition that media rely more on governmental sources than other sources in a crisis situation was supported. Two major sources were identified in the coverage: government officials (including former goverment officials and eyewitnesses). Slightly less than 18% of the stories used government officials as sources, whereas 11% of the stories quoted witnesses (see Table 9.5). However, ABC (22%) and NBC (22%) used government sources more often than CBS (14%) and CNN (13%). On the other hand, CBS (6%) and CNN (6%) used experts substantially more than the other networks. When government officials were sources, the stories addressed government reaction and policies. Key issues associated with governmental sources include terrorism, government reaction, rescue efforts and safety concerns. When witnesses were quoted, the stories focused mostly on a recount of what happened at the WTC and the Pentagon and severity of disaster.

The proposition that the media shift their focus of key issues during stages of the crisis was supported. From 8:45 a.m. to 11 a. m., the coverage was devoted mostly to descriptions of the disaster (31%), severity of disaster (18%), terrorism (16%), and safety concerns (13%). During Stage 2 of the coverage, from 11 a.m. to 3 p.m., descriptions of the incident (11%) declined dramatically. Coverage of U.S. government reactions (18%) and rescue efforts (10%) increased significantly, whereas safety concerns remained approximately the same (11%). Severity of disaster (19%) and terrorism (17%) continued to be dominant issues. After 3 p.m., government reaction (13%) and rescue efforts (7%) declined; severity of disaster (18%) remained high; and safety concerns (16%) and victims of the tragedy (6%) increased (see Table 9.6).

Table 9.4. Percentage of Coverage Frames in Networks' First 8 Hours of Coverage

Frames	Network					Total
	ABC	CBS	NBC	CNN	Fox	
Disaster	38	45	54	44	43	44
Political	22	16	17	26	25	22
Criminal	14	18	5	12	12	12
Safety	8	10	18	6	7	9
Human interest	5	3	1	4	4	4
Economy	1	3	1	1	2	2
Environment	3	1	0	0	1	1
Religious	0	0	1	1	0	0
Other	9	4	2	5	5	6

Table 9.5. Percentage of Sources Used

Sources	Network					Total
	ABC	CBS	NBC	CNN	Fox	
Government official	22	14	22	13	18	18
Witness of the incident	9	11	12	11	11	11
Expert	4	6	3	6	2	4
President	3	4	4	1	1	3
Airline officials	2	1	4	1	1	2
International	1	2	3	2	0	2
Arab group	0	0	0	0	0	0
Business	1	1	1	0	0	0
Non-Arab group	0	0	0	0	0	0
Relative of victims	0	0	0	1	0	0
Other	4	2	4	1	1	2

Note. The percentage reflects how each source was used in 1,117 stories. Sources were not identified in some of the stories and thus total frequency does not add up to 100%.

Table 9.6. Shift of Focus in Key Issues During Stages in First 8 Hours of Coverage

Key Issues	Coverage Stage			Total
	8-11a.m.	11a.m.-3p.m.	3-5p.m.	
Description of incident	31%	11	8	18
Severity of disaster	18	19	18	18
Terrorism	16	17	12	15
U.S. government reaction	10	18	13	14
Safety concerns	13	11	16	13
Rescue effort	5	10	7	7
Victim of the tragedy	2	2	6	3
Muslim or Arab	2	3	5	3
Economic impact	1	1	3	1
International reaction	0	1	2	1
Arab community in the U.S.	0	0	0	0
Other	3	6	10	6

Patriotism was not a visible theme in the coverage. There was no demonstrated patriotism in 96% of the news stories, some patriotism in 3% of the stories, and high patriotism in less than 1%. Among the networks, ABC (4%), CBS (6%), and NBC (4%) demonstrated more visible patriotism in their coverage than CNN (1%) and Fox News (3%).

American values demonstrated through the use of specific words and expressions were not a frequent occurrence in the news coverage. Only 3% of the stories emphasized freedom/liberty. However, NBC (5%) had significantly more stories emphasizing freedom/liberty than ABC (3%), CBS (3%), and CNN (3%). Two other values—democracy and justice—were both below 1%. Almost none of the stories emphasized human interest (0.1%).

DISCUSSION

During the first 8 hours after the first plane hit the WTC the networks had no time to plan, so coverage was dictated by instinct and based on professional experience and media values.

We found a number of associations between what the media professionals said they were trying to produce and the content of the actual news programming. For example, news executives stressed repeatedly that their goal in the first few hours was to provide information and verify facts. Content analysis showed 76% of the coverage dealt with presentation of facts and another 19% with analysis of those facts.

Furthermore, in the early stages, both content analysis and interviews confirm that it was not possible for the networks to put much emphasis on human interest stories. Both study methods confirm that government officials were the most sought after and used sources of information. Both methods indicate the focus of the coverage shifted after the first 3 hours to less descriptive coverage of the attacks and more coverage of rescue efforts. And, finally, both content analysis and interviews confirm that the journalists did not focus their attention on democratic values or patriotism during the first 8 hours of coverage.

News people at CNN and Fox News said they felt an obligation to inform the public about the magnitude of the event on September 11 but couched these obligations in terms of their journalistic values. Reliance on those values and on experience produced the 9/11 coverage. That the public was reassured and that government was able to use the media as a conduit for its point of view were natural outcomes from that process.

10

The Dynamics of Electronic Media Coverage

Kevin J. Dooley
Steven R. Corman
Arizona State University

Because of their horrific magnitude and historical precedence, the attacks of September 11 on the World Trade Center (WTC) and the Pentagon represent an ideal opportunity to study a terrorist act's impact on media communication. Media organizations allocated significant resources to sensemaking, tracking, and investigation of the event (Finkel, 2001). The purpose of this chapter is to describe and explain the dynamics of news coverage by Reuters, a "traditional" wire service with a significant Internet presence. To do this, we apply a novel form of text analysis, Centering Resonance Analysis (CRA), which automatically quantifies the influence of words within texts based on their position in a network structure of other words making up the text. We examine influential words in Reuters' texts across a 66-day period (from September 11 to November 15), and also analyze temporal patterns of influence within this period. This enables us to identify themes and their dynamical patterns, and subsequently hypothesize a process model linking two different terrorist triggering events to internal and

121

external institutional responses, and to sense-making about societal impact.

METHODS

We chose to examine the content of the Reuters articles because Reuters is the largest international news organization in the world, and has a very significant online readership. Reuters employs more than 2,000 staff, producing more than 30,000 headlines per day in more than 200 bureaus. Concerning its electronic news on the Internet, Reuters (2001) claims that more than 80 million unique users access its articles on the Internet per month. Reuters has the operational traits of both a newspaper and television media organization. Like a newspaper organization, it provides its news in written form, which means it has to pay particular attention to word choice (because texts are explicit) and content accuracy (because explicit texts are hard to recall for correction). Like a television organization, it releases stories on a quasi-continuous basis, enabling it to put down "place-holder" articles that outline a bare minimum of the story in as rapid a manner as possible, and then build on the text in the place-holder as new information is uncovered and emerging news events unfold. This creates a certain amount of path dependency in their content, over shorter periods of time.

We collected data in the following manner. The time horizon of the sample is from September 11 to November 15, encompassing 66 days. To put the end date in historical perspective, the Taliban had just lost control of Kabul, Afghanistan several days before. We used two different data collection approaches. From September 11 through the end of the month, we collected all articles available on Yahoo.com's news Web sites. A sample check verified that Yahoo.com carried more Reuters articles than any other online portal (except for Excite.com, which carries an almost identical list of articles). Various paths of links found at the bottom of these stories were followed to ensure that all possible articles were identified. We then identified cases of incremental story building as just described and kept only the latest and most lengthy version. On October 1, Yahoo.com changed the way it organized the relevant articles. After this date, we collected all relevant articles from Yahoo's listing of "Reuters Top Stories." In this case, the list is a sample of all of Reuters releases, selected by Yahoo. In selecting the stories we erred on the side of inclusion, for example, even though it was not known whether the New York City plane crash in October, or the anthrax story were "connected" to the September 11 attacks, we included them in the sample. We tested one particular day (November 12, 2001) to see how the list from Yahoo's "Reuters Top Stories" compared to the stream of Reuters articles more generally available on Yahoo.com and found that their sampling method was comparable to what we had done manually with September's article sets.

We analyzed the manifest content of the selected Reuters stories using CRA, a representational method that is a form of network text analysis (Corman, Kuhn, McPhee, & Dooley, 2002). CRA assumes that competent authors/speakers generate utterances that are locally coherent by focusing their statements on conversational centers (Lecoeuche, Roberston, Barry, & Mellish, 2000). Centers are noun phrases constituting the subjects and objects of utterances. In CRA, concepts are first selected using linguistic analysis that identifies noun phrases. Second, the nouns and adjectives making up these phrases are linked sequentially within sentences, and all possible co-occurrences of words within the larger noun phrases are linked. This yields a network of words. Third, CRA indexes the *influence* of each word by analyzing its position in the network generated in the previous step. The final step in CRA is mapping, whereby the words in the network are spatially co-located and visualized.

The *influence* index calculated in Step 3 of CRA is of particular importance because it provides the means to identify crucial concepts in the network based on their place in the entire structure of concepts in a text. We operationalize a word's influence as its betweenness centrality (Anthonisse, 1971; Freeman, 1979) in the CRA network. The betweenness measure, as compared to some other measures of centrality, takes into account the position of a node in the entire network rather than just its local connections. Words with high betweenness, and thus influence, add coherence to the text by connecting strings of words that otherwise would not be connected.

An example of a CRA network is shown in Fig. 10.1, a map for an aggregate text containing all relevant articles released between 9 a.m. and 12 p.m. EST on September 11. All of the nodes shown in Fig. 10.1 are highly influential, the more influential terms being located near the center. Less than 1% of all the words present are shown in the graph. Lines connecting the nodes indicate that I have connected those words in meaningful ways within their discourse.

In the map, we see that the event is being immediately framed as an attack on the United States. Nodes toward the bottom show that the articles emphasized the locale, *New York*, *WTC*,

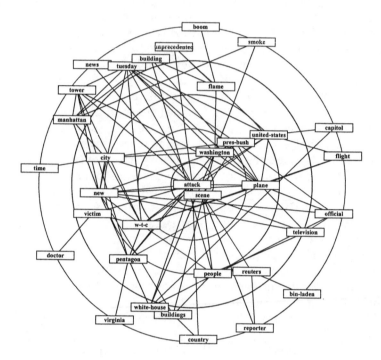

Fig. 10.1. Reuters 900-1200 September 11: CRA map

Washington, Pentagon. In the upper middle part of the map, there is emphasis on the scene itself: *eyewitness, smoke, scene, Manhattan, explosion.* Note directly to the right of that cluster is *Saudi-born bin Laden* (we examine this framing in more depth later). *Bin Laden* is connected to *attack,* and the *attack* is primarily being described as *unprecedented.*

The sequence in which articles occurred is critical to our analysis. Patterns in sequences imply underlying dynamics, and dynamics are important to understand because different ways of organizing and behaving lead to different dynamical patterns. The examination of these patterns can indicate the nature of the underlying, fundamental generative mechanisms that recreate the system on an on-going basis (Dooley & Van de Ven, 1999). In order to examine how the content of Reuters' articles changed over the next 2 months, we aggregated articles within a given day into a single text, and performed CRA analysis on those texts. Following this, we pursued inductive modeling of the CRA results using the following steps:

1. Identify themes by performing factor analysis on the influence value time series data for each word. Each theme is composed of multiple words, whose influence values are highly correlated with one another over time.
2. Determine an influence score for each theme by taking the average influence across words within the theme; a time series is then constructed.
3. Perform statistical analysis on the thematic time series, including identification of change points, and thus dynamical epochs.
4. Propose generic model to account for the dynamical behaviors observed, and apply this to the data.

RESULTS

Influence Analysis

Space limitations prevent us from showing the influence analyses for all 66 days. As a substitute, we show here the most influential words, in descending order of magnitude, across the whole period (words connected with "=" are treated as a single word; "days," i.e., "Saturday," have not been included):

> united=states, attack, taliban, people, afghanistan, pres=bush, anthrax, bin=laden, official, washington, country, new=york, american, city, government, security, military, force, war, day, week, leader, group, time, terrorism, world, plane, afghan, pakistan, kabul, office, bomb, new, worker, mail, letter, terrorist, air, man, airport, support, muslim, percent, foreign, spokesman, police, troop, minister, president, report

These words, according to CRA, are those most responsible for making Reuters' coverage coherent. Readers can judge the face validity of the list for themselves, but we find it hard to imagine writing a sensible story about the terrorist attacks and subsequent events without using at least some of its words.

Themes

Given the abundance of words, we used factor analysis of the daily influence values to determine groupings of words that indicate themes within the texts. The factor analysis is under specified as there are almost 5,000 words, and only 66 different influence values for each word variable. We performed analysis with the 20, 50, 66, and 200 most influential words, and then also investigated the pairwise correlation between the most influential (240) words (those that had an average influence of more than 0.002). We also used nonrotated, rotated (varimax), and oblique methods to see what differences existed. In all of the variations of factor analysis, two strong themes emerged: one associated with the main terrorist attack issues (WTC, anthrax), and one associated with the war in Afghanistan.

The factor analysis served as a starting point for a number of further iterations. By coupling an analysis of the pairwise correlations with the factor analysis results, we were able to identify six themes. No doubt there are more, but these six appeared to largely capture, from a face validity standpoint, the major events over the 2 months. They also involved about one sixth of the words within the top 240 of influence. For each theme hypothesized, Cronbach's alpha was calculated as a measure of the theme's (factor's) intervariable reliability in measuring a common, underlying construct, and further factor analysis was performed to ensure that each factor was cohesive (i.e., it had convergent validity). This resulted in the dropping of some variables until a final set of word variables for each theme emerged.

The results are in Table 10.1. *WTC Attack* focuses on the weapon (*plane, hijack, passenger, hijacker*) and its target (*world_trade_center, tower*). *Military response* deals with the war in

Table 10.1. Factors Representing Themes Within Reuters' Content

Factor	Cronbach Alpha	Words
Military response	0.83	Afghan, Kabul, south, Taliban, northern, opposition, u.n., fighter, force, political
Air security	0.71	security, airport, passenger
Political response	0.88	Palestinian, Islamic, Israel, Israeli, foreign, minister
WTC_attack	0.71	plane, hijack, passenger, hijacker, world_trade_center, tower
Economic_impact	0.83	financial, business, bank, trade, market
Anthrax	0.79	anthrax, bacterium, spore, mail, letter, office, postal, capitol, tom_daschel, health, test, antibiotic

Afghanistan, including locales (*afghan, kabul, south*), players (*taliban, northern, opposition, u_n, fighter*), and the context (*force, political*). It is interesting to note that the word *war* itself is not within the military response factor, perhaps indicating the government's semantic positioning of the events. *Air security* obviously relates to *security* within aviation (*airport, passenger*). *Political response* has to do with the international context of the war on *terrorism,* including the countries outside of Afghanistan (*palestinian, islamic, israel, israeli*) and their conduit (*foreign, minister*). *Economic impact* deals with the market and its components (*financial, business, bank, trade, market*). Finally, *anthrax* describes the material (*anthrax, bacterium, spore*), its mode of transport (*mail, letter*), the locale of its discovery (*office, postal, capitol, tom_daschel*), and its effects (*health, test, antibiotic*).

Time Series Analysis of Themes

To understand the ways these themes changed over time, we determined an influence score for each theme for each day by averaging influence across words within a theme. A plot of each theme's time series is shown in Figure 10.2. In order to discern specific dynamical epochs in these series (also in Fig. 10.2), we applied statistical change point methods (Poole, Van de Ven, Dooley, & Holmes, 2000). We used a temporally local measure of variation, the moving range, to estimate the amount of random variation in any short time frame; this was estimated across all 66 days. We then

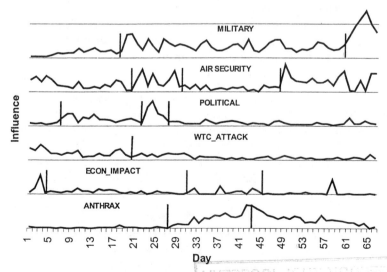

Fig. 10.2. Themes and change points

calculated the mean influence over the 66 days. This, coupled with the estimate of short-term variation, yielded prediction limits for both the influence value and its moving range (see Montgomery, 1996, for details). Applying these prediction limits to the data, we found "outliers," the presence of which indicates that the data do not likely stem from a singular distribution, or system. These estimated change points bounded potential dynamical epochs, where the dynamical behavior of a theme's influence within an epoch is constant, and its influence across epochs is different. We then iterated this procedure: New means and moving ranges were calculated for each potential epoch, and outliers identified. We concluded that a valid change point existed when we found few or no outliers within each epoch. Next we comment on the dynamics of each theme before proposing an explanation of the process underlying them.

Military Response. This theme has low influence until Day 16, corresponding to the U.S. decision to wage a War on Terrorism. It undergoes another major spike at Day 60 when the first major town in Afghanistan fell to the Northern Opposition. During the second epoch, *military response* is best modeled as a first-order autoregressive model with a first-order lag autocorrelation of 0.79. This means that the concept has a strong "memory" from day to day, and its impact decays exponentially over time.

Air Security. This theme is immediately influential, and decays in a linear fashion until Day 18, when major new initiatives involving airport and passenger security are unveiled, and partially implemented. It moves into the background after Day 30, as the news turns to the anthrax attacks. It increases again around Day 47, as new initiatives become more fully implemented and the impact on traveling passengers becomes more pronounced.

Political Response. This theme has little influence until Day 6, as world leaders begin to respond to the longer term issues implied by the attacks. It has a significant increase over a 4-day period, peaking at Day 23, corresponding to the reaction in the Middle East and Islamic countries concerning the potential of Afghan air strikes and U.S. retaliation. This ends at Day 27, and these contextual issues remain more in the background throughout the rest of the time period.

WTC Attack. This theme begins with quite large influence values as one would suspect. Then it slowly (and linearly) decays over time, except for a blip around Day 18, corresponding to new discoveries about the identities and actions of the hijackers. It remains in the background after that; only more local news agencies such as *The New York Times* continued to carry extensive news concerning the WTC clean up.

Economic Impact. This theme shows an immediate influence spike on Day 3 as international markets respond. Then it remains small in influence until Day 32, where over the next 9 days there are three spikes. It remains small in influence again until a spike on Day 58. Each of the four spikes relate to discussions about the side effects of anthrax attacks. It is interesting to note that economic impact, like fear, is associated with bioterrorism, rather than the September 11 attacks.

Anthrax. Dynamically, this theme acts as a basic ramp-up and ramp-down phenomenon. It remains small in influence until Day 28 when the first Florida anthrax case was discovered, and increases linearly until Day 42, and then decreases linearly after that. The peak on Day 42 corresponds to the death of two U.S. postal workers, the last deaths associated with anthrax.

Looking at all six themes together, we observe roughly three times when three or four of the time series change within close time proximity of one another: (a) around Day 18 (changes in political response, air security, military response, WTC attack), (b) around Day 28 (air security, political response, economic impact, anthrax), and (c) around Day 45 (air security, economic impact, anthrax). That yields four different micro-historical epochs, each lasting about 2 weeks. One might also consider the change point in military response around Day 60 as indicative of a fifth epoch.

A Model of Terror and Communication

Next we propose a model that could account for the dynamical behavior we observe in the influence of the different themes. Specifically, a basic stimulus–response model (Fig. 10.3) says that a triggering event (terrorist act) causes an institutional response that has both internal and external components, and both in turn lead to sense-making about societal impact. Furthermore, the institutional response revolves around a certain set of key actors.

In the Reuters data there are two realizations of this process. First, the WTC attack is followed by an institutional response. The response has internal (air security) and external (political response, military response) components. The attack is also followed by an economic impact, and a general discursive turn of attention to *threat.*

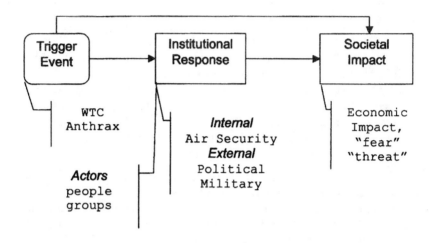

Fig. 10.3. Model of terrorist act and effect on media content

Second, the *anthrax* attack generates an institutional response, but the response is not separable from the triggering event itself. It causes an *economic impact*, and a general discursive turn of attention to *threat* and *fear*.

Figure 10.4 shows the thematic data, and data on two other singular terms (*threat, fear*) in the framework of the model. The lines represent the "mean" value of the theme across that epoch. For the WTC attack, we signify two basic phases. The first encompasses the trigger event and its immediate consequences. We observe WTC Attack start at a high level of influence at the beginning of the phase, and linearly decrease in influence over the next 18 days. There is a political response during this phase, of moderate magnitude, that took about one week to materialize. There is an immediate spike in the Economic Impact theme, which decays to background noise after 1 week. The WTC attack theme also generates on-going waves of discursive attention to *threat*.

A second phase is identified as starting at the point where there are simultaneous, significant changes in the themes representing the institutional response. Specifically, military response, political response, and air security all undergo a significant increase in their mean level, around Day 18. All three responses differ from one another dynamically. The military response theme

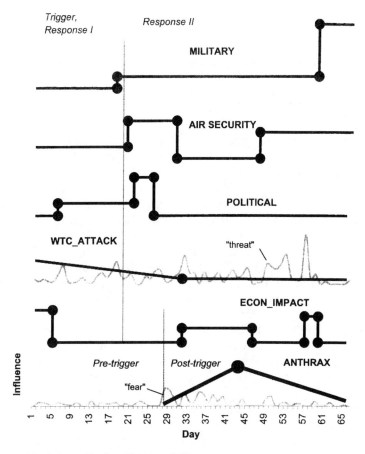

Fig. 10.4. Model applied to Reuters' themes

remains moderate in strength until around Day 60, when coordinated attacks against the Taliban begin and the theme increases greatly in influence. The political response theme spikes at the very beginning of the second phase and then falls to background. The air security theme undergoes changes in influence at three different times. The time lags (about 2 weeks) between the two changes in military response, and the three changes in air security, give some indication as to the "speed" of these institutional elements. There is discursive attention to threats throughout the period. Some peaks correspond to official warnings of possible new attacks: Days 7, 32, 53 (the bridge threat in California), and Day 57 (smallpox, Florida ports). The peak on Day 18 corresponded to the confluence of several international protests of threatened U.S. action, from the Muslim world, or from Muslims (Indonesia, Britain, Pakistan).

For the anthrax attack, there are two waves of economic impact, and an increase in discursive attention to *fear*. The institutional response cannot be separated from the event itself. The terrorist event was not singular, but rather involved multiple sites across several weeks of time. Likewise, the institutional response was very much entangled with the threat itself, which was delivered through the mail. Within the theme, words denote both nature of the event and the response. Discursive attention to *fear* is almost solely associated with anthrax, as it reaches its maximum values at the onset of the anthrax attacks (correlation with *anthrax* equals 0.21); *threat* also is associated with *anthrax* (0.21), but *threat* and *fear* tend not to be associated (0.05). In this case, it may be that *threat* is associated with the WTC attacks because the "enemy" was known, while *fear* is associated with the anthrax attacks because the enemy was not known.

The words associated with the actors involved in these events are shown in Fig. 10.5. The top plot shows U.S. officials, and bin Laden. We note that (New York City Mayor) *guiliani* and (Secretary of State) *powell* remain relatively low in influence (despite Guiliani later being named "Times Man of the Year"). *tom_daschle* is directly associated (only) with the anthrax attack, as his office was one of the targets of the attacks. Change point analysis indicates that *rumsfeld* remains small in magnitude until Day 25, and then peaks on Day 29 as "U.S. Claims Control of Afghan Skies" (headline of the relevant Reuters' article). Moving forward, *rumsfeld* has a great deal of volatility, corresponding to specific times when Rumsfeld made public appearances. The dynamical behavior of *vp=cheney* is more interesting. It is common knowledge that Cheney was located in a separate, secure position and kept a low profile, for U.S. national security reasons. The plot shows the specific times when he surfaced. On Day 6, he came forward for the first time to discuss the details of Bush's odyssey across the country on Air Force One on September 11. On Day 38, he made his "first major appearance" since September 11, to announce, "the war will enter a covert phase."

Both *pres=bush* and *bin=laden* are highly influential throughout the entire period. *Pres=bush* peaks on Day 13 when Bush announces the War on Terrorism. On Day 18, both spike, as the Reuters headline says "U.S. in Hot Pursuit of Prime Suspect." *Bin=Laden* spikes again on Day 24, with the headline "West Unveils Evidence on bin Laden." *Pres=bush* reaches its second and third largest values on Day 61-62, corresponding to Afghanistan's Northern Alliance taking control of the key city of Mazar-I-Sharif, and *bin=laden* follows on Day 65 as Reuters announces "Cheney Sees End of Taliban Rule, bin Laden on Run, and bin Laden Denies

Actors

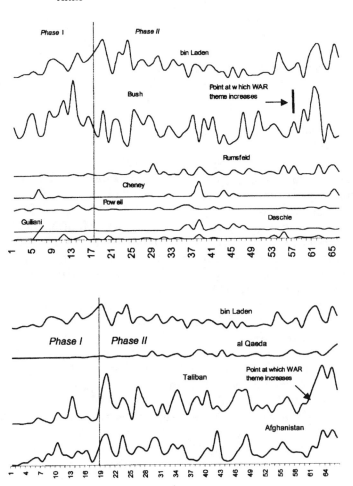

Fig. 10.5. Actors

Knowledge of Anthrax Mail." Interestingly, *bin=laden* and *anthrax* have a statistically significant correlation of -0.45, meaning that when one is influential in the news, the other is not.

In the case of both *pres=bush* and *bin=laden*, no distinct epochs can be discerned. Their dynamical behavior is constant throughout the 66 days. ARMA analysis (Poole et al., 2000) indicates that *bin=laden* is best described by a periodic model, with a period length of 4 days; lag one autocorrelation is 0.46. *Pres=bush* is best described by a simple moving average (MA) model; lag one autocorrelation is 0.22, and autocorrelation decays to zero at lag 4.

Examining the cross-correlation, we find that the two are moderately correlated on the same day (0.17), and then lagged by one day (0.32, *bin=laden* leading *pres=bush*).

These two findings suggest that *bin=laden* is best described as a "leading" concept, and *pres=bush* as a following concept (Dooley & Van de Ven, 1999). More specifically, the influence of *bin=laden* increases at a given point in time, triggered by his own actions/ communications and those from U.S. government officials. The "discursive wave" this creates has periodic elements to it, perhaps indicating that either bin Laden and/or U.S. officials were releasing news about bin Laden according to a schedule. The influence of *pres=bush* often increases just after that of *bin=laden,* indicating that some of the discourse surrounding *pres=bush* is a reaction to that surrounding *bin=laden.*

The second graph in Fig. 10.5 shows attention paid to the groups generally thought of as responsible for the WTC attacks. We see that the influence of the *taliban* and *afghanistan* increased during Phase II of the process, and that taliban increased significantly at the same time that the *military response* theme did. We note that although *al qaeda* was denoted as the target of the military response, its discursive influence is consistently small during the study period.

In summary, the WTC attack is an example where the triggering event is immediate and short-lived, and the responses are both discursively and temporally distinct from the event itself. On the other hand, the anthrax attack is an example where the trigger event is temporally extended, and responses are neither discursively nor temporally distinct from the event itself. This suggests that the duration of a news event might be a generic trait that determines the dynamics of the response as enacted in media content.

DISCUSSION

In this chapter we examined the content of 66 days of Reuters articles related to the attacks of September 11. We can make several concluding remarks. First, we demonstrated the methodological efficacy of CRA, and its ability to identify key words and themes within vast amounts of text, and the ability to use those data to determine change points and micro-historical epochs. In terms of media content, we showed that words could have interesting and insightful dynamical histories, that certain words lead and others follow, and that "news events" enacted as words can have "memory" in terms of their impact on media content. Second, we identified six major themes embedded in Reuters' content: the WTC attack itself, air security issues, international and political issues relating to the War on Terrorism, a military response, an economic impact, and anthrax. Furthermore, we found that these themes also had change points indicating four or five different dynamical epochs, each lasting about 2 weeks. This led us to propose a stimulus–response process for terrorism coverage, in which a terrorist event (WTC attack, anthrax) leads to an institutional response (military, political, air security), and sense-making about the impact on society (economic impact, discursive attention to "threat," and "fear").

11

Dehumanizing the Enemy in Editorial Cartoons*

William B. Hart, II
Fran Hassencahl
Old Dominion University

The first purpose of this chapter is to integrate the literature on war and metaphor. Since 1980 three authors, George Lakoff, Robert L. Ivie, and Sam Keen, have made significant progress in understanding how metaphor is used in the framing of a war-time enemy and how metaphor is used to justify war, but there is very little cross-referencing among the authors.[1] All three focus on the use of metaphor in justifying war. Lakoff, Ivie, and Keen use a slightly different terminology in their analyses, but they all address the same

---

*We wish to thank James Baesler, Alicia Rountree, Heather Wiest, Amy Ouellette and Elise Robbins for their assistance with this study. A bibliography, a list of a Internet links, and other information relevant to this study can be found at http://www.odu.edu/enemycartoons.

[1]Keen (1991) did mention the work of Ivie in a selected bibliography at the end of his book. "Professor Ivie's explorations of the decivilizing rhetoric used in American political speech parallels my explorations of the visual metaphors of the faces of the enemy" (p. 193). However, there is very little integration of Ivie's work into the main text of Keen's book.

concepts. The second and main purpose of this chapter is to apply the work of Lakoff, Ivie, and Keen to understand how U.S. editorial cartoonists used visual metaphor when drawing Osama bin Laden, the al-Qaida, and the Taliban. Through a content analysis of editorial cartoons related to the current war, we empirically test claims generated specifically from the work of Keen (1991).

METAPHOR AND WAR

Early scholars of metaphor held that metaphors were the tools of poets and rhetoricians. However, as Lakoff and Johnson (1980) observed, metaphors are also important in everyday language and thought.[2] Metaphors are commonly used in various forms of communication from everyday discourse, to film, to presidential rhetoric to editorial cartoons. We often understand one thing in terms of another. We speak, for example, of arguments in terms of war. We may say "My *opponent's* critique was *right on target*. She just *shot down* every one of my arguments. She *attacked* every weakness." Lakoff and Johnson (1980) argued that in addition to being commonplace, metaphors shape thought and justify action.[3]

International relations is one context in which metaphors are commonplace and are used to justify policies and actions (Chilton & Lakoff, 1995; Lakoff, 1991). Lakoff examined the metaphors used by the George Bush, Sr. administration during the Gulf War. Lakoff argued that the metaphors used by the Bush administration helped justify the military actions that the U.S. and coalition forces took during the war. The "state is a person" metaphor, which suggests that "war is a fight between two people," framed the war as a struggle between Bush and Saddam Hussein. The state-as-a-person metaphor brings about "the fairy tale of the just war" with a common cast of characters: a hero (sometimes seen a law official, e.g., the police), a villain, and a victim (Lakoff, 1991). The common plot begins

---

[2]Others, too, have pointed to the importance of metaphor. Grassi (1980), the Italian humanist, drew on the earlier work of Vico to posit that "the metaphor lies at the root of our human world. Insofar as metaphor has its roots in the analogy between different things and makes this analogy immediately spring into 'sight,' it makes a fundamental contribution to our world." Metaphors privilege the seeing of new relationships (K. Burke, 1984).

[3]Perry's (1983) study of Hitler's rhetoric during World War II illustrates well how metaphor justifies action. Perry explained how the parasite and infestation metaphors used by Hitler in reference to Jews justified for Hitler and his followers the act of killing millions of Jews during World War II.

with an evil, monstrous villain committing a crime against an innocent victim. The honorable, moral hero then defeats the villain, rescues the victim and thus righting the world again. The villain is cunning, but not rational and must be dealt with by force. In the case of the Gulf War, the United States was the hero, Hussein was the villain, and Kuwait was the victim. By falling into the fairy-tale view of the war Lakoff suggested, we may lose sight of the realities of the war. With its focus on one individual (Hussein) the fairy-tale metaphorical framework hides from us the death and damage the war brought to Iraqi citizens and others in the region. More recently, Lakoff (2001) applied his form of metaphorical analysis to the U.S. War on Terrorism. He identified within the rhetoric of the George W. Bush, Jr. administration such metaphors as the enemy as animals (such as rodents and snakes) and the enemy as evil-doers.

In his study of the presidential rhetoric of the Vietnam War, Cold War, and the Gulf War, Ivie (1980, 1984, 1996) argued that the metaphors used by past presidents serve to justify war. In times of war, presidents can "help rationalize the proposed mobilization by calling up a cluster of rhetorical forms which themselves stimulate the nation's belief in its cultural superiority as the foremost proponent of civilization" (p. 292). Ivie's (1984) analysis of Ronald Reagan's foreign policy discourse revealed how Reagan drew on a "cluster" of archetypal metaphors to "decivilize" the Soviets. Ivie found the following metaphors used by Reagan: Soviets-as-natural-menace (e.g., storms and fires), Soviets-as-animals, Soviets-as-primitives (e.g., barbarians), Soviets-as-machines (e.g., instruments or machines of war), Soviets-as-criminals who murder and steal, Soviets-as-mentally-disturbed, Soviets-as-fanatics-and-ideologues, Soviets-as-satanic-and-profane (e.g., evil empire).

Like Lakoff and Ivie, Keen (1984) observed metaphors being used to justify military actions in foreign policy rhetoric. The metaphors initially found by Keen are enemy-as-barbarian, enemy-as-rapist, enemy-as-animal, enemy-as-enemy-of-God, and enemy-as-death. Keen's (1986) book, *Faces of the Enemy,* is an historical analysis of the visual metaphors used by artists in times of war. In that book's more than 300 propaganda posters, editorial cartoons, and other artwork, the artists, according to Keen, draw on "archetypes of a horrible imagination" to dehumanize the enemy.[4] Keen's three main propositions are:

---

[4]See also Keen's (1991) edition of *Faces of the Enemy* and the 1987 documentary, also called Faces of the Enemy, for an overview of the main points of Keen's book along with some additional material (Jersey & Friedman, 1987).

Proposition 1. In times of war the enemy is dehumanized through visual metaphor.[5] (This proposition has two corollaries: (a) This process is universal. Each side dehumanizes the other. (b) This process has occurred in past wars and appears to continue.)

Proposition 2. There are 13 types of dehumanizing visual metaphors.

Proposition 3. Dehumanization of the enemy justifies the killing of the enemy. (If the enemy is not a civilized human like us, then, according to Keen, the guilt associated with killing the enemy is greatly lessened.)

More recently, Keen (2001) observed that the fear and hate triggered by the al-Qaida attacks have driven the public to dehumanize the new enemy as atheists, barbarians, and animals, but his essay did not specifically address visual metaphor. This chapter serves as an update to Keen's earlier work through an analysis of editorial cartoons related to the current war.

EDITORIAL CARTOONS, VISUAL METAPHOR, AND WAR

Editorial cartoons also have been analyzed using a variety of rhetorical or persuasive frameworks. Bormann, Koester, and Bennett (1978) studied the use of rhetorical fantasies in the cartoons covering the 1976 election. Benoit, Kluykouski, McHale, and Airne (2001) used fantasy theme analysis in a study of President Clinton's second term in office. Editorial cartoons have also been studied using metaphorical analysis. DeSousa and Medhurst (1982) drew on the five canons of Aristotle's *Rhetoric* to create a taxonomy of graphic discourse and recommend that critics of cartoons tap into the commonplaces or *topoi*, as Aristotle labeled them, which are the basis for cultural metaphors. By virtue of their visual images and limited text, cartoons do not present chains of formal reasoning, but function enthymatically. The audience is expected to recognize the symbolism and to fill in the Gestalt. If readers do not connect the "dots," they may lack familiarity with political commonplaces/ issues or the events have little salience beyond their appearance in that day's cartoon.

---

[5]Keen's term *dehumanizing* could be used synonymously with Ivie's term *decivilizing.*

Two studies (Conners, 1998; DeSousa, 1984) specifically used metaphorical analysis to study depictions of enemies in editorial cartoons. DeSousa, in his study of 186 cartoons depicting Ayatollah Khomeini during the 1979-1980 U.S.–Iran hostage crisis, draws upon "commonplace images within American culture to explain what was happening in a foreign land" (p. 217). The metaphors used for Khomeini were Khomeini-as-madman, Khomeini-as-religious-fraud, and Khomeini-as-manipulator. DeSousa suggested the metaphorical images in the cartoons gave the American public a venue for venting their hostilities in a situation where little else could be done. Conners' (1998) study of cartoonists' portrayal of Saddam Hussein during the Gulf War used Keen's categories of enemy images. Conners surveyed 965 cartoons in three large circulation newspapers and *Newsweek* over a period of 7 months (August 1990–March 1991). Of the 397 cartoons that dealt with the Gulf War, 170 (43%) dehumanized Hussein (i.e., used one of Keen's dehumanizing visual metaphors). Hussein was most frequently portrayed as an aggressor (48%) and criminal (24%). Conner concluded that the cartoons "reflected Bush administration rhetoric labeling Hussein as a threat that the United States needed to control" (p. 110).

Research Questions

This chapter analyzes how U.S. editorial cartoonists in the month following the September 11 attacks used metaphor in their depictions of the current U.S. enemy. For the purpose of this chapter, the enemy is defined as Osama bin Laden, the al-Qaida, and the Taliban. The Bush administration has also defined the enemy in this manner. Based on the work of Lakoff, Ivie, and more specifically Keen, and following in the research path of DeSousa and Conner, we propose the following research questions:

RQ1: To what extent is the enemy shown in the editorial cartoons?

RQ2: To what extent is the enemy dehumanized in the editorial cartoons?

RQ3: Which types of dehumanization (Keen's visual metaphors) were most prominent? How often are each of dehumanization types used?

RQ4: What trends emerge? Were different types of dehumanization used at different times?

The research questions serve to empirically test the claims (or propositions) of Keen (1986) and verify whether the types and amount of dehumanizing metaphor that Conners (1998) found in Gulf War cartoons is the same in cartoons about the current war.

METHODS

Sample

The American Association of Editorial Cartoonists has approximately 150 members categorized as full-time editorial cartoonists employed as cartoonists for newspapers and other periodicals (American Association of Editorial Cartoonists, 2002). Typically, past studies of cartoons relied on small samples of cartoonists found in a few major newspapers and news magazines. Current technology allows for a much wider, near-census sample.

We analyzed 1,070 cartoons drawn by 85 cartoonists available in an online database of editorial cartoonists, *Daryl Cagle's Professional Cartoonist Index* at Slate.com (Cagle, 2001). The 85 cartoonists studied had cartoons in the database between September 11 and October 8, 2001. They included 17 Pulitzer Prize winners such as Tony Auth (*Philadelphia Inquirer*), Paul Conrad (*Tribune Media Services*), Pat Oliphant (Universal Press Syndicate), Mike Ramirez (*Los Angeles Times*), and Ann Telnaes (Tribune Media Services). They represented such geographically diverse newspapers as the *St. Paul Pioneer Press*, the *Savannah Morning News*, the *Sacramento Bee*, the *Richmond Times-Dispatch*, the *Albuquerque Journal*, the *Palm Beach Post*, and the *Honolulu Bulletin*. Cartoonists also represented both large circulation newspapers and those newspapers with smaller circulations.

Of the 1,070 cartoons gathered, the researchers identified 317 that contained representations of the enemy. Two independent coders (seniors in an advanced research methods course) agreed in their coding of 242 cartoons (coefficient of reliability = .76). Because cartoonists could include more than one metaphor into any single cartoon, coders were allowed to code cartoons into more than one category. When coders agreed on at least one metaphor within a cartoon this was counted as agreement.

For the purposes of this study Keen's dehumanizing types were operationally defined as follows:[6]

---

[6]Keen (1986) also included two additional metaphor categories: enemy-as-stranger and enemy-as-worthy-opponent. The enemy-as-stranger category was excluded from the present study because it is not a mutually exclusive category. Enemy-as-stranger would be subsumed in all categories. By

Enemy-as-animal: Cartoon with repulsive animals (e.g., rat, reptile, insect, germ), including plants such as weeds; showing the enemy doing animal-like actions (e.g., hiding or living under a rock); a character doing actions toward the enemy that are typically done to repulsive animals.

Enemy-as-desecrator-of-women-and-children: Cartoon with Taliban or Afghani women (and/or children) who have been (or are being) harmed (physically or psychologically) through physical contact, intimidation, repression, and so on.

Enemy-as-torturer-of-prisoners: Cartoon containing U.S. soldier(s) or civilian(s) being tortured by the enemy (e.g., hanging by thumbs, being beaten).

Enemy-as-barbarian: Cartoon with an image of the enemy as primitive/uncivilized/not modern (e.g., wearing clothing associated with prehistoric cave people); as a small or tiny person; as a "brute/ monster" (e.g., with exaggerated features like elongated/sharp teeth or with claws and/or is oversized).

Enemy-as-criminal:[7] Cartoon with an image of the enemy as criminals (e.g., shown on a wanted poster, or in a criminal line-up).

Enemy-as-greedy: Cartoon containing an image of the enemy taking (from others) land, money or other resources.

Enemy-as-enemy-of-God: Cartoon with an image of the enemy as a desecrator of Christian religious symbols (e.g., the Holy Bible); as an opponent of Christianity (e.g., being the Devil or being associated with the Devil); as a desecrator of Islamic religious symbols (e.g., the Koran); as an opponent of Islam (e.g., not a true follower of Islam).

---

definition when an enemy is dehumanized, he or she is not like us, a stranger. The worthy-opponent category was excluded because it was not a dehumanizing category. In the enemy-as-worthy-opponent, the enemy is made superhuman.

[7]Keen (1986) included "terrorist" within the enemy-as-criminal category. Because most of the cartoons would be coded as enemy-as-criminal if "terrorist" was included, the terrorist aspect of the enemy-as-criminal metaphor was excluded during the coding process.

Enemy-as-death: Cartoon containing an image of the enemy as a skeleton (or skull) or as the Grim Reaper.

Enemy-as-faceless: Cartoon with an image of the enemy who has only one or no facial features (e.g., only eyes); images of more than one enemy, who all look alike or identical.

Enemy-as-aggressor: Cartoon containing images of the enemy carrying weapons (e.g., gun, knife). Cartoon containing the enemy in the military (e.g., army) or the enemy protesting or demonstrating (e.g, fists in air or carrying signs).

Enemy-as-abstraction: Cartoon with an image of the enemy as a nonliving object (e.g., robot, target, smoke).

Enemy-as-human: Cartoons containing the enemy, but not falling into any of the categories just presented (i.e., enemy that is not dehumanized).

In addition to the images within the cartoons, cartoons also were coded into the categories just described based on words used within the cartoon (e.g., within captions).

RESULTS

Portrayal and Dehumanization of the Enemy in Editorial Cartoons

The enemy (Osama bin Laden, al-Qaida, or the Taliban) was represented in 242 (23%) of the 1,070 editorial cartoons studied. When the enemy was represented, it was dehumanized in 91% of the editorial cartoons (220 of 242).[8] Of the large percentage of cartoons that dealt with the attacks and their effects, but did not show the enemy, common themes emerged. In the first few days after the attacks, grief and anger were shown in the many images of the Statue of Liberty crying and in the enraged stare and clinched fists of Uncle Sam images. Other themes included financial effects of the attacks, criticism of the CIA and airport security, and concerns over civil liberties.

---

[8]In 18 cartoons, the enemy was dehumanized into two of Keen's visual metaphors (e.g., enemy-as-animal and enemy-as-aggressor). A total of 260 dehumanizing visual metaphors were used in 242 cartoons.

Fig. 11.1. Under Our Noses by David Reddick, *The Herald Bulletin*, September 30, 2001, all rights reserved. Reprinted with permission.

Fig. 11.2. Bluebird to Nest. Copyright, Tim Menees/*Pittsburgh Post-Gazette*, 2002, all rights reserved. Reprinted with permission.

Types of Dehumanization Used

When the enemy was dehumanized, certain of Keen's types were more prominent than others ($\chi^2 = 257.7$, 11 df, $p < .001$). As shown in Table 11.1, the enemy-as-animal and enemy-as-aggressor metaphors appeared prominently in the editorial cartoons, whereas the enemy-as-torturer metaphor appeared only once and the enemy-as-greedy metaphor did not appear at all.

Enemy-as-animal (29%).[9] The enemy-as-animal metaphors consisted of such subcategories as enemy-as-rat, enemy-as-reptile, and enemy-as-insect. Within this category, the enemy was most frequently depicted as a rat and reptile (e.g., snake).[10] The enemy was also portrayed as an octopus, a germ, and a weed.

Enemy-as-aggressor (21%). The next most prominent metaphor was enemy-as-aggressor. All but a few of the aggressor cartoons showed the enemy carrying a weapon (e.g., a knife or gun). A few cartoons showed the enemy carrying a bomb. No cartoons showed the enemy in other aggressor roles.

Enemy-as-abstraction (12%). The two abstraction metaphors used were the enemy-as-target and the enemy-as-smoke. Bin Laden occasionally appeared with a bulls-eye target on his head, body, or on the ground near him. Cartoonists using a bin Laden-as-smoke metaphor drew bin Laden's face within plumes of smoke coming from burning Twin Towers.

Enemy-as-barbarian (8%). The fourth most frequent metaphor used was the enemy-as-barbarian metaphor. Within this category, the enemy was portrayed almost equally as a brute, a miniature person, and as primitive (or uncivilized person). The enemy-as-brute appeared in the form of a monster (e.g., bin Laden-as-Frankenstein). The enemy-as-miniature-person was depicted by showing a large Uncle Sam stepping on miniature Taliban and a large

---

[9]The percentage in the parentheses is the percentage of enemy metaphors fitting the category under discussion out of total number of enemy metaphors used ($N = 260$). Also see Table 11.1. This pattern continues for the other metaphor types.

[10]In the enemy-as-animal cartoons there were 22 times in which the enemy was depicted as hiding (e.g., in turbans, under clothes, in holes or under rocks). The images of the enemy hiding were coded as enemy-as-animal and are included in the total of 76. If the hiding enemy depictions were removed from the total count, then the percentage of enemy-as-animal cartoons would be 21%.

Table 11.1. Frequencies of Visual Metaphors used by Editorial Cartoonists between September 11 to October 8, 2001

Enemy Metaphor	Freq.	% of Total[a]	Week 1	Week 2	Week 3	Week 4	CS 4wks[b]	CS 2wks[c]
Animal	76	29%	21	17	24	14	3.05	0.00
Desecrator	11	4%	0	2	4	5	5.36	4.45[d]
Torturer	1	0%	0	0	1	0	3.00	1.00
Barbarian	20	8%	4	6	6	4	0.80	0.00
Criminal	11	4%	1	8	2	0	14.09[e]	4.45[f]
Greedy	0	0%	0	0	0	0		
Enemy of God	16	6%	6	3	5	2	2.50	0.25
Death	6	2%	2	2	1	1	0.67	0.67
Faceless	12	5%	5	4	3	0	4.67	3.00[g]
Aggressor	54	21%	6	16	16	16	5.56	1.85
Abstraction	31	12%	11	9	5	6	2.94	2.61
Humanized	22	9%	2	6	7	7	3.09	1.64
Total	260	100.0%	58	73	74	55		
Chi-Square (χ^2)	257.7							
Significance	$p < .001$ $df = 11$							

[a]Percentage of all metaphors used within editorial cartoons containing a representation of the enemy ($N = 260$).
[b]Chi-square (χ^2) for analysis using four time periods (each of the 4 weeks).
[c]Chi-square (χ^2) for analysis using two time periods (first 2 week and last 2 weeks).
[d]$p < .05$, $df = 1$ for two time periods.
[e]$p < .01$, $df = 3$ for four time periods.
[f]$p < .05$, $df = 1$ for two time periods.
[g]$p < .10$, $df = 1$ for two time periods.

American eagle attacking a small figure of the enemy. Bin Laden was portrayed as a primitive (or uncivilized person) when dressed in animal hides like early cave people. The enemy also was portrayed as a primitive by means of the words in some cartoon captions, for example, references to the enemy living in the "stone-age."

Enemy-as-enemy-of-God (6%). Enemy-of-God cartoons most frequently depicted as the enemy of the Christian God. For example, some cartoons depicted the enemy (particularly the al-Qaida hijackers) as being in hell with the devil. Bin Laden was also associated with or compared to the devil. The enemy also was portrayed as being an enemy of the Islamic God (Allah) who sometimes punished or banished bin Laden.

Enemy-as-faceless (5%). Enemy-as-faceless takes two forms: (a) all members of the enemy group look the same, and (b) enemy missing facial features. Some cartoons depicted the enemy looking alike. For example, one had several al-Qaida members sitting around a table, but all members looked like bin Laden. Most of the faceless cartoons, however, showed the enemy with missing facial features. One cartoon, in particular, showed bin Laden sitting cross-legged as has been shown in news coverage, but with missing eyes, nose, and mouth.

Enemy-as-desecrator-of-women-and-children (4%). No cartoons contained depictions of the enemy desecrating American or coalition women. However, some cartoons did depict the enemy as a desecrator of Taliban and al-Qaida women. A few of them showed images of Taliban men harming or threatening Taliban women and children. In most cases, the enemy was portrayed as desecraters of women and children by the words the cartoonists used in their captions.

Enemy-as-criminal (4%). Two common themes occurred within the enemy-as-criminal category. Several cartoons showed bin Laden on wanted posters. President Bush appeared as a sheriff in some of the wanted poster cartoons. The enemy was also shown as part of a criminal line-up.

Enemy-as-death (2%). Most of the cartoons using the enemy-as-death metaphor depicted the al-Qaida hijackers as a grim-reaper. A couple showed skulls with the words "terrorist" or "terrorism" on them.

Trends

When the enemy cartoons are analyzed over the 4-week period, some
trends emerged. Cartoons were divided into four 1-week periods
(Tuesday, 9/11 to Monday, 9/17; 9/18 to 9/24; 9/25 to 10/1; and 10/2 to
10/8). Cartoons also were divided into two 2-week periods (Tuesday,
9/11 to Monday 9/24 and 9/25 to 10/8). As Table 11.1 shows, in the
analysis with two time periods, there is a significant difference
between the amount of cartoons in the first period and the second
period for three of the metaphor types. There were less enemy-
desecrator-of-women-and-children metaphors used in the first 2
weeks than in the last 2 weeks ($\chi^2 = 4.45$, 1 df, $p < .05$). There were
more enemy-as-faceless metaphors in the first 2 weeks than in the
last 2 weeks ($\chi^2 = 3.0$, 1 df, $p < .10$). There were more enemy-as-
criminal metaphors used in the first 2 weeks than in the last 2 weeks
($\chi^2 = 257.7$, 1 df, p < .05). A significant difference also appeared for
the enemy-as-criminal metaphor in the four 1-week analyses ($\chi^2 =
14.1$, 3 df, $p < .05$) with significantly more enemy-as-criminal
cartoons in the second week than the other 3 weeks.

DISCUSSION

The work of Lakoff, Ivie, Keen, DeSousa, and Conner suggest that
metaphors play an important role in war-time rhetoric. Likewise, the
results of this study indicate that dehumanizing visual metaphors
continue to appear in war-time editorial cartoons. Conners (1998)
found that, of the cartoons covering the Gulf War, 18% dehumanized
the enemy. Similarly, this study found that, of the cartoons covering
the current war, 23% dehumanized the enemy. Such results suggest
that when drawing cartoons about war, editorial cartoonists
dehumanize the enemy approximately in one out of every five
cartoons. This apparent pattern should be studied further.

The present study prompts two other areas of future
research. Further study is needed to test Keen's claim that
dehumanizing metaphors lead the general public to support the
killing of enemies (Keen's Proposition 3). This study, like all content
analyses, focuses on the construction of messages and not on the
reception of messages. An experimental media effects study would
better address Keen's Proposition 3. Another issue is the influence of
President Bush's speeches on cartoonists. The appearance of certain
metaphors (e.g., enemy-as-criminal and enemy-as-barbarian) and the
appearance of certain trends (e.g., the number of enemy-as-criminal

metaphors higher in the second week of study) appear to be linked to President Bush's references to the new enemy as "evil-doers" and "barbaric criminals" who "burrow deeper into caves" (Bush, 2001a, 2001b). Further study is needed on the relationship between the cartoonists' visual metaphors and the metaphors in presidential rhetoric.

The link between editorial cartoons and presidential rhetoric shows that metaphors are not the mere tools of artists, but play an important role in foreign policy. Metaphors are used in presidential rhetoric to frame enemies. Furthermore, as noted by DeSousa (1984), Keen (1986), Lakoff (1991), and Ivie (1996) the use of metaphor in foreign policy is both "dangerous" and "dysfunctional" because metaphor may over-simplify or hide the realities of a complex international relations situation. Metaphors help to create the myth of the leader as the protector against despicable villains or creatures (Ivie, 1996; Lakoff, 1991). In the case of the current war, no longer are al-Qaida human beings, who might have a rationale for their behavior, but insects and rodents to be exterminated.

Edelman (1971) described metaphors as devices that simplify and give meaning "to complex and bewildering sets of observations that evoke concern"(p. 65). Edelman saw the use of metaphor by leaders as a means to build mass support for political violence. Definitions of the enemy as a stranger, an alien or a subhuman are repeated themes which "will most potently create and mobilize allies" (p. 114). Edelman (1971) explained that the causes and remedies for wars are complex, but metaphors "permit [people] to live in a world in which the causes are simple and neat and the remedies are apparent" (p. 83). Metaphors can quickly define the bad guys in the black hats or in this situation, the guys in the turbans and the good guys in the white hats.

Along with being a "powerful legitimizer" of governmental policy, Edelman (1971) warned that metaphor dampens dissent (p. 72). Metaphors become an organizing principle around which "the public thereafter arranges items of news that fit" (p. 72). Thus, a viewpoint is constantly revalidated and appears to be a legitimate way of behavior. Consequently metaphors may silence those who would question or dissent from the administration's handling of the current war. Dissenting views were noticeably absent in the cartoons analyzed in the present study. Astor (2002), in *Editor and Publisher,* noted that most cartoonists "sensibly backed the Afghanistan war." An additional danger to metaphor, then, may be that dehumanizing metaphors dampen dissent (or alternative perspectives to current policies and actions).

In the present study, we have shown that dehumanizing metaphors continue to be used in war-time and we have argued that there are some important dangers to using metaphor in foreign policy discourse. However, to argue that metaphor use in times of war is "dangerous" and "dysfunctional," is not to side with the enemy or condone, in any way, their actions. The point is, as Keen noted,

> There are real enemies and we can't make conflict go away by pretending that we are all friends, but the world has become too dangerous to portray those enemies as monsters and evil empires and ourselves as God's righteous warriors (Keen, cited in Jersey, 1987)

> We have to develop empathy for our enemy. It doesn't mean sympathy. It doesn't mean compassion. It means you have to have the imagination to get inside his skin, and see how the world seems from his point of view. (Keen, 2001)

In order to better and more completely understand the motives and future actions of Osama bin Laden and the al-Qaida, we may find value in not accepting too quickly oversimplifying metaphor.

12

Representing Patriotism:
The Blurring of Place and Space in
an "All-America City"

Donnalyn Pompper
Florida State University

This chapter focuses on nonmediated representations of patriotism. It is of interest because the process and *cultural context* of ordinary people's[1] lives seldom capture social science researchers' interest (Frake, 1996; Shore, 1996) beyond base/superstructure power issues. Furthermore, historians have devoted little attention to the process of how symbolic complexes form (Hobsbawm, 1983). Finally, the September 11, 2001 event is timely, offering a multifaceted lens by which to examine a variety of phenomena—including the construction of collective memory about a "critical incident"[2]

[1]*Ordinary people* are defined as "a diverse lot . . . invariably include individuals from all social stations. . . . They acknowledge the ideal of loyalty in commemorative events and agree to defend the symbol of the nation but often use commemoration to redefine that symbol or ignore it for the sake of leisure or economic ends" (Bodnar, 1992, p. 16).

[2]*Critical incidents* are what Levi-Strauss (1966) called "hot moments, phenomena or events through which a society or culture assesses its own significance" (p. 259).

unrivaled in U.S. history. Scholarship relevant to this study is reviewed in four sections: fusing setting to situation, representation and meaning making, symbolic vocabulary of patriotism, and constructing new memory.

FUSING SETTING TO SITUATION

As both physical realities and social constructs, *place* and *space* are essential components of culture as we live our lives in common. These multipurpose terms vary according to discipline, defying operationalization. Looseness of both terms facilitates a discovery of meaning-making among Americans who lived the September 11, 2001 tragedy.

We lack a theory of *place* and the term has little meaning separated from its materializations (Geertz, 1996). Place is expressed in the literature in both general and in particular terms. Harvey (1993) posited that there are generic places like *location, neighborhood, region,* and *territory*—and particular places such as *city, village, town,* and *state.* Moreover, words like *home, community, nation,* and *turf* convey an implied meaning that constructs and maintains place by virtue of the gestures, prevailing practices, rituals, ceremonies, and commemorations that take place there (Duncan & Ley, 1993; Tuan, 1991). It is suggested here that Americans made sense of a unique event by using place to put traditional rituals to work in new ways.

Space is bound parcels of physical geography that take on political meaning and are categorized by how they are used and who has access to them. Henaff and Strong (2001) defined *private space* (ownership and standards for entering), *sacred space* (presence of God), *common space* (not owned or controlled), and *public space* (democratic forum for the common good). The relationship between spheres is not reciprocal, and boundaries are flexible. For purposes here, *place* refers to a "metaphorical territory" (Harvey, 1993, p. 3), and *space* refers to the "relational act" of drawn boundaries (Featherstone, 1993, p. 176).

Postmodernists and cultural critics in recent decades lament that public space is shrinking and its value has been exchanged for greater privacy. Public space has been encroached by popular culture (streets), mass culture (malls), high culture (museums), corporate culture (office buildings), and official culture (government structures; Lippard, 1997). Furthermore, public space is becoming obsolete as institutions seek to control and close "the open dimension of public space" (Norton, 2001) because people covet privacy, wanting to insulate themselves and disconnect from their surroundings (Gumpert & Drucker, 1998). Radical critiques cast remaining public spaces as "militarized" zones of surveillance where the affluent fortress themselves in gated communities segregated from the "criminalized poor" (Davis, 1992, p. 224).

Some researchers indict the mass media for forever altering place and space. Featherstone (1993) suggested that "everywhere is the same as everywhere else" (p. 177) and Meyrowitz (1985) posited that bombardments of messages and images leave us with "no sense of place." As a "window on the world" (Hutchinson, 1948, p. ix), mass media erase sharp distinctions between indoors–outdoors and private–public life (Gumpert & Drucker, 1998; Prost & Vincent, 1991; Spigel, 1992). Newly designed and wired domestic spaces enable people to overcome time–space barriers with large-pane glass windows and telecommuting technology. Regardless of agency, public space historically used for interacting with others has become an anomaly. Certainly, Americans huddled around their televisions for live information and used cyberspace as they sought to sort out details of September 11, 2001. However, as this chapter illustrates, Americans' also used nonmediated fora to connect with others and make the national tragedy *mean*.

REPRESENTATION AND MEANING-MAKING

Communication scholars have placed a high premium on language as both a producer of culture and as a cultural product. Language works through a "representational system" that incorporates signs and symbols—words, sounds, images, and objects—as stand-ins for one's "ideas and feelings" (Hall, 1997, p. 1). Individuals use this system—this signifying practice—to regulate and organize our acts and order social life. Thus, language belongs neither to senders nor receivers, but resides in the "shared cultural space" in which representation takes place (Hall, 1997, p. 10).

Moreover, Shore (1996) argued that shared cultural models offer "salience-enhancing templates" to help with meaning making (p. 315). However, these templates suffer limited parsimony in bridging texts with mental models—especially when there is no appropriate cultural model to account for an extraordinary situation. In such events, individuals develop their own models. Similarly, people act on an innate "narrative impulse" (Bird, 2002) to create and share stories to explain unknowable answers to questions. Narrative is both a

ng and a mode of representation (Richardson, 1990)
ople together" (Johnstone, 1990, p. 127) through
ws (Bruner, 1984). Therefore, it is posited here that
to terms with an unprecedented happening on
001—by using place and space to represent their
patriotic spirit and thereby connect with other Americans.

SYMBOLIC VOCABULARY OF PATRIOTISM

Patriotism is represented by and defined as "the American flag and
love of country" (Kosterman & Feshbach, 1989). To examine the
symbolic vocabulary of patriotism is to acknowledge that the red-
white-and-blue American flag is the most respected and revered
symbol in the United States—a personification of free speech,
democracy, freedom, independence, sacrifice, honor, and other deeply
held values. Since the late 1800s, the American flag has served as
part of a daily ritual in public schools (Kammen, 1991) and is
displayed over courthouses, ball parks, and war memorials.
Americans celebrate Flag Day[3] annually to promote patriotism
(Bodnar, 1992). Moreover, desecration of the flag is a cultural taboo
and consequently, the source of U. S. Supreme Court free speech
decisions.

Discovering how this symbol serves as a stand-in for
patriotism involved examining the social history literature on
incorporated practices. To understand humans' relation to their past,
Hobsbawm (1983) drew on old traditions—specific and strong binding
social practices, and invented traditions—"unspecific practices vague
as to the nature of the values, rights and obligations of the group
membership they inculcate" (p. 10). He categorized *patriotism* among
traditions *invented* since the Industrial Revolution that use history
as a "legitimator of action and cement of group cohesion" (p. 12).

The communication, sociology, and political science literature
underscored patriotism's links to social forces that affect public
opinion. Patriotism (ethnocentrism) serves as an enduring news
value (Gans, 1979), routinely attended to in journalists' news
production acts. Patriotism's opposite—"otherness"—emerges from
public opinion, represented in stereotypical "we-images" and "they-
images" as defensive "mobilization of nationalism" reactions during
international conflict (Featherstone, 1993, p. 184). Moreover, a "rally
around the flag" effect—the aggregation of individual patriotic

[3]Woodrow Wilson established Flag Day, a national celebration, in 1916.

responses (Mueller, 1970)—is strongest during international conflicts when the enemy is dehumanized, stereotyped, and headed by a villifiable leader (McLeod, Eveland, & Signorielli, 1994). The effect translates to a spike in popular confidence of authority figures and promotes social solidarity. It was germane to this study, therefore, to explore patriotism as an invented tradition represented in many nonmediated forms following the September terrorist attacks.

CONSTRUCTING NEW MEMORY

Patriotism and its symbolic vocabulary is central to a vital cultural construction—public memory.[4] Memories help us make sense of the world we live in (Gillis, 1994) and provide a heuristic for understanding the past, present, and future (Bodnar, 1992; Kammen, 1991). The study of public memory formation and maintenance may be traced back to the conscience collective work of Emile Durkheim. It involves probing "acts that make remembering in common possible" (Connerton, 1989, p. 39). In particular, certain moments stand out, challenging people to make them mean as they enter private and public records on the spot (Irwin-Zarecka, 1994)—such as the assassination of John F. Kennedy and the Oklahoma City bombing. Nonmediated representations of patriotism, undoubtedly, will play a role in shaping collective, public memory of the September 11, 2001 domestic terrorist attacks.

Researchers across social science disciplines agree that public memories are not created or sustained in a vacuum. They are subjective, selective, often contested, and shaped by ideological systems that serve particular interests.[5] However, the memory formation landscape is changing; no longer the exclusive domain of elites. Americans and Europeans are more interested in the past than ever before (Gillis, 1994), localizing national commemorations, tracing their family genealogy, purchasing artifacts of the past, and using new technologies to record their own memories (Nora, 1996). Kammen (1991) discovered that popular opinion supports anointing the private

---

[4]Public memory is produced from discussion of fundamental issues about a society's existence—its organization, structure of power, and the meaning of its past and present (Bodnar, 1992, p. 14).

[5]For example, dramatic citizens rights events rarely are commemorated because they threaten authority and threaten to disrupt a stable social order (Bodnar, 1992). He noted that the colonists of 1776 are the notable exception among commemorated dramatic episodes of citizens asserting their rights.

sector, rather than government, as stewards of tradition and memory. This finding underscores a recent shift in people's preference for local, personalized memory (Gillis, 1994; LeGoff, 1992)—even when issues and events begin at a national level. Old holidays and monuments "have lost much of their power to commemorate" (Gillis, 1994, p. 20) as Americans use July 4 and other public ritual time for recreational purposes in their local communities (Bodnar, 1992). Thus, Americans increasingly record their own history, construct new memories, and represent patriotism their own way.

METHODOLOGY: IN SEARCH OF REPRESENTATIONS OF PATRIOTISM

This analysis was designed to discover how ordinary people used place and space to represent patriotism in Tallahassee, the Florida state capital, in the wake of the domestic terrorist attacks.

In the tradition of grounded theory emerging from data and then illustrated by characteristic examples of data (Glaser & Strauss, 1967), a descriptive approach—"where theories hover in the background while the complex phenomena themselves occupy the front stage"—was used to observe and document representations of patriotism (Tuan, 1991, p. 686). Fieldnotes recorded over the course of 6 months (September 2001 through February 2002) during drives and walks among Tallahassee places and spaces were reviewed for setting and context.

The city of Tallahassee was selected for its proximity to the primary researcher. Furthermore, Tallahassee's catapult into the international news spotlight in 2001 framed the city as a hotbed of democracy in the wake of the controversial "election night that never ended" (Hickey, 2001). The election's outcome hinged on Florida's vote, which had been misstated by network news media due to closeness of the presidential race and the state's vote tabulation challenges. Finally, Tallahassee might be expected to represent its patriotism more zealously than some other cities because it is home to U.S. President George W. Bush's brother—Florida Governor Jeb Bush—and routinely welcomes the brothers' parents, former U.S. President George Bush and First Lady Barbara Bush. Like many U.S. cities, Tallahassee hosts diverse neighborhood clusters defined by socioeconomic status, ethnicity, proximity to place of worship, and distance from the downtown commercial district. From the African-American-dominated close-in "Frenchtown" section, to the outlying pockets of Seminole Native Americans, to the mansions of Governor

Jeb Bush and national champion FSU Seminoles' football coach, Bobby Bowden—Tallahassee is a community of many neighborhoods. Moreover, Tallahassee's 57,800 college students call Greek and apartment housing home. Once inhabited by the Apalachee Native Americans, Tallahassee now is a mid-sized southern city of nearly 151,000 residents—an economic hub of a 13-county area covering North Florida and South Georgia. Geography includes moss-draped oaks, hills and valleys, more so than flat land and tropical foliage native to the state's southern half. Yet among so much diversity, Tallahasseeans used place and space in quite similar ways as they represented patriotism in weeks and months following September 11, 2001.

RESULTS

Representations of patriotism among everyday Tallahasseeans' places and spaces clustered into three distinct categories: (a) Patriotism at home: American flags in fabric and sticker forms; buntings, red-white-and-blue holiday lights; decorated front doors of homes; tri-color flower gardens; words of inspiration and solidarity plastered on posters, signs, and banners; (b) patriotism on the go: automobile bumper stickers; and (c) patriotism as personal adornment: home-made remembrance ribbons, red-white-and-blue pins, and patriotic clothing.

DISCUSSION

Patriotism at Home

Humans' adornment of place and space has captivated anthropologists in search of clues about "what it is to be human in this world we all live in" (Frake, 1996, p. 230)—as well as sociologists who analyze the "manifest and latent functions" of acts, rituals and ceremonies (Merton, 1968). For example, the manifest intent in displaying an American flag is to announce one's love of country—but the latent function of this act is to support authorities and institutions charged with maintaining political and social order. Rituals also contribute to public-collective memory maintenance—as "the batteries which charge up the emotional bonds between people and renew the sense of the sacred" (Featherstone, 1993, p. 177).

Tallahassee residents tapped into their reservoir of patriotic representations traditionally reserved for the Fourth of July, Labor Day, Veterans Day, and Memorial Day. Post-September 11, red-white-and-blue colors dotted nearly every private, sacred, common, and public place and space, blending into one seamless nonmediated expression of empathy, sorrow, and solidarity. Boundaries containing spaces became invisible amidst patriotic representations—flags and buntings were hung and flown in yards and tri-colored flowers of the season were sown in family gardens and outside state buildings. Greek organizations on both of Tallahassee's university campuses painted half-walls at well-traveled intersections with "God Bless America" and "God Bless the U.S.A." instead of promoting their usual crushes, formals, and fundraisers. Indeed, Tallahasseeans treated place and space as sites where articulation of meaning could take place—shifting from passive spectators of local, regional, and national commemorative ceremonies—to engaged, expressive participants.

The "home," a "historically situated concept" (Gumpert & Drucker, 1998, p. 424), was a canvass for patriotic representation across semi-gated community entrances and front doors throughout Tallahassee. Locals abandoned their traditional red-and-green holiday yard decorations for red-white-and-blue lights and stars on trees—and outlines of rooftops—several weeks earlier than usual. In December, wreaths of greenery and wicker were tied with red-white-and-blue ribbons and competed first with Rudolph the Red-Nosed Reindeer and Santa for space on homes' doors—and then later with Cupid and heart-shaped wreaths on Valentine's Day.

Everyone seemed to circulate and swap patriotic artifacts. The daily newspaper, The *Tallahassee Democrat*, distributed cardboard stock posters with patriotic themes. Local grocery stores and other commercial enterprises distributed posters inscribed with words of inspiration and solidarity, including: "United We Stand," "One Nation Under God," and "We Stand United. We Will Not Tolerate Terrorism." These posters were fastened to trees, telephone poles, lamp posts, mailboxes, storefronts, U.S. post office branches, and schools. Some Tallahasseeans even downloaded from the Internet and displayed photos of Osama bin Laden with a bull's eye superimposed on his face. Hall (1997) reminds us that "culture is about shared meanings" (p. 1). Tallahassee residents were united in their attempts to interpret meaningfully what had happened on 9/11.

Patriotism on the Go

Beyond representing patriotism on and outside the home, Tallahassee residents also took their messages on the road—

decorating automobiles, pickup trucks, and SUVs. School buses, TalTran (public bus system), and taxi cabs also featured patriotic messages. Quite popular were 12-inch American flags mounted on a plastic pole clipped to vehicle windows.[6] Throughout October, nearly every car in Tallahassee featured these—waving furiously on both driver and passenger sides of vehicles—until they blew off and littered the sides of major roads. Drivers of pick-up trucks used the open slots on either side of the tailgate to hold long poles that supported very large flags—creating a parade-like ambiance all across the Capital City wherever the trucks with flags-in-tow traveled. This spacial practice underscores the salience of mobility in our culture—and our use of vehicles as moving private space.

American flag stickers and bumper stickers—a traditional means for communicating one's political views, spreading humor, and promoting school and church institutions—also enabled Tallahassee residents to maximize the illusory power of representation beyond the boundaries of their home and immediate neighborhoods. The cardboard stock posters also could be seen duct-taped to doors of SUVs, pick-ups, and utility trucks. Finally, Tallahassee's police squad cars portrayed a bumper sticker that read, "Don't Be Afraid. Be Alert."

Patriotism as Personal Adornment

Beyond their private spaces and vehicles, Tallahasseeans also used their bodies as nonmediated means to represent patriotism. A cadre of children dressed as Uncle Sam marched along Tallahassee streets gathering Halloween treats—and students and others wore their "Old Navy" American flag T-shirts with greater regularity while exercising out of doors. Local hobby and fabric shops hosted "make and take" classes for children and adults to create patriotism-themed crafts—safety pins threaded with red-white-and-blue seed beads for lapels and tri-color ribbon loops secured with a straight pin as one would wear a corsage.

During the weekend after 9/11, a drive through one of Tallahassee's "canopy roads" neighborhoods included observation of a family of four (mom, dad, and two young girls) standing at the corner of their yard where intersecting streets meet, holding a sign that read "God Bless America," and brandishing July 4 sparklers while waving to passers by. The vision evoked a slice of Norman Rockwell

---

[6]Tallahassee's college sports fans—FSU Seminoles and FAMU Rattlers—fly similar flags and windsocks featuring school colors and mascot/logo, as well as team-spirit stickers.

Americana. Behaviors such as these, undoubtedly, contribute to a great sense of belonging and solidarity among community members and contribute to public-collective memory.

CONCLUSION

Why should we be concerned with everyday Americans' nonmediated representations of patriotism? How did this participant-observation research conducted in Tallahassee bring us closer to understanding the processes of fusing setting to situation, meaning-making, culture production and new memory construction?

Americans' desire for privacy over public interaction in recent years proved to have negative ramifications as people struggled to make sense of the domestic terrorism acts. Gone are the traditional town meetings and gathering places where neighbors used to meet and resolve issues through dialog. Comfortable in their wired homes with substantial views of the outdoors, Americans have insulated themselves from neighbors and find it difficult to reach out in time of need. Thus, it is posited here that boundaries separating places and spaces blurred as everyday people—regardless of ethnicity, gender or socioeconomic status—expressed support for their country's leaders and empathy for victims in the wake of September 11. They did so by invoking symbols and by using place/space that clearly would be understood by others for the purpose of fostering shared meaning that will greatly contribute to formation of new public-collective memory of the terrorist attacks.

13

*"Plane Wreck with Spectators": Terrorism and Media Attention**

Bernhard Debatin
Ohio University

Attention is the most precious good of mass communication because only a few issues can be processed at once. Additionally, the attention spans of audience members are short. But the media depend on the same economy of attention as their audience. Attention to one topic is edged out by its competitors in the marketplace of public issues. News selection criteria (*news values*) can be understood as *media attention rules*: sensationalism, violence, negativism, surprise, dynamics, identification, and spatial and cultural proximity.

In the following analysis, I unfold the thesis that terrorist action usually satisfies these criteria and that the September 11 terrorists planned their attacks with a clear understanding of these media attention rules: They organized and executed their attacks anticipating the media impact and the symbolic power that the worldwide broadcasted images would have. Thus, the terrorists, who

*The author extends his gratitude to Stephanie Hay and Patricia Stokes for research and editorial assistance. Parts of this paper were presented at the AEJMC Regional Conference in February 2002.

despise modern technology and the democratic media society, are simultaneously experts in the use of them.[1] There is a *media semiotics of terror* that worked exactly as the terrorists intended.

My following four theses explain different aspects of this complex topic: First, I discuss the temporal dimension of the events and their media coverage. I then analyze their aesthetic aspect, particularly with respect to fascination with the dreadful images. This is followed by some reflections on the meaning of the ritualistic repetition of the images. Finally, I discuss the relationship between mystification and glorification of terrorist action. In closing, I raise some questions concerning the media ethical dimension of these events and their media coverage, followed by an outlook on media coverage of terrorism and the war in Afghanistan.[2]

TIMING

Thesis: *The terrorists reached the largest live audience possible because most people around the globe were awake. Instantaneously, the shocking events profoundly interrupted the normal flow of time. Moreover, real-time coverage guaranteed immediate global information on the events, yet greatly hindered thoughtful journalism.*

The symbolic space of time is, to a large extent, constructed by the synchronizing effects of modern technology and particularly the media (Elias, 1992). Consequently, this interruption of time would not have been possible without the media. The psychological earthquake of the events sent its shockwaves through the media into the farthest regions of the globe.[3] The sudden interruption of the flow of time by the 9/11 attacks had apocalyptic elements. Time seemed to

---

[1]This is, however, nothing new: "In innumerable instances in the past and doubtless more to follow, terrorist outrages have been planned and timed so as to exploit the media to its absolute limits and to attract maximum publicity. . . . The terrorists show no hesitation or lack of skill in exploiting the benefits of democracy—in this case an open press—in order to subvert democracy" (Hermon, 1990, p. 38).

[2]I am using the form of an essayistic explanation of *theses* rather than that of a research report because this chapter is a *theoretical analysis* of semiotic and philosophical aspects rather than an empirical study.

[3]Again, this is not a new phenomenon: "Modern media technology has made the terrorists' task all too easy. In a few minutes, a terrorist group can place its signature on an atrocity and have its claims beamed around the world. The Munich Olympic massacre of 1972 was beamed to an estimated worldwide audience of more than 500 million" (Wilkinson, 1990, p. 31).

have come to an end, or at least to a sudden stop. Interruption of the normal flow of time by a shocking event has always been regarded as a sign of a new beginning. The reaction to this interruption was that nothing would be the same as before the incident. This disruption of the temporal structure of our media-synchronized society has to be understood as an important part of terrorist strategy. It guarantees and focuses media attention and, at the same time, creates an ubiquitous and diffuse atmosphere of insecurity, fear, and terror:

> Terrorists use news organizations as their advertising agencies, recruiting them into providing intense coverage to increase the societal impact of an attack. Terrorists use sensational and innovative methods of attack, select high-profile targets, submit prepared messages directly to news organizations, and even attack the news organizations themselves to boost coverage. (Dietz, 2002, para. 4)

In the case of the 9/11 events, the global media system—the infosphere—created a worldwide synchronization of attention, thus establishing an extraordinary order of time and life: The whole world was watching the events in real time or very shortly after the events occurred. The urgency and sheer enormity of the events caused an extended period of mostly live coverage and improvised voice overs with little editorial filtering. Thoughtful journalism, analytical reflection, and detachment were almost impossible, partly because of the powerful, horrific images and partly because the events were still unfolding. Real-time coverage leaves little space for reflection and in-depth information. The lack of background is, in fact, characteristic of the coverage of terrorist action and has to be understood in the context of a situation where television reports generally "concentrate on violence at the expense of background contextualization" (D. Miller, 1994, p. 72). This tendency was obviously exacerbated by the monstrosity of the events and the extraordinary time pressure that they created. The broadcast media were mostly confined to real-time coverage of the crude facts, without much consideration of why all this could happen and what it actually would mean. Thus, real-time coverage paid a high price for its advantages and it took days before more in-depth analysis surfaced in these media.

AESTHETICS

Thesis: *The aesthetic effect of the airplanes crashing into the World Trade Center (WTC) towers was so horrific that the event was perceived as impossible. The terrorists created new signifieds without signifiers—objects with incomprehensible meanings. The aesthetics of terror has striking similarities with Burke's and Kant's notion of the "sublime."*

ᴐ   The sheer magnitude of the events was incomprehensible. There were no words and no signifiers that would have been adequate to describe the events. Whereas postmodern media philosophy is concerned with the flood of signifiers without signifieds, these events showed the power of the reverse situation: signifieds for which there were no signifiers. Therefore, most TV networks restricted their immediate coverage to a repetition of the images.

Additional images were shown when new footage was available, yet there was no other language available to describe the meaning of the events than metaphors and similes, such as the often-repeated comparison to Pearl Harbor.[4] The lack of appropriate language was not restricted just to the attacks but also included the response: The linguistic confusion turned into embarrassment when President Bush used the highly charged *crusade* metaphor for retaliation, as well as when the planned military action was dubbed "Infinite Justice." Even after this name was dropped, Wild West metaphors dominated and continue to dominate the discourse on the military response.

As remarked by Weigel (2001), the fascination of the horrible images can be explained with Edmund Burke's concept of the sublime. In his essay on the origin of the ideas of the sublime and the beautiful, R. Burke (1756–1757/1901) proclaimed:

> Whatever is fitted in any sort to excite the ideas of pain and danger, that is to say, whatever is in any sort terrible, or is conversant about terrible objects, or operates in a manner analogous to terror, is a source of the sublime; that is, it is productive of the strongest emotion which the mind is capable of feeling. (p. 36)

● [4]I am currently conducting a research project on the metaphors that were used by the media in the context of the 9/11 events. A typical example is the "Special Report" from *U.S: News and World Report* (September 24, 2001, p. 10 ff.), which has the headline: "The terrorists flew on *devil's wings* in a horrifying moment, singular in history. They changed the course of a presidency, a nation, and, quite likely, the world" (italics added). The article repeats the Pearl Harbor reference, and goes through a variety of different metaphors to describe and capture the events.

He pointed out that "terror is in all cases whatsoever, either more openly or latently, the ruling principle of the sublime" (p. 52). Burke finally asserted that "the sublime is built on terror," which seems to be contrary to delight and pleasure (p. 112). He claimed it is physiological strain exerted by impressive objects on the organs of perception that ultimately causes the feeling of terror and subsequently the idea of the sublime. ∅

Immanuel Kant, however, criticized the idea of a direct connection between terror and the sublime. Like Burke, he stated "We call that *sublime* which is *absolutely great*" (Kant, 1790/1961, p. 86), and continued "if nature is to be judged by us as dynamically sublime, it must be represented as exciting fear" (p. 99). But then he emphasized that "it is impossible to find satisfaction in a terror that is seriously felt" (p. 100). Instead, he stated that the sight of a terrifying object or event

> is the more attractive, the more fearful it is, *provided only that we are in security*; and we willingly call these objects sublime, because they raise the energies of the soul above their accustomed height and discover in us a faculty of resistance of a quite different kind, which gives us courage to measure ourselves against the apparent almightiness of nature. (p. 100)

There seems to be an intriguing dialectic between the degree of terror and the degree of security that enables us to withstand and even enjoy the terrifying object.[5]

Kant differed from Burke in his emphasis on the *unharmed observer*. In his renowned book "Shipwreck with Spectator," Blumenberg (1997) argued that aesthetic pleasure is derived from the consciousness of a secure, detached perspective that allows the spectator to observe the troubled ocean and the shipwreck from a safe distance. In the case of the September 11 attacks, this globally televised *plane wreck with spectator* is the ultimate form of reality television, for which disaster movies (such as *Armageddon* and *Deep* ∅ *Impact* with their crumbling skyscrapers and fleeing masses) provided the background imagery. Thus, the position of the unharmed observer of the catastrophic disaster has been ingrained in the audience in an almost behaviorist way. At the same time, the authenticity[6] and tragedy of the events enable the observer to

---

[5]Local news about criminals, and also the whole genre of suspense, disaster, and horror movies, seem to built on this very dialectics.

[6]Luhmann (1984) held the view that the "quasi-oral relationship to time" as is found in real-time filming adds a particular "credibility bonus" to the media by letting the event appear more authentic.

become sympathetically absorbed in the creation of a community feeling that is based on identification with the victims of this *mythic tragedy* (Lule, 1990):

> News reports on terrorism perhaps can be studied and understood as part of a larger process of purification and degradation, a social drama of victimage in which the death of the terrorist victims becomes an opportunity for a people to acknowledge and affirm community life. (p. 44)

REDUNDANCY

Thesis: *The media society reacted with full attention to and ritualized repetition of the dreadful images. Background information that might have helped to create a more nuanced understanding of the events was scarce in the hours after the attacks.*

The terrorists knew that they could count on the full attention of the media. Nothing could satisfy *media attention rules*[7] more than a terrorist mass murder that is brought about by a collision of the two main symbols of the Western world: mass transportation's advanced technology represented by large capacity airplanes, and the capitalist economy's advanced bureaucracy represented by high-tech skyscrapers. Laqueur (1999) pointed out that the media are in a strange, almost symbiotic relationship with terrorism because of the high news value of terrorist action:[8]

---

[7]See, for example, the classic study of Galtung and Ruge (1965), and for a typical analysis of news values Peltu (1985), who presented the following list of news values:

1. immediacy and event-orientation,
2. drama and conflict,
3. negativity (bad news has drama and conflict),
4. human interest,
5. photographability,
6. simple story lines,
7. topicality (current news frames),
8. media cannibalism,
9. exclusivity,
10. status of information source,
11. local interest.

[8]For similar arguments on the role of the media, see also the contributions in Alexander and Latter (1990).

The terrorists need the media, and the media find in terrorism all the ingredients of an exciting story. . . . Media coverage has supplied constant grist to the terrorist mill; it has magnified the political importance of many terrorist acts out of all proportion. (p. 44)

Only this media attention, of course, allowed the terrorist attacks to turn into a globally disseminated *plane wreck with spectators*. The media as our "window to the world" have made the position of the unharmed observer conveniently available to a worldwide audience. There was a strange fascination of the images that glued millions of people to their TV sets, even though they would not learn anything new and would only see the same horrible sequence again and again. During the first week, public voices gradually started to express growing unease with the repetition of these images, as illustrated by Howard Kurtz' editorial in the *Washington Post* (September 14, 2001):

Will the networks please—please—stop showing the planes crashing into the World Trade Center as scene-setters for their opening credits? As "bumpers" before commercial breaks? As video wallpaper while talking heads are being interviewed? As split-screen diversion while Ari Fleischer is briefing reporters? The sheer repetition trivializes and dehumanizes the tragedy.

This protest against familiarization and trivialization of tragic events by the media is nothing new, and it is—paradoxically enough—usually expressed by the media themselves (Deledalle-Rhodes, 1997). There was a ritual element in the repetition that seemed continuously to conjure up the events. It was as if the ritual made them understandable as real events:

Graphic form, rhythmic form (the footage of the jet smashing into the second tower repeated up to 30 times per hour), and increasingly, narrative form—all gave coherence to events that were still difficult to comprehend. (Uricchio, 2001)

The most frequently repeated image of the attack was the ABC footage in which the second plane approached the South Tower from the right and then crashed into it.

The *directionality* of the plane in this sequence is of particular interest. As semiotic studies on the meaning potential of images have shown,[9] a person or object moving from the left to the

---

[9]See Jewitt and Oyama (2001) and Landsch (1981).

right indicates "going away," or "leaving," at least in the Western culture. Contrary to this, moving from the right to the left indicates "coming back from," or even "coming home." Thus, the incidental camera perspective of this particular sequence created a powerful connotation that strongly underscored a feeling that terror has finally come to us—to our homeland.

Yet the media did not provide much context: The main contextualization offered by them was a "simple narrative of good versus evil" (Uricchio, 2001) instead of an explanation of the complex situation:

> the choice of an antagonist who embodies the antithesis of our values (a multi-millionaire who has rejected consumerism, a terrorist who seems deeply religious) helped to mute the complexity of the 18 or so terrorists who destroyed themselves along with their helpless victims. Bin Laden's casting helped to keep narrative causality elegantly simple: evil.

As Uricchio (2001) furthermore pointed out, the framing of the events as an "American story" with an emphasis on domestic coverage (*Attack on America* and *America's New War*, etc.) reduced the events to a confrontation between "us" as a nation and "them," without exploring alternative points of view.[10] This constellation set the tone for the subsequent war in Afghanistan as a matter of American decision making. This simple narrative remains the guiding principle of the public discourse on this topic. The implicit identification of the Taliban with bin Laden and the al-Quaida organization is the most striking example of this principle.

MYSTIFICATION AND GLORIFICATION

Thesis: *This faceless, baseless, and authorless terrorism leaves nothing but disturbing insecurity. It is pure terrorism in that it seems to have neither rational goals nor an actor claiming accountability, and only aims at maximizing material and symbolic wreckage. Its demonization in the Western media, however, is the source for its simultaneous glorification in (parts of) the Islamic World.*

---

[10]This, of course, raises the difficult "what if" question. Would there have been other alternatives? What could a different media coverage have looked like? Yet, these questions are not just pointless. For an interesting discussion of the possibilities of alternative coverage of the Gulf War, see Halliday (1999).

The attack had strong mystifying elements, ranging from the complete surprise effect that this attack had on a wholly unprepared nation, to the fact that almost nothing was known about the terrorists, their goals, and their motivation. This was aggravated in that the government and the media seemed to be completely unprepared for any such event. Both politicians and pundits were taken by surprise and reacted with fruitless questions, such as "why are they doing this to us?" and "why do they hate us so much?" This inability to provide any explanatory information and background analysis demonstrated not only a failure of military and civil intelligence but also an unfamiliarity with the phenomenon of international terrorism.

Beyond cultural explanations (such as the inconceivability of the United States being attacked on its own soil), this lack of information and understanding can be interpreted as a communication failure between different societal subsystems. There already existed a plenitude of studies on international terrorism, its means and goals, and its relation to the media. In the terminology of systems theory, there was a lack of exchange of information among the scientific system, the political system, and the media system.

Kushner (1998) extensively discussed the various groups and forms of international terrorism and the danger they pose to the American society. In retrospect, it is ironic that the author referred repeatedly to the bombing of the WTC in 1993 and stated that "the World Trade Center bombing and the plot to destroy other New York City landmarks are prime examples of IRT [international radical terrorism]" (p. 49). An even more chilling irony is that the cover of this very book shows a schematic drawing of the two towers and one of them as a target in a red crosshair. The author also held the clear-sighted view that "the World Trade Center bombing shattered the illusion that the United States is immune from the hands of the new terrorists" (p. 51).

Mystification also pertains to the terrorists' seeming lack of rational goals and accountability. However, this kind of asymmetrical warfare only profits from its irrational barbarism, unpredictability, and maximized material and symbolic wreckage. As Wilkinson (1990, p. 30f) pointed out, terrorist action has four main objectives:

1. Convey the propaganda of the deed and create extreme fear among the target group.
2. Mobilize wider support for their cause among the general population and international opinion by emphasizing such themes as the righteousness of their cause and the inevitability of their victory.

3. Frustrate and disrupt the response of the government and security forces, for example, by suggesting that all their practical antiterrorist measures are inherently tyrannical and counterproductive or an unnecessary overreaction.
4. Mobilize, incite, and boost their constituency of actual and potential supporters and in so doing to increase recruitment, raise more funds, and inspire further attacks.

It is most likely that the global media coverage helped to fulfill these goals despite—or maybe even because of—its mystifying qualities. The second goal does not apply directly and was not fulfilled because it is international rather than domestic terrorism (therefore this goal is identical, in this case, with the fourth objective). This is why the constant media coverage inevitably indicated the attack's success— merely broadcasting the symbolically highly charged images of the collapsing towers can already be read as successful instances of the *propaganda of the deed.* Potential sympathizers would understand the terrorists' martyrdom as heroic and as an incitement to follow them. Moreover, the worldwide dissemination of the terrorists' names and pictures turned them into media stars, which only magnified their glory. Thus, the demonization of the terrorists in the Western media, at the same time, provides a source of their *glorification* in their home base.[11]

CONCLUSION AND OUTLOOK

Media coverage of the events has received mostly positive reviews. Yet, there is an unsettling pattern in the coverage that can be described as *abstention from background analysis* and *taming by narration.* The understandable attempt to make sense of these disruptive events rapidly led to a simplifying and mainstreaming narrative centered on a desire for retaliation in the "monumental struggle of good versus evil," as President Bush proclaimed and the media echoed. Looking back, one might ask whether shock, anger, and grief were channeled too conveniently into a "New War" without exploring other options. At the same time, the terrorists were able to

---

[11]This is of course an intended effect, which refers back to the previously discussed symbiosis between terrorism and the media.

send a powerful signal through their globally broadcast *propaganda of deed*. The human, material, and symbolic damage of the attacks was so unfathomable that it received full and unparalleled media attention. The undivided attention of audience members in their position as unharmed spectators was the necessary complement to the media's attention.

This poses some media ethical questions, such as: How can the media cope with and understand events of this magnitude? Do we need to reconsider the basic habits and conventions of our media society? Are there ways for the media to deal with such events that neither abet the terrorists, nor create a falsely comforting narrative of patriotism and counterstrike?

There are certainly no easy answers to these questions. It is quite possible that the media, particularly real-time media, are in fact *necessarily* overwhelmed with events of this dimension. Background information and analysis requires some time for reflection and research, and time is scarce when dramatic events rapidly follow one another. Nevertheless, the media's almost naive and superficial approach to the events indicates a lack of understanding of foreign affairs and cultures that seems to be as widespread within the media as in politics. There may be two structural reasons for this:

First and generally, U.S. media have increasingly concentrated on domestic news and drastically cut down on foreign coverage throughout the past decades. This is, of course, a vicious circle where the dearth of information produces audience indifference, and vice versa.

Second, and more specifically, the 9/11 events happened at a time when CNN and "Fox News" were already competing fiercely for audience share. This race intensified as events unfolded.

One cannot claim, however, that this situation was completely new with respect to media ethics. There are in fact specific ethical guidelines in place that address the questions raised here. The "CBS News" Standards, for instance, recognize that coverage of terrorist action is indispensable but that "there must be thoughtful, conscientious care and restraint" (Alexander & Latter, 1990, p. 139). Coverage should neither "provide an excessive platform for the terrorists" (p. 139), nor should it "unduly crowd out other important news of the hour/day" (p. 140). The sheer dimension of the events certainly made restraint and thoughtful coverage more difficult than for other terrorist events. Yet, it seems that such media ethical criteria were not much considered at the time.

Additionally, the call for patriotism and counterstrike led very quickly to a situation in which critical words were stigmatized by the government as unpatriotic and intolerable, even when they were clearly satirical. Such was the case of Bill Maher's remarks on the American use of cruise missiles. *Salon.com* editor Talbot's (2001) account of the reaction of White House spokesperson Ari Fleischer is unsettling:

> Fleischer used the Maher controversy to issue this creepy Orwellian pronouncement: "Americans need to watch what they say, what they do, and this is not the time for remarks like that; there never is." (Creepier still, someone in the White House then took scissors to the official transcript of Fleischer's remarks to make them less chilling.)

Instances like this have brought the media and the political opposition in a position where any critical thought could be regarded as unpatriotic and as posing danger to the fight against terrorism.[12] However, the real danger lies in the possibility that the American media—who have been known for their incorruptible search for truth and their critical approach to government action—may find themselves increasingly in a situation where the lines are blurred between independence and patriotism, as well as between war coverage and propaganda.[13]

---

[12]See, for example, the firestorm that surrounded Tom Daschle's measured criticism of the war's prosecution in early March 2002, which spread beyond conservative pundits and swept up even mainstream media figures such as Peter Jennings (see Keefer, 2002, and Nyhan, 2002).

[13]I am alluding to the disturbing trend that government spokespersons, retired generals, and self-appointed war specialists constitute the "experts" in almost all TV and radio networks. Critical voices, not to mention outspoken pacifists, are usually not among these experts.

III

RESPONSES AND REACTIONS TO NEWS OF THE TERRORIST ATTACKS

14

National Studies of Stress Reactions and Media Exposure to the Attacks

Leslie B. Snyder
Crystal L. Park
University of Connecticut

People who experience or witness traumatic events, such as disasters, wars, violent crimes, and terrorism, can be deeply affected. Studies of war veterans, concentration camp and disaster survivors, people who lived in war zones, and crime victims have documented that extreme stress due to terrible traumas can lead to acute and sometimes chronic mental health difficulties (e.g., Fullerton & Ursano, 1997). It is important to understand how a national traumatic event such as the September 11 terrorist attacks affected the psychological health of the U.S. population, and to examine the role of the media in exacerbating or alleviating this distress.

This chapter draws on 30 surveys sponsored by different organizations between September 14 and March 13, 2002, to explore American adults' emotional and stress-related responses to the September 11 attacks and their aftermath. The study also examines the relationship between news exposure and stress, which has largely been overlooked in past studies.

STRESS REACTIONS

As with other traumatic events, the September 11 terrorist attacks had the potential to cause widespread emotional responses and psychological stress. An extreme stress reaction to the trauma of the attacks could qualify as posttraumatic stress disorder (PTSD). PTSD is a clinical condition arising when a "person experienced, witnessed, or was confronted with an event or events that involved actual or threatened death or serious injury, or a threat to the physical integrity of self or others" and when the person has an intense reaction to the event (American Psychiatric Association, 1994, p. 467). PTSD is often associated with depression and substance abuse, and may persist over long periods of time (APA, 1994).

Prior studies of PTSD have focused almost exclusively on events that are witnessed or experienced first-hand, or on populations geographically proximate to the event and therefore more likely to know victims personally. However, several studies have shown that the level of emotional response to an event is more important than geographic proximity in determining PTSD (Lonigan, Shannon, Taylor, Finch, & Sallee, 1994; Schwarz & Kowalski, 1991). People geographically distant from the World Trade Center (WTC), Pentagon, and Pennsylvania crash site may have had strong emotional responses to the attacks.

It is vital that clinicians know the extent of stress and PTSD so that they can be sensitive to stress and PTSD symptoms in their patients and plan appropriate outreach and intervention strategies. Research has shown that early interventions among people at risk of developing PTSD reduces the incidence of PTSD in a traumatized population (Keane, 1998). In the case of 9/11, outreach efforts were mounted immediately after the attacks in New York City, Washington, DC, and Boston (the origin of two of the flights), but were rare in the rest of the country. An awareness of the rate of stress and PTSD nationally after the 9/11 attacks may help mental health professionals create a nationally recommended strategy for future terrorist attacks.

Thus, we expect to find measurable amounts of stress and PTSD symptomatology related to the attacks in the 3 months post-event. As time passes, the extent of stress in the general population should dissipate (Shalev, 2000); it is valuable to describe the population levels of various stress symptoms over time to understand which types of stress symptoms remain problematic for more people.

COMMUNICATION AND STRESS

The few studies that have examined television viewing and PTSD have done so with people located in the area of the traumatic event (e.g., Oklahoma City), rather than with remote populations. Interestingly, the studies do find a media effect—greater viewing of trauma-related television is positively related to greater estimates of PTSD in such diverse populations as Kuwaiti children after the Gulf War, Oklahoma children after the Timothy McVeigh bombing, and adults who lost a friend or relative in the Mount St. Helen's volcanic eruption (Morland, 1999; S. Murphy, 1984; Nader, Pynoos, Fairbanks, Al-Ajeel, & Al-Asfour, 1993; Pfefferbaum et al., 2000). The studies of PTSD and media exposure in small geographic areas have weak exposure measures and are not generalizable to national populations.

However, events that individuals learn about through the media and that happened in a distant location may also invoke strong emotional responses (e.g., Cantor, Mares, & Oliver, 1993; Hoffner & Haefner, 1993; Riffe & Stovall, 1989; Wober & Young, 1993). One study comparing the effects of the Oklahoma City bombing among local and Indianapolis residents found the expected higher rates of stress and select PTSD symptoms in the proximate city, but also found substantial amounts of stress in the more remote city (D. Smith, Christiansen, Vincent, & Hann, 1999).

The strength of the emotional response is positively related to the amount of television viewing. Frequency of television viewing was related to increased worry for children in the Netherlands, Britain, and the United States during the Gulf War (Hoffner & Haefner, 1993; van der Voort, van Lil, & Vooijs, 1993; Wober & Young, 1993). Exposure to coverage of the *Challenger* shuttle disaster was also related to greater emotional responses by U.S. adults (Riffe & Stovall, 1989). The studies of emotional responses to televised traumas are limited, however, by weak measures of stress responses, small sample sizes, or specialized populations.

This chapter examines the link between witnessing traumatic events through the media and stress reactions by examining national responses to the 9/11 attacks. It overcomes limitations of prior studies by using large national samples, more standard assessment instruments, and multiple measures.

In summary, the present chapter addresses two issues:

1. What is the extent of stress symptoms due to the September 11 attacks?
2. What is the relationship between exposure to news coverage and stress?

METHODS

This chapter reports data from national telephone surveys and polls collected by various organizations after September 11. The surveys were reported by the media, and most are available in the Roper Center for Public Opinion Research online archives—iPoll—at the University of Connecticut (2002). Additionally, we collected original national survey data specifically to measure stress, PTSD, and communication. Data from New York City are also used for a few variables for comparative purposes (Galea et al., 2002). The details on the national surveys are presented in Table 14.1.

Table 14.1. September 11 Studies Containing Stress or Media Questions

Short Name and Date	Sponsor	Data Collection Organization	Sample Size: # Adults	Reference
PRC 9/12-13	The Pew Research Center	Princeton Survey Research Associates	1,226	Roper Center, 2001
PRC 9/13-17	The Pew Research Center	Princeton Survey Research Associates	1,200	PRCa, 2001
LA Times 9/13-14	*Los Angeles Times*		1,561	Roper Center, 2002
Newsweek 9/13-14	*Newsweek*	Princeton Survey Research Associates	1,001	Roper Center, 2002
Schuster 9/14-16	Rand		557	Schuster et al., 2001
ISR 9/15-10/7	University of Michigan	The Institute for Social Research	668	University of Michigan, 2001
NBC 9/20	NBC News	Hart and Tweeter Research Companies	513	Roper Center, 2002
PRC 10/1-3	The Pew Research Center	Princeton Survey Research Associates	891	PRCa, 2001
Fox 10/3-4	Fox News	Opinion Dynamics	900	Roper Center, 2002
NMHAC 9/26-10/2	The National Mental Health Awareness Campaign	Greenberg Quinlan Rosner Research	1,010	Roper Center, 2002
Newsweek 9/27-28	*Newsweek*	Princeton Survey Research Associates	1,000	Roper Center, 2002
PRC 10/1-3	The Pew Research Center	Princeton Survey Research Associates	1,001	PRCb, 2002
Fox 10/3-4	Fox News	Opinion Dynamics	900 registered voters	Roper Center, 2002

Table 14.1. September 11 Studies Containing Stress or Media Questions (con't.)

Short Name and Date	Sponsor	Data Collection Organization	Sample Size: # Adults	Reference
CBS 10/8	CBS news		436	Roper Center, 2002
PRC 10/10-14	The Pew Research Center	Princeton Survey Research Associates	891	PRCb, 2002
Newsweek 10/11-12	Newsweek	Princeton Survey Research Associates	1,004	Roper Center, 2002
Galea 10/16-11/15	Grants from United Way, New York Community Trust, National Institute on Drug Abuse	New York Academy of Medicine	1,008 New Yorkers	Galea et al., 2002
Newsweek 10/18-19	Newsweek	Princeton Survey Research Associates	1,006	Roper Center, 2002
Snyder & Park, 10/22-11/12	University of Connecticut	Center for Survey Research and Analysis	1004	Snyder & Park, 2002a, 2002b
CBS 10/25-28	CBS News		1,024	Roper Center, 2002
Newsweek 10/25-26	Newsweek	Princeton Survey Research Associates	1,005	Roper Center, 2002
Newsweek 11/1-2	Newsweek	Princeton Survey Research Associates	1,001	Roper Center, 2002
Time 11/7-8	Time and Cable News Network	Harris Interactive	1,037	Roper Center, 2002
Newsweek 11/8-9	Newsweek	Princeton Survey Research Associates	1,001	Roper Center, 2002
LA Times 11/10-13	Los Angeles Times		1,995	Roper Center, 2002
Harris, 11/14-20	Harris Poll	Harris Interactive	1,001	Roper Center, 2002
Newsweek 11/15-16	Newsweek	Princeton Survey Research Associates	1,000	Roper Center, 2002
CGE 11/27-29	Center for Gender Equality (CGE)	Greenberg Quinlan Rosner Research	999 women	Roper Center, 2002
Fox 2/12-13, 2002	Fox News	Opinion Dynamics	900 registered voters	Roper Center, 2002
CNN 3/8-9, 2002	Cable News Network, USA Today	Gallup Organization	802	Roper Center, 2002
Fox 3/12-13,2002	Fox News	Opinion Dynamics	900 registered voters	Roper Center, 2002

Measures of PTSD

PTSD diagnosis depends on the presence of a minimal number of symptoms within each of three specific categories of symptoms. First, an individual must have been exposed to the traumatic event and to have responded to it with "intense fear, helplessness, or horror" (APA, 1994, p. 467). Second, the traumatic event is "persistently reexperienced" in at least one way, such as intrusive thoughts, recurrent dreams, flashbacks, intense distress, or physiological reactions when exposed to internal or external cues about the event (APA, 1994, p. 468). Third, the individual persistently tries to avoid stimuli related to the trauma; and is psychologically numb, exhibiting at least three of the following: avoiding thoughts, feelings, or conversations about the trauma; avoiding people, places, or activities associated with the trauma; inability to recall important aspects; decreased interested in activities; detachment from others; flat affect; sense of foreshortened future. Fourth, the individual is aroused more than before the trauma, as evidenced by two or more symptoms: difficulty sleeping, irritability, difficulty concentrating, hyper-vigilance, or exaggerated startle response. Fifth, the symptoms must be present for at least a month, or another type of stress diagnosis is given (APA, 1994). Finally, the individual with PTSD exhibits "clinically significant distress or impairment in social, occupational, or other important areas of functioning" (APA, 1994, p. 468).

Standard scales have been developed for rapid assessment of PTSD symptomatology and validated against longer clinical interviews. The Snyder and Park data used a scale by Foa, Cashman, Jaycox, and Perry (1997). The response options for each item were *none, a little, some, quite a bit,* or *a great deal,* and the cutoff for having a symptom was at least some. We also present some results based on the severity of PTSD symptoms summed across the interval measures (alpha = .88). The Galea et al. (2002) study used a modified version of the Diagnostic Interview Schedule for PTSD (Resnik, Kilpatrick, Dansky, Saunders, & Best, 1993). For both studies, people needed at least one re-experiencing, three avoidance, and two arousal symptoms to qualify as symptomatic of PTSD.

RESULTS

Extent Of Stress Symptoms

The first question concerned the extent of psychological trauma experienced by the nation after the 9/11 attacks. Because only a small percentage of people nationwide witnessed the events first-hand, widespread trauma would be evidence that mediated events can deeply affect people.

Fear. The first PTSD diagnostic criterion is that a person exposed to a trauma feels intense fear, helplessness, or horror. Current fear, anxiety, and worries were measured in some of the surveys.

In October, 20% of adults said they were nervous or edgy (CBS, October 25). By mid-November, 10% described themselves as very anxious and 37% as somewhat anxious about their personal safety considering what had happened in the world, and 42% said they were more concerned about their personal safety than they were before 9/11 (Harris Interactive, 11/14). Similarly, 21% were a great deal or quite a bit, and 23% somewhat afraid when they thought of the terrorist attacks and aftermath in late October and early November (Snyder & Park, 10/22-11/12).

A series of *Newsweek* surveys asked repeatedly about personal vulnerability, "Do you personally feel a lot less safe where you live and work, somewhat less safe, only a little less safe, or not at all less safe than you did before?" Vulnerability declined slightly over time, but increased again during the last measurement wave in mid-November, when another government warning was issued (Fig. 14.1).

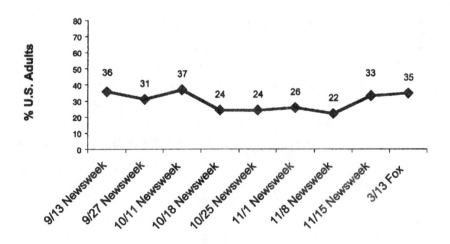

Fig. 14.1. Percentage of adults personally feeling somewhat or a lot less safe where they live and work than they did before September 11 over time

A similar question asked around the 6-month anniversary of the attacks found that 35% felt less safe (Fox, 3/12/2002). We cannot be certain whether this high level was due to a continued perceived vulnerability, or whether levels dropped and then went up again due to the renewed coverage and reminders surrounding the anniversary. It seems likely, however, that high levels of vulnerability were maintained throughout the intervening months: A February poll found that 73% of people thought it at least somewhat likely that there would be another terrorist attack causing large numbers of losses in the "near future" (Fox, 2/12/2002).

Fear was somewhat related to gender. The percentage of women afraid quite a bit or a great deal was 31%, as opposed to 11% of men (Snyder & Park, 10/22-11/12). In a poll of women, 20% described themselves as having anxiety or panic in late November (CGE, 11/27).

Worry about another attack declined very little over the first 2 months, from about 30% (CBS, 10/8; NBC, 9/20) to 26% (CBS, 10/25). More people (53%) admitted to being concerned a great deal or quite a bit about another attack (Snyder & Park, 10/22-11/12). The difference in wording between *worry* and *concern* may explain the difference in results because *concern* has a milder connotation and may be more socially acceptable to men.

By November, subjective stress levels due to the attacks were judged to be a little higher than normal for 24% and much greater than normal for 11% of respondents (*LA Times*, 11/10/2001). Most people (64%) said retrospectively that their stress had decreased since the day of the attack, whereas 13% said it had increased (Snyder & Park, 10/22-11/12). Nineteen percent said they were stressed quite a bit or a great deal currently, but 55% said retrospectively that they were stressed that much on September 11 (Snyder & Park, 10/22-11/12).

Re-Experiencing the Event. Snyder and Park (2002a) found that 49% of the population had at least one re-experiencing symptom some of the time in the week prior to the survey.

Many people said they were upset quite a bit or a great deal when reminded of the event (30% on September 14-16, in Schuster et al., 2001; and 14% in Snyder and Park, 10/22-11/12). Repeated memories occurred in the initial period to 16% of adults (Schuster et al., 2001), and 6 to 9 weeks later, 11% said they had images they could not get out of their minds quite a bit or a great deal (Snyder & Park, 10/22-11/12). Fewer people said they relived the attacks (7%), relived other traumas (6%), or had physical reactions (3%) quite a bit or a great deal when reminded of the attacks (Snyder & Park, 10/22-11/12).

The extent of the population having any recent nightmares related to the attacks hovered around 10% (Fig. 14.2). Slight differences in question wording could account for the slight differences in the responses. Women were slightly more likely to have nightmares, with 13% of women and 7% of men reporting them in late October (Snyder & Park, 10/22-11/12; $\chi^2 = 13.4$, $p < .01$), and 14% of women still reporting them at the end of November (CGE, 11/27).

Psychic Numbing. Of the PTSD symptom categories, psychic numbing was experienced by the fewest people. Only 9% of the U.S. adult population said they experienced at least three symptoms some or more (Snyder & Park, 2002a). The most common symptoms related to avoidance of thoughts and feelings (19%) and activities, places, or people (17%), and feeling emotionally numb (17%). Only 11% said they felt cut off from others, and the same percentage lost interest in normal activities. Only 1% reported three psychic numbing symptoms quite a bit or a great deal. Psychic numbing was not measured in other national surveys.

Arousal. Arousal symptoms declined as time passed. Having difficulty concentrating, which was asked in seven surveys, declined from around half the population exhibiting the symptom right after

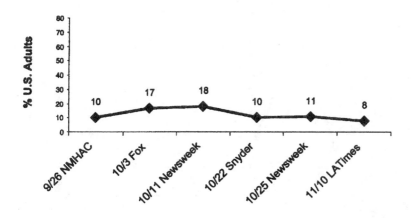

Fig. 14.2. Percentage of adults experiencing nightmares over time

September 11 to around 20% 2 months later (Fig. 14.3). Trouble
sleeping because of the attacks also declined over time (Fig. 14.4).
The Schuster et al. (2001) survey found that only 9% of respondents
said they were quite a bit or extremely irritable; 6 weeks later
Snyder and Park found that 8% were irritable quite a bit or a great

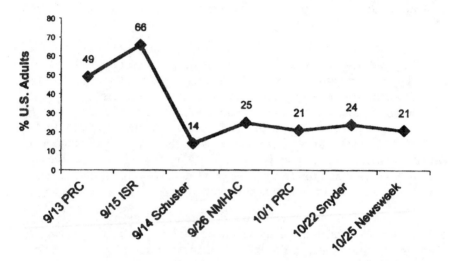

Fig. 14.3. Percentage of adults having difficulty concentrating over time

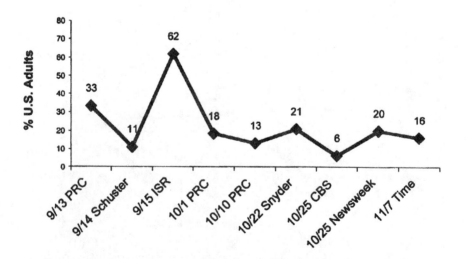

Fig. 14.4. Percentage of adults having trouble sleeping over time

deal (30% at least a little) in the last week. Men were slightly more likely to report quite a bit or great deal of irritability (6% of women vs. 10% of men; Snyder & Park, 10/22-11/12; $\chi^2 = 27.2$, $p < .001$). By the end of November, 20% of women experienced unexplained anger (CGE, 11/27-29).

Two months after September 11, about one third of the population (34%) said they had at least two arousal symptoms sometimes or more often in the prior week, and 14% had the symptoms quite a bit or a great deal (Snyder & Park, 2002a).

Depression and Dysfunction. Depression dropped dramatically as time passed. The first poll on September 13 found that 71% of people said they were depressed by the terrorist attacks. This figure dropped to about 20% in November (Fig. 14.5). By the 6 month anniversary, 21% said that they had cried in the previous 2 weeks as a direct result of thinking about the terrorist attacks (CNN, 3/8/2002).

The percentage who were clinically depressed in the previous month in New York City was 10%, with higher rates among those who suffered a personal loss (11%-28%) and less among those who did not (around 6%; Galea et al., 2002). The measure in the New York City study used a much stricter criterion to establish depression

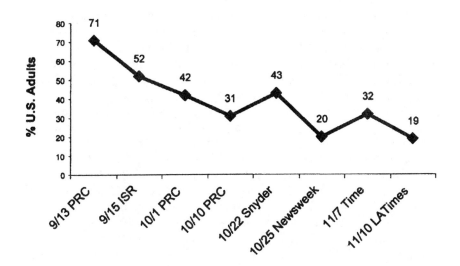

Fig. 14.5. Percentage of adults feeling depressed in the past few days or week, over time

(a version of the *DSM-IV* Structured Clinical Interview for major depressive episode) than the national studies, and we could extrapolate that the national rate of major depression in late October/early November may be close to 6%.

Only a small percentage of the population sought professional help to deal with their reaction to the attacks: 5% consulted a doctor, psychologist, or physician (*Newsweek*, 10/25-26/2001), and 2% saw a mental health professional (*LA Times,* 11/10). A similar percentage (4%) began taking prescription medications for anxiety, whereas other people (4%) self-medicated with over-the-counter sleep aids (*Newsweek*, 10/25-26). By the end of November, 7% were taking prescription or over-the-counter drugs (*Newsweek*, 11/15-16).

PTSD. Schuster et al. (2001) estimated that 44% of the population had at least one of five stress symptoms to a substantial degree (quite a bit or extremely) within 3 to 5 days of the attacks. Several months later, Snyder and Park (10/17-11/12) found that 39% had at least one of 15 stress symptoms to a substantial degree (quite a bit or a great deal). Estimates of PTSD for both New Yorkers (Galea et al., 2002) and the US population (Snyder & Park, 2002a) were about 7%, with higher estimates (11%-28%) for people who suffered a personal loss.

Television Viewing on September 11

People watched tremendous amounts of television on September 11. A few days after the attacks, people reported viewing a mean of 8.1 hours (Schuster et al., 2001). About 2 months later, people remembered viewing about 7.5 hours on September 11 (Snyder & Park, 2002b). When asked directly about where they got most of their information, people overwhelming said television (81%, PRC, 9/12/2001; 90%, PRC, 9/13/2001). Many people reported keeping their television tuned to the news that day (81%) and feeling as if they "can't stop watching news about the terrorist attacks" (PRC, 9/13/2001). More people preferred cable stations over network news (50% vs. 33%, respectively, PRC, 9/13/2001).

By the beginning of October, 67% of U.S. adults were still tuned to the news (PRC, 10/1/2001). Whether because of displacement by news or a temporary change in tolerance for violent content, 33% reported watching less violent television in early October, compared to 12% who watched more (Fox, 10/3/2001). However, overall viewing time was down to an average of about 2 hours by 2 months after the attacks (Snyder & Park, 2002b).

Stress and Communication

Two studies directly related stress to the amount of television viewing on September 11. Schuster et al. (2001) compared reports of one substantial stress symptom with a categorical measure of hours of television viewing. From Table 14.2 reported in Schuster et al. (2001), it is possible to compute the effect size as $r = .09$ ($n = 556$, $p = .001$).

Snyder and Park (2002b) found that television was the most important medium in predicting subjective stress levels on September 11, subjective stress 2 months later, and PTSD severity. Retrospective assessments of the hours of television viewed on 9/11 was correlated .18 with stress on 9/11, .16 with stress 2 months later, and .20 with PTSD severity (Snyder & Park, 10/17-11/12). Television viewing 2 months later continued to be related to stress; the correlations were .15 with stress on 9/11, .12 with stress 2 months later, and .16 with PTSD severity (Snyder & Park, 10/17-11/12). All these correlations are significant at $p < .001$. The effects of television viewing on the three stress outcome variables remained significant when both TV variables were entered into a regression, controlling for age, education, gender, personal loss, and near loss (Snyder & Park, 2002b).

PTSD severity was also predicted by exposure to two types of content. The more people saw news about ways to keep safe and the greater their exposure to graphic images, the greater the PTSD severity, controlling for the quantity viewed (Snyder & Park, 2002b). Other types of content that were not significant included news about the support and rescue efforts; acts of terrorism, threats, and victims; America fighting back; and ways to cope.

DISCUSSION

This research analyzed stress responses to the 9/11 attacks, and linked the degree of stress reactions, in part, to media exposure. It was the first nationally experienced traumatic mediated event in the United States for which researchers have gathered PTSD data on adults. The study drew on 30 studies and polls conducted at different points in time, most ranging from immediately after the attacks to almost three months afterward, plus three polls conducted 5 to 6 months later. Despite the fact that the measures varied slightly from study to study, the body of results paints a fairly consistent picture.

The first research goal was to document the extent of stress symptoms due to the September 11 attacks in the U.S. population. The research indicated surprisingly high levels of stress regarding the attacks: 6% to 7% of the population had symptomatology severe enough for a diagnosis of PTSD after the attacks. As a baseline, an epidemiological study conducted in the midwest estimated *lifetime* prevalence of PTSD may be around 1% of the population (Helzer, Robins, & McEvoy, 1987), and therefore estimates of current PTSD symptomatology would be even lower. Thus, PTSD rates after the attacks were much higher than health professionals would have expected.

Furthermore, research indicated that mediated events can cause extreme stress. Contrary to the current assumptions of PTSD, many people experienced traumatic stress symptoms for an event that they did not witness first-hand nor for which they talked directly to a victim (Snyder & Park, 2002a). Media effects researchers and mental health professionals should be aware of the possibility that people may experience significant stress due to traumatic mediated events.

It is also noteworthy that many specific stress reactions were widespread. For example, people reported feeling unsafe in their home and work environments and reported significant levels of depression. The emotional reactions may have been due to the terrorist attacks or other stressful occurrences in the months after the attacks, such as the cleanup at Ground Zero, fears of future attacks, anthrax scares, and military strikes. Most reactions declined over time, which is consistent with psychological literature on stress (Green, 1996). Some reactions persisted, such as feelings of increased personal vulnerability.

The second research question was whether exposure to more media coverage of the 9/11 events led to greater stress. We found that it did—more media exposure was related to experiencing more stress reactions in two studies. Note that the effect sizes were larger in the Snyder and Park study (2002b) than those found by Schuster et al. (2001). The larger effect sizes may be due to better measures— Snyder and Park used continuous measures of television exposure and stress, whereas Schuster et al. used categorical measures. Or, the relationship between stress and television exposure to information about the terrorist attacks may have grown stronger over time; the Schuster study was conducted 3 to 5 days after the event, and the Snyder and Park study was conducted 6 to 9 weeks after the event.

In addition to the sheer amounts of viewing, two types of content proved important: Viewing more graphic images of the terrorist attacks and the aftermath and exposure to more news about ways to keep oneself safe were both related to higher levels of stress reactions. Because two of the attack sites were major media markets, people were able to see live broadcasts of the devastation as it occurred in New York City, and they could follow the chaos and gradual loss of hope in New York and Washington, DC. The graphic images were repeated throughout the day, and many newspapers and newsmagazines used similar images in the following week. This repetition enhanced the effects of these graphic images on people's psychological reactions, perhaps by serving as a cue to recall the initial horror and dread.

Interestingly, the news broadcasts were presented along with a heavy emphasis on mental health awareness and expected trauma reactions, ways to volunteer and give help, and where and how to get help. Such content may be particularly sought out by individuals who are having difficulties and stress reactions. On the other hand, it is possible that viewing such content may increase one's expectations that such distress is to be expected. The extent of viewing of such content was, perhaps unexpectedly, unrelated to stress symptoms. It may be that such information did have benefits for some viewers, but because those who were more distressed may have been seeking out this information as well, evidence for beneficial effects were essentially "washed out" in the analyses.

Not only were stress and PTSD levels high after the mediated event, but the amount of media exposure was directly linked to severity of symptoms, a finding that extends previous research on this question (e.g., Riffe & Stovall, 1989). The views put forth by the television broadcasters may have influenced the way that the September 11 events were framed, understood, and responded to. In the future, individuals may want to consider self-regulation of types of content and amounts of viewing in order to temper their reactions.

Limitations

The research is limited by the fact that there was no near baseline measuring stress and PTSD levels prior to September 11. The collection of studies together constitutes an independent time series design, but with a limited number of data points for each item. The answers to the question about amounts of stress generated by the September 11 attacks were largely consistent across the independent samples, indicating reliability of the results. The key analysis relating amounts of media use to stress, while yielding consistent findings, were measured in only two studies. However, the causal direction is not certain. It may be that people who tend to watch a lot of media are also prone to stress reactions, or perhaps predisposed toward greater stress reactions from mediated events. Similarly, viewing graphic images might create more distress, but those who are experiencing more distress may seek out more information in their attempts to cope with the trauma, and may thereby be exposed to a greater degree of graphic images. It is likely that both of these occurred to some extent after September 11.

Recommendations for Future Research

Many social scientists and polling organizations were mobilized almost immediately to conduct research. Not only were large-scale polls initiated, but many others began gathering data either in close proximity to the attacks or at remote locations. Apparently, within the research community, there is a heightened awareness that such occurrences, although horrific, also present opportunities to better understand people's responses to them. The present findings suggest that it is worthwhile to examine stress reactions outside of the immediate area of a stressor that is cast as a national assault rather than a localized one.

An important avenue for future research would be to explore the nature of the relationship between viewing news regarding the trauma and stressful reactions to it. More sophisticated research designs may shed light on the direction of these relationships. Furthermore, the mechanisms of effect should be delineated. What is it about specific types of content that influence people? Is some content more upsetting or soothing to particular types of individuals? For example, is the viewing of graphic images more disturbing to someone who is already dealing with another life crisis or has experienced trauma, although perhaps helpful to someone who is less distressed but is searching for an understanding or way to make meaning? Future research should also address the role of interpersonal communication within family and friendship networks, and how interpersonal communication relates to stress and media exposure.

15

Parents' Perceptions of Children's Fear Responses

Stacy L. Smith
Emily Moyer
Aaron R. Boyson
Katherine M. Pieper
Michigan State University

On September 11, 2001, Americans were bombarded with horrific televised images of catastrophic death and destruction. Depictions of planes crashing, the Twin Towers collapsing, and the emotional pain and suffering of missing victims' friends and family members were virtually inescapable for days. Given the graphic nature of the news footage surrounding the terrorists attacks, there has been a great deal of public concern about the impact of exposure to such dreadful portrayals on children (ABC News.com, 2001). Indeed, as distress specialist Dr. Jeffery Mitchell recently stated, "it can be very traumatizing for children to see these images on television. They don't understand what this is all about . . . that's why I'm suggesting that we not allow an excessive amount of television for children at this particular point" (Cable Network News, 2001).

To date, only a few public opinion surveys have been conducted on youngster's emotional reactions to these events. For instance, the Pew Research Center (2001b) randomly sampled 331 parents of 5- to 12-year-olds across the country and found that 46% of the children had reportedly expressed fears about the attacks. Another nationwide survey of parents conducted by ABC/*Washington Post* (Gallup News Services, 2001) on September 13 revealed that one third of the children expressed concern for their personal safety.

Beyond these public opinion polls, there is very little empirical evidence regarding children's fear responses to the attacks. As a result, our purpose was to conduct an in-depth phone survey with a random sample of parents of 5- to 17-year-olds about their children's exposure and fear responses to news coverage immediately after 9/11. The survey was conducted within 7 days of the attacks. Research and theory on children's exposure and fright reactions to television news in general and catastrophic events in particular provided direction for this inquiry.

CHILDREN'S EXPOSURE TO TV NEWS

Given the magnitude of this national tragedy, we suspected that most children were exposed to at least some coverage of the terrorist attacks. We also anticipated age-related differences in youngsters' patterns of exposure, because many parents may have limited their younger children's exposure to television in an effort to shield them from the disturbing visual images surrounding the attacks. The Pew Research Center (2001b) survey found that 48% of parents with 5- to 12-year-olds tried to restrict their child's viewing of the news coverage. Older children, on the other hand, may have sought out TV news on their own to learn more detailed information about the dreadful events. Consistent with this reasoning, Siegel (1965) found that high school students were more likely to seek out and watch TV news surrounding President Kennedy's assassination and funeral proceedings than were either junior high or elementary school students. Based on this rationale, we predicted the following:

H1: Children's exposure to the terrorists' attacks will increase linearly with age.

CHILDREN'S FEAR REACTIONS TO TV NEWS

In addition to exposure, we were primarily concerned with children's fear reactions to the news coverage. It was expected that children's fright responses to the news would be influenced by their age or level of development. There are three major reasons why age-related differences were anticipated. The first is based on exposure. Older children were more likely to have been exposed to the news footage of the terrorist attacks than were younger children. As a result, older children were more likely to have witnessed repeatedly the horrific visual images of airplanes exploding, individuals jumping to their deaths, and the towering inferno that ultimately led to the collapse of the World Trade Centers (WTC). Studies show that heavy viewing of catastrophic events in the news is positively associated with children's increased fear and emotional upset (Hoffner & Haefner, 1993a; Siegel, 1965; van der Voort, Van Lil, & Vooijs, 1993).

The second reason is based on comprehension. Although the actual attacks were presented visually, many of the subsequent dangers surrounding 9/11 were communicated verbally on the news. Stories about future terrorists attacks on our country and the possibility of world war were common on TV news. Such stories contain abstract dangers that are presented orally by news anchors and thus may be too complicated for younger children to understand (Cantor, Wilson, & Hoffner, 1986; Paris & Upton, 1976).

The third reason is based on the ability to differentiate fantasy from reality. Because younger children are likely to think that everything that "looks" real on television is real (M. Brown, Skeen, & Osborn, 1979), they are more responsive to fantastic dangers that visually appear scary, such as monsters, ghosts, and witches (Cantor & Sparks, 1984; Sparks, 1986). With age, children evaluate TV content based on notions of possibility and then probability (Dorr, 1983). Thus, older children are more responsive to realistic dangers that could possibly occur in the world (Cantor & Sparks, 1984; Sparks, 1986). Because the September 11 attacks were not only real but they also communicated that other terrorist attacks on innocent people in this country are possible, older children are more likely than their younger counterparts to be upset by what they saw and heard in the news. Based on this reasoning, the following hypothesis is advanced:

H2: Children's fear responses to the news coverage of the terrorists' attacks will increase linearly with age.

Another factor that may influence children's fear responses to the terrorist attacks is gender. Research reveals that girls respond with more fear to television news than do boys (S. Smith & Wilson, 2002; Wright, Kunkel, Pinon, & Huston, 1989). Such findings may be due to the fact that girls are more likely than boys to be taught that expressing emotions is normative or socially appropriate. Thus, girls simply may be more willing than boys to express fear reactions to television news with their parents. Based on this reasoning,

Hypothesis 3 posited:

H3: Girls will be more frightened by the news coverage
of the terrorist attacks than boys.

Besides the prevalence of fear, we also were interested in the
features of news stories that children perceived as scary. Research
reveals that younger and older children respond with fear to very
different aspects of televised news threats (S. Smith & Wilson, 2000,
2002). Cantor, Mares, and Oliver (1993) interviewed a random
sample of parents of 1st, 4th, 7th, and 11th graders about their
children's fear reactions to the televised news coverage of the Gulf
War. The researchers found that younger children (Grades 7 and 11)
were more likely to respond to stories featuring concrete, visual
images, whereas older children (7th and 11th graders) were more
responsive to abstract threats that communicated danger verbally.
Cantor et al. (1993) argued that these differences can be
explained by a shift from perceptual to conceptual processing of
information. Younger children are stimulus bound and thus have a
tendency to focus on dangers that are the most perceptually vivid
(Cantor et al., 1993). As such, graphic visual images from the Gulf
War were specific sources of fear for younger children—although
such portrayals presented no real-world threat of harm to viewers in
the United States (Cantor et al., 1993). Given that the September 11
attacks were very visual in nature, we expected that such depictions
would be sources of fear for younger children. Thus, Hypothesis 4 is:

H4: Younger children will be more frightened by the
visual aspects of the news coverage from the
terrorists' attacks than will older children.

Older children, on the other hand, are more likely to focus on
the conceptual information presented in news stories, such as
whether the threat could result in some personal real-world harm
(Cantor et al., 1993). Older viewers were more frightened by abstract,
verbally presented stories from the Gulf War involving the threat of
terrorism or the possibility of nuclear war. Since September 11, these
types of stories also have been very common on TV news. For
example, the threat of biological and chemical weaponry and the
inability of United States to locate the agents responsible for
initiating the terrorists' attacks have been featured routinely at the
top of every news hour. Because such stories not only feature a
current threat to U.S. citizens but are also communicated verbally,
we predicted the following hypothesis:

H5: Older children will be more frightened by the verbal aspects of the news coverage from the terrorists' attacks than will younger children.

Finally, the last aim of this study was to examine how exposure to the news surrounding the terrorists' attacks influenced a variety of children's concerns. At least one study with children found a positive relationship between viewing news coverage of the Gulf War and concern for self. That is, as viewing of Gulf War news increased so did children's concern for their personal safety (Hoffner & Haefner, 1993a). They explain these findings by arguing that "exposure to threatening events can increase the salience of potential dangers and can enhance their perceived likelihood of occurrence" (p. 367). Based on these findings, we anticipated that repeated exposure to news coverage of the terrorist attacks would have a similar effect on children's safety concerns. Therefore, the final hypothesis was advanced:

H6: Exposure to television news coverage of the terrorist attacks will be a positive predictor of children's concern for their personal safety.

METHOD

A total of 212 parents (77 males, 131 females, 4 missing) of 5- to 17-year-old children (115 girls and 97 boys) were surveyed for this study. The sample of parents was divided into three groups by children's age. Altogether, 63 were parents of 5- to 8-year-olds (M = 6.78, SD = .92), 60 were parents of 9- to 12-year-olds (M = 10.48, SD = 1.10), and 89 were parents of 13- to 17-years-old (M = 14.9, SD = 1.29). These age-related categories are generally consistent with research investigating children's fear reactions to TV news (S. Smith & Wilson, 2000, 2002). All the parents lived in Ingham County, Michigan. In terms of parental ethnicity, 86% were White, 4% black, and 3% Hispanic.[1] The median annual family income was $50,000 to $60,000.

Two days after the terrorist attacks, the 15-minute telephone survey began and continued for 6 contiguous days (September 13–18). Toward this end, a list of page numbers from the local

---

[1]Of the remaining 7% of respondents, 1% were Asian, 1% were Middle Eastern, and 5% were from "other" ethnicities.

telephone directory was generated randomly. From this list, every 11th telephone number was selected and called by one of 24 trained interviewers. A total of 334 calls reached parents with at least one child 5 to 17 years of age. Of these calls, 64% of the parents agreed to complete the survey. Parents with more than one child within the age range of interest were asked to focus on the child who had the most recent birthday for all the questions in the survey. Age, grade, and gender of that child then were established.

Throughout the interview, parents were asked a series of open-ended and forced-choice questions. Many were taken from or directly modeled after the measures used in Cantor et al.'s (1993) parent survey of children's responses to the Gulf War. This was done so that comparisons could be made across events regarding children's fright reactions to national tragedies. First, parents were asked about their child's emotional reactions to the news coverage of the terrorist attacks. In particular, the parents were asked how frightened their child had been by the news coverage of the attacks, what specific aspects of the coverage frightened their child, and how their child's upset manifested itself. Second, the child's concerns about specific issues and events (i.e., safety, future terrorism, flying) surrounding the terrorists' attacks were assessed. Third, parents were questioned about their child's exposure to the news coverage of the attacks on September 11 as well as the days following that tragedy. Additionally, parents were asked about their own fear reactions.

RESULTS

Exposure to TV News

Hypothesis 1 predicted that children's exposure to the terrorist attacks would increase linearly with age. To test this, parents were asked, "On the first day of the terrorists' attacks, how much exposure to the TV news coverage did your child have at home? *0 hours, 1 hour, 2 hours, 3 hours, 4 hours, 5 hours,* or *6 or more hours.*" An analysis of variance yielded a significant main effect for exposure by age group, F (2, 202), 31.38, $p < .01$, $n^2 = .24$. When compared to the middle age group ($M = 2.22$), children in the oldest age group watched significantly more TV news coverage of the terrorists' attacks ($M = 3.5$), whereas children in the youngest age group watched significantly less ($M = 1.27$; see Table 15.1).

Next, parents were asked about their child's daily exposure to TV news after September 11. Specifically, the interviewer asked, "After the first day, how much exposure has your child had to TV news coverage each day? *0 hours, 1 hour, 2 hours, 3 hours, 4 hours, 5 hours,* or *6 or more hours.*" An analysis of variance yielded a significant main effect for age group, F (2, 200) = 14.43, $p < .01$, $n^2 = .13$. Partially supporting Hypothesis 1, 13- to 17-year olds reportedly watched more TV news after the first day of the attacks ($M = 2.27$) than did 9- to 12-year olds ($M = 1.35$) or 5- to 8-year olds ($M = 1.13$). The results from the exposure analyses support Hypothesis 1.

Fear Reactions to TV News Coverage

It was expected in Hypothesis 2 that children's fright reactions would increase linearly with age. To test this hypothesis, parents were first asked a forced-choice (no, yes) question, "Has your child expressed any concern, fear, or upset over the TV news coverage of the terrorists' attacks in the United States?" A log-linear analysis revealed a significant main effect for age group, G^2 ($N = 212$) = 6.81, $p < .05$, $V^* = .01$. When compared to those in the youngest age group (48%), a greater proportion of children in the oldest age group reported being upset over the news coverage (67%; see Table 15.1).

Parents were then asked to rate their child's fear responses. In particular, the interviewer stated, "How concerned, frightened, or upset has your child been? Was your child *a little bit concerned* (1), *pretty concerned* (2), *very concerned* (3), or *very very concerned* (4)."[2] An analysis of variance yielded a significant main effect for age group, F (2, 204) = 8.17, $p < .01$, $n^2 = .07$. As noted in Table 15.1, children in the middle and older age groups ($M = 1.46$, $M = 1.54$, respectively) experienced significantly more intense fear than did those in the youngest age group ($M = .73$). The analysis also yielded a main effect for gender that approached significance, F (1, 204) = 3.18, $p < .10$, $n^2 = .01$. Supporting Hypothesis 3, girls ($M = 1.40$) were reportedly more frightened by the news coverage of the terrorist attacks than were boys ($M = 1.08$). The interaction between age group and gender was not significant.

---

[2]Parents who indicated that their children were not at all frightened by the news coverage of the terrorists attacks were included in the analysis. These children were assigned a "0" on the interval level scale.

Table 15.1. Parents' Perceptions of Children's Exposure and Reactions to the Terrorists' Attacks by Age Group

	5-8 Years	9-12 Years	13-17 Years
Exposure			
Mean rating of news viewing on September 11	1.27_a	2.22_b	3.50_c
Mean rating of news viewing after September 11	1.13_a	1.35_a	2.27_b
Fear			
Percent experiencing fear	$48\%_a$	$65\%_{ab}$	$67\%_b$
Mean rating of fear	0.73_a	1.46_b	1.54_b
Manifestations of upset			
Percent experiencing behavioral upset*	$21\%_a$	39%	$46\%_b$
Percent indicating discussion as upset	$55\%_b$	$21\%_a$	$27\%_a$

Note. Tabled values represent mean responses or percentages as a function of age group. All age group comparisons are significant at the $p < .05$ except for the asterisked measure, which is significant at $p < .10$.

Parents also were asked three questions regarding their own reactions to the terrorist attacks.[3] First, parents were asked "How frightened, concerned, or upset have you been by TV news coverage of the terrorists' attacks? *Not at all* (0), *a little bit* (1), *pretty* (2), *very much* (3), or *very very much* (4)" ($M = 2.64$, $SD = 1.20$, range 0-4). A one-way analysis of variance was computed by parents' gender, resulting in no significant differences. Almost two thirds of the parents (63%) reported being *very* or *very very* frightened by the news coverage of the terrorist attacks.

---

[3]Parents were asked what they said to their children about the terrorist attacks. Next, we asked about how each parent comforted his or her child if he or she expressed concern over the attacks. In addition, we also asked parents a forced-choice question about whether or not they discussed the attacks with their children. We asked "Did you talk to your child about the terrorists' attacks?" A chi-square analysis yielded a significant effect by gender, $\chi^2 (1, N = 208) = 6.35, p < .05$. Although a high proportion of parents discussed the attacks with their children, females (98%) were more likely to talk about the events than were males (90%).

Manifestation of Fear

Children's manifestations of fear also were evaluated. Parents who stated that their child had been frightened by the TV news coverage of the attacks were asked, "Please describe the ways in which your child showed him or herself to be upset. That is, how did the concern, fear, or upset manifest itself?" The spontaneous responses to this question were coded for the presence or absence of four attributes: behavioral upset (i.e., sleep disturbances, nightmares, eating difficulties, or anxiety attacks), negative affect (e.g., mad, sad, bad, angry), discussion about the attacks (e.g., question-asking, initiating conversation), and specific mentions of fear (e.g., anxious, scared, afraid, nervous). Coding of all responses was performed by two independent judges and disagreements were resolved through discussion. Using Scott's (1955) Pi, intercoder reliabilities were 91% for behavioral upset, 97% for negative affect, 85% for discussion, and 92% for fear.

The most frequently reported manifestation was behavioral upset (38%) followed by negative affect (35%), discussion (32%), and fear (17%). To assess whether these measures differed by age group and gender, log-linear analyses were conducted. For behavioral upset, the analysis yielded a main effect for age group that approached significance, G^2 ($N = 123$) = 5.59, $p < .10$, $V^* = .02$. As in Table 15.1, post hoc comparisons revealed that the prevalence of behavioral upset was reportedly greater among 13- to 17-year-olds (46%) than 5- to 8-year-olds (21%).

In terms of negative affect, a log-linear analysis revealed no significant main effects or interactions. However, the analysis of spontaneous mentions of fear yielded a significant main effect for gender, G^2 ($N = 123$) = 6.02, $p < .05$, $V^* = .03$. Girls were more likely to manifest fear ($24\%_b$) than were boys ($8\%_a$), which is consistent with Hypothesis 3. No other effects emerged in this analysis.

Finally, a log-linear analysis on the presence versus absence of initiating discussion revealed a significant effect for age group, G^2 ($N = 123$) = 9.01, $p < .05$, $V^* = .03$. Children in the youngest age group ($55\%_b$) were more likely to initiate discussion about the terrorist attacks than were those in the middle (21%) or oldest age group (27%).

News Features Contributing to Fear

It was anticipated in Hypotheses 4 and 5 that developmental differences would be observed in the aspects of TV news coverage of the terrorist attacks that were reportedly scary. To test these predictions, we asked parents this open-ended question: "Please describe any specific aspect of the TV news coverage that concerned, frightened, or upset your child." The parents' responses were coded first for specific visual aspects of the news coverage (Cantor et al., 1993). Examples include "explosions," "seeing the burning of the buildings," and "planes going into building." The responses also were coded for verbal aspects of danger/threat in the news such as concern about the death toll/missing victims, future terrorist attacks, and the possibility of war. Instances of this category include "numbers of dead victims," "the talks of war," and "family, lost people." Using Scott's (1955) Pi, intercoder reliabilities were 83% for visual threats and 81% for verbal threats.

A log-linear analysis on visual threats revealed a significant main effect by age group, G^2 ($N = 125$) = 6.23, $p < .05$, $V^* = .02$. Consistent with Hypothesis 4, the proportion of children mentioning visual images as specific sources of fear decreased with age (62%, 58%, 38%, respectively). However, it must be noted that the pair-wise comparisons fell just short of significance. The analysis on verbal threats revealed a significant difference by gender, G^2 ($N = 125$) = 5.49, $p < .05$, $V^* = .03$. Girls were reportedly more scared by verbal dangers (31%) than were boys (13%). Contrary to Hypothesis 5, no significant differences emerged by age group. Almost 25% of the children reported the verbal aspects of the news coverage as specific sources of fear.

Concerns About Specific Issues and Events

Hypothesis 6 predicted that exposure to television news coverage of the terrorists' attacks would be a positive and significant predictor of children's concern for their personal safety. To this end, the parents were asked "How concerned has your child been about her or his own personal safety? Has she or he been *not at all concerned* (0), *a little bit concerned* (1), *pretty concerned* (2), *very concerned* (3), or *very very concerned* (4)." Parents also were asked three similarly formatted questions about their child's concerns regarding the safety of their family, future terrorist attacks on their city, and future terrorist attacks in their state. The responses to these four questions were summed to form an overall index of personal concern ($M = 3.72$, $SD = 4.18$, $\alpha = .90$). Finally, parents were asked about their child's concern regarding flying in commercial airplanes. Using a single item and the same response categories, we asked "How concerned has your child been about flying in airplanes?" ($M = 1.32$; $SD = 1.97$; range 0-4).

Hierarchical regression analyses were conducted on both of these concern measures (i.e., overall concern index and flying concern). In three steps, five predictor variables were entered into each analysis. To control for demographic variables, age group and gender were entered on the first step. Parents' fear reactions to the terrorists' attacks were inserted on the second step. On the third and final step, two news exposure variables (i.e., news viewing at home on and after September 11) were entered.

Table 15.2 features the results from these analyses. Consistent with Hypothesis 6, exposure to television news after September 11 was a significant and positive predictor of children's personal concerns about safety and flying. The observed relationship remained significant after controlling for the influence of age group, gender, and parental fear level. Two other aspects of the regression analyses are worth noting. First, exposure to the terrorist attacks on

Table 15.2. Multiple regression analyses for concerns surrounding terrorists' attacks

	Variable	Safety Scale		
		B	SeB	Beta
Step 1	Age Group	0.49	0.37	0.10
	Gender	0.93	0.55	0.11
Step 2	Parents' fear reactions	0.97	0.23	.28*
Step 3	News exposure on September 11	0.01	0.17	-0.04
	News exposure after September 11	0.52	0.22	.18*
	Adjusted R^2 = .13			
		Flying Concern		
Step 1	Age Group	0.50	0.17	.27*
	Gender	0.40	0.21	0.13
Step 2	Parents' fear reactions	0.27	0.09	.21*
Step 3	News exposure on September 11	0.01	0.05	-0.20
	News exposure after September 11th	0.26	0.09	0.24*
	Adjusted R^2 = .13			

Note. All tabled values represent the third and final step of the regressions. For Safety Scale, $F(5, 199) = 6.90$, $p < .01$.

For Flying Concern, $F(5, 185) = 6.95$, $p < .01$. Asterisks denote significant betas at $p < .05$

the day of September 11 did not predict children's concerns. These findings are consistent with the idea that repeated viewing may exacerbate children's fright responses over time. Second, parental fear responses were a significant and positive predictor of children's concerns in both regression analyses. Similar findings have been observed in other studies of catastrophic news events (Cantor et al., 1993; van der Voort et al., 1993). It has been argued that children may learn fears or social concerns by imitating their parents' reactions to a variety of threatening events (Muris, Steerneman, Merckelbach, & Meesters, 1996).

Correlations Among Measures

To assess the relationship between measures of exposure, fear, and concern, partial correlations were computed controlling for age group and gender. As shown in Table 15.3, a few significant findings emerge. First, parents' fear reactions are related to children's fright responses as well as their manifestation of behavioral upset. These findings suggest that children may be modeling their parents' emotional reactions to the terrorists' attacks (Muris et al., 1996).

Second, safety concerns are positively related to exposure to TV news and fear responses. These results suggest that exposure may heighten children's concerns for their personal safety. It may also be the case, however, that children who are concerned may seek out television news for reassurance and information. Interestingly, discussion about the terrorists' attacks is inversely related to behavioral upset.

DISCUSSION

Overall, the purpose of this survey was to examine children's responses to the news coverage of the terrorists' attacks. The results revealed that there are strong developmental differences in children's patterns of exposure and fear responses to the attacks on September 11, 2001. In addition, repeated exposure to terrorist news coverage after the day of the incident was a significant and positive predictor of children's concerns about their personal safety.

In terms of specific predictions, it was expected in Hypothesis 1 that exposure to the news footage of the attacks would increase linearly with age. This hypothesis was generally supported across two independent exposure measures. When compared to 9- to 12-year-olds, 13- to 17-year-olds were exposed to more TV news coverage of the attacks on 9/11 and 5- to 8- year-olds were exposed to less. In terms of watching TV news after that day a similar trend by age group was observed.

Although there were significant differences in viewing by age, it is important to note that only 13% of the children reportedly were not exposed to any news coverage of the terrorist attacks on 9/11. Put another way, a full 87% of the children in this sample were exposed to horrific images of planes exploding, fires burning, and the collapse of the WTC buildings. Exposure to such depictions, as was argued earlier, may be traumatizing and have long-term effects—especially for young children. Thus, parents may be advised to shield their younger children from television altogether when such cataclysmic national tragedies occur.

A second prediction of developmental differences in fear was strongly supported by the data, especially when children's fright responses in the oldest age group were compared with those in the youngest. It was argued earlier that older children's fear responses may be a function of exposure. That is, older children were more likely to view news coverage of the terrorist attacks both at home and school (S. Smith, Suding, Boyson, Moyer, & Pieper, 2001). Yet the correlation between exposure and fear was small and nonsignificant (see Table 15.3). Consequently, older children's fear responses are more likely to be a function of their understanding of the magnitude of this national tragedy rather than their sheer exposure to it on television.

As predicted, gender also influenced children's fright reactions to the coverage. We had anticipated that girls would react with more fear to this national tragedy than would boys. Furthermore, these findings are consistent with other research examining children's reactions to television news in general and catastrophic events in specific (S. Smith & Wilson, 2002; Wright et al., 1989).

Overall, two other points are worth mentioning regarding children's fear responses. In terms of prevalence, about 60% of the parents sampled reported that their children experienced fear as a function of exposure to news coverage of the terrorist attacks. As a point of comparison, Cantor et al. (1993) found 45% of the parents they surveyed reported youngsters' fear reactions to news footage from the Gulf War. Because the September 11 attacks took place on domestic soil and featured more graphic images than those depicted during the Gulf War, one would anticipate children's responses to be more prevalent and intense.

In addition to fear, almost one quarter of all the parents in the sample reported that their children experienced behavioral upset

Table 15.3. Partial Correlation Coefficients Among Exposure, Fear, and Concern Measures

	Exposure September 11	Exposure After September 11	Fear September 11	Fear Rating	Behavioral Upset	Discuss	Safety Concerns	Flying Concerns	Parents' Fear Ratings	Parents' Talk Terrorism
Exposure September 11	1.00	0.42[a]	0.11	0.09	-0.17	-0.04	0.06	0.12	0.07	-0.06
Exposure After September 11		1.00	0.07	0.11	0.01	-0.14	0.18[a]	0.19[b]	0.10	0.08
Fear (Y, N)			1.00	0.78[b]	0.04	0.09	0.35[b]	0.4[b]	0.27[b]	0.00
Fear rating				1.00	0.32[a]	-0.09	0.53[b]	0.51[b]	.32[b]	0.01
Behavioral upset					1.00	-0.32[b]	.24[a]	0.07	.22[a]	-0.06
Discussion						1.00	-.26[b]	-0.06	-0.17	0.16
Safety concerns							1.00	.57[a]	.28[a]	0.03
Flying concerns								1.00	.21[a]	0.05
Parents' fear ratings									1.00	-0.06
Parents' talk terrorism										1.00

Note. All partial correlation coefficients have been controlled for age group and gender of the child. Correlations with an "a" are significant at the $p <$ .05 level and those with a "b" are significant at the $p <$ .01 level.

after the terrorists' attacks. One parent even indicated that her child reacted so severely (i.e., crying, hard time breathing, chest pains, sleep disturbance) that she thought he was having a heart attack. Other parents reported their children crying, withdrawing, and asking lots of questions about the events. Such findings are consistent with a survey done by ABC/Washington Post indicating that 15% of the parents of 5- to 12-year-olds reported that their children had cried after viewing coverage of the terrorists' attacks and 4% had nightmares (cf. Gallup News Service, 2001). These are just some of the short-term manifestations of exposure to the news coverage. Perhaps more disturbingly, we do not know what long-term repercussions exposure may have on the socio-emotional development of children.

We also predicted that visual and verbal aspects of the news footage would be frightening to children at different stages of development. This did not hold for the verbal features but did for the visual. Parents of younger children were more likely to report the visual aspects of the news footage as specific sources of their youngsters' fear. These types of stories are scary to younger children because they are not only visually striking but they are also very easy to comprehend. Examples some of the parents gave of younger children's responses include "he didn't enjoy seeing people jump," "planes going into [the] building[s] [are] very frightening to him" and "mostly the flames." These findings are strikingly similar to Cantor et al.'s (1993) results that showed that visual features from the Gulf (e.g., bombs dropping) were specific sources of fear among elementary school children. Taken together, these trends suggest that the easiest way to prevent fear responses to television news during a time of national crisis is to restrict younger children's news viewing. However, many parents may not want to prevent even young children from viewing informational programming. The results from the correlational analyses suggest that parental discussion of catastrophic events is inversely related to behavioral upset and concern for personal safety. Thus, parental co-viewing and mediation of news content may be one way to ameliorate or control children's fear responses.

The final prediction was that exposure to television news coverage of the terrorist attacks would be a significant and positive predictor of children's concern for their personal safety. However, the only exposure measure that predicted both safety and flying concerns was viewing news coverage after September 11. Why was exposure on the day of the attacks not related to children's concerns? One explanation for the findings is that only repeated viewing of the event over time heightens children's worries, which is consistent with a cultivation perspective. Another explanation has to do with parents' own emotional reactions on 9/11. Public opinion polls reveal that many adults in this country experienced strong affective reactions to the attacks (ABC News.com, 2001; Pew Research Center, 2001b). Research reveals that strong emotional responses can have a powerful and negative impact on memory (Nabi, 1999; Zoellner, Sacks, & Foa, 2001). As such, parents may have had difficulty accurately recalling how much exposure their child had on the day of the attacks. Consistent with this explanation, the two news exposure measures were only moderately correlated ($r = .42$).

This study has some limitations. First, a random sample of parents in a single Michigan county was surveyed about their children's responses. These parents may be very different than parents elsewhere. Thus, the generalizability of the findings is limited. Second, we relied on asking parents about their children's reactions to the news coverage rather than interviewing children more directly. Research reveals that parents tend to underestimate their children's reactions to television (Cantor & Reilly, 1982). As such, our estimates of children's patterns of exposure as well as fear may be conservative. Third, we only assessed youngsters' fear responses. Several other emotional reactions may have been evoked by the news coverage. For example, children may have expressed anger, sadness, and disgust over this tragedy. Future research needs to be conducted on the full range of children's affective responses to different tragedies.

In summary, the findings of this study reveal pronounced developmental differences in children's patterns of exposure and fright responses to such coverage of the terrorists' attacks on television and news.

16

Hopes and Fears of 6- to 11-Year-Olds

Susan Royer
Kelly L. Schmitt
Sesame Street Workshop

The sudden, unexpected terrorist attacks on September 11, 2001 shook the nation, causing disbelief, anxiety, and deep grief. As adults attempted to come to terms with what had happened, a key concern was how children would cope with the events. It is no longer believed that children are immune to nightmares and the type of stress that adults experience after suffering psychological trauma (Green et al., 1991; Sleek, 1998; Solomon & Green, 1992); nevertheless, little is known about how American children react to terrorism because so few instances have occurred in the United States.

The most recent terrorist attack, the Oklahoma City bombing in 1995, provides the most updated understanding of the reaction of children. A large study of the critical needs of children in Oklahoma City conducted 7 weeks after the attack indicated that knowing someone who was killed, or heavy viewing of bomb-related television, was associated with posttraumatic stress disorder (PTSD) symptoms such as trembling or a faster heartbeat (Pfefferbaum et al., 1999). Children's reactions mirrored those of the adults around them, suggesting that adults' reactions may be contagious to children (Klingman, 2001; Schuster et al., 2001).

Additional research evidence is available about how children react to a distant trauma that is not personally threatening. For example, Terr and colleagues (1997) examined children's processing of the *Challenger* explosion in 1986. They interviewed children from Christa McAullife's New Hampshire hometown and from a demographically similar town in California. Those authors argued that children's processing of the tragedy followed patterns similar to those of other types of trauma; children initially denied the reality of the explosion, later fantasized about it and afterward tried to cope by seeking additional information at home, school, and on their own. Furthermore, research by Monaco and Geier (1987) indicated that children were confused about the explosion. Five- to 15-year-olds were able to think more realistically and abstractly about the explosion. Older children, but not younger children, became more realistic after factual talks given by their teacher. In a similar vein, Wright, Kunkel, Pinon, and Huston (1989) also indicated that older children (Grade 6) were better than younger children (Grade 4) in distinguishing their fantasies about the explosion from the actualities.

Finally, one study on children's reactions to September 11 has already been reported (Schuster et al., 2001). 560 adults, 170 of whom were parents of 5- to 18-year-olds, were interviewed via phone 3 to 5 days after the attack. This research indicated that adults coped by turning to their community and religion, with high percentages of adults reported talking with others, turning to religion, participating in group activities, and making donations. According to the parents, 35% of their children exhibited signs of stress and 47% were worried about their own or their family's safety. Although the individuals who were closest to New York had the highest rate of substantial stress reaction, other people throughout the country, in large and small communities, also reported stress reactions (Schuster et al., 2001). Proximity to the event tends to be related to intensity of symptoms (Horn & Trickett, 1998). However, those who are more susceptible to PTSD may also include children who visited the affected buildings, whose parents fly frequently, or who had recently experienced another loss.

METHOD

The study reported here is based on qualitative research that provides an in-depth exploration into the thoughts and feelings of 6-

to 11-year-old children after a massively threatening tragedy, September 11.

Sample

There were 87 children (ages 6 to 11) who participated in this study, with an average of 14 participants at each age. The 87 were recruited from a potential sample of 120 children (73% response rate.)[1] Only children who were aware of the events of September 11 were included. Five children were eliminated by responding negatively to the question: "Recently there has been a lot of news about Washington DC and New York City. Have you heard the news about Washington DC and New York City?" Of the 82 participants (39 girls, 43 boys), 73% were White, 20% were African American, 5% were Hispanic, and 2% were Asian American. The majority of the children (76%) had parents who were married, with the remainder having single, divorced, or a widowed parent. Approximately one third of the mothers had some high school education or a high school diploma, another one third had some technical or college education, and the rest of the mothers had college or postcollege education.

Participants were recruited from shopping malls in 16 geographically dispersed markets. Of the 16 markets, 5 were in urban areas and 11 were within 30 miles of a major city. The criteria for selecting a specific shopping mall within each area was: (a) the mall population represented a broad range of incomes; (b) the mall population was ethnically diverse; and (c) an experienced interviewing organization existed within the mall.

Although this was not a purposive sample, only children with indirect exposure to the events were interviewed (i.e., they were not present at the attacks, and at the time of completing the interview did not know anyone who died as a result of the terrorist attacks). This is worth noting because children directly exposed to the events, such as those who lost a loved one or were displaced from their home or school, deal with different issues (Pfefferbaum et al., 1999). Nevertheless, research conducted after the Oklahoma City bombing indicated that children were "not immune to the effects of witnessing violence whether their exposure was direct or indirect" (Groves, Weinreb, & Augustyn, cited in Castle, Beasley, & Skinner, 1996, p. 1).

---

[1]An additional 458 potential respondents were approached who were not given booklets. 334 because they did not meet the age quota, were not a legal guardian, did not live in town, or did not read or write English; 76 qualified refusal and 48 were not given booklets because we already had enough participants of a particular age or race.

We oversampled (n = 38) from the New York and Washington, DC metropolitan areas (hereafter referred to as affected areas) to determine whether proximity would influence reactions because the literature is contradictory as to whether being in closer proximity is or is not related to increased stress (e.g., Fraser, 1973; Horn & Trickett, 1998). Younger children (6- to 8-year-olds) were paid $50, whereas older children (9- to 11-year-olds) were paid $75 for their participation.

Procedure

Children were asked to document their lives for a time capsule study. They were asked to help create a self-portrait by using cameras, artwork, and mini essays to describe their lives. The questionnaire booklet that children were given was entitled *All About Me*. This booklet contained 18 questions intended to give us insight into their internal and external lives.

In addition to the *All About Me* booklet, 9- to 11-year-olds were given a disposable camera and a second booklet entitled *Kid's View*. In the *Kid's View* booklet there was an archetype framework. This group of children was instructed to take a photograph of the person who fulfilled certain roles in their lives (including a caregiver and hero), places in their world (the heart of the home and the safe place), and their view of the future (hopes, concerns, and sources of pride).

All children were given a booklet to complete on their own without parent or interviewer intervention. Parents were given a letter instructing them to feel free to help their child with writing or spelling if they ask for it, but not to "improve" on their child's responses. The opportunity to discuss, write, draw, and express their views seemed to be welcomed by the children.

Participants were instructed to return booklets in person and one-on-one in-depth interviews were then conducted. None of the booklets had any specific reference to September 11, terrorists or violent events. It was only after the booklets were turned in that interviewers inquired about (a) knowledge of the events of September 11, (b) their reactions to the events, and (c) media exposure to the events. Parents were present for the interviews and answered questions concerning (a) changes in behavior after the events and (b) other background information. All the interviews were completed between September 21, 2001 and October 10, 2001.

Interestingly, most trauma studies are not conducted until after the acute phase of response or solely rely on parental report (Pynoos et al., 1987). By contrast, this study elucidates the feelings of children to the terrorist attacks of September 11, 2001 (2 to 4 weeks) after the event. During this initial reaction period, children may have exhibited intense responses. Our approach relied almost solely on children's own reactions and did not attempt to diagnose PTSD.

It is worth noting that the instruments in this study were used in prior research with 233 different 6- to11-year-old children during the spring of 2000 (Royer, 2001). This earlier research indicated that many children, particularly 9- to 11-year-olds, had anxieties about guns, death, and violence. The anxieties and fears expressed in those booklets were coupled with a strong yearning for the presence of an engaged adult. Grandparents were especially prominent, appearing in nearly half the kid's view booklets. The most common reason for identifying someone as an archetypal figure was, in each case, because "they take care of me." Although the aforementioned sample of 6- to 11-year-olds were different from the present study, they allow for a cross-sectional comparison at two different historical times.

RESULTS

When asked whether they had heard the news about Washington, DC and New York City, 82 of the 87 said they had. The following is based on their responses.

Understanding of September 11 Attack

Approximately three quarters of the children reported that planes hit buildings, with some children naming the specific buildings that were hit or targeted.

> The plane crashed into the Pentagon. I know that a lot of people died and it was very evil. It was a dumb plane crash. It crashed into one of the tallest buildings in the world, but I don't know the name. (6-year-old girl, Washington, DC)

> A plane was going to the Twin Towers and hit them, and one was going for the White House and it crashed in Pennsylvania, and one hit the Pentagon. I think bin Laden is to blame. (11-year-old girl, Washington, DC)

Nearly two fifths of the children also reported that terrorists or bad or evil men were involved.

> A terrorist was in a plane and it had lots of fuel and it crashed into the two twin towers. (10-year-old boy, Florida)

> Bad guys crashed a plane into a building—I think we should go beat the bad guys. (6-year-old boy, Denver)

The next most frequent responses (almost one fourth of the children) concerned the visually striking aspect of the terrorist attacks—the fire or the buildings coming down. Children were equally likely to talk about this as to talk about people dying or being injured.

> The World Trade Center and the Pentagon blew up. (6-year-old boy, Washington, DC)

> The Twin Towers broke down. (8-year-old girl, Florida)

> Bad men crashed into buildings and all the people inside were hurt. (7-year-old boy, New Jersey)

Feelings About September 11 Attack

When children were asked about how they felt about what had happened, about half reported feeling sad. Younger children (6- to 8-year-olds) were especially likely to say that they were sad. Some of the children felt bad for the victims, others felt sad for America, and others were sad for the rescuers.

> Sad because all those people died. I also feel surprised because I didn't know that people would do that horrible thing. I also feel kind of frustrated. I feel frustrated because there is so much going on. There is nothing else to think about since that thing happened. (8-year-old girl, Washington, DC)

> I feel sad. Sad for the other people, the ones who died and the ones who don't have their homes any more. (9-year-old girl, Rochester)

> I feel really, really sorry for the people in NY and the firemen. (8-year-old girl, Florida)

The next most commonly expressed emotion was fear, particularly among older children and those in close proximity to New York or Washington, DC. As one 11-year-old boy from New Jersey said, "I get scared and hope nothing bad happens to me." Another boy from Washington, DC, aged 6, said that he felt "kind of scared, kind of worried, and afraid to fly because I am going to Disney World."

One fifth of children had another defensive reaction, feeling angry or frustrated, which was sometimes expressed as vengeance.

I think we should go beat the bad guys. (6-year-old boy, Denver)

I think we should kick butt, I think that it was wrong what they did. (10-year-old boy, Memphis)

I'm mad because I don't like people to die and we shouldn't hijack planes and I'm sad because people have died. (10-year-old boy, Washington, DC)

Only a few children preferred not to discuss the events, possibly to avoid feeling any emotions related to the events.

Talking About Attack

Children also were asked how often parents, teachers, grandparents, or other adults discussed what had happened with them. Almost all the 9- to 11-year-olds reported that adults talked to them *sometimes* or *a lot*, whereas approximately half of the 6- to 8-year-olds reported talking to adults *not very much* or *not at all*. Presumably, the more frequent conversations with older children reflect their developmental capacity to understand more, as well as the likelihood that they have more questions about what happened. Alternatively, some parents may assume that young children are immune to suffering psychological trauma.

A similar pattern of talking with friends was observed, with 9- to 11-year-olds reporting talking *a lot* much more frequently than younger children. In fact, almost half the 6- to 8-year-olds didn't talk to their friends very much or at all about the events. Conversations with peers also were slightly more frequent in the affected areas.

Acquiring More Information

Children's media consumption regarding the terrorist attacks was comprised mostly of television viewing, followed by listening to the radio or reading newspapers or magazines. Older children were more likely than younger ones to consume each of these communication media.

Children of all ages watched TV news with adults, especially their mothers. Only two children watched the news by themselves, and four children watched with other kids with no adults present. It appears that children were very interested in watching TV news,

despite expert advice to limit children's exposure to reports of
terrorism (Cantor, 1998; Tassey, 1996). This interest may appear as
a way to cope by acquiring more information (Terr et. al., 1997). In
fact, some research indicates that adults watch television as a way of
coping with stressful life events, even though it is only a temporary
means of doing so (Anderson, Collins, Schmitt, & Smith-Jacobvitz,
1996). As an 8-year-old girl from the DC metropolitan area said:

> When the big accident happened I just really wanted to see it on TV.
> I know a lot about it but I don't think I know a lot of stuff that other
> people know.

Changes in Child's Behavior

Some behavioral indications of being affected by the terrorist attacks
were observed by parents. According to the parents, 39 of the
children woke up in the middle of the night and 32 slept in their
parent's room. All but two of the children who watched "a lot" woke
up in the middle of the night or slept in their parent's room.

One third of the parents noticed other behavioral changes.
Children in the affected areas were described as being worried, with
younger children having trouble sleeping, being more quiet or more
nervous than usual.

IMPROMPTU REPORTS ABOUT SEPTEMBER 11

Prior to the interview, children were not directly asked about the
attacks. Even so, children exhibited a range of responses to them in
their booklets: some directly referred to them (e.g., fear of war), others
reflected them in more oblique ways (e.g., fear of flying), and about
half made no mention of what had happened (mostly 6- to 8-year-
olds). However, a cross-cutting theme was the importance of adults as
role models and the community as a support system for children.

Fears and Worries

The *All About Me* booklet included a question to ascertain children's
anxieties: "Do you have any fears or worries? Draw a picture below
and, on the opposite page, write about what you drew." The majority
of the children in the younger age group, aged 6 to 8, cited things
that might be considered routine childhood fears or worries, such as

reptiles, bugs, darkness, and imaginary threats like monsters. In addition, however, about one quarter drew pictures of planes hitting a building, images of war or other types of violence. Older children, aged 9 to 11, were less likely to cite "normal" fears and instead, over half cited more alarming ones which may be related to the terrorist attack (see Fig. 16.1 for a sampling of 6- to 11-year-olds' fears). There was almost no difference in these responses between boys and girls. A closer look at the other violent anxieties (not clearly related to September 11) show guns or getting shot (reported by five children aged 9 to 11 and three children aged 6 to 8).

More than half the children expressed some concern for personal safety or the safety of their family members. Consistent with Terr et al. (1999), children tend to move from concerns about their own safety to family safety, extended family, and then to the safety of the community, the state, and the nation. The entire spectrum of these concerns was exhibited in this data.

Despite fears of death and violence and feelings of sadness, some children also expressed empathy.

My worries is that terriest will harm my Family and I will be left with no family like the kid in NY. (11-year-old boy, Atlanta)

the world trade center explosions because I don't want to have a world war III plus we had to many people die and I don't want to see more people die. I just don't want to go throw this again. (10-year-old boy, Florida)

a airplane hit a building. Because my mom and dad work in building and my papa is in the army and might have to go to war. (8-year-old girl, Atlanta)

Nine- to 11-year-olds also were asked to describe "Worries about the future." Research by Terr et al. (1997) indicates that children's negative views about the future increase over time after a disaster. Would children's concerns about the future be influenced by September 11?

Royer (2001) indicated that 9- to 11-year old children were most concerned about the environment, especially litter and trash. Children in this study were more concerned about war, bombing, and other types of terrorism. A 10-year-old boy from Brooklyn, who took a picture of nothing, explained that he was worried because "we might have a nuclear war and our world could look like this." A 10-year-old boy from Florida took a picture of a newspaper article describing the World Trade Center attack because "I don't want to have another world war. Too many people die. Children get hurt. So do moms and

2) Do you have any fears or worries? Draw a picture below and, on the opposite page, write about what you drew.

PICTURE OF MY FEARS OR WORRIES:

Female, age 11

2) Do you have any fears or worries? Draw a picture below and, on the opposite page, write about what you drew.

PICTURE OF MY FEARS OR WORRIES:

Male, age 10

Fig. 16.1. Children's fears or worries

2) Do you have any fears or worries? Draw a picture below and, on the opposite page, write about what you drew.

Female, age 11

2) Do you have any fears or worries? Draw a picture below and, on the opposite page, write about what you drew.

Female, age 8

Fig. 16.1. Children's fears or worries (cont.)

dads too. It is a scary thing." These fears were personalized to children's own neighborhoods. One child took a picture of the block where she lives because "I worry about terrorists dropping a bomb where I live or crash a plane" (10-year-old girl, Minneapolis). Concerns related to the terrorist attack also came out in response to the question "What are you ashamed of?" The majority of the children talked about the environment (e.g., litter, urbanization), but a small segment expressed being disturbed by the fighting. As one child said, "People who are fighting for no good reason. Because we should be all living together in peace and not fighting about things that don't mean anything" (10-year-old girl, Houston). Another child said "because people kill other people for no reason" (9-year-old boy, Washington, DC). Environmental concern in relation to the terrorist attack was also expressed when an 11-year-old girl from Brooklyn explained she was ashamed of "Burned paper from the world trade bombs. It shows war and destruction."

Heroes

According to Erikson (1980), heroes teach children about their culture and their relationship to society. Heroes may exert their most profound influence on children as examples of possible selves. Oyserman and Markus (1990) contended that possible selves operate as motivators for children. Possible selves include those selves we would like to become, as well as those we fear becoming (Markus & Nurius, 1986).

To address this issue, we asked 6- to 11-year-olds: "Cut out a picture or draw someone famous you would like to be for one day." Children in our previous study wanted to be like pop culture icons such as Britney Spears and The Rock. Girls, in this study, also wanted to be like pop culture icons, especially musicians. Interestingly, boys not only wanted to be like pop culture icons or sports figures. Instead, evidence of wanting to be like real and imaginary heroes such as the president, policemen, firefighters, and even Batman was expressed.

> [I chose] George W. Bush [because] of the bad things going on with the terrorists. (8-year-old boy, New Jersey)

> [I chose] Police Officer [because] They are heros. They help find people. They stop traffic. (6-year-old girl, Washington, DC)

Nine- to 11-year-olds also were asked to photograph someone whom they consider to be a hero. In addition to family members, a small segment of the boys and girls took pictures of firefighters, policemen, and teachers, all of whom may have helped to restore their feelings of safety and security.

> Firemen. This person is a hero because with all of the things that have been going on, these firemen are the heroes to all of us. (11-year-old girl, Brooklyn)

It is interesting to note that before September 11, teachers were the only local public figure identified as heroes. The methodology specified photographing the hero, which all of the children did in the previous study (Royer, 2001). However, in this study, children sometimes cut out pictures to represent heroes or other archetypes, displacing some of the local heroes with firefighters or policemen (not necessarily from the local area).

Special Powers

Children want to help. The desire to help was expressed in a variety of ways. When asked what special power they would like to have, children expressed an interest in flying, mystical powers or helping powers in order to "save the world," "keep my family safe," or stop "the bad guys" (see Fig. 16.2). One girl in Los Angeles told us she would like the special power of flying and fighting bad guys "So every one will be safe." A 6-year-old boy from Denver said "I'd like to make a big blast come out of my hand. So I could help people. I could bomb the bad guys." An 8-year-old boy from Rochester wanted to predict the future so that "I would know what's going to happen before it actually happens and that way I can help them by warning them." It is worth noting that although children in our previous study frequently reported wanting to fly or change things with their mind (Royer, 2001), the reasons for wanting to do so infrequently concerned helping others.

Expressions of wanting to help also came out in response to the question "What do you do best." Some children said that what they do best is to "take care of others." Children were also asked to "explain about a time you helped someone." All of the children gave examples of helping their parents or friends, but a small segment also displayed a sense of the world around them. As a 9-year-old girl from Rochester said "3 weeks ago many people died. I gave money at my school to help those who lost everything."

9) MY "SPECIAL POWERS" COLLAGE

Male, age 8

9) MY "SPECIAL POWERS" COLLAGE

To be a good Mom

To bring all people together

To make sad people feel better

Female, age 8

Fig. 16.2. Special powers children would like to have

Male, age 8

9) MY "SPECIAL POWERS" COLLAGE

To be like these men and try
To stop the War.

Female, age 9

Fig. 16.2. Special powers children would like to have (cont.)

Hope for the Future

Our research suggests that national and community connectedness immediately after the terrorist attacks gave children strength. Although a study conducted by Terr et al. (1997) after the *Challenger* explosion indicated that negative views about the future increased over time, in our study children expressed hope for the future, evidenced by mentions of communities rallying together, displays of charity, and a new sense of patriotism. For example, a typical response to a question in our prior study such as "Hopes for the Future" would be "Football. This makes me feel excited because I'm going to play football in High School" (9-year-old boy, Washington, DC). However, about half the children in this study talked about the flag or life in America representing their hope. In our previous research none of the children mentioned America itself as a hope for the future.

Specifically, two fifths of the children talked about the flag representing their hope for the future, and the importance of everyone coming together.

> When I see everybody with Flags. [It shows] that everybody can be friends and help one another. (11-year-old boy, Atlanta)

> American flag. Each star represents a state. Our country comes together in a time of need. (9-year-old boy, Houston)

> American Flag. It show the very best of America because we are United. (10-year-old girl, Houston)

> To see American flags. Because we are all putting American flags out and it shows we're all one! (10-year-old girl, Brooklyn)

In addition, when asked "What makes you proud?" more than one third of the children said the American flag, especially kids from nonaffected areas. A smaller segment of children in the previous study (Royer, 2001) did talk about the flag making them proud, although they did not talk about it as a hope for the future.

Some other children in this study talked about America making them proud, or how their view of America had changed.

> I'm proud to be an American. I'm proud to be an American because we are a powerful nation and we won't let anything take away freedom. Our neighborhood has shown a lot of support since the attack in New York and Washington, DC. (11-year-old boy, Phoenix)

Proud to be an American because all of the Americans stand together no matter where were at. (11-year-old boy, San Diego)

I think it is stupid for people to feel we are better than them, but as the song goes "and our flag was still there." We are Americans, we have our rights. (11-year-old girl, Florida)

Children seemed to gain strength in seeing other people help out. One girl expressed her optimism for the future by taking a picture of a Twin Towers plexiglass model in her home. This child's resilience shines through in her explanation of why this picture gives her hope for the future:

When I look at what happened to these buildings, I think of myself. I think that I could rebuild myself if I ever go down. (11-year-old girl, Brooklyn)

Social Support

The *Kid's View* booklet asked 9- to 11-year-olds to identify individuals and places that fit archetypal descriptions, and their answers revealed what they think of the people and places around them as well as what concerns and delights them. The descriptive archetypes included in the study were: the caregiver ("Who takes care of us?"), the excluded or forgotten one ("Who has been left out"), a hero, rebel, troublemaker, magician, wise one, joker, and a regular kid.

The results elicited by these archetypes demonstrated the vital role of adults, especially family members and teachers in a child's life. The people children most often selected as fitting different archetypes were family members, teachers, and sometimes a neighbor. Not surprisingly, immediate family members were most frequently identified as children's heroes, but extended family members were also of crucial importance in children's lives, appearing frequently even though they were not specifically asked about. Grandparents appeared in 23% of the booklets, mentioned in very positive terms as a friend of kids, magicians, wise ones, or heroes. Aunts and uncles also were valued, appearing in 13% of the booklets. Teachers also were presented in a positive light in a small segment of the books as heroes, a friend of kids, and wise ones.

When asked to identify the "safe place," most children responded with an answer like this one: "My house. I feel nothing bad can happen to me because my house is really safe and I just don't think anything can happen to me" (10-year-old boy, Florida). However, other children identified church and school as a "safe place."

> A church. I feel nothing bad can happen to me because I am in God's hands. When I'm here I fell that nobody can take me away from anything. (11-year-old girl, Brooklyn)

> A school is for learning. Because every year we are there we learn more and more. When we are adults we will be able to run the USA better and safer. (10-year-old girl, Minneapolis)

One other child talked about religion in terms of his hopes for the future. He said that God is his hope for the future, "Cause he created America and everything on Earth. He is so great."

DISCUSSION

Children from across the country appeared to have been affected by the terrorist attacks, which was expressed in their hopes and fears. Proximity to the terrorist attacks was only rarely related to stress reactions. Some of the children, particularly older ones, expressed fears related to September 11, which is understandable because their sense of safety and security was clearly violated. Expressions of hope for America also indicated youngsters' potential to exhibit resiliency, with older children appearing to draw from the strength of the collective community. This is heartening because collective trauma allows one to better cope with the personal impact by knowing others' reactions. Children's feelings appeared to have been validated, which provides reassurance that one is not alone and actively developing an expressive sense of fellowship in grief.

Additionally, children received the message that many more people help than do harm by seeing people across the nation try to join in the efforts to help save lives—by donating blood, money, or time. One way that children can be helped to cope is by allowing them to feel that they are part of the solution. This study suggests that the meanings we assign to events and messages are important to how people respond to events (Berson & Berson, 2001).

Older children had more fears concerning the real-world violent terrorist attacks they had heard about or watched on television not only because of more exposure, but perhaps also because they are better able to understand cause and effect relationships and can think prospectively about many possible frightening outcomes and motives (Muris, Merckelback, Gadet, & Moulaert, 2000; Owen, 1998). Thus, it is not surprising that children in our previous study (Royer, 2001) exhibited fears of guns, death, and violence, but in this study those fears appeared less frequently, and instead real-world fears related to the September 11 terrorist attacks appeared.

There was some indication that boys' role models were influenced by the September 11 terrorist attacks, with reports of firefighters, police officers, and the president as heroes, replacing some of the sports stars and pop culture icons. Role models may be particularly influential for school-age children's self-esteem. Previous research also has demonstrated that self-esteem can be increased after exposure to role models that are not gender-stereotyped (Jennings, Geis, & Brown, 1980; Ochman, 1996; Parish, Bryant, & Prawat, 1977).

Social support is especially important to children's healing (Baker & O'Neill, 1993). It is important to foster an atmosphere in which anything can be talked about. Most parents did have conversations with their child about the terrorist attacks, and not surprisingly, appeared in children's booklets as important persons in their lives. Additionally, teachers may have been a source of social support, as many classrooms attempted to get involved in the helping effort by writing letters of sympathy or thanks. This may have been especially important, as children in our study expressed a desire to help. Those who feel empowered through action may feel less despair and uncertainty about the future. Thus, it is important to provide age-appropriate opportunities for children to get involved.

Although the results of this study provide us with insight into children's hopes and fears one month after the terrorist attacks, it does not allow us to know the long-term effects. However, we might surmise that one way children may be influenced in the future is by shared experiences influencing their attitudes. Terr et al. (1997) hypothesized that a generation's commonalities in thought may be set up by disasters. Children may lose their innocence in the wake of one traumatic event and subsequently be labeled by that connection—for instance "the depression generation," the "war generation," and the "60s generation." More research is needed to determine whether the degree to which the short-term fears and worries and the positive sense of hope that children expressed shortly after September 11 persist.

17

Emotion and Coping with Terror

Cynthia Hoffner
Yuki Fujioka
Amal Ibrahim
Jiali Ye
Georgia State University

A small body of research has examined people's responses to news coverage of tragedies and crises, such as the assassination of President Kennedy, the explosion of the *Challenger*, and the Persian Gulf War (e.g., Greenberg, 1964a; Hoffner & Haefner, 1994; Kubey & Peluso, 1990). Yet the events of September 11 were different than most crises studied. The attacks caused massive destruction and loss of human life within a few hours. Many Americans felt personally involved because they had relatives, friends, or acquaintances who were in New York or Washington, DC, or on an airplane during the time of the attacks. Additionally, concern about the possibility of additional terrorist attacks elsewhere increased uncertainty and stress, making nearly everyone feel vulnerable.

This chapter focuses on the role of emotion and coping in the news diffusion process among college students. Despite the fact that many of the events studied have had a strong emotional impact on people, little diffusion research has examined the role of emotion in this process (Kubey & Peluso, 1990). Additionally, relatively few studies have explored the factors that influence whether individuals pass the news to others. This chapter addresses these issues.

Emotional Responses

The events of September 11 aroused a range of emotions in people, including shock and disbelief that the events occurred in the United States, sadness for victims and their loved ones, fear of additional terrorist attacks, and anger at the perpetrators. This chapter examines four emotions: upset, sadness, fear, and anger.

Several diffusion researchers have considered whether emotional responses vary based on when people first learn of a disturbing news event. Pettey, Perloff, Neuendorf, and Pollick (1986) reported that early learners were more saddened by the *Challenger* explosion than those who learned later, possibly due to witnessing the events as they happened. Riffe and Stovall (1989) hypothesized the same results, but found the opposite: Those who learned of the explosion later were actually more upset. These authors argued that those who learned later had the nature of the event defined for them as a tragedy by newscasters or interpersonal sources, which may have increased their negative affect. Given the unique nature of the 9/11 events, and conflicting prior evidence, the following research question was posed:

RQ1: Will the time that individuals learned of the events
be related to their emotional responses?

The source from which people first learned of the attacks also may have influenced their emotional reactions. Mass media coverage of news is uniquely suited to arouse emotions. Live media coverage, especially visual television images, creates a sense of drama that attracts and holds attention. Live coverage gives audience members the sense of participating in an event, or witnessing it personally. These characteristics make it easier for them to identify with the people and situations depicted, and to become emotionally involved (Graber, 1996). Thus, one can expect that learning of the events from the mass media may have facilitated identification and involvement, resulting in greater negative emotional responses.

Interpersonal sources also may have influenced how people felt when they first heard the news. Learning from another person may have been less disturbing than learning from the mass media, in part because talking with others can ease aversive emotions (Kubey & Peluso, 1990). Interpersonal contact, however, might exacerbate negative emotions if the person who shares the news appears emotionally upset or distressed. Thus, receiving the news interpersonally may either reduce or increase negative affect in the receiver, depending on the context.

Research examining the effects of information source on emotion is scarce and results seem inconclusive. Riffe and Stovall (1989) hypothesized that people would be more upset if they first learned of the *Challenger* explosion from the mass media, rather than an interpersonal source. However, they did not find any difference in emotion based on the initial source of the news. Pettey et al. (1986) reported that individuals were sadder if they heard about the *Challenger* explosion from another person, rather than the mass media. Based on this review, a research question was posed:

RQ2:   Will emotional responses differ for those who learn of the events from mass media versus interpersonal sources?

Interpersonal News Diffusion

Gantz and Trenholm (1979) found that expressing emotion is one reason that people pass news along to others. Two studies have shown that people's emotional response to a news event is an important factor that can facilitate the news diffusion process. Riffe and Stovall (1989) examined the relationship between people's emotional upset in response to news of the *Challenger* explosion and their subsequent communication behavior. Although emotion was unrelated to people's behavior immediately after they learned of the events, those who were most upset were ultimately more likely to share the information with others. Kubey and Peluso (1990) found that those who informed others of the explosion reported more negative emotion when they first learned of the accident than those who did not inform others. Informers were also more likely to say they felt better after talking to others.

These findings suggest that when people are emotionally upset after learning of a tragic event, sharing the news can function as a coping strategy. Research shows that people tend to seek social contact with others when they are under stress (e.g., Shaver & Klinert, 1982). Other research has found that the experience of negative emotion facilitates sharing of the emotional experience with others (e.g., Luminet, Bouts, Delie, Manstead, & Rime, 2000). Based on this research, we hypothesized:

H1: Stronger negative emotions will be associated with
      greater interpersonal news diffusion.

Individuals who have a personal connection to news events
should also be more likely to share the news with others. Rogers
(2000) argued that the salience or importance of news events varies
across people. News events are perceived as important when they
involve people or issues that individuals care about, or that may
affect them personally. Several studies have shown that people are
more likely to contact others to talk about news events when they
perceive those events as personally relevant or important (e.g.,
Adams, Mullen, & Wilson, 1969; Gantz, Trenholm, & Pittman, 1976).
Basil and Brown (1994), for example, reported that Magic Johnson
fans were more likely to talk to other people about the news of
Johnson's HIV positive condition than were non-fans. On September
11, people who had a personal connection to anyone who was or
might have been directly affected by the attacks should have
perceived the events as more personally important, and should have
been more motivated to contact others about the events. Thus, it was
predicted that:

H2: A stronger personal connection to the event will be
      associated with greater interpersonal news
      diffusion.

It seems logical that those who learn of a news event earlier
would be more likely to pass the news on to others, in part because
they may assume that others do not yet know about the event.
Research has shown that one reason for sharing news is the desire to
keep others informed (Gantz & Trenholm, 1979; Gantz et al., 1976).
However, there does not appear to be any direct evidence regarding
the influence of timing on interpersonal news diffusion. Thus, we
asked:

RQ3: Will the time that individuals learned of the events
       be related to interpersonal news diffusion?

The initial source of the news also may be related to
interpersonal news diffusion. Based on the two-step flow model, Basil
and Brown (1994) predicted that individuals who first learned of
Magic Johnson's HIV positive condition from the mass media (rather
than from another person) would be more likely to share the news
with others. However, they found no difference in informing others
based on the initial source. Moreover, prior research reports

conflicting results. Some studies found that those who learned of a news event from another person were more likely to talk with others (e.g., Greenberg, 1964a; Larsen & Hill, 1954), whereas other studies found more interpersonal communication by those who were first informed by the mass media (e.g., D. Miller, 1945). Rogers (2000) argued that research still needs to explore how the source of first knowledge affects interpersonal news diffusion. We asked:

RQ4: Will the initial source of knowledge be related to interpersonal news diffusion?

COPING RESPONSES AND INTERPERSONAL NEWS DIFFUSION

The predicted association between emotional response and interpersonal news diffusion was based, in part, on evidence that social contact can function as a coping strategy (e.g., Rime, Finkenauer, Luminet, Zech, & Philippot, 1998). Studies of people's responses to news coverage of crises have often focused on how people felt and how they interpreted the events, but only a few have explicitly examined how they coped with their feelings (e.g., Hoffner & Haefner, 1993b; L. Murphy & Moriarty, 1976). On September 11, there were a variety of ways people could have coped with their responses to events that were beyond their control. Three types of short-term coping strategies seem likely, and were examined in this study: (a) seeking information, in an effort to gain understanding or perceived control over the events; (b) seeking social or emotional support; and (c) emotion-focused or cognitive coping, which attempts to change attention to or interpretation of the events (Eckenrode, 1991; Lazarus, 1991; S. Miller, 1990). We asked the following research question:

RQ5: Which coping responses will individuals report using most often?

Lazarus (1991) argued that different emotions are associated with different action tendencies (e.g., anger leads to attack; fear leads to avoidance). Research has rarely examined whether the nature of the emotional response affects choice of coping strategies, but the few studies that have done so found different patterns of coping for different emotions (e.g., Beaver, 1997; Laux & Weber, 1991; Saarni, 1997). The range of emotions elicited on September 11 provides an ideal context for asking the following:

RQ6: Will coping responses vary based on emotional responses?

Interpersonal contact could facilitate any of the types of coping examined in this study, although coping could be accomplished in other ways as well. In particular, seeking information and seeking support seem similar to two of the motivations for sharing news that were identified by Gantz and Trenholm (1979): to satisfy informational needs and to express affect. Thus, we asked the following:

RQ7: How will the different coping responses be related to interpersonal news diffusion?

METHOD

Respondents

Undergraduates (107 men, 269 women) at a large, urban university in the southeastern United States participated in the study.[1] The students reported more than 40 different majors. They ranged in age from 18 to 56 years (M = 22.8 years), and 94% were U.S. citizens. Out of this sample, 53% identified themselves as White/caucasian, 31% as Black/African American, 7% as Asian/Pacific Islander, 2% as Hispanic /Latino, < 1% as Native American, and 6% reported mixed ethnicity or did not respond.

Procedures

Beginning 3 weeks following the September 11 attacks, students completed anonymous, self-administered questionnaires about their reactions to the events. Data were collected from October 1 to October 18.

Measures

Learning About the Events. Respondents estimated the exact *time* that they first found out about the attacks. A chronology of the events of that day was provided to help them make an estimate. They also indicated how they initially learned of the attacks, by checking one of several *sources* listed (television, radio, Internet site, personal contact, telephone, e-mail), or by writing a response.

---

[1]The distribution of males and females in the sample was very similar to the gender distribution within the classes that participated in the study.

Emotional Responses. Respondents rated the extent to which they experienced several different emotions soon after the attacks, using a 7-point scale ranging from 0 (*not at all*) to 6 (*very much*). Two emotions (angry, outraged) were averaged to form an *anger* index (α = .86), two emotions (sad, depressed) were averaged to form a *sadness* index (α = .66), and one emotion (frightened) was used as a single-item measure of *fear*.[2] Respondents also rated how upset they felt, in comparison to others, on a 7-point scale ranging from -3 (*much less upset*) to +3 (*much more upset*; adapted from Riffe & Stovall, 1989). Responses to this item were recoded to correspond to the other emotion scales (i.e., 0 to 6).

Interpersonal News Diffusion. Respondents were asked whether they contacted others when they learned of the attacks, to pass along the news. If yes, they were asked to list *who* they contacted, and what *medium* they used (e.g., personal contact, telephone, e-mail). Two independent coders achieved high reliability for both questions (> 90% agreement). Coders also counted or estimated the number of people respondents contacted (r = .96).

Coping Responses. Respondents rated the degree to which they used each of eight coping responses in the first few hours after they learned of the attacks, using a 7-point scale ranging from 0 (*no/not at all*) to 6 (*yes/a great deal*).[3] Three items were averaged to form the *discussion* scale ("talked with friends and family members," "discussed events with others," "sought more information"; α = .68), and three items were averaged to form the *support-seeking* scale

---

[2] Six emotion items were designed to measure three emotions: fear (frightened, anxious), sadness (sad, depressed), and anger (angry, outraged). A principal axis factor analysis with oblique rotation produced a two-factor solution. The anger items loaded on one factor, and frightened, sad, and depressed loaded on the second factor (all primary loadings over .60, no cross loadings over .20). "Anxious" loaded on neither factor, and did not form a reliable scale with the fear item. However, because fear is a basic emotion that is conceptually distinct from sadness, "frightened" was used as a single item.

[3] The eight coping items were chosen based on both prior research (e.g., Hoffner, 1995) and observations of people's responses to this specific event. In an initial principal axis factor analysis with oblique rotation, the two emotion-focused coping items (distraction, positive thinking) did not load on any factor and did not form a reliable subscale. They were dropped from the factor analysis and used as single items. A subsequent factor analysis yielded two factors, which were labeled "discussion" and "support seeking." All primary factor loadings were over .45, with the exception of the prayer/religion item, which had a loading of .37. There were no cross loadings over .20.

("sought emotional support from others," "sought the company of others," "prayed or sought religious guidance"; $\alpha = .66$). Single items measured *distraction* ("tried to keep your mind on other things") and *positive thinking* ("told yourself things would be OK"). As a measure of media information seeking, respondents rated their use of news on TV, radio, and the Internet in the first few hours after they learned of the events, using the same 7-point scale. Because many people relied primarily on one medium, a measure of primary *news media use* was created by using each respondent's highest score across the three news media.

Personal Connection. Respondents were asked to describe any personal connection they had to anyone who was directly affected by the attacks, or whom they initially thought may have been affected. Two independent coders classified the strongest personal connection each respondent described, using a 6-point scale ranging from 0 (*no connection*) to 5 (*very high level of connection; r* = .96). The coding scheme considered both the closeness of relationship and the likelihood that the other person was affected.

RESULTS

Analyses of covariance (ANCOVAs) compared groups on interval- or ratio-level data, using four variables as controls (unless those variables were factors in the design): gender, personal connection, when respondents learned of the events, and from what source (mass media, interpersonal). Adjusted means are reported in the text, and means with no subscript in common differ at $p < .05$ by the Scheffé method. Partial correlations use the same four control variables.

Learning About the Events

Just over half of the respondents (52%) learned of the events within 30 minutes of when the first plane crashed into the World Trade Center (WTC). Approximately three quarters (73%) had heard within 60 minutes, and nearly all (99%) were informed within 2 1/2 hours. One half learned of the events from an interpersonal source: 30% were told personally, 17% learned from a telephone call, 4% heard an announcement in class or overheard others talking, and < 1% received an e-mail. The other half were informed by a mass media source: 27% learned from television, 22% heard on the radio, and 1% learned from an Internet site.

Emotional Response

The four emotions (upset, sadness, fear, anger) were analyzed in a 4 x 2 x 2 mixed ANCOVA, with emotion as a within-subjects variable, and gender and contacting others as between-subjects variables. Results related to contacting others are reported in the section on interpersonal news diffusion.

The analysis revealed a main effect of gender, which was qualified by an interaction between sex and emotion, F (3,1089) = 25.18, p < .001. Scheffe comparisons showed that, compared to men, women reported significantly more upset (men, M = 3.23; women, M = 3.68), more sadness (men, M = 3.28; women, M = 3.90), and more fear (men, M = 2.87; women, M = 4.15). In contrast, men reported significantly more anger (M = 4.24) than did women (M = 3.78).

Factors Predicting Emotional Response

To examine the factors affecting emotional responses to the events, separate regression analyses were conducted for each of the four emotions. In addition to gender, the predictors included personal connection to the events, when respondents first learned of the events, and from what source. These results are reported in Table 17.1, in the first step of each analysis.

The effects of gender reported earlier also emerged in these analyses, although the effect for anger only approached significance. Those with a stronger personal connection were marginally more upset. Regarding RQ1, individuals who heard about the events earlier were also more upset. For RQ2, learning about the events from the mass media was associated with more upset and more anger.

To further clarify the influence of initial source on emotion, additional analyses compared three different sources: television, other mass media (radio, Internet), and interpersonal sources. Separate 2 x 3 ANCOVAs included gender and initial source as independent variables. Again, initial source had no effect on sadness or fear. However, the main effects of source were significant for both upset, F (2,362) = 3.18, p < .05, and anger, F (2,361) = 4.80, p < .02. The same pattern emerged for both emotions. Respondents who learned of the events from television reported more upset (M = 3.84_b) than those who learned from another person (M = 3.37_a), with those learning from another mass medium in the middle (M = 3.60_{ab}). Similarly, those who learned from television were angrier (M = 4.60_b) than those who learned interpersonally (M = 3.84_a), with those informed by another mass medium in the middle (M = 4.24_{ab}).

Table 17.1. Hierarchical Regression Analyses Predicting Emotional Responses

Upset			Sadness		
	beta	R^2 change		beta	R^2 change
Step 1			Step 1		
Gender	.17**	.08***	Gender	.21**	.06***
Personal connection	.09+		Personal connection	.07	
When heard	-.14**		When heard	-.07	
Initial source	-.10*		Initial source	-.02	
Step 2			Step 2		
News media use	.08	.16***	News media use	.13**	.21***
Discussion	.06		Discussion	.09+	
Support seeking	.36***		Support seeking	.39***	
Positive thinking	-.11*		Positive thinking	-.03	
Distraction	-.12**		Distraction	.07	
Adjusted R^2 = .22***			Adjusted R^2 = .25***		

Fear			Anger		
	beta	R^2 change		beta	R^2 change
Step 1			Step 1		
Gender	.35***	.13***	Gender	-.09+	.03*
Personal connection	.04		Personal connection	.06	
When heard	-.02		When heard	-.08	
Initial source	-.05		Initial source	-.12*	
Step 2			Step 2		
News media use	.09+	.17***	News media use	.10+	.11***
Discussion	.04		Discussion	.19***	
Support seeking	.39***		Support seeking	.16**	
Positive thinking	.00		Positive thinking	.04	
Distraction	.06		Distraction	.00	
Adjusted R^2 = .28***			Adjusted R^2 = .12***		

Note. Gender was coded: men = 0, women = 1. Initial source was coded: mass media = 0, interpersonal = 1.

+ $p < .10$; * $p < .05$; ** $p < .01$; *** $p < .001$

Interpersonal News Diffusion

Nearly three quarters of respondents (72%) contacted others to pass along news of the events. Three quarters of those who contacted others (75%) used the telephone, 39% did so personally, and 8% used e-mail. Respondents contacted: friends, 44%; parents, 42%; siblings, 11%; other family members, 17%; coworkers, 14%; roommates, 10%; classmates, 6%; and others, 11%.

Emotion and Interpersonal News Diffusion. Hypothesis 1 was supported in analyses involving both whether respondents contacted others, and how many people they contacted. The 4 x 2 x 2 mixed ANCOVA described earlier revealed a main effect of whether respondents contacted others, $F(1,361) = 15.59$, $p < .001$, but no interaction with emotion or gender. Those who contacted others reported stronger emotional responses ($M = 3.93$) than did those who did not make contact ($M = 3.35$). Separate one-way ANCOVAs confirmed that the main effect of contacting others was significant for all four emotions.

Partial correlations revealed that the number of people contacted was positively correlated with all four emotions: upset, $pr = .14$, $p < .01$; sadness, $pr = .11$, $p < .05$; fear, $pr = .15$, $p < .01$; anger, $pr = .19$, $p < .001$. The relative contribution of the four emotions was examined in a regression analysis. Four control variables were entered in the first step (gender, personal connection, time respondents learned of the events, and from what source), and the four emotions were entered in the second step. In this analysis, only anger was a significant predictor of the number of people contacted ($\beta = .15$, $p < .01$).

Other Factors Affecting Interpersonal News Diffusion. Hypothesis 2 was not supported. Personal connection did not differ based on whether or not respondents contacted others, and was unrelated to the number of people they contacted. Overall, a low degree of personal connection was reported ($M = 1.20$).

In answer to RQ3, interpersonal news diffusion was greater among those who learned of the events earlier. In a one-way ANCOVA, those who passed on the news to others learned of the events earlier ($M = 9:29$ a.m.) than those who did not ($M = 9:42$ a.m.), $F(1,366) = 7.12$, $p < .01$. In addition, those who learned earlier passed the news on to more people ($pr = -.14$, $p < .01$).

Regarding RQ4, respondents who learned of the events from the mass media were more likely to contact others (77%) than were those who learned interpersonally (67%), $\chi^2(1) = 4.90$, $p < .03$. The percentages for TV and the other mass media were nearly identical

(76%, 79%). The number of people contacted did not differ based on respondents' initial knowledge source.

Coping Responses

Use of Coping Responses. A 5 x 2 x 2 mixed ANCOVA was conducted to examine the use of five coping responses: news media use, discussion, support seeking, positive thinking, and distraction. Gender and whether people contacted others were between-subjects variables. Regarding RQ5, the analysis revealed a main effect of coping response, $F(4,1444) = 8.34, p < .001$. The most common way of coping was news media use ($M = 5.69_d$), followed by discussion with others ($M = 4.86_c$). Both of these responses were used more often than positive thinking ($M = 2.70_b$) and seeking support ($M = 2.51_b$). Distraction ($M = 1.90_a$) was used least often.

The analysis also revealed a main effect of gender, $F(1, 361) = 12.43, p < .001$, and an interaction between gender and coping response, $F(4,1444) = 5.39, p < .001$. Overall, women reported greater use of coping responses than men, but this difference was primarily limited to two ways of coping. Compared to men, women reported significantly higher levels of support seeking ($Ms = 3.03$ vs. 2.00) and positive thinking ($Ms = 2.95$ vs. 2.44), but the two genders did not differ in the other coping responses.

Regarding RQ6, Table 17.1 shows that use of the five coping responses differed across the four emotions (see the second step of each analysis). Upset was associated with more support seeking, and less positive thinking and distraction. Both sadness and fear were associated with more support seeking and news media use. Finally, anger was associated with more discussion and support seeking, and with marginally more news media use.

Coping and Interpersonal News Diffusion. Regarding RQ7, the ANCOVA also revealed a main effect of contacting others, $F(1,361) = 17.41, p < .001$, which was qualified by an interaction with coping response, $F(4,1444) = 3.62, p < .01$. As Table 17.2 shows, individuals who contacted others to share the news were significantly more likely to cope through discussion, support seeking, and positive thinking. Whether respondents contacted others was unrelated to their use of news media or distraction. Partial correlations between the number of people contacted and each of the five coping responses revealed two significant correlations. Respondents who coped by discussing the events ($pr = .32, p < .001$) and by seeking support ($pr = .21, p < .001$) contacted a greater number of people. There were no

Table 17.2. Adjusted Means Associated with the Interaction Between Coping Response and Personal News Diffusion

	Personal News Diffusion	
	No	Yes
Use of news media	5.63_e	5.74_e
Discussion	4.45_d	5.20_e
Support seeking	2.12_{ab}	2.91_c
Positive thinking	2.42_b	2.98_c
Distraction	1.89_a	1.91_{ab}

Note. Scores could range from 0 to 6. Means with no subscripts in common differ at $p < .05$ using Scheffé comparisons.

differences between men and women in any of the relationships between interpersonal news diffusion and coping.

DISCUSSION

News of the terrorist attacks diffused very quickly among the participants in this study. More than half learned of the events within 30 minutes, and diffusion was nearly complete within 2 1/2 hours. Half of the respondents were informed by an interpersonal source. The rapid diffusion of news and the importance of interpersonal communication in this process are consistent with prior research on diffusion of dramatic news events (Greenberg, 1964b; Rogers, 2000).

In this study, upset was associated with more significant predictors than were sadness, fear, or anger. Upset is also the only measured response that is not generally considered a primary emotion (Izard, 1991). Rather, *upset* usually refers to a more generalized form of personal distress, a high-arousal, self-focused response to suffering (e.g., Batson, Fultz, & Schoenrade, 1987; Tomkins, 1984). Perhaps this emotion label more fully captured the range of affective responses that people experienced simultaneously in response to the terrorist attacks.

Individuals who learned of the events earlier felt more upset. Being aware of the sudden, unexpected events as they transpired may have contributed to more intense feelings of emotional distress (cf. Pettey et al., 1986). The other three emotions are linked more closely to knowledge that emerged over time: the massive loss of life (sadness), the fact that terrorists intentionally targeted the United States (anger), and the possibility of future attacks (fear).

Those who learned of the events from television were more upset and angrier than those who learned from an interpersonal source. Television may have produced stronger emotional responses through its ability to provoke "direct responses" similar to those in nonmediated experience. The pictures and sounds of television create relatively accurate representations of objects, places, and people, and allow viewers to vicariously experience events (Lombard, 1995). When people learned of the attacks from television, they were able to watch and hear the events almost as if they were involved in a nonmediated experience. Research also shows that negative images, in particular, increase negative emotional responses and arousal (Lang, Newhagen, & Reeves, 1996). In contrast, the portrayal of the events by other sources (e.g., radio, interpersonal communication) would have lacked the visual immediacy and verisimilitude of television. It is not clear, however, why the initial source did not influence fear or sadness. Perhaps the factors that were most likely to induce these emotions (i.e., death, threat of future attack) were more abstract and thus were not depicted on screen, especially in the first few hours after the attacks. In contrast, the sight of the planes crashing into buildings may have had a strong influence on both anger and more generalized feelings of emotional upset.

Consistent with prior research on responses to tragic news (e.g., Cantor, Mares, & Oliver, 1994; Javaratne, Flanagan, & Anderman, 1996), this study found that women experienced more upset, sadness, and fear than did men. Additionally, anger was greater among men than women. Literature on emotion in other contexts shows similar gender differences. Inwardly focused negative emotions, such as sadness, fear, and anxiety, tend to be higher among females and, at least in some contexts, outwardly directed negative emotions such as anger tend to be higher among males (Brody & Hall, 2000).

Replicating prior research (Kubey & Peluso, 1990; Riffe & Stovall, 1989), this study found that individuals who experienced stronger emotional responses were more likely to engage in interpersonal news diffusion. These results are consistent with evidence that negative affect motivates people to affiliate with others (see Luminet et al., 2000). In this study, individuals who experienced stronger emotions, especially anger, also contacted a greater number of people to pass along the news. Anger is associated with an external focus and a high level of activation, which may have motivated people to contact others. In fact, anger was the only emotion that was significantly associated with using discussion as a way of coping.

Of course, it is possible that the link between emotion and interpersonal news diffusion reflects the influence of personal contact on emotion rather than the reverse. Talking about tragic news events can be either comforting or distressing, depending on the circumstances. When people are upset or angry, they may seek and receive support and reassurance. On the other hand, through conversation, others may express their own distress or inflame already existing feelings of anger.

Although this study did not measure reasons for interpersonal news diffusion, people's coping responses provided some insight into why they shared the news with others. Specifically, individuals who contacted others were more likely to cope using discussion, support seeking, and positive thinking. Additionally, those who used discussion and support contacted a greater number of people. Thus, it appears that seeking information (through discussion) and support were among the reasons that people in this study diffused the news. These findings support Gantz and Trenholm's (1979) position that interpersonal news diffusion is the result of several needs, including informational needs, affective needs, and social needs.

This study also found that both the time individuals heard the news and the source from which they heard influenced interpersonal news diffusion. Those who learned earlier were more likely to contact others, and contacted a greater number of people. This pattern may reflect a desire to keep others informed (Gantz & Trenholm, 1979). Those who learned from the mass media were more likely to contact others, although they did not contact more people. Similar to the early learners, those who were informed via the mass media (e.g., TV at home, radio in the car) may have been more likely than those informed personally to assume that other people did not yet know what had happened. Many early studies found that learning of crises interpersonally led to more interpersonal communication. Greenberg (1964a), for example, argued that some people tend to place themselves in situations that maximize interpersonal contact, where they can be reached and can reach others. However, in the past, more interpersonal news diffusion undoubtedly occurred by word of mouth. Today, the widespread use of cell phones means that people can easily reach others by telephone from virtually any location.

Participants clearly wanted more information during the first few hours after the attacks. News media use and discussion with others were by far the most common coping responses that people reported using. Other methods that could help reduce emotional responses, but yet allowed people to maintain attention to the developing story, were used somewhat less often: thinking positively and seeking social support. Given the magnitude of the events and the continuing uncertainties, it is not surprising that distraction was the least used way of coping.

Consistent with several studies (e.g., Laux & Weber, 1991), coping responses differed across the four emotions. When coping with upset, sadness, and fear, respondents primarily sought support. Anger was associated with more discussion, and to a lesser extent, support. Although angry individuals may have been motivated to discuss the events, it is possible that discussion also contributed to their anger. News media use was significantly associated only with sadness. Again, individuals who felt more intense sadness may have sought news media in an effort to obtain reassuring news (e.g., about rescues and reunions), but it is also possible that continued exposure to the news increased sadness.

Some limitations of this study should be noted. The use of a convenience sample of college students limits the generalizability of the results. Although the goal of this study was not to provide descriptive data, it is possible that the role of emotion and coping in the diffusion process would be different within different subgroups of people. Additionally, the 3-week delay between the events and the initial data collection raises the question of whether respondents were able to accurately recall their responses that first day. Although we asked people whom they contacted and how, we did not ask them their reasons for contacting others, what they spoke about, or how their conversations affected their emotions. This type of information would further elucidate the process of interpersonal news diffusion. Future research should explore these issues, and should examine the role of emotion in the diffusion of other types of news stories.

18

Fear, Grief, and Sympathy Responses to the Attacks

William J. Brown
Regent University
Mihai Bocarnea
Regent University
Michael Basil
University of Lethbridge

There are relatively few moments in history that are so dramatic that people remember where they were and what they were doing when they first learned of the event through the news media or interpersonal communication. Such events for those living today include the Japanese attack on Pearl Harbor, the assassination of President John F. Kennedy (Greenberg, 1964a, 1964b; Hill & Bonjean, 1964; Mendelsohn, 1964), the *Challenger* space shuttle disaster (Kubey & Peluso, 1990; Riff & Stovall, 1989), the tragic death of Princess Diana (W. Brown, Basil, & Bocarnea, 1998), and now, the September 11, 2001 terrorist attacks on the United States. Since D. Miller's (1945) seminal work on news diffusion, there have been more than five decades of studies on how news disseminates, particularly for dramatic events. DeFleur (1987) noted the spontaneous way in which most of this research has been conducted, asking questions of different groups of participants in different sociocultural settings about different news stories, making it difficult to advance our understanding about why news stories diffuse the way they do. Equally important is our need to better understand how news stories influence people's attitudes, beliefs, and behavior.

The purpose of this chapter is to provide an analysis of the initial public responses to these terrorist attacks. First, we discuss why news diffusion is different today as compared to 20 or 30 years ago. Second, we explain the nature of media events and discuss why the news of the September 11 attacks should be studied within this context. Third, we discuss the emotional nature of media events and why researchers should focus more attention on emotion rather than almost exclusively on cognition. Fourth, we provide an analysis of the diffusion of the September 11 story and an analysis of the cognitive and affective responses to the story through a large sample of people who completed a Web-based survey posted the day after the attack. Finally, we discuss the implications of these findings.

The first of six generalizations about news diffusion that DeFleur (1987) offered after analyzing four decades of news diffusion studies was that changing media technologies in the United States have influenced the way in which important news is diffused. This has been more clearly apparent since the advent of 24-hour cable news networks such as CNN. What has been learned about news diffusion from 1991 through 2001 is different in some aspects as compared to what was learned from 1945 through 1990. We have known that studying interpersonal and mass communication as separate processes is theoretically and pragmatically disadvantageous (Reardon & Rogers, 1988; Rosengren, 1973), but recent studies in the past decade have provided evidence that shows the complex ways in which people communicate and seek information through a web of interrelated communication networks, both mediated and face to face (Basil & Brown, 1994; Bocarnea, 2001; Kiesler & Kraut, 1999; Tardy & Hale, 1998).

The proliferation of new communication technology around the world has given us access to more news stories than at any time in history. We can now read the *Indian Straight Times* in the morning, check the weather in Hong Kong before going to lunch, read a European stock market report from London in the afternoon, and monitor the war against terrorists in remote mountain regions and jungles in the evening. We also can communicate with people across the globe in real time or asynchronously. The connectivity of the Internet with print news services, radio, and television networks has blurred the distinctions between mediated and nonmediated communication.

When major events in the world do occur, the great breadth of connectivity gives individuals much more timely access to information. Shortly after the terrorist attacks, one author received e-mails offering prayers and condolences from friends and acquaintances who lived in Thailand, India, Hong Kong, Taiwan, the Philippines, and Australia, to name a few. These e-mails arose out of spontaneous emotional reactions to news of the attacks that had reached people within minutes from the time that the first plane struck the towers. News today travels very rapidly, across great distances and across cultural, economic, social, political, and religious boundaries, through a complex web of interpersonal and mediated relationships enabled by interlocking communication networks.

NEWS DIFFUSION DURING MEDIA EVENTS

Planned news coverage of a major public event or spectacle was first referred to by Jun and Dayan (1986) as a media event. These authors described *media events* as being characterized by news coverage that (a) interrupts regularly scheduled programming, (b) is broadcast simultaneously by competing media outlets, and (c) is experienced with other people as a group activity. Brown, Duane, and Fraser (1997) extended the concept of media events by noting unplanned media coverage of relatively spontaneous events, such as the *Challenger* disaster, the bombing of Baghdad during the Persian Gulf War, and the police chase of OJ Simpson in June 1995, can have the same influential characteristics as planned media events.

Beginning with the Persian Gulf War in 1991, CNN began to systematically produce programming to foster media events by using techniques common in the production of entertainment programs. For example, CNN began titling their news coverage of specific events the way entertainment serials are titled, such as "Crisis in the Gulf" and "The Simpson Trial." CNN's coverage of the September 11 attack on the United States followed this pattern, with in-depth attention given to heroes and villains, defined plots, familiar sets, and even background music. It is no accident that news networks incorporated the production values and techniques of serial dramas to boost audience ratings of their news coverage. The use of drama is also intended to increase the propensity of individuals to tell other family members and friends to join them in their media consumption.

News stories diffuse much more rapidly, more extensively, and through more communication channels during media events than do ordinary news stories. Ongoing news coverage of the September 11 attacks made it nearly impossible to avoid repeated exposure to this story. It is important to analyze how individuals learn about news during media events and how that news affects them. Unlike many previous studies of how various communities of media consumers learn about a major news event, our focus here is on how individuals react when confronted with a major news story, or in this case, when enveloped in a major media event.

Some individuals who are exposed to a major story may not do anything in response to their exposure. Others will immediately seek to tell their family members, friends, and co-workers about the event. Additionally, many individuals will seek out more information from the news media or from other individuals about the event. Some will spend a considerable amount of time talking to other people about the event and consuming more media coverage. Through the analysis of individual responses, we can learn more about the process of how news stories influence people's communication behavior and subsequent media consumption.

EMOTIONAL RESPONSES TO NEWS STORIES

The dramatic nature of major news events such as the sacrifice of national heroes (Riffe & Stovall, 1989), the fall of a sports celebrity (Brown, Duane, & Fraser, 1997), and the death of a princess (W. Brown et al., 1998), produces strong emotional reactions. The investigation of the role of emotion in news diffusion has received very little scholarly attention as compared to the study of cognition. News carries emotion, especially when communicated verbally and visually. The paralinguistic characteristics of broadcast journalists and the powerful influence of still and moving pictures have important affective dimensions that can reinforce or change the attitudes, beliefs, and behaviors of news consumers.

After the assassination of President Kennedy, Banta (1964) documented a range of emotions experienced by those who had received the news, including anger, excitement, grief, and nervousness. Riffe and Stovall (1989) measured the degree to which people were emotionally upset by the fatal crash of the space shuttle *Challenger*. Gantz and Trenholm (1979) discovered that one of the primary motives for passing on news to others was emotional in nature. The visits by hundreds of thousands of people to the World Trade Center (WTC) site in New York has much more to do with emotional responses to the September 11 news story than to cognitive responses. Here, we seek to assess how the emotional reactions to the September 11 attacks might have influenced the diffusion of this news story.

RESEARCH QUESTIONS AND HYPOTHESES

Consistent with the early work of Katz and Lazarsfeld (1955) and numerous news diffusion studies (DeFleur, 1987), it is expected that both the mass media and individuals are responsible for the diffusion of information through a community. Specifically, research has shown that the importance of a news event affects the extent to which the news is diffused. Learning about a major news story that moves people emotionally is expected to enhance its diffusion and influence.

Three research questions that focus on three emotions were posed in the study discussed here:

RQ1: Will learning about the terrorist attacks through the news media be associated with greater degrees of grief, fear, and sympathy than when learning about the attacks through interpersonal communication?

RQ2: Will people's degree of grief, fear, and sympathy be positively associated with their propensity to pass the news of the attacks on to others?

RQ3: Will people's degree of grief, fear, and sympathy be positively associated with the amount of time they discuss the attacks with others?

One additional question compares the patterns of learning about the terrorist attacks with the propensity to pass the news on to others, as follows:

RQ4: Are there any associations between sources of learning about the terrorist attacks and the propensity for people to pass on the news of the attacks to others?

Based on previous news diffusion research and the timing of news events, it is expected that the mass media will provide the initial means of learning about the terrorist attacks, but then interpersonal communication channels will dominate the means of diffusion. Because of the time of the attacks, we expect that most people will learn of the news through co-workers. The following hypotheses test these expectations:

H1: The diffusion of the September 11 news story will more likely occur through an interpersonal

communication channel than through any single
media channel.
H2: Among those who learn of the attacks through an
interpersonal communication channel, more people
will learn the news from a co-worker than from any
other interpersonal source.

The next set of hypotheses test relationships between
information sources and emotion in the news diffusion process.
Television news images can illicit powerful emotional responses
(Newhagen, 1998). Previous research has suggested that television is
better able to evoke emotional responses than other media (Haudhuri
& Buck, 1995). Lang, Newhagen, and Reeves (1996) found that
negative news images produced greater effects on news consumers,
including increases in message attention, message processing, and
message retrieval. The added dimension of motion alone, not present
in print or radio news, has strong emotional effects (Simons,
Detenber, Roedema, & Reiss, 1999). Initial support for Lang's (2000)
information-processing model also suggests that television news has
a greater capacity to produce emotional responses as compared to
other media.
We expect that those who learn the news of the attacks
through television will respond with greater emotion than those who
learn of the attacks through interpersonal interactions or other
media sources. We also expect that television news will create
greater detailed knowledge of the attacks as compared to other
information sources. These expectations were tested as follows:

H3: Television news viewing of the terrorist attacks will
be more positively associated with emotional
responses to the attacks than will other sources of
following the news story.
H4: Television news viewing of the terrorist attacks will
be more positively associated with detailed
knowledge of the attacks than will other sources of
following this news story.

Finally, we also sought to assess the relationship between
sources of learning about this news story and people's subsequent
beliefs and communication behaviors. Because television can
generate high degrees of audience involvement, we expect that those
who watch the television news coverage will be more motivated to
discuss the terrorist attacks with others than those who follow the
story through other information sources. We also expect that

television coverage of the attacks will have a greater influence on forming people's attributions of who caused the attacks than will other information sources. We tested the following hypotheses:

H5: Exposure to television news coverage of the terrorist attacks will be positively associated with the amount of time people discuss the attacks with others.

H6: Exposure to television news coverage of the terrorist attacks will be positively associated with attributions that Islamic radicals are responsible for these attacks.

METHOD

A survey questionnaire was posted on a university Web site and advertised with various search engines in the United States on September 12. More than 1,000 people from more than 30 countries responded to the survey. For this study, we only report the U.S. data ($N = 734$). Because of the unusual nature of this media event, the nonrandom sample is not expected to be as much of a limitation in addressing our research objectives as would normally be the case. Demographic comparisons of people who use the Web versus people who do not use the Web in our own research shows that differences are narrowing over time. MSNBC (2002) reported that 143 million people (54% of the total U.S. population) are now online. Most data were collected in the first few days of the terrorist attacks; therefore, the accuracy of recall is expected to be high.

Survey Questionnaire

The survey questionnaire consisted of 49 questions. The survey included 11 categorical fixed-response items, 10 open-ended quantitative questions, 20 fixed alternative questions using a standardized 5-point Likert scale (agree–disagree), seven categorical demographic items, and one qualitative open-ended question at the end of the survey.

Measured Variables

Two composite variables were constructed through the analysis of the Likert-scale questions based on factor and reliability analyses. The resulting factor structure of these 20 items revealed three factors. The first factor (with 6 items), which explained 26% of the total variance, was labeled as the Belief that foreign Islamic radicals had carried out the September 11 terrorist attacks, with a Cronbach alpha of .73. The range for this scale was 1 to 5, where 1 represents a strong attribution of blame for the attacks to foreign Islamic radicals. The mean of this scale was 1.98 and the standard deviation was 0.64. The second factor (with 4 items) explained 15% of the total variance and was labeled Fear, with a Cronbach alpha of .74. The range for this scale was also 1 to 5, where 1 represents a strong degree of fear, with a mean of 2.98 and a standard deviation of 0.97.

Three questionnaire items loaded on the third factor, which explained 9% of the variance and was labeled Emotional Concern for victims of the attacks. The Cronbach coefficient alpha of this scale was below .60 and deemed unreliable. Thus, all variables other than attribution of blame and fear were measured by single questionnaire items.

Decision Rules

The reliability criterion used was a minimum Cronbach coefficient alpha of .60. Also, because three different emotions are being evaluated on individual hypotheses, predicted associations for at least two of the three emotions must be supported by the analyses in order for the overall hypothesis to be supported. We used $p < .01$ level to support statistical significance because of our large sample size. Finally, all beta coefficients reported are standardized regression coefficients.

RESULTS

Before analyzing the research questions and hypotheses, a correlation analysis was conducted with all the primary continuous variables in the study. Correlations among the independent variables in the study were checked for multicollinearity. No problems were found. Less than 10% of the correlation coefficients reported among the variables are above .20 and none are above .40. The correlation matrix resulting from this analysis is provided in Table 18.1.

Diffusion of the News Story

The second analysis provides an understanding of how this news story diffused among the respondents in the study. Results indicate

Table 18.1. Pearson Correlation Coefficients Study Variables

	PASSNEWS	TVNEWS	RADNEWS	NETNEWS	TALKNEWS	BELIEF	FEAR	GRIEF	SYMPATHY	AWARE
PASSNEWS	1.00									
TVNEWS	.01	1.00								
RADNEWS	.23**	.16**	1.00							
NETNEWS	.01	.00	.20**	1.00						
TALKNEWS	.11**	.28**	.04	.06	1.00					
BELIEF	.05	.22**	.05	.03	.09*	1.00				
FEAR	.01	.12**	.00	.05	.08	.21**	1.00			
GRIEF	.04	.08*	.04	.02	.01	.18**	.25**	1.00		
SYMPATHY	.04	.21**	.00	.04	.04	.23**	.16**	.36**	1.00	
AWARE	.02	.20**	.01	.06	.02	.10**	.02	.11**	.13**	1.00

$*p < .05; **p < .01$

PASSNEWS = passing news of the attacks on to others
TVNEWS = hours watching TV news coverage of attacks
RADNEWS = hours listening to radio coverage of attacks
NETNEWS = hours reading Internet coverage of attacks
TALKNEWS = hours discussing attacks on September 11

BELIEFS = Islamic radicals responsible
FEAR = personal fear because of attacks
GRIEF = personal grief because of attacks
SYMPATHY = identifying with attack victims
AWARE = awareness of details of the attacks

that those who learned about the first plane striking the WTC towers were more likely to learn through television (40%) than through an interpersonal interaction (35%) or any other media source. Those who learned about the second plane striking the towers were more likely to hear first through an interpersonal communication source (54%), than through radio (23%) or television (21%). Learning the news through interpersonal communication continued to be the primary source of learning for the remainder of the morning. After lunch, however, television then retook the top spot as the number one source of learning the story, slightly ahead of interpersonal communication. Radio faded into the background as the third most popular information source from 10 a.m. and on throughout the day. Only 1% of the total sample learned the news through the Internet. Table 18.2 provides these results.

Based on these results, we collapsed the data into two categories, those who learned the news through a media source and those who learned the news through interpersonal communication. We then conducted a chi-square analysis, which verified our expectation that this news diffused in significantly different patterns across both interpersonal and mass media channels over time (χ^2 (8) = 46.6, $p < .001$ for Table 18.2; χ^2 (4) = 34.1, $p < .01$ for Table 18.3). A comparison of the story's diffusion through interpersonal and media channels is in Table 18.3.

Research Questions

The first research question explored the relationships between the information sources by which people learned of the terrorist attacks and the emotions they experienced. Results of an analysis of variance indicate that there is no relationship between how a person learned about the attacks and the strength of his or her emotional reactions [$F(5,724) = .40, p = .78$]. Post-hoc comparisons using Bonferroni t-tests further verified that different information sources did not produce significant differences in respondents' degree of grief, fear, and sympathy.

A correlation analysis was conducted to explore the second research question. Results indicate there is no significant association between respondents' emotional reactions and their propensity to pass the news of the attacks on to others. None of the correlation coefficients were significant at the $p < .01$ level and only one coefficient was significant at $p < .05$, as indicated in the correlation matrix in Table 18.1.

Table 18.2. Cross Tabulations of the Number of Respondents who Reported How They First Learned the News of the Attacks and the Time Period (EST) When They Learned It

Source of News	8-8:59	9-9:59	10-10:59	11-11:59	Afternoon	Total
Someone told me	46	211	106	21	7	391
Television	53	82	26	5	8	174
Radio	29	88	18	7	4	146
Internet	2	3	4	10	10	
Totals	130	384	154	34	19	721

Table 18.3. Cross Tabulations of the Number of Respondents who First Learned the News Through Media and Interpersonal Communication Channels and the Time Period (EST) When They Learned It

Source of News	8-8:59	9-9:59	10-10:59	11-11:59	Afternoon	Total
Interpersonal	46	211	106	21	7	391
Mass media	84	173	48	13	12	330
Totals	130	384	154	34	19	721

The third research question also was explored by a correlation analysis. Results indicate there were no significant relationships between the strength of respondents' emotional reactions to the attacks and the number of hours they spent discussing the attacks with others. None of the correlation coefficients between these variables in Table 18.1 were significant at $p < .01$.

Finally, we analyzed the relationship between sources of learning of the terrorist attacks and the propensity to tell others about the attacks. Analysis of variance results indicate there is no significant relationship between these two variables [$F(5,724) = .50, p = .78$].

Hypotheses

The first hypothesis, which predicted that the diffusion of the September 11 news story would more likely occur through an interpersonal communication channel than through any single media channel, was not supported by the results.

The second hypothesis, which predicted that among those who learn of the attacks through an interpersonal communication channel, more people will learn the news from a co-worker than through any other type of interpersonal relationship, was supported [$\chi^2 (df = 4 = 141.08, p < .01$].

Hypotheses 3 and 4 predicted that television news viewing of the terrorist attacks would be more positively associated with emotional responses to the attacks and detailed knowledge of the attacks as compared to other media coverage. Regression analysis results indicate that respondents' exposure to the television coverage of the attacks was not significantly associated with their degree of grief ($\beta = .08, p = .03$), but was significantly associated with their degree of fear ($\beta = .12, p < .01$) and sympathy ($\beta = .21, p < .01$). Other media and interpersonal communication sources did not exhibit significant associations. Therefore, the third hypothesis was supported.

The fourth hypothesis also was supported by regression analysis results. Those who watched more hours of television coverage of the attacks had more detailed knowledge of the attacks as compared to learning through other information sources ($\beta = .18, p < .01$). This was not the case with other media or interpersonal communication sources. Television news coverage explained 4% of the total variance in detailed knowledge of the terrorist attacks.

Hypothesis 5, which predicted that exposure to television news coverage of the terrorist attacks would be positively associated with the amount of time people discussed the attacks with others, also was supported by regression analysis results ($\beta = .28$, $p < .01$). Respondents' exposure to television news coverage explained 8% of the total variance in discussion time on the day of the attacks.

The last hypothesis predicted that exposure to television news coverage of the terrorist attacks would be positively associated with attributions that foreign Islamic radicals were responsible for these attacks. Regression results provide support for this hypothesis ($\beta = .224$, $p < .01$). Exposure to television news explained 5% of the total variance in attributing blame to Islamic radicals outside the United States.

DISCUSSION

Some results are consistent with previous research findings and some provide new understanding of how emotion relates to news diffusion. Three of the research questions covered the same ground as Riffe and Stovall's (1989) study of the *Challenger* disaster. They hypothesized that emotional responses to this tragedy would be prompted by learning about it through the media, and those who saw the disaster on television would be more emotionally upset and more likely to pass the information on to others. Consistent with our findings, none of their hypotheses were supported by their data.

We expected that those who saw the planes crash into the WTC towers would experience more grief, fear, and sympathy than those who learned about the attacks another way. This was not the case. We also expected that stronger emotional reactions would produce stronger communication behavior in terms of passing the story on to others and talking to others about the attack for longer periods of time. This also did not occur. We attribute both our findings and those of the *Challenger* study to the characteristics of a dramatic media event. People were emotionally shocked by both tragedies, regardless of how they first learned of the story. We talked with a number of people who said they had to watch the television footage of the planes crashing into the towers over and over again because it was difficult to accept that the attacks actually had occurred. Our respondents could only report their emotions at the time they completed the survey. By then, those emotional effects seemed to have found a common level.

Those who were glued to the television in the morning after hearing of the attacks likely stayed there. Those who first saw the planes hit the towers on television were not more likely to tell others about it during the next hour. However, those who first learned about the attack on radio were more likely to tell others. We suspect that once those listening to the radio while traveling or working heard the news, they wanted to contact someone immediately to get more information, particularly someone who had access to a television.

Although interpersonal communication clearly played an important role in the diffusion of this story, it was not the dominant role through all phases of the diffusion process. Most of the earliest learners of the story learned through television. These results provide support for a statement we posed earlier, that news diffusion occurs through a complex web of mediated and nonmediated communication channels. One cannot easily conclude that one communication channel is more important than another channel in the diffusion of a major story like the September 11 attacks.

Television news plays an important role in influencing beliefs and emotions. Exposure to other media and interpersonal communication sources was not significantly associated with respondents' beliefs about the terrorists responsible for these attacks. This is a rather striking finding and demonstrates the power of visual images. Seeing the terrorist attacks and pictures of the terrorists provided a persuasive argument that foreign Islamic extremists carried out these attacks. Other information sources did not produce that persuasive effect. Although television news provides less information than many other news sources, the visual information seems to have been more persuasive than the nonvisual information.

One implication of our study is that the patterns of mass media use and interpersonal communication may be much more complex today than in the past. New communication technology allows people many options in learning about historic events and provides many options of how they can pass on their knowledge and emotional reactions to others. In hindsight, we wish we had also measured telephone and cell phone use, because these networks undoubtedly provided important channels for interpersonal communication.

A second implication is that instantaneous visual communication may enhance awareness and learning and even the emotional force of a news story, but more emotion does not necessarily enhance the diffusion of news. Certainly more research on emotion is needed, but what we assumed with the *Challenger* disaster and with the September 11 attacks was not supported. Future studies should continue to assess the emotional content and affective attributes of news stories and the role that emotion plays in the diffusion of knowledge and beliefs. Like previous studies of dramatic historic events, the intersection of emotion and communication behavior provides a rich testing ground for the study of news diffusion.

19

Emotional Involvement in the Attacks

Mary M. Step
Case Western Reserve University
Margaret O. Finucane
John Carroll University
Cary W. Horvath
Slippery Rock University

The media cover a variety of crisis events (e.g., assassinations, natural disasters, technical disasters) as if viewers were really there (Katz, 1980; Perse, 2001). As real as these events can seem, viewers perceive them through the conventions and lens of media organizations. However, this does not make viewers responses to them any less real. People experience deep emotional responses to mediated traumatic events (Zillmann & Bryant, 1994). Individuals' involvement with disaster stories reflects the universality of loss and their shared emotional experience as humans.

Media involvement can reflect both cognitive and emotional participation with media content (Perse, 1990; A. Rubin & Rubin, 2001). In the case of disaster coverage, emotional involvement may be a much more encompassing event, coloring our thoughts, attitudes, and actions for an indefinite time. Although researchers have studied various media processes immediately after a disaster or crisis, few have focused on audience responses to mediated versions of the event. Our purpose here is to try to understand emotional involvement with media during a disaster from a psychological perspective, particularly that of appraisal theory.

Appraisal theory is an explanation of emotions that suggest they result from evaluations of events and situations (Roseman & Smith, 2001). Furthermore, the appraisal process assumes a motivational component to emotions. Communication researchers have successfully used this theory to explain affective experiences in both interpersonal communication and media (Dillard, Kinney, & Cruz, 1996; Step, 1998).

Emotional involvement is an important predictor of media effects and a signature experience for audiences (Perse, 1990; Zillmann & Bryant, 1994). Without emotional involvement, drama, humor, and even documentary, would be empty and one dimensional. In the case of a mediated disaster we have an opportunity to tap into a communal experience with emotional involvement across a large audience.

DISASTERS AS MEDIA EVENTS

Disasters have been defined as "overwhelming events and circumstances that test the adaptational response of community or individuals beyond their capability, and lead, at least temporarily, to massive disruption of function for community or individual" (Raphael, 1986, p. 5). Disasters can be man-made (e.g., chemical spills) or natural (e.g., earthquakes) occurrences, however, both types are threatening and necessitate a return to stability.

Disasters not only disrupt a community, but, paradoxically, tend to bring people together (Raphael, 1986). Diffusion researchers noted an increased willingness among respondents to become involved with others following an unanticipated news event (Kubey & Peluso, 1990; Riffe & Stovall, 1989). Following the *Challenger* disaster, those who experienced stronger emotional reactions to the news were more likely to inform others, talk in order to feel better, and spend more time talking (Riffe & Stovall, 1989).

Disasters and unexpected crisis events are major news stories that captivate audiences (Zillmann & Bryant, 1994). These stories break media routines, are high in uncertainty and are rooted, at least at the onset, in eyewitness versus official facts (Fensch, 1990; Wilkens & Patterson, 1987). In this sense, the coverage is likely to emphasize the emotional response of victims and relatives, typified by shock, anxiety, and excitement. Clearly, viewing disaster coverage is likely to be characterized by high audience levels of emotional involvement.

EMOTIONAL INVOLVEMENT

Emotional involvement is the degree to which a media user is emotionally engaged with a media experience, content, or characters (Perse, 1990; Step, 1998). This engagement is the result of experiencing any of a number of distinct positive or negative emotions in response to media stimuli, and these emotional responses can vary in intensity and duration.

Initial research conceptualized emotional involvement as part of the larger construct of media involvement (Perse, 1990). People's emotional responses during news viewing were positively related to instrumental motives (e.g., information-seeking) as well as increased elaboration (i.e., thinking). However, people also can experience emotions through mediated interpersonal behavior.

Parasocial interaction also has been used to represent emotional involvement (A. Rubin & Step, 2000). Parasocial interaction is the feeling of interpersonal connection to a specific media persona (A. Rubin, Perse, & Powell, 1985). Media users turn to interpersonal contacts in times of crisis. Thus, emotional involvement with media may be experienced interpersonally as well as intrapersonally.

Television viewing can be thought of as a social activity (Babrow, 1990; Lemish, 1985; Lull, 1980). People viewing together in the same room (i.e., co-viewers) construct a shared reality through their common experience. Co-viewing research in communication focuses primarily on everyday television viewing by parents and children (Nathanson, 2001), and in marriages (Finucane & Horvath, 2000). No research to date has considered co-viewing in a crisis or disaster situation. It is expected that co-viewing during a disaster would be a rich opportunity to share emotions, reduce uncertainty, and reinforce pre-existing relational bonds.

In summary, emotional involvement with media is experienced as a sense of engagement with media content that can be facilitated by parasocial responses to media persona, or co-viewing activities with other media users. Emotion theorists provide further assistance in explaining how emotions function in psychological models of media use.

APPRAISAL THEORY

Appraisal theorists see emotions as the outcome of continuous appraisal of the environment (e.g., Frijda, 1993; Scherer, Schorr, &

Johnstone, 2001). The appraisal model is simple. When an event or stimulus is perceived, a person automatically makes judgments about features of that event (e.g., potential harm). The patterned set of judgments that emerge constitute an appraisal. Although universal appraisals have not been established (Schorr, 2001), smaller sets, applicable to specific social contexts have (Dillard, Kinney, & Cruz, 1996; Dillard, Plotnick, Godbold, Friemuth, & Edgar, 1996). Appraisals that have consistently emerged include valence, attentional activity, certainty/predictability, relevance, novelty, and legitimacy/fairness (Dillard, Kinney, & Cruz; Scherer, 1993). Different patterns of appraisals correspond to distinct emotional experiences.

The appraisal model is compatible with audience-centered explanations of media effects. Emotions are responses to environmental appraisals. In this sense, emotions mediate message effects. On an individual level, emotion intensity defines media involvement. On an interpersonal level, co-viewing also provides a setting for testing emotions. During a crisis, appraisals and emotions will likely be discussed by co-viewers as salient features of the event. In this way, co-viewers may facilitate or inhibit emotional responses and subsequent outcomes.

We applied this logic to a naturally occurring, emotionally charged event witnessed by hundreds of millions of television viewers. This unprecedented event offered a unique opportunity to investigate intense emotional involvement with media experiences.

Appraisal theory assumes that features of an event produce appraisals that result in emotions. This raises the question as to what features of the event were salient enough to produce an emotional response. In other words, what were some of the structural features of the story that constituted common appraisals among television viewers that day? Therefore, we posed the following research question:

RQ1: What were some common aspects of the 9/11 story
       that produced emotional response?

Appraisal theorists suggest that emotions are also accompanied by a motivational component (Frijda, Kuipers, & ter Schure, 1989; Roseman, Wiest, & Swartz, 1994) sometimes referred to as an *action tendency* (Izard, 1991). One of the most useful applications of appraisal theory to media use models is in providing a potential explanation for effects. If consistent action tendencies are associated with distinct emotions, then we may have a powerful explanatory mechanism for a variety of media effects. Media involvement in general is associated with a greater likelihood of content related media effects (A. Rubin, 1994). Our second research question was:

RQ2: What behaviors or activities were motivated by emotional responses to 9/11 television coverage?

Given that crisis content tends to bring people together interpersonally, we were interested in why people would want to coview the event with others. Although interpersonal communication motives are well documented, we did not expect the same reasons to be salient (R. Rubin, Perse, & Barbato, 1988). For example, communicating for pleasure, escape, or relaxation did not make much sense in this context.

Second, we were particularly interested in the conversational topics generated during coviewing. Initial descriptions of these topics should provide information about the role and expression of emotional response during a mediated disaster. Therefore, the final two research questions were:

RQ3: What are the reasons people co-view during a mediated disaster?
RQ4: What kinds of topics are expressed while co-viewing a mediated disaster?

In sum, we explored emotional involvement with media via individual appraisal, emotion intensity, action tendency, and co-viewing experience.

METHOD

Similar to media effects models, appraisals are investigated primarily through retrospective self-reports (Schorr, 2001). Although there is criticism that accumulated memory may contaminate recollection of original emotional experiences, most appraisal researchers ask respondents to recall a "salient and recent emotional encounter" (Schorr, 2001, p. 337). This method is supported by evidence that emotional events are better remembered than other events, especially when focused on central details (A. Burke, Heuer, & Reisberg, 1992). Here, we distributed questionnaires within 1 week of the September 11 attacks.

Sample

Data were gathered at two small private colleges in the Great Lakes area, using students to obtain survey responses from friends, family, and acquaintances over 18 years of age. The resultant group ($N = 251$) included 146 women (58%) and 100 men (40%). Age was distributed as follows: 18–29 (25%), 30–49 (38%), 50–69 (33%), and 70 or above (3%). Education level varied with 1% completing only grade school, 38% completing high school, 38% completing college, and 19% completing graduate or professional school.

Measurement

Emotional involvement was the degree of affective participation with the media coverage of the events of 9/11. We operationalized this by asking people to state their first emotion upon hearing of the events, that emotion's intensity, and ongoing amounts of several basic emotions as the event unfolded. A person's higher emotion intensity was interpreted as a greater engagement with the depiction of events.

Emotions. We chose emotions based on simplicity and utility in light of the events. They included surprise, sadness, fear, interest, anger, and disgust. Respondents were asked what their first emotion was on hearing the news. They responded by circling the emotion. A follow-up question asked the respondents to rate the intensity of their initial emotion on an interval scale of 0 (*none of this emotion*) to 10 (*the most of this emotion I could have*). Intensity for each ongoing emotion was measured the same way.

Appraisals. There are no standard appraisal scales for all situations. In fact, it is difficult to simply convert items used in other studies to mediated stimuli (see Step, 1998). Previous appraisal research tends to focus on directly experienced, individual, and interpersonal emotional events. For most people, the events of 9/11 were witnessed, not directly experienced. Here, appraisals were measured by first asking respondents, "What aspects of the story caused the intensity of your most prominent emotion?" and then examining the open-ended responses for regularities and content-analyzing them according to recurring themes. Two investigators coded all open-ended responses for the presence or absence of certain appraisals (i.e., content features). Interrater agreement was .80.

Action Tendencies. Appraisal theory assumes that emotions have motivational components (e.g., avoidance) that can be enacted in behavior (e.g., leave the premises). There is little precedent to measuring this concept in a mediated situation. People watch a variety of television content and experience many, sometimes intense emotions without leaving their sofas. We asked respondents "Did your emotional response motivate you to engage in any specific behaviors or activities?" Two investigators content-analyzed open-ended responses for recurrent themes, and interrater agreement was .92.

Motivated Co-Viewing. Another indicator of emotional involvement, motivated co-viewing conversation, was assessed by first asking respondents if they watched alone or with someone else. This was followed up by: "If you watched with someone else, describe your reasons for wanting to watch the events with the other person." Intercoder agreement in coding these reasons was .90.

RESULTS

Of this sample, 70% relied on network television or cable for information about the event. Although 42% could not pinpoint the exact number of hours they watched, another 40% watched between 5 and 14 hours that first day.

Research Questions

Research questions were addressed through content analysis of open-ended responses. Few people responded in complete sentences, and we differentiated between different objects/actors and their corresponding actions. In this way, long sentences were often broken down into thematic units (Weber, 1990). We also defined categories that we thought were mutually exclusive yet encompassing the entire range of responses.

There is some uncertainty, both in the content analysis literature and the appraisal literature as to how to code first-person accounts. In some cases, respondents answered in great detail. Others were terse, yet mentioned very different ideas that spanned categories. Coders identified the presence or absence of themes across all open-ended responses. Each respondent could mention more than one theme.

Appraisals. In the first research question, we asked what story features were producing people's emotional responses. There were 272 stated appraisals across all open-ended responses.

Four appraisal themes were identified. They included:

1. *Empathic response*, which represents an imagined connection with the experiences of others involved first hand in the event (e.g., "people jumping from the top of the WTC," "the bravery of the rescuers").
2. *Magnitude of the devastation,* which refers to the overall scope of the event (e.g., "all of the deaths and their families," "the destruction and devastation").
3. *Crash / collapse* of the buildings/Pentagon refers to the actual physical acts that defined the event (e.g., "seeing the plane go through the building," "watching the WTC collapse").
4. *Security violation*, which reflects the personal feeling of self or nation being violated by others in some way (e.g., "that certain groups feel their actions are justified," "unsafe security on the plane").

Response frequencies are provided in Table 19.1. Appraisal categories were coded only once, but respondents could mention more than one appraisal category.

Action Tendencies. The second research question concerned the motivational component or action tendency of emotional response. We asked respondents if their emotional response motivated them to engage in any specific behaviors or activities. Again, open-ended responses were content analyzed, this time using seven categories. Participants felt motivated to

1. *Help others* (e.g., "donated blood", "gave money").
2. *Connect to others interpersonally* (e.g., "talk to people," "e-mailed family and friends").

Table 19.1. Percentages of Appraisals

Appraisal	Percent (N = 272)
Empathic response	34
Magnitude	31
Crash/collapse	21
Security violation	14

3. *Watch more television* (e.g., "I was glued to the TV", "I didn't want to turn the TV off").
4. *Be more patriotic* (e.g., " displayed flag").
5. *Pray* (e.g., "began to pray," "went to prayer service").
6. *Disrupt normal activities* (e.g., "frozen for days," "cancelled plans").
7. *Elaborate* (e.g., "reflected on events," "thought about implications").

Coders identified the presence or absence of these action tendencies across all open-ended responses. Response frequencies for action tendencies (n = 270) are illustrated in Table 19.2. Some responses did not fit the category scheme. For example, 18% answered "no" to the question because they did not think their emotional responses motivated them to think or do anything. Again, action tendency categories were coded only once, but respondents could have mentioned more than one category.

Emotion Intensity

The overall initial average emotion intensity was high (M = 7.9, SD = 2.00). Not surprisingly, 66% of the sample indicated their first emotion was between 8 and 10 on the scale. The most commonly reported initial emotion on hearing the news was surprise (M = 7.68, SD = 2.07, 44%) followed by sadness (M = 8.37, SD = 1.59, 25%), fear (M = 8.22, SD = 1.36, 15%), interest (M = 6.00, SD = 2.32, 7%), anger (M = 8.27, SD = 3.00, 5%), and disgust (M = 8.22, SD = 1.71, 4%). As the event unfolded, surprise (M = 8.03, SD = 2.56) succeeded in

Table 19.2. Percentages of Action Tendencies

Action Tendency	Percent (N = 270)
Didn't motivate me	18
Help others	17
Interpersonal connection	15
Heavy television	14
Patriotic activity	12
Prayer	12
Disrupt normal routine	8
Elaboration	4

intensity by interest (M = 8.89, SD = 1.80) and sadness (M = 8.76, SD = 1.88). Overall, ongoing emotions remained high (disgust, M = 8.00, SD = 2.62; anger, M = 7.80, SD = 2.37; fear, M = 6.50, SD = 2.87). In summary, most people experienced high levels of surprise that evolved into interest or sadness.

Co-Viewing

Across the sample, 71% indicated they watched the coverage with at least one other person. Respondents also were asked to describe their reasons for watching the event with someone. Three themes emerged: *proximity* (e.g., "I was with family," "just because the other person was in the room with me"), both giving and receiving *comfort* (e.g., "someone to share the disbelief," "I wanted to be held"), and *sensemaking* or helping another understand reality (e.g., "So we could have discussion about the events," "to get more opinions"). The response frequencies are in Table 19.3.

DISCUSSION

Disasters and crises are unique media events characterized by uncertainty and emotional response. Previous research suggested interpersonal communication as a companion to witnessing mediated crisis. We identified the appraisals, emotional responses, and action tendencies of an audience that viewed an unfolding disaster as well as their reasons for co-viewing.

Appraisals are the initial component of emotions. The appraised story features include empathic responses, the magnitude of devastation, the actual crash/collapse, and security violations. It is interesting to note the appraisals vary in concreteness and specificity. For example, appraisals of the crash or collapse are tied to very specific images. On the other hand, appraisals that reflect the magnitude of the event are more diffuse and abstract.

Table 19.3. Percentages of Co-viewing Motives

Appraisal	Percent (N = 303)
Proximity	37.5
Comfort	23.5
Sensemaking	14

Previous appraisal sets have included constructs such as valence, certainty, attentional activity, relevance, novelty, and fairness (see Dillard, Kinney, & Cruz, 1996; Step, 1998). These appraisals were thought of as applying specifically to oneself, rather than a witnessed event. Although appraisals such as valence, certainty, and novelty might be easy to apply to this sample, it is also possible to find some connection to appraisals of relevance and fairness. For example, audience members were able to mentally connect to certain experiences such as being on an airplane, or being at work. This may be a way of making the disaster relevant to their own lives. More directly, fairness can be compared to the security violation appraisal. In summary, data appear to validate some of these earlier, person-based notions of appraisal.

The appraisals also appear to correspond with previous research describing disaster coverage. The appraisals reflect events of the story (crash/collapse), eyewitness accounts (empathic response), and high uncertainty (security violation). The fact that the crisis spanned a broad geographic area may account for the perceptions of magnitude. Other disaster stories/coverage should be examined in order to confirm these themes.

The second component of emotions is intensity. Emotional intensity was consistently high for both initial and ongoing responses. Surprise was the most frequent initial emotional response. Judging from the ongoing emotion scores surprise appears to give way to feelings of interest and sadness.

There may be some uncertainty about including interest as a basic emotion. Izard (1991) referred to interest as being the feeling of being "caught up, fascinated, or curious" (p. 100). Others suggested it was a guide to processing and influenced attention (Grimes & Meadowcroft, 1995). Although this issue is not put to rest by these data, it is important to note that the high intensity of interest in this study may represent a state of active heightened perception motivated by a potential threat. Many researchers have suggested that emotions have evolutionary roots and serve to protect the individual (see Izard, 1991). In this case, interest may be a more primitive emotional response, driving perceptive processes. Leventhal (1984) suggested multiple tiers of emotional and cognitive processing that represent this view. Future models of emotional involvement should consider this phasic or multi-tier model featuring interest as a guide to more complex emotions.

Action tendencies, that is, the motivational component of emotions, represented the third component of emotions. Paradoxically, the most frequent action tendencies in this sample were not being motivated to do anything at all, or, being motivated to help others. These were followed by heavy television viewing and seeking an interpersonal connection.

In order for the action tendencies to be considered a dimension of emotional experience, they need to be associated with emotions in a more precise, controlled way. These data provide limited, evidence of a motivational component to emotions. Persuasion researchers have consistently maintained that affect produces intentions and ultimately behavior (McGuire, 1985). In this study, the responses do not differentiate between intentions and behavior. Therefore, it is not clear whether we are identifying a component of a person's emotion or an outcome to watching television. If action tendencies are to be considered an aspect of emotion then a simpler solution is warranted.

Respondents also indicated a need for interpersonal connection as a result of their emotional experience. It may be that the emotional response associated with viewing this kind of coverage is the mediating variable in this relationship. Many respondents specifically stated that they needed to check up on their loved ones and wanted to be with others while they watched the coverage. Co-viewing, and other interpersonal activity (e.g., phone calls, e-mails) functioned as an important form of social support in a time of high uncertainty and emotional intensity. Future research needs to explore the relative contributions of coviewing partners to the construction of mediated realities during serious social threats.

We investigated the experience of coviewing as emotional involvement with a mediated disaster. After accounting for simple proximity, giving or seeking comfort is the predominant reason for co-viewing. Furthermore, the most frequent topics while co-viewing were to reduce uncertainty and *express* emotion. Although exploratory, this suggests that co-viewing is a context for emotional experience while viewing a disaster. It is likely that emotional involvement is facilitated or even inhibited by a viewer's choice of partners. Theories of emotional contagion may be useful in explaining this experience (Hatfield, Cacioppo, & Rapson, 1994).

One advantage of this study lay in the immediacy of its distribution to the respondents. Paradoxically, this also is a limitation. It was noted several times that responses to open-ended questions were being used by respondents as a means of releasing emotional tension or venting political views. These responses were not directly associated with the questions asked. We discerned that the respondents were using the questionnaire as a way to express emotion. Although we believe that respondents were able to remember and document things like story features and emotion intensity, it is possible that their answers reflected a measure of ego involvement with the issue not considered in designing the study. This may have resulted in some inflated emotion intensity scores and may account for people's inability[1] to accurately estimate how much television they had viewed.

In general, the findings support an important area of communication research that focuses on the intersection of mass and interpersonal communication (A. Rubin & Rubin, 2001). The fundamental assumption of this approach is that communication is functional, serving to gratify social and psychological needs. Within this perspective, media involvement and interpersonal communication motives are key constructs that mediate communicative and other outcomes.

Emotional involvement with media is experienced as affective participation or engagement with mediated content (Perse, 1990). In the past, this concept has been represented by emotional intensity, parasocial interaction, and attraction. We explored a new avenue for emotional involvement, coviewing. Given strong interpersonal needs during a disaster, we found co-viewing to be an appropriate and important context for emotional experience and expression.

These data support the idea that emotional responses are prompted by features of the event emphasized by news media and reinforced by interpersonal communication. In the experience of disaster coverage it is important to consider the interface of these sources to various communication outcomes.

---

[1]Although respondents encountered a very direct question concerning the amount of viewing, many were unable or unwilling to respond. The question reads "On September 11, approximately how many hours did you follow broadcast media coverage of the explosion?" The response option was an open line for a number followed by the term *hours*. Many answers exceeded the 24-hour limit, were accompanied by comments such as "I'm still watching," or were simply checked to represent the more abstract concept of *hours*.

20

Gender Differences in Perceptions of Media Reports of the Gulf and Afghan Conflicts

Robert A. Baukus
Susan M. Strohm
The Pennsylvania State University

In times of crisis, questions about media reporting often come to the forefront of the public agenda. The ubiquitous television coverage of the events beginning on September 11 and CNN's coverage of the 1991 Gulf War (especially Peter Arnett's broadcasts from Baghdad) were almost as much a part of the story as the events themselves (Brookings/Harvard Forum, 2001; *Newsweek,* 1991, February 4 & February 11). In both the Gulf and Afghan conflicts, similar questions about the nature of the coverage were raised. Elements of the controversy included the public's assessment of media performance, including the media's responsibility to provide fair, accurate, and complete coverage of war-related events, the nature and extent of government censorship, and the impact of media reporting on the Allied war efforts.

℮ Gender has long been an important factor in understanding American public opinion on war-related events. In fact, the most striking and consistent public opinion gap in the post-World War II era has been on issues of war, peace, and the use of force—men have been consistently more likely than women to support the foreign and domestic use of force and are more likely to see war as a valid means of conflict resolution (Shapiro & Mahajan, 1986; T. Smith, 1984).

As past polls on the use of force would predict, men and women felt differently about the 1991 Gulf War and the conflict in Afghanistan. A 1991 *Washington Post*–ABC News poll found that women supported then President George Bush's policies in the Gulf to a lesser extent than did men (85% of men; 71% of women; Williams, 1991). A Times-Mirror poll suggested that women worried about the Gulf War more than men did and more women reported they were depressed about the war (64% of women, 33% of men; reported in Williams, 1991). Similar attitudes were reported in a RAND study conducted after the events of September 11, 2001, in which 50% of women said they experienced substantial stress in the days following the attacks, compared to 37% of men (Schuster, 2002). Differences in perspectives of men and women regarding war were summed up by *Washington Post* writer Marjorie Williams (1991):

> Men do consequences; women do burning flesh.
> Men do technology; women do husbands and brothers,
>   mothers and sons.

Some have suggested that, within a broader Western cultural imperative, fundamental value orientations and modes of moral reasoning may account for some of the differences between men and women on issues of conflict and conflict resolution (Beutel & Marini, 1995; Gilligan, 1993; Gilligan, Ward, & Taylor, 1988). Harvard psychologist Carol Gilligan outlined two modes of moral reasoning, a morality of responsibility in which human needs and human connections are emphasized and which empirically is more often associated with women, and a morality of rights in which justice and due process are emphasized, which is more often associated with men (Gilligan 1993; Gilligan et al., 1988).

The morality of responsibility places greatest weight on human needs and connections when balancing competing values. In this mode, the social world "coheres through human connections, rather than a set of rules" (Gilligan, 1993, p. 29). Moral conflicts tend to be viewed more "as a problem of inclusion, rather than one of balancing claims" (Gilligan,1982, p. 160). Social conflict and aggression are seen in this mode as a "fracture of human connection" (Gilligan, 1993, p. 43). Communication is viewed as a process which creates inclusion and connectedness, and draws its value from the discovery, description, and resolution of underlying tensions and issues in conflict situations.

The morality of rights, on the other hand, places greatest emphasis on established forms and meanings of justice and pre-existing commitments when balancing competing values. Resolution of conflict flows not from communication, but from established notions of "rights" and "fairness." Rights and fairness tend to be understood in terms of preferred outcomes, established power relationships, and the consistent application of formal policies and rules for conflict resolution.

MORAL REASONING AND PERCEPTIONS OF MEDIA REPORTING

Differences in perceptions of media reporting and the appropriate role of media in times of war may flow from these broader differences in mode of moral reasoning, and parallel perceptions of the broader meaning of conflict and the role of communication in conflict resolution. An extension of Gilligan's paradigm suggests that in times of war, women may be more likely to see media reporting as a crucial channel of information, essential for the creation of understanding, connectedness, and eventual resolution of conflict. The process of communication per se may be seen as a "binding element," serving to create a sense of connectedness among the parties to the conflict (see Coser, 1956, p. 121).

For women, the creation of connectedness may require a communication process that is inclusive and unfettered, allowing all parties to have a voice in the production of shared meaning about the conflict. Unfettered communication not only provides relevant information, it gives context to the conflict and helps create understanding about the subtle and interwoven issues surrounding the conflict. This full and fair exchange of ideas may be seen as an essential step in the process of producing a just resolution of the conflict.

From this perspective, women may be more likely to take an expanded view of both media rights and responsibilities, even in times of war. Comprehension and the production of a shared understanding is a function of relevant and credible information, which requires a news media relatively free from censorship. The responsibility of media to engage in accurate and objective reporting may also be seen as central to the process of creating shared meaning and a just resolution of the conflict. To the extent women see the media reports as a credible and relevant source of information, they may be more likely to seek out "knowledge-generating messages" (Bradac, 1989, p. 8) to satisfy their needs for increased understanding of the event.

The extension of Gilligan's paradigm suggests that men, on the other hand, may view censorship and responsibility issues quite differently. Because moral reasoning in the morality of rights mode is grounded in the use of pre-existing formal policies and procedures to understand and resolve conflicts, media reporting may be seen as playing a less central role in this process. Instead, conflict resolution is seen as intertwined with those outcomes that function to maintain power hierarchies and work within established policies designed to mitigate threats.

This suggests that men may be more willing to accept news media censorship as part of the "rules of the game" for war. Men may be more accepting of restricted information flow because they may view mediated communication as a tool useful to maintain defensive advantages against potential aggressors. This suggests the interests of government in maintaining military secrets in wartime may be less troubling for men than for women. As parties move toward war and engagement begins, men may perceive media reports more in terms of the impact of the reports on the war effort, rather than in terms of the accuracy and inclusiveness of the relevant information.

This chapter begins by looking at gender differences in the level of support for the use of force in the 1991 Gulf War and in the conflict in Afghanistan. These overall beliefs create an important framework for perceiving, understanding, and evaluating the media reporting of these conflicts. Gender differences in perceptions of the media reporting, including the duty of media to report regardless of impact of the coverage, are then examined and related to the theoretical perspective outlined by Gilligan.

RQ 1: Are there significant differences between men and women on beliefs related to the use of force in the Gulf and Afghan conflicts?

RQ2: Are there significant differences between men and women on perceptions of media reporting and media responsibility in the Gulf and Afghan conflicts?

METHOD

To examine perceptions of media reporting in times of war, two waves of surveys were conducted over a 10-year period. In both cases, the two nonrandom purposive samples consisted of undergraduate juniors and seniors enrolled in a college of communication at a large mideastern university. Age and race were not recorded, but students were required to be 18 years or older. The only recorded demographic characteristic was gender. The purposive convience sample used in this study risks external validity. It was used because, as Singletary (1994) noted, this study only requires that two groups of respondents be comparable, not necessarily representative of the population.

Two sets of surveys were collected during the 1991 Gulf War. Surveys were first administered between January 28 and February 1, approximately 2 weeks into the air war phase of the military campaign in the Gulf region. This provided 450 respondents, 210 women (47%) and 240 men (53%). A second set was collected on February 26–27 during the ground war phase of the Gulf conflict and yielded 166 respondents, 112 women (68%) and 54 men (33%). Key attitudinal indicators such as support for the war and media use and evaluations showed no differences between the two sets of subsamples and they were combined to produce the Gulf sample ($N = 616$, 52% women).

The Afghan sample was collected between September 27 and October 9 and consisted of 621 respondents, 389 women (62%) and 232 men (37%).

Respondents in both the 1991 and 2001 samples completed a self-administered questionnaire. Topics covered in the survey included amount and type of television news exposure, approval ratings for the sitting president, the general level of support for the war, and perceptions of the media coverage of the war. The Gulf and Afghan survey instruments were virtually identical in form and content. Each survey consisted of 40 questions. All questions were identical except questions which referred to individual events. For example, the question, "The U.S. should be at war with Iraq" was changed to, "The U.S. should be at war with Afghanistan."

Respondents were asked to rate on a Likert-type scale, from 5 (extremely well) to 1 (not well at all), how well each of 52 single-word descriptors described their opinion of the media coverage of the war in the Gulf or, in the 2001 survey, media coverage of the attack on America. Amount of TV news exposure was indicated by asking, "How many hours per week do you watch television news coverage of the war (or attack)?" Respondents had eight half-hour choices ranging from none to 3.5 hours. Type of media exposure was indicated by respondents' rank ordering of a set of identified national news networks. Approval ratings for the sitting President were measured on a 7-point, approve–disapprove semantic differential. All remaining questions about the respondents' feeling, beliefs, and attitudes toward the conflicts were measured on a 5-point scale ranging from strongly agree (1) to strongly disagree (5).

RESULTS

Almost all U.S. military conflicts have seen strong expressions of support at their start for the sitting president (Blendon & Benson, 2001). Respondents in both the Gulf and Afghan samples echoed the strong approval ratings for the sitting president expressed in national public opinion polls at the time. During the Gulf War, national public opinion polls gave President George Bush approval ratings in the low- to mid-80% range (Clymer, 1991). Student respondents in the 1991 Gulf War sample, conducted at the same time as the national polls, gave President Bush an 82% approval rating. In the Afghan sample, student sentiment again echoed public support for the president. Students gave George W. Bush a 62% approval rating; among the general public, approval ratings ranged from 84% to 91% (Blendon & Benson, 2001).

Within this broader context of approval for the sitting president, systematic gender differences appeared on more specific questions related to the president's positions, the war effort and media reporting of war events. As suggested by the data in Table 20.1, men were consistently more supportive of force as a means for resolving the Gulf conflict.

Table 20.1. Support for Use of Force by Gender

	1991 Sample: Gulf			2001 Sample: Afghanistan		
	Males (n = 294)	Females (n = 322)	t value	Males (n = 232)	Females (n = 389)	t value
Support president's position	1.96	2.24	-2.91**	2.09	2.37	-3.05**
Support U.S. retaliation	1.27	1.29	-0.32	1.97	2.28	-3.48***
Should be at war	2.26	2.72	-4.46***	2.99	3.03	0.37
Use only non-military options	3.80	3.34	-5.35***	3.80	3.44	-4.07***
Worry war will escalate	2.53	2.17	-3.94***	2.20	2.11	-1.06

* $p < .05$; * * $p < .01$; *** $p < .001$

Note. Mean Agreement Scores on Likert Items (1 = *strongly agree*, 5 = *strongly disagree*)

In the 1991 Gulf War survey, men more strongly supported President Bush's position on the war, felt more strongly that the United States should be at war, and were more likely than women to reject the use of nonmilitary options alone as a means for resolving the Gulf conflict. Women, however, were more likely than men to worry the war would escalate.

In the 2001 Afghan war survey, men also showed stronger levels of support for the President's position and were more favorable to U.S. retaliation. Men also were more strongly opposed to a strategy using nonmilitary options by the United States.

Gender differences also were found on perceptions of media reporting and media responsibilities in the Gulf and Afghan wars, as shown in Table 20.2. In both the Gulf and Afghan conflicts, men were more likely to disagree that news media have a duty to report all attack or war-related events, regardless of the impact on the U.S. war effort. In both the Gulf and Afghan conflicts, women were more likely than men to say they wished they had more time to watch the

Table 20.2. Support for Use of Force by Gender

	1991 Sample: Gulf War			2001 Sample: Afghanistan		
	Males ($n = 294$)	Females ($n = 322$)	t value	Males ($n = 232$)	Females ($n = 389$)	t value
Report regardless of impact	3.73	3.39	-3.13**	3.35	2.91	-4.19***
Bias toward military perspective	2.33	2.09	-3.01**	2.36	2.46	-1.21
Government distorting truth	2.91	2.69	-2.56*	3.28	3.20	-1.11
Can believe media reports	2.86	3.07	-2.74**	2.86	2.73	-1.69
Getting whole truth	3.82	4.07	-3.60***	3.78	3.83	-0.64
Reports increase understanding	2.79	2.98	-2.27*	2.77	2.59	-2.30*
Want more time to watch	2.88	2.58	-3.39***	3.32	3.06	-2.77**
I understand reasons for war	2.37	2.98	-6.40***	2.42	2.80	-4.04***

* $p < .05$. ** $p < .01$. *** $p < .001$.

Note. Mean Agreement Scores on Likert Items (1 = strongly agree, 5 = strongly disagree)

coverage. Men, on the other hand, were more likely to say they already had a clear understanding of why the United States was at war.

For the Gulf War, women perceived more one-sidedness in the media reports than did men. Women were more likely to agree that the reporting was biased toward the U.S. military perspective and that government spokespersons were distorting the truth about the conflict. Women were more skeptical about whether they could believe the media reporting and were more likely to say that they were not being told the whole truth about the war. Perhaps as a result of these concerns about the accuracy and inclusiveness of the reporting, women were less likely than were men to say that the media reporting gave them a better understanding of the situation.

The Afghan conflict presented a much different scenario. The Gulf conflict was a military operation carried out in a foreign location—combatants were primarily military personnel. There was a long lead time during which media had ample time to present information about the situation. The ensuing war took the more familiar form of an organized, military operation. In contrast, television coverage of the September 11 events was often confusing and chaotic, as the media sought to provide comprehensive coverage of the unexpected attacks. As the event unfolded and the Afghan connection came into focus, coverage tended to include more discussion of the ensuing U.S. response to the attack, which ultimately led to the use of force against Afghanistan. Due to the time period in which the data were collected, both the initial attack and the U.S. response framed respondents' perceptions and operationally defined the Afghan conflict.

Not surprisingly, in the weeks following September 11, respondents expressed a need to keep informed about the unfolding events—69% watched 2 or more hours of television coverage per week; 45% cited CNN as their most frequently watched source for media reports of the events. Media reporting generally was perceived very favorably—95% rated the media coverage as "worthwhile." This result was echoed in the national opinion poll data collected after September 11, where 89% gave the press a rating of either "excellent" or "good" and ratings for accuracy of the press were the best since 1992 (Brookings/Harvard Forum, 2001). Nationally, nearly 70% said the leading news organizations "stand up for America," up from 43% in the days before September 11. Andrew Kohut, director of the Pew Center for the People and the Press, attributed the post-September 11 upswing in public attitudes toward the media to an increase in trust "at a time where they feel a great need to know" (Brookings/Harvard Forum, 2001).

These more favorable national attitudes toward media were reflected in differences in responses about media reporting in the Gulf and Afghan samples. Concerns about media performance expressed by women in the Gulf sample were less evident in the women's perceptions of the reporting of the Afghan conflict. In the Afghan sample, women's perceptions were no different from men's on questions of military bias, distorting of truth by government spokespersons, believability of the media reporting and whether or not they were getting the whole truth about the attack. With fewer concerns about accuracy and completeness, women in the Afghan sample were more likely than men to say that media reporting increased their understanding of the situation.

To further explore gender differences in perceptions of the accuracy and relevance of the media reporting, respondents rated a set of 52 descriptors on a 5-point Likert type scale (5 = describes media reporting extremely well to 1 = describes media reporting not well at all). The descriptors were factor analyzed using principal components analysis with varimax rotation. The first derived rotated component identified a coherent set of concepts related to the accurate and relevant information concept (this set and their associated factor loadings included: valuable .711, informative .678, orderly .672, thorough .661, truthful .660, resourceful .658, honest .639, organized .606, and fair .570). This concept set was used to create an "information relevance" scale (operationalized as the mean score of the nine individual descriptors, α = .88) and gender differences were examined.

Significant differences between men's and women's perceptions of the relevance of information appeared in both the Gulf and Afghan samples (Gulf sample, M for males = 3.40, M for females = 3.24, t = 2.95, $p < .003$, Afghan sample, M for males = 3.47, M for females = 3.61, t = 2.55, $p < .01$). The direction of the difference was consistent with the differing perceptions of the bias and credibility of the media reporting. As shown in Table 20.2, women in the Gulf sample saw more military bias and placed less trust in media reports than did men—women in the Gulf sample also had lower scores on the information relevance scale. In the Afghan sample, where gender differences on questions of military bias and media credibility disappeared, women had higher scores on the information relevance scale than did men.

When comparing each gender's information relevance scores for the two events, men in the Gulf and Afghan samples had virtually the same mean score (Gulf sample M = 3.40, Afghan sample M = 3.47). Women's scores, on the other hand, increased significantly. Women in the Afghan sample had a significantly higher information relevance mean score than did women in the Gulf sample (Afghan sample M = 3.61, Gulf sample M = 3.24, t = 6.77, p < .001).

A second scale was derived using the factor analysis procedures discussed previously. This factor dimension used three of the 52 descriptors—each of the three descriptors, "shocking" .797, "scary" .795, and "overwhelming" .640, had a unique factor loading (α = .76). This scale was then used to compare men's and women's perceptions of the September 11 attacks. Women found the September 11 events to be more shocking, scary, and overwhelming than did men (M for females = 4.08, M for males = 3.84, t = 3.08, p < .002). This sense of fear and uncertainty may have precipitated a greater information search for the women in the Afghan sample and may account for the improved media performance scores and their higher scores on the information relevance scale.

DISCUSSION

The pattern of data in both the Gulf and Afghan samples suggests that men were more supportive of the use of force as a means to resolve the conflicts. Men in the Gulf War sample tended to ascribe more credibility than did women to established sources of information, both government and media sources. When asked to respond to this item, "*War coverage should be censored by the U.S. and Allied military,*" men were more likely than women to agree (M for males = 2.68, M for females = 3.20, t = 491, p < .001). When asked to respond to this item, "*There is enough coverage of anti-war demonstrations,*" men in the Gulf sample were more likely than women to think there had been enough coverage of anti-war demonstrations (M for males = 2.17, M for females = 2.49, t = 3.52, p < .001). These data suggest that men may place a greater importance on the impacts of media reporting when balancing media freedoms against military objectives.

Women, on the other hand, were more supportive of inclusive and open communication about war-time events than were men. In the Gulf sample, women were more concerned than were men about a possible escalation of war and were more critical of the media reporting. Even so, women were more likely to say that media has a duty to report all war events, even if the reporting might have a negative impact on the United States and Allied war efforts. Even in the Afghan sample, where women found the events to be more scary, shocking, and overwhelming than did men, women were still more supportive of the news media's duty to report, regardless of the impact of the reporting.

In both the Gulf and Afghan samples, men and women differed in their perceptions of the utility of the media reporting. In both samples, men felt they already had a clear understanding of why the United States was at war. This is consistent with the morality of rights mode of reasoning, in which conflicts are seen through the lens of established policies and procedures for achieving just resolution. This lens may serve the same function as the sense-making and shared understanding process in the morality of responsibility mode of reasoning—men may have a pre-existing acculturated commitment to action. The "understanding" type of cognition has already occurred; preludes to conflict may serve as a catalyst point which initiates a defensive orientation, rather than information search and contemplation.

In both samples, women, on the other hand, wanted more time to watch the media coverage. Women nationally were more stressed and worried about the events of September 11 than were men—similarly, women in the Afghan sample said the events were more scary, overwhelming, and shocking than did men. As worry about future terrorism has been linked with liking the media coverage (Brookings/Harvard Forum, 2001), this worry may account for the disappearance of the gender differences in the media bias questions in the Afghan sample. Here, men and women had the same assessments of the accuracy and completeness of the coverage and women were more likely than men to say that the media reporting increased their understanding of the situation.

At the same time what might explain why the information relevance scores for the men in these samples were relatively consistent, whereas the same scores for women changed so dramatically? The nature of the Afghan scenario itself, reinforced by gender differences in reactions to the September 11 attack, may have heightened women's need for understanding and intensified the "great need to know" factor suggested by Kohut. As Abramson of *The New York Times* suggested, "this is a story that the public feels fundamentally impacts their lives quite directly . . . they crave information because they see that information as essential to their safety" (Brookings/ Harvard Forum, 2001). Worrying about the prospect of future terrorism has been associated with liking the media coverage and searching for more information about the events (Brookings/Harvard Forum, 2001). As noted, women and girls were more likely than men or boys to have experienced a substantial stress reaction to the September 11 attacks (Schuster, 2002)—73% of women worried that further attacks would occur, with women under the age of 30 expressing the highest levels of concern (Center for Gender Equality, 2002).

Dilemmas raised by the conflict of media rights and responsibilities may have different meanings and different solutions for men and women, due to differences in modes of moral reasoning. In this study, women were both more supportive of the idea that media have a duty to report and a right to operate unfettered by government censorship. These attitudes are in line with the paradigm outlined by Gilligan in which women are more likely to use a morality of responsibility mode of moral reasoning, which sees communication as central to conflict resolution. In this case, women may have seen the media reporting as a tool for the creation of connections and as means for the discovery of underlying tensions and eventual resolution of the long-standing conflicts in the Gulf and Middle East regions.

Men, on the other hand, are more often associated with the morality of rights mode of moral reasoning that draws on concepts of established rights, due process, and established power arrangements in the resolution of conflicts. Men's greater support for pro-force options, greater investment of credibility in authority sources, and greater concern about the effects of media reporting of war-related events are in line with this approach to moral reasoning.

Results of this study also suggest that personal orientation to the conflict may be an important modifying factor when extending Gilligan's paradigm to perceptions of media reporting. Fear and a sense of being overwhelmed by events may have intensified information needs for the women in the Afghan sample and enhanced their perceptions of media performance.

Overall, men may have used media reporting of the conflict events to discover and confirm that hostilities had occurred and that appropriate government responses were taking place. Women may have used media reporting to seek out information related to the events that would detail and explain the nature of the conflicts. Based on their mode of moral reasoning, men and women may have used different routes to develop understanding of the events.

The sampling procedures used in this study limit the external validity of the findings. Although generalizing beyond the young adults surveyed in this research was not a goal of this pilot project, the results suggest there is sufficient evidence to warrant a national survey to examine the degree to which the gender differences outlined by Gilligan hold within the broader population.

Further work is needed to extend the moral reasoning approach to understanding gender-based differences in perceptions of mediated conflicts, how information is sought and interpreted in conflict situations, and to perceptions of media reporting, media duties, and broader first amendment issues. Differences between the two modes of moral reasoning in the meanings and salience of concepts such as fairness, justice, inclusion, and communication make for useful research questions.

21

Communication Infrastructure and Civic Actions in Crisis

Yong-Chan Kim
Sandra J. Ball-Rokeach
Elisia L. Cohen
Joo-Young Jung
University of Southern California

After September 11, 2001, news reports detailed a laundry list of civic-minded reactions to the national tragedy including people attaching American flags to their cars; contributing money to relief funds; attending churches, synagogues, and mosques with new regularity; standing and waiting in long lines to donate blood; and greeting strangers on streets and buses (e.g., McMahon, 2001). Such collective civic actions, as opposed to individualistic coping strategies (e.g., escaping from strangers or staying away from public places), during a time of crisis raise important questions for social research. Specifically, are such civic actions merely transient reactions to the crisis or are they embedded in a more stable community base?

There has been great debate about the state of civic community in the United States after 9/11. Social researchers exploring community capital formation offer differing bases for understanding individuals' civic-minded responses to 9/11. One prominent figure, Robert Putnam (2002), maintained that the September 11 crisis reshaped American attitudes toward one another and reinforced a broader sense of social justice.

Putnam argued that such psychological reactions may be fleeting and transient responses to crisis, leaving little lasting impression: "though the crisis revealed and replenished the wells of solidarity in American communities, those wells so far remain untapped." Such interpretations are consistent with Putnam's (1995, 2000) prior research examining how America's stock of social capital has declined, and with other scholars' findings that American social and political institutions have not succeeded in encouraging civic participation.[1]

Some researchers tend to believe that individuals' civic-minded responses to 9/11 were tapped from latent reservoirs of social capital, having more significant linkages to civic society. Studies that have observed the restructuring of civil society suggest alternative indicators of social capital, or latent capacities for civic participation (e.g, Ball-Rokeach, Kim, & Matei, 2001; Paxton, 1999; Sampson, Raudenbush, & Earls, 1997). Such research lends support for the argument that civic-minded actions and feelings of community after the 9/11 tragedies were reactions embedded in more stable social or communication resources in local communities.

The main inquiry in this chapter is to examine whether the post-September 11 civic-minded responses provide evidence of community capital deeply rooted in an established communication opportunity structure in residential communication environments. Our previous work uses the concept of a neighborhood *storytelling system* to examine the relationship between community-level communication opportunities and the possibility of civil society (Ball-Rokeach et al., 2001). *Storytelling* is a communication process where storytellers—large and small media, organizations, and individuals, and so on—interact with one another to produce and exchange stories that are essential resources for building and maintaining communities. That research developed and tested a storytelling model of neighborhood belonging in the context of seven different "geo-ethnic"[2] communities in Los Angeles. Individuals' feelings of

---

[1]Research supporting the thesis of a decline in social capital include studies evidencing the decline in party loyalty and political membership across generation cohorts (e.g., Bartels, 2000), the evisceration of linkages among political parties, institutions, and community-based organizations (e.g., Walker, 1991), market-driven journalism at the expense of public interest (e.g., McChesney,1997), public distrust of government and politics (e.g., Cappella & Jamieson 1997), and the growth of interest group politics and narrow issue conflicts in urban communities (e.g., Warren, 1998).

[2]*Geo-ethnicity* is defined as ethnically identified attitudes and behaviors grounded in a specific temporal and spatial situation. See Kim, Ball-Rokeach, Jung, and Loges (2002) for a more elaborated discussion.

attachment and actions that indicated belonging to their neighborhoods were closely related to their level of connection to the storytelling network in their geographically defined communication environment. This model includes three storytelling levels—macro, meso, and micro. Mainstream media are *macro-level* storytellers because their usual storytelling referents are on the state, national, or global level rather than the neighborhood level. Local community media and community organizations are two important *meso-level* storytellers; they work as liaisons between macro and micro storytellers by translating macro-level topics to *micro-level* storytelling and converting micro-level community concerns to higher level issues. The most critical micro-level storytellers are the residents who talk about their neighborhoods with their neighbors. Dynamic interplay among these multilevel storytellers constitutes an integrative storytelling network where each storyteller stimulates the other to imagine community, which builds and maintains community belonging (Ball-Rokeach et al., 2001).

To understand civic participation after September 11, we examine the extent to which individuals were embedded in a vibrant local storytelling network. In so doing, we aim to test our hypothetical model wherein civic actions after 9/11, although first activated by specific crisis events outside residential communities, were evidence of the latent potential for community building that arises from an established residential "communication infrastructure." Through testing this storytelling model, we hope to better understand the relationship between community-level communication resources and national-level civic actions in situations wrought by uncertainty and ambiguity (e.g., Ball-Rokeach, 1985, 1998; Hallman & Wandersman, 1992).

COMMUNICATION INFRASTRUCTURE AND CIVIC ACTIONS

Our inquiry into civic actions after 9/11 is theoretically guided by communication infrastructure theory (CIT),[3] developed by the ongoing Metamorphosis Project at the Annenberg School for Communication at the University of Southern California (http://www. metamorph.org). A communication infrastructure is *a storytelling*

---

[3]Our concept of communication infrastructure builds on the assumptions of media system dependency theory (Ball-Rokeach, 1998), and goes beyond to a more inclusive consideration of the interplay between interpersonal and mediated storytelling systems and their contexts.

system set in its communication action context (Ball-Rokeach et al., 2001, p. 396). It consists of the everyday conversations and stories that people, media, and grassroots organizations create and disseminate (*storytelling system*), and the resources of residential areas that promote or constrain communication between residents (*community action contexts*; e.g., parks, safe streets, libraries, schools).

Practical application of the CIT approach affords a way to articulate and to empirically unveil the communication infrastructure in diverse urban communities. CIT is based on the premise that communication resources are just as, if not more, important than economic resources in building civic society (Ball-Rokeach, 1998). Just as an entrepreneur relies on access to the financial features of an economic infrastructure to build a successful business, the individual citizen or family relies on access to a supportive communication infrastructure to build their sense and reality of community. The vast landscape of communication flows produced by storytellers—people talking with one another, media producing stories, and local organizations bringing people together—are the milieu of daily life. A belonging community has an integrated network of storytellers where each player stimulates the other to story-tell their community (Cocke & McGarvey, 2001). When various storytellers help one another to imagine and talk about community (Anderson, 1991), there is an infrastructure that people can use to build civic society (Ball-Rokeach et al., 2001; Wytte, Katz, & Kim, 2000).

As with other infrastructures, communication infrastructures are usually invisible until something happens to impair their functioning (Starr & Bowker, 2002). For example, when electrical failures or transportation shutdowns occur inhibiting our everyday media connections, acute awareness of the communication system as a precondition to attain everyday goals quickly emerges (e.g., Ball-Rokeach, 1998; Hirshbury, Dillman, & Ball-Rokeach, 1986). After 9/11, we observed a turning point where a usually invisible community-based communication infrastructure became visible.

HYPOTHESES

By extending the local storytelling model to the case of civic actions after September 11, we illustrate the ways in which people's connections to a local storytelling network form the basis for civic reactions to a national event. The model of storytelling paths to civic actions after 9/11, shown in Figure 21.1, presents linear flows from structural storytelling conditions through macro, meso, and micro storytelling connections to civic actions. These multilevel connections to storytellers are important communication resources that, once activated by community residents, spur motivation to participate in civic activities during crisis situations.

Our model in the Fig. 21.1 is based on the following hypotheses.

H1: The positive effects of structural characteristics (residential tenure, home ownership, immigration history, age, male, income, and education) on civic actions in response to the 9/11 tragedies will only be indirect through connections to either macro-level storytelling agents (mainstream media) or meso-level storytelling agents (community organizations and local media).

This basic hypothesis follows from the argument that structural variables have force through the impetus they give to establish connections to macro- and meso-level storytelling agents (Ball-Rokeach et al., 2001, p. 403).

H2: The positive effects of connections to macro storytelling agents (mainstream media) on civic actions in response to the 9/11 tragedies will be both direct and indirect through connections to meso-level storytelling agents (local media and community organizations) and micro-level storytelling agents (interpersonal storytelling).

After 9/11, all important storytelling agents turned to a shared referent—in this case, a national referent. The civic actions taken after 9/11 reflected intersecting local and national concerns as civic-minded responses often had links to various national activities including blood donation drives organized by the Red Cross, and the "rallying around the flag" symbolic gestures encouraged by media. Therefore, there should be a correspondence between what mainstream media referred to and what individuals did in local communities to achieve collective goals during the crisis. In addition, when mainstream media stories overlapped with local concerns, they were likely to encourage broader connections to meso-level storytellers (local media and community organizations) and micro-level storytellers (interpersonal storytelling). Therefore, we

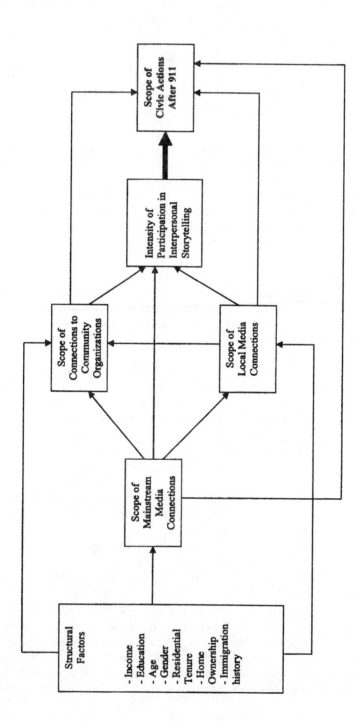

Fig. 21.1 Hypothetical storytelling model of civic actions after 9/11

hypothesize that mainstream media have both direct and indirect influences on the scope of civic actions.[4]

H3: The positive effects of connections to meso-level storytelling agents (community organizations and local media) on civic actions after 9/11 tragedies will be both direct and indirect through connections to each other and to micro-level interpersonal storytelling.

People's connections to community organizations or local media can operate directly to enhance civic actions after the 9/11 incidents by heightening both the knowledge and the salience of 9/11-related local news and events taking place in their communities. Connections to these meso-level storytelling agents also precipitate a carrying forward of these stories through interpersonal storytelling.

H4: Connection to micro neighborhood storytelling (interpersonal conversation) will have a stronger positive direct effect on civic actions after 9/11 than connections to macro-level storytelling (mainstream media) and meso-level storytelling (local media and community organizations).

This hypothesis follows from our view that an agentic potential exists in neighbors talking with neighbors about local-level concerns, issues, or events, which in some circumstances can be transformed to other civic actions. Such interpersonal conversations may mobilize participation in national-level collective actions in response to the September 11 incidents.

METHODS

Sample

As part of the multi-year Metamorphosis Project, 331 households were selected before and after September 11, by random digit dialing

---

[4]In the original storytelling model (Ball-Rokeach et al., 2001), connections to mainstream media as macro-level storytelling agents had only an indirect path to belonging through local media. This can be attributed to the types of referents of mainstream media that usually concern places beyond people's neighborhoods. That is, the breadth of connections to mainstream media mainly contribute to increasing individuals' chances of connecting to local

for participation in a telephone survey assessing a range of social and communication variables. The sample frame was all residential telephone numbers ringing into zip code qualified households that fall into known banks of working residential numbers for a city in Los Angeles County. In order to reach the diverse populations of this incorporated residential community on the cusp of Los Angeles, the survey was administered in the language of respondents' choice (English, Spanish, and Armenian).[5] These data were gathered at two points in time. The first began on August 30 and was stopped on September 11 after 141 participants were interviewed. The survey resumed on September 21, with additional items added to the survey to assess media connections and civic actions during and after the tragedies. It is the second wave data (n = 191) that we use to test the present model.[6]

Dependent Variable: Scope of Civic Actions

A scope of civic actions variable was constructed by summing the number of affirmative responses to ten civic action items presented in our survey (range = 0 to 10, M = 3.9, SD = 1.84). The ten civic action items include "buying or displaying an American flag" (73%), "talking about the 9/11 incidents with neighbors" (67%), "contributing money to a relief fund" (66%), "talking about the 9/11 incidents with strangers" (48%), "phone calling to check on the welfare of a person you know who might have been injured" (41%), "attending a memorial service for the victims" (31%), "donating blood" (20%), "attending a candlelight vigil" (18%), "posting a message on an Internet public message forum" (5%), and "writing a letter to the editor or calling in to a radio talk show" (5%).

---

media that cover community-related referents without having direct effects on interpersonal storytelling or neighborhood belonging.

[5]A survey research firm was employed using trained bilingual interviews (the survey was translated and back translated in each language) programmed for Computer Assisted Telephone Interview administration. These unusual multilingual data collection procedures afford inclusion of non-English-speaking new immigrants often excluded from survey research.

[6]Our survey response rate was 54% when calculated by dividing the number of completed interviews by the number of theoretically eligible phone numbers. Eligible phone numbers were calculated by examining the total number of study phone numbers excluding phone numbers for which eligibility could not be determined, inappropriate/duplicate phone numbers, nonqualified household phone numbers (e.g., outside study area), and the estimated number of initial refusals not likely to qualify for our study.

Exogenous Variables

Residential tenure was a continuous measure of years of neighborhood residence. Home ownership was a dichotomous measure, as was gender. Respondents were asked their age on their last birthday, and household income for the previous year (in ranges staggered from less than $20,000 to more than $100,000). The highest grade or year of school completed was used to indicate educational level, ranging from eighth grade or less to receipt of a graduate degree. Immigration history was measured by the generation of a respondent's first family member to immigrate to the United States (see Table 21.1 for means, standard deviations, and coded response categories).

Intervening Variables

The intensity of participation in interpersonal storytelling was measured by asking respondents to indicate, on a scale from 1 to 10, where 1 represents *never* and 10 *all the time*, how often they "have discussions with other people about things happening in their neighborhood" ($M = 5.08$, $SD = 2.80$).

Assessing scope of connections to community organizations involved a two-step process. Respondents were asked if they belonged to any of five different types of organizations:

1. sport or recreational
2. cultural, ethnic, or religious
3. neighborhood or homeowner's
4. political or educational
5. other

Having a membership was coded as "1," and responses were summed to form a synthetic variable ranging from 0 to 5. However, initial inspection showed that many people were not a member in a religious organization at the same time as they reported regularly attending religious services. For these respondents, we credited "1" to their religious organization scores if they attended a religious service more often than once every few weeks. By summing these scores, we created a final synthetic variable assessing the scope of the respondent's connections to community organizations (range: 0 to 5; $M = 1.60$, $SD = 1.73$).

To measure respondents' scope of connections to local media, we examined whether respondents spent any time connecting to local newspapers, radio, or television in the prior week. Local media were

Table 21. 1. Zero-Order Correlation Between Variables in the 9-11 Storytelling Model

	(1)	(2)	(3)	(4)	(5)	(6)	(7)	(8)	(9)	(10)	(11)	Mean (SD)
(1) Age												3.38 (1.33)
(2) Gender	-.01											.42 (.50)
(3) Income	.11	.14										4.22 (2.47)
(4) Education	.06	.08	-.04									4.92 (6.24)
(5) Residential Tenure	.46***	.04	.13	-.02								5.41 (2.21)
(6) Home Ownership	.33***	.06	.41***	-.02	.43***							.45 (.50)
(7) Immigration History	.19**	-.02	.07	-.06	.14*	.13						2.46 (1.50)
(8) Mainstream Media	.01	.08	.26***	-.07	.13	.17*	.04					2.18 (.87)
(9) Local Media	-.00	-.09	.01	-.06	-.02	.02	-.09	.07				1.59 (1.50)
(10) Organizational Participation	.05	.02	.39***	-.01	.16*	.32***	.22***	.14*	.03			1.60 (1.73)
(11) Interpersonal Storytelling	.06	-.11	.15*	-.07	.10	.18*	.22**	.27***	.10	.31***		5.08 (2.80)
(12) Civic actions	-.02	-.02	.16*	-.05	-.08	.03	.04	.17*	.04	.27***	.28***	3.90 (1.84)

Note. **Age** was measured with the following categories: 1 = between 18 and 25 years old, 2 = between 26 and 35 years old, 3 = between 36 and 45 years old, 4 = between 45 and 59 years old, and 5 = more than 60 years old. **Gender** is a dichotomous variable, with 1 = male and 0 = female. **Income** was measured with the following annual income categories: 1 = less than $20,000, 2 = between $20,000 and $35,000, 3 = between $35,000 and $45,000, 4 = between $45,000 and $60,000, 5 = between $60,000 and $75,000, 6 = between $75,000 and $100,000, and 7 = more than $100,000. **Education** was measured with the following categories: 1 = eighth grade or less, 2 = some high school, 3 = high school graduates, 4 = some college or technical school, 5 = college graduates, 6 = some graduate study, and 7 = graduate degree. **Residential tenure** was measured with the following categories: 1 = less than 1 year, 2 = between 1 and 2 years, 3 = between 2 and 3 years, 4 = between 3 and 5 years, 5 = between 5 and 20 years, 6 = more than 10 years, and 7 = entire life. **Homeownership** is a dichotomous variable, with 1 = own home and 0 = rent. **Immigration History** was measured with the following categories: 1 = first generation, 2 = second generation, 3 = third generation, and 4 = more than fourth generation.

* $p < .05$; ** $p < .01$; *** $p < .001$

defined in our survey as either community media targeted to a particular ethnic group in the study area or public/noncommercial media oriented to the specific area. We summated the number of affirmative connections to create a scope variable that reflects the breadth of connectedness to different types of local media (range = 0-3; M =1.59, SD = 1.50).

A parallel procedure was used to assess the scope of connections to mainstream media, the relatively large, commercial, and English-language media that are not targeted to any particular ethnic or residential area audience. Affirmative responses for connecting to mainstream newspapers, radio, and television were summed to generate a score (range = 0–3; M = 2.18, SD = .87).

DATA ANALYSIS

We used structural equation modeling (Jöreskog & Sörbom, 1989) to test the theoretical model in Fig. 21.1. The unfolding procedure began by testing our hypothesized structural model using EQS/Window, a statistical program that tests structural equation models (Bentler, 1995). Then we conducted a WALD test against the hypothesized model. The WALD test checks all the estimated paths, and selects those that are not contributing to the fitness of the model. Non-significant (p > .05) paths are eliminated. This resulted in a revised structural path model in which all paths were significant.

RESULTS

The zero-order correlation matrix of all variables in the model is in Table 21.1, along with their respective means and standard deviations.

Relationships between the five types of variables (structural, macro, meso, micro storytelling, and civic actions) were organized in a structural equation model. Maximum likelihood estimation was used to estimate the model. The independence model, which assumes that the variables in the model are uncorrelated, was rejected. That is, the chi-square difference test indicated significant improvement in fit between the independence model and the hypothesized model (Fig. 21.1).

Post hoc model modifications were performed in an attempt to develop a more parsimonious model. On the basis of the WALD test, nonsignificant paths were deleted. In the final model (see Fig. 21.2), the predictors account for 12% of the variance in civic actions after September 11. This revised model satisfies all of the model test criteria[7] (χ^2 = 32.26, df = 7, p = ns, Comparative Fit Index [CFI] = 0.96, Non-NFI = .98, NFI = .98, RMSEA = .04), which means that the revised model fits well to the data (Bentler, 1995).

This post hoc model confirms most of our hypotheses. First, structural variables have indirect effects on civic actions via connections to macro- or meso-level storytellers (H1). Income, homeownership, and immigration history have indirect effects on civic actions through scope of participation in community organizations. Income also has an indirect effect on civic actions through scope of connections to mainstream media. Residential

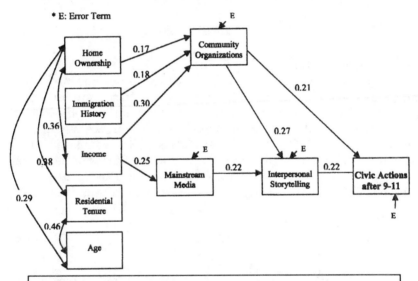

Mainstream Media: Scope of Mainstream Media Connections
Local Media: Scope of Local Media Connections
Community Organization: Scope of Connections to Community Organizations
Interpersonal Storytelling: Intensity of Participation in Interpersonal Storytelling
Civic Actions after 9/11: Scope of Civic Actions after 9/11

Fig. 21.2. Post hoc structural model of 9/11 storytelling

[7]The following criteria were used to evaluate how well the proposed model fit the observed correlation matrix (Bentler, 1995): (a) chi-square statistic (nonsignificant), (b) the Bentler–Bonett Normed Fit Index (NFI) (greater than .90), (c) the Non-Normed Fit Index (Non-NFI) (greater than .90), and (d) the root mean square error of approximation (RMSEA, less than .05).

tenure and age are correlated with home ownership, but they do not have a direct effect on connections to macro- or meso-level storytellers. Education and gender are excluded from the final model because the WALD test indicates that they do not make a significant contribution to the model.

Second, scope of connections to mainstream media as a macro-level storyteller has an indirect effect on civic actions by stimulating connections to interpersonal storytelling. However, it has neither a direct effect on civic actions nor indirect effects through connections to any meso-level storytellers—local media or community organizations. Therefore, H2 is partially confirmed.

Scope of connections to community organizations has both a direct effect and an indirect effect via intensity of participation in interpersonal storytelling on scope of civic actions (H3). However, scope of local media shows neither direct nor indirect effects on civic actions and is dropped from the final model.

Finally, intensity of participation in interpersonal storytelling has a stronger direct positive effect on civic actions (β = .22, p < .001) than macro or meso-level storytelling variables. H4 is supported.

DISCUSSION

The corrected model (Fig. 21.2) shows an integrated storytelling network in our study area where macro-level (mainstream media), meso-level (community organizations and local media), and micro-level storytellers (residents talking with their neighbors) work together to stimulate residents' participation in civic actions in response to the September 11 tragedies. The integrated storytelling network in this local area works as a supportive milieu for participation in national-level civic concerns and actions after the 9/11 tragedies. Among the key storytellers identified in our previous work on neighborhood storytelling (Ball-Rokeach et al., 2001), however, local media were not included as one of the major players in the storytelling network with regard to this nationwide crisis. Local media did not have significant connections to other storytellers and to civic actions in the revised 9/11-storytelling model, and there was no significant link between mainstream media and local media. The lack of local media influence can be explained by considering the stories told by mainstream and local media on and after September 11. In such a nationwide crisis, most key storytellers shared referents, resulting in overlapping stories across different levels of storytellers. Thus, local media, whose niche is to report local or ethnically targeted stories, mainly retold stories about the September 11 events that also were covered by the mainstream media. This type of storytelling may have blurred the boundaries between mainstream media and local media. It also may have weakened the position of local media that are usually inferior to mainstream media in terms of the resources they may devote to covering a national crisis (Ball-Rokeach, 1985, 1998).

Our model testing has several implications. First, it supports the contention that civic actions taken after September 11 were grounded in the multileveled activation of individuals' latent tendencies to engage in civil society. This model shows that the civic actions after the 9/11 tragedies are built on the established storytelling network in a community communication infrastructure. Overall, the 9/11 storytelling model suggests that people who had stronger connections to the existing storytelling network were more likely to participate in various types of civic actions in response to the September 11 crisis than those who had weaker or no connections to the community storytelling network.

Second, the level of participation in interpersonal storytelling is the strongest factor among key storytellers. This result supports the importance of strong interpersonal communication as a driving force for civic actions in response to crises. This also is consistent with what we found in the original storytelling model for neighborhood belonging in noncrisis situations (Ball-Rokeach et al., 2001).

Third, the scope of individuals' connections to community organizations is an important factor for the scope of civic actions. This result suggests that people who had established linkages to community organizations had a better chance of being involved in these civic actions. This may be due to the fact that many civic actions organized after September 11 were led by various kinds of local as well as national organizations. This finding is consistent with previous studies suggesting that individuals' involvement in organized collective actions—by way of continuing relationships with community organizations, community leaders, or local governments—predicts their level of participation in collective activities organized in response to various natural and social disasters (Hallman & Wandsersman, 1992; Stone & Levine, 1985).

Fourth, the positive effect of mainstream media on interpersonal storytelling is consistent with the findings of previous communication studies where the importance of mass media as an information resource, compared to smaller scale targeted media or interpersonal communication, increased in ambiguous situations

(Ball-Rokeach, Rokeach, & Grube, 1984; Loges, 1994). Our findings go one step further to indicate that even in the extremely ambiguous situation wrought by the September 11 tragedies, the effect of mainstream media is mediated by interpersonal storytelling processes to effectively influence the level of participation in civic actions (Wyatt et al., 2000). Put simply, mainstream media cannot be the sole factor for civic participation in crisis situations despite their large-scale capacities for delivering crisis information. The contribution of mainstream media to promoting civic actions is made most effective when people also have strong ties to interpersonal storytelling in their communities.

22

Public Opinion Responses in Germany

Elisabeth Noelle-Neumann
Allensbach Institute

Two days after the terrorist attacks in the United States—on Thursday, September 13, from 5:30 to 9 p.m.—the Allensbach Institute completed 506 telephone interviews with a representative cross-section of the German population. The goal of the survey was to capture the feelings, expectations, assumptions, and opinions of the German population in the immediate aftermath of the attacks, as depicted in veritable marathon broadcasts by German television and radio and in German newspapers, particularly those newspapers that are mainly sold at the newsstand.

All of the people who answered the telephone calls had heard about the terrorist attacks in New York and Washington, DC. Never before had we recorded such a finding! The only time we came close to obtaining such a result was when we asked Germans in the mid-1960s whether they had ever heard of Konrad Adenauer, who had gained renown as West Germany's first chancellor—but even then, only 99% said they had heard of him.

So many times in the days after the attacks we heard people say: "Nothing will ever be the same as it was before." A great majority of the German population perceived the suicide pilots' demolition of the two towers of the World Trade Center (WTC) as the start of a new era. The following question was posed in this context: "The World Trade Center in New York was destroyed by these acts of terror. Would you say this means the end of half a century of peace for Europe and America or will everything be the same as usual in a few months' time?" Only one out of four Germans could imagine that life would go on as usual after a few months had passed.

A large segment of the population viewed the attacks as something that the American political scientist Samuel Huntington, prophetically foresaw in 1982 (i.e., as a clash of civilizations). The representative cross-section of Germans was asked the following question: "The president of the United States has said, 'This is a monumental battle of good against evil.' Do you agree with him or wouldn't you put it that way?" Here, the Germans were split almost evenly: 44% agreed with Bush and 47% disagreed.

When asked, "Do you think Europe will be drawn into the conflict between America and the Arab world or don't you think so?" 65% expected this would happen, whereas only 23% did not think so. Another question on Germany's possible involvement in the conflict read: "NATO has now decided that the attacks on the United States are to be viewed as an attack on all NATO members, in other words, as an attack on Germany too. Would you say this is the right decision or is it wrong?" A majority of Germans (57%) supported this decision, 25% felt it was wrong, and 20% was undecided.

The great slogan in the days following the attacks was coined by the Social Democrats' leader in the Bundestag, Peter Struck, who declared, "Now we are all Americans!" Almost half of the population (47%) felt this was "Well put," whereas 42% expressed reservations.

In the months to come, it became clear just how deeply shocked the German population was by the events of September 11, as the findings of more and more trend questions pointed to a profound change in the social climate in Germany in the wake of the terrorist attacks. This shift was clearly evidenced by responses to the question, "Is it with hopes or with fears that you view the coming 12 months?" a question that has been posed regularly by the Allensbach Institute since 1949 and one that we have included in our omnibus surveys practically every month for several decades. Within a few days from early to mid-September, the percentage of respondents who said they viewed the coming 12 months "with hopes" plunged from 50% to 30%—the lowest level recorded since 1950. In recent decades, a similarly dramatic reaction was only seen in connection with the oil crisis in 1974 and the outbreak of the Gulf War in 1991.

The attacks in New York and Washington released a multitude of fears and set off a wave of grief. The destruction of the WTC was perceived by many as the start of a new era—an era that took on a different countenance in various parts of the world, as recognized by sensitive observers. Regular travelers reported different reactions in Italy, England, Israel, Germany, and throughout the world. The Germans' reaction is probably best described as a sort of symbolic grieving—the weeks following the attacks were characterized by nationwide moments of silence.

Yet it is also remarkable how quickly the Germans appeared to recover from the initial shock. Again, this is most clearly indicated by the findings of the trend question: "Is it with hopes or with fears that you view the coming 12 months?" The curve resembles a seismograph recording of a short but powerful earthquake: After having fallen to 30%, the share of respondents who said they were looking forward to the future with "hopes" rose constantly in the following months, ultimately returning by January 2002 to the level prior to the attacks (Fig. 22.1).

The same pattern (i.e., shock directly after the attacks followed by a gradual calming process over the next 3 months) is evidenced by a number of trend questions, even though the fluctuations do not always appear so dramatic. One example is the following question: "Generally speaking, would you say that the situation following the terrorist attacks in the United States scares you or would that be going too far?" In the poll conducted on September 13, 2001, 60% admitted the situation scared them. The findings obtained in October and November remained at this level. By December, however, the share of people who felt scared by the situation had fallen to 54%. A similar pattern was observed in response to the question: "Do you feel that the situation in Germany today is cause for concern?" Here, 64% said the situation was "cause for concern," in December, 2001, a figure that had dropped to 50% by January 2002.

The follow-up question, "What is it that concerns you most? What particularly comes to mind?" reveals a reduction of tension practically across the board. The share of respondents who feared that Germany might be drawn into a war declined especially dramatically, dropping from 49% to 37%.

In the wake of the attacks, the Germans were particularly concerned about the potential for conflict between the native population and immigrants from Muslim countries living in Germany. Although it is little known internationally, Germany has a far higher share of immigrants as a percentage of the resident population than

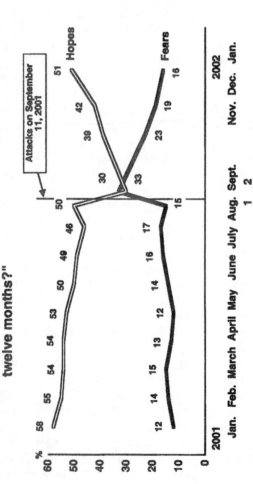

QUESTION: "Is it with hopes or with fears that you view the coming twelve months?"

When figures do not add up to 100, the remaining percentage points correspond to the responses "with scepticism" and "undecided."

SOURCE: Allensbach Archives, IfD Surveys 7001 to 7017

Fig. 22.1. Optimism plunges in Germany in the wake of the September 11 attacks

any other European country except Switzerland. Some 8% of people living in Germany are not German citizens. The real number of immigrants is even higher—immigrants make up as much as 30% of the population of large German cities. Roughly half the immigrants living in Germany are Muslims, mainly of Turkish descent. Until the attacks in America, Germans had experienced remarkably few problems living together with Turkish immigrants. Contrary to what is often assumed, conflicts between the two groups are exceptionally rare—far rarer than in other countries in a comparable situation. After September 11, however, the Germans became aware of the potential for conflict in their own country, a potential perhaps made more apparent by the fact that three of the perpetrators of the attacks had lived and studied in Hamburg for a long time prior to the attacks without drawing any attention to themselves.

Most Germans do not hold Islam responsible for the terrorist attacks in the United States. In October 2001, only 25% of the population agreed with the statement: "I consider Islam to be a dangerous religion; the terrorist attacks were after all carried out in the name of Islam and directed against the western world." The great majority, 65%, said that Islam could not be held responsible for the terrorist attacks carried out in its name. Responses to related questions, however, shed a different light on this issue. In the same survey, conducted in October 2001, 41% of those questioned agreed with the statement: "There are just so many Muslims living in Germany. Sometimes I fear that there may also be many terrorists amongst them." When asked on September 13, "Do you think that tensions will arise between the German population and Muslims living here in Germany, or is there no need to fear this?" 49% said that they did fear tensions; in October, the figure even rose to 55%, but, as in the cases just discussed, emotions then calmed noticeably. In December, the number of those expecting tensions between Germans and Muslim residents in Germany had fallen to 39% (Table 22.1).

The findings presented here could easily lead to the impression that the German population had recovered from the initial shock and returned to its normal everyday life, and that in the middle of 2002, everything was back to the way it had been before the attacks. It is true to say that normality returned to many areas. After all, a nation cannot maintain an emotional state of emergency for a period of months. Another event of the century, namely the introduction on January 1, 2002 of the common European currency, which eclipsed the attacks of September 11 and the war in Afghanistan that followed, may also have contributed to this reduction in tension. After a long period of not being able to get accustomed to the idea of the euro, the end of the year saw a sudden reverse in attitudes in Germany.

Table 22.1.

Question: "Do you think that tensions will arise between the German
population and the Muslims living here in Germany in the
near future, or is there no need to fear this?"*

	Total Population		
	September 13, 2001 %	September/ October 2001 %	November/ December 2001 %
Think tensions will arise	49	55	39
No need to fear this	43	28	36
Undecided, no response	8	17	25
	100	100	100
n =	506	2,049	2,030

---

*September and September/October: "Do you think tensions will now arise between." For
Tables 22.1-22.6, the sample is derived from the population 16 and over in the Federal
Republic of Germany.

Source. Allensbach Archives, IfD Surveys 5165 (Telephone survey), 7012, 7014

People began to look forward to the new currency and
hundreds of thousands of them stormed into banks when the first
coins were released in advance at the end of December, 2001. People
wanted to see the new currency and to hold it in their hands for the
first time. When the Allensbach Institute asked which topics families
had talked about under their Christmas tree, 69% said the euro. When
one considers that the topic of Christmas presents was only in second
place with 55%, it becomes obvious how dominant an issue the euro
was at the turn of the year. In contrast, the war in Afghanistan and
the terrorist attacks were pushed into the background (Table 22.2).

Nevertheless, it would be wrong to assume that the Germans
went through a phase of trauma lasting for 3 months and then
returned to normality. The attacks in the United States accelerated a
series of changes in opinion toward central political issues; changes
that, although already in progress, had not been completed. In many
respects the German population can be seen to have finally "come of
age" in the wake of the attacks. This applies especially to the younger
generation (under the age of 30). One of the fashionable slogans of the
1990s in Germany was *spaßgesellschaft* or "fun society," which stood for
a social development prevalent mainly among the younger generation
that was not at all typical of Germany. The bitter political seriousness

Table 22.2

Question: "What topics did you talk about a lot when you got together
with your family and friends over the holiday season?"
(Presentation of a list)

	Total Population % (n = 1102)
We talked about:	
The introduction of the euro	69
Christmas presents	55
The war in Afghanistan	50
Unemployment	39
The economic situation in Germany	31
The Middle East conflict, clashes between Israelis and Palestinians	31
The danger of terrorist attacks	26

Source. Allensbach Archives, IfD Survey 7016, January 2002

still characteristic of youth culture in the 1980s was replaced by a carefree demeanor devoid of anxiety or tension; by a feeling that anything goes because nothing really matters. It was a development underpinned by irony. Politics was above all something to joke about.

The end of this *spaßgesellschaft*, often heralded since the turn of the century, may well have arrived in the form of the terrorist attacks of September 11, which were at the same time a gripping and a sobering experience for the younger generation. Although the older generations' responses to many central political questions remained completely unaffected by the attacks, this certainly cannot be said of the younger generation. When asked about areas of interest before September 11, 41% of respondents 30 and under said that domestic policy was of little or no interest to them. When the question was posed after September 11, this figure was only 27% (Table 22.3). The same is true of the younger generation's attitude toward foreign policy. Prior to September 1, 43% of Germans under the age of 30 said that foreign policy was of little or no interest to them. After September 11, only 28% of this group turned their back on foreign policy issues.

The Germans' attitude toward the issue of interior security has changed dramatically. Political developments the 1980s have lead to Germany having one of the strictest data protection laws in the world. The exchange of personal records between different public authorities is, for example, subject to extremely tight restrictions.

Table 22.3

	Young People Under 30	
	Before the Attacks %	After %
Young people who-		
Are interested in domestic policy	59	73
Are interested in foreign policy	56	70
Like Americans	47	57
Like the sight of the black, red, and gold German flag	43	53

Source. Allensbach Archives, IfD Surveys 6076, 7012

The spirit of the 1980s made even the most harmless of statistical surveys practically impossible to conduct in Germany. A national census that had already been prepared had to be abandoned, revised, and postponed for several years because of angry public protests. Citing George Orwell's *1984*, protest groups succeeded in giving broad sections of the population the impression that the federal government would use data ascertained on income, family, and living conditions to establish a "big brother" state with all-encompassing control over its citizens.

The Germans had already begun to moderate their stance toward data protection issues during the 1990s, but now, after the assassinations in New York, the public is calling for measures that would have triggered furious protests just years earlier. The federal government's plans to combat terrorist activities have found almost universal approval in all political camps. In October 2001, 76% of the German population approved of the office for the protection of the constitution investigating foreigners wanting to take up residence in Germany; 66% spoke out for a more extensive regulation requiring banks to provide information about any suspect transactions; 65% were in favor of unhindered data exchange between security and other public authorities; and 58% were in agreement with a general slackening of data protection regulations. Only 25% of the population voiced worries that such measures might pose a threat to an open and free society.

The German population has also completely changed its attitude toward the military. Defense expenditure was cut back enormously after German reunification and the army was reduced in size from almost 500,000 to 370,000. The army also was not modernized and the political climate tended toward further cuts in the defense budget. The Germans wanted nothing more to do with the military. A substantial minority—in east Germany even a relative majority—of the population were of the opinion that the end of the cold war had rendered NATO completely unnecessary. When the Gulf War broke out in 1991, Germany's participation was unthinkable. The thought of German soldiers being deployed on military action in a foreign country was unbearable for many on purely historical grounds. Instead, moral indignation about America's handling of the situation became widespread within many sectors of the population. Tens of thousands of Germans took to the streets bearing candles and formed pickets, called "chains of light" in protest against the military action.

After the Gulf War, the Germans slowly became accustomed to fulfilling military obligations, even international ones. It no longer caused a stir when, finally, Germany took an active part in military action in the Kosovo Conflict in 1999 nor when it established itself as one of the leading peace-keeping forces in the region thereafter. September 11 greatly strengthened this re-found support for the military. October 2001 was the first occasion on which the majority of the German population agreed that the German army needed to be better equipped to fulfill its obligations within NATO (Table 22.4) and only 10% of the west German population and 24% of east Germans considered NATO to be redundant (Table 22.5).

Table 22.4

| Question: | "If someone were to say: 'The German army must be better equipped in future. Otherwise, it will not be able to fulfill its obligations as a member of NATO (i.e., to come to the aid of other NATO partners in conflict situations).' Would you agree with this statement or would you disagree?" |

	Total Population	
	August/ September 2001 %	October/ November 2001 %
Agree	42	53
Disagree	25	19
Undecided, no response	33	28
	100	100

Source. Allensbach Archives, IfD Surveys 7010, 7013

Table 22.5

Question: "Two people are talking here about NATO, the western defense alliance. Which of the two would you tend to agree with, the one above or the one below?" (Presentation of illustration)

	Total Population					
	November 1991 %	April/May 1994 %	May 1995 %	August 1997 %	August/ September 2001 %	October/ November 2001 %
"Now that the eastern European states and the former Soviet Union no longer pose any threat to us, NATO is no longer important at all as a military alliance"	27	16	15	18	17	12
"NATO must continue to be a strong alliance so that we will be prepared for any emergency. You never know where in the world trouble might arise next."	57	74	71	69	70	75
Undecided	16	10	14	13	13	13
	100	100	100	100	100	100
n =	2,119	999	453	2,028	1,035	980

Source. Allensbach Archives, IfD Surveys 5055, 5094, 6015, 6047, 7010, 7013

This tendency goes hand in hand with a clear rise in Germans' self-confidence regarding their country's role in the world. It is as if the nation has for the first time managed to shake off a few of the shadows of its past. Throughout the 1990s, when asked the question, "Should Germany take on more responsibility in the world, or should it keep a low profile?" the majority agreed with the statement: "Germany should keep a low profile." Now, in January 2002, the majority of those who expressed an opinion for the first time believe that Germany should take on more responsibility in the world (Table 22.6).

Finally, a completely unexpected effect of the terrorist attacks: The ideological differences between east and west Germans, which had remained stubbornly intact ever since reunification, have been noticeably reduced in response to this exterior threat. Despite all the joy about reunification and, notwithstanding the economic problems, the immeasurable progress since made in developing the east German states, many people who grew up in east Germany continued to hold a skeptical opinion of western Germany and the new political system. During the decade after German reunification, whenever asked, "Is our social order worth defending?" the east German population was split in its response. Only in July of last year, 39% of East Germans said that they doubted whether the social

Table 22.6

Question: "Should Germany take on more responsibility in the world or should we keep a low profile?"

	Should Take on More Responsibility %	Should Keep a Low Profile %	Undecided %
1991: September	31	56	13
December	23	59	18
1992: June	28	55	17
1993: March	37	49	14
1994: October	41	46	13
2002: January	41	29	30

Source. Allensbach Archives, IfD Surveys 5055, 5059, 5067, 5078, 6007, 7016

order of the Federal Republic of Germany was worth defending. After the attacks, there was a noticeable change in perspective. For the first time since the early 1990s, the clear majority of the east German population feels that the social order of their country is worth defending (Table 22.7). The Germans pull together in the face of a threat.

Table 22.7. East Germany: Population 16 and Over

Question: "Thinking of life in Germany, would you say that our social order in its present form here in the Federal Republic is worth defending or do you have doubts about this?"

	East Germans	
	Before the Attacks July 2001 %	After the Attacks October 2001 %
Is worth defending	42	55
Have doubts about this	39	29
Undecided	19	16
	100	100

Source. Allensbach Archives, IfD Surveys 7008, 701

23

Summary and Discussion

Bradley S. Greenberg
Linda Hofschire
Michigan State University

Chapters in this volume have been organized according to their primary emphasis. However, some variables of significant interest, particularly those dealing with individual responses to news of the terrorist attacks, overlap across sections. This summary then crosscuts where necessary to bring together relevant findings.

The first section of this volume highlights the importance and excellence of television in conveying information, providing a communal meeting place and stimulating interpersonal communication in response to the tragedies of 9/11. At the same time, it identifies the strong need and role of interpersonal relationships in not only sharing and interpreting the news, but also in coping with troubling information. Related research deals with general media roles and gratifications in time of crisis, the present role of the Internet, and the spontaneous emotions emanating from the 9/11 experience.

TELEVISION AND INTERPERSONAL COMMUNICATION

These two go in tandem with crisis events, particularly if the crisis is "made for television," as were the terrorist attacks. When we think of 9/11, it's a good bet that we think first with the pictures in our head that originated with television—one or both planes crashing into the World Trade Center or one or both towers collapsing onto themselves (Greenberg, Hofschire, & Lachlan, Chap. 1).

Television and interpersonal contacts combined for prominence as initial sources of information about the tragedies. In one national sample conducted for 1 week beginning on September 12, 44% of those surveyed reported that television had been their first source of information, with 31% finding out from others, and 22% hearing it first on the radio (see Jones & Rainie, Chap. 3). These figures closely match another national sample study conducted 5 weeks later, 50% reporting that television was their initial source, 30% finding out from others and 17% first hearing from radio (Stempel & Hargrove, Chap. 2). One localized study done in Michigan on September 12 and September 13 pegged the interpersonal channels even more strongly, as fully 50% reported first hearing from others, one-third from television, and 15% from the radio (Greenberg et al., Chap. 1). A second study done in three university communities also pinpointed the initial interpersonal connection at 48%, with television at 28% and radio at 24% (Ruggiero & Glascock, Chap. 6).

Regardless of how we first found out, we immediately turned to (or remained with) television for an average of 7 hours (Greenberg et al., Chap. 1). In the Scripps studies, 69% indicated that television was most useful (Stempel & Hargrove, Chap. 2); in the Michigan study, 88% said they relied most on television (Greenberg et al., Chap. 1), and television remained the primary source of information across the first week (Ruggiero & Glascock, Chap. 6). Why television? In addition to the visual nature of the event, television was determined to be best for its surveillance (informative) function and best for accessibility over radio, newspapers, and the Internet (Ruggiero & Glascock, Chap. 6). In Germany, where the broadcasts began about 2:45 p.m., television was deemed most important by 80% of a national sample (Roeser & Schaefer, Chap. 8).

Then we started talking with others about what was happening. Half the Pew national sample phoned family and 40% phoned friends (Jones & Rainie, Chap. 3). Fully two thirds of another sample tried to tell someone else what was happening. Then, later on Tuesday or on Wednesday, one half told one or two others, but 14% talked with nine or more other people. Young people talked more with others than older people did. E-mail activity soared and is discussed in another section of this chapter. Talking with others was reported by one fifth as a primary means of coping with what they were watching and hearing. The same proportion reported that praying provided their main coping mechanism (Greenberg et al., Chap. 1).

MEDIA ROLES, INFORMATION NEEDS, AND GRATIFICATIONS

The relative importance of different media roles was examined by Perse and her colleagues (see Chap. 4). Providing information, explaining the significance of the events, and building solidarity were equally and highly important to a national sample by the second week in October. How much the respondents feared terrorism was a positive predictor of the importance of all three of these roles. Stronger endorsement of media openness positively predicted the importance of providing information and explaining the significance of events, but was a negative predictor of building solidarity (i.e., media depictions of anti-war images work against solidarity-building).

Less prominent but still important media roles were reducing tension and providing comfort. Predictors of these two roles included overall approval of the job the media were doing and reliance on the media for information.

These general media roles may have their counterparts in the specification of what information was most desired. Within five days of 9/11, large majorities of respondents (from 97% to 78%) from three cities wanted to know foremost about the cause of the attacks, continuing threats, damage, the broader implications of what was happening, who was affected, and the nature of rescue efforts (Seeger et al., Chap. 5).

Gratifications sought from the 9/11 news experiences provide another means of sorting out information needs (Ruggiero & Glascock, Chap. 6). The primary gratification sought was that of surveillance, referring to timely, informative, and detailed news. A second need was that of news accessibility, (e.g., readily available), and a tertiary need of *communication* with others, best satisfied outside of traditional media with e-mail, telephone, or face-to-face contacts.

THE INTERNET

Several studies explored the role of the Internet in the public's efforts to deal with the news of 9/11. Overall, Internet activity lessened in the immediate aftermath of the attacks, in terms of total users, as well as senders and receivers of e-mail (Jones & Rainie, Chap. 3). About one fourth of those with Internet access spent some time online on 9/11, and the majority of those spent 30 minutes or less (Greenberg et al., Chap. 1). One fourth of those online were found to be multitasking with television or radio (Jones & Rainie, Chap. 3).

E-mail activity was pervasive, with estimates ranging from 42% who sent or read e-mail (Jones & Rainie, Chap. 3) to 59% e-mail usage (Ruggiero & Glascock) to 68% receiving and 48% sending (Greenberg et al., Chap. 1). E-mail use immediately after 9/11 centered on receiving or sending patriotic material (46%), prayer requests (33%), and notes of consolation (25%) (Jones & Rainie, Chap. 3).

The Internet was the first or primary source of information for only 1%-2% of the public (Jones & Rainie, Chap. 3). The highest estimate of the Internet as the most useful source of information—6%—came from a national study conducted 6 weeks after 9/11 (Stempel & Hargrove, Chap. 2).

The two Pew Center national surveys (the weeks of September 12 and September 20) offer the most comprehensive examination of the Internet (Jones & Rainie, Chap. 3). Overall, they found that all Internet functions—e-mail, browsing, purchases, hobby efforts, and work-related research—save one—getting news—decreased in the week following 9/11. And all these functions were found to be restored to normal levels by the time of their second survey 1 week later. Getting news online was not easy as 43% had trouble accessing Web sites, in part because the increase in unique visitor traffic ranged as high as 680% for CNN's Web site.

The news sought online was primarily information about the attacks (50%), but one third wanted financial information, one quarter wanted information about Osama bin Laden, and one fifth about Afghanistan. In addition, one fifth downloaded pictures of the American flag!

INITIAL REACTIONS

The research in this volume showed that the most common initial response to news of the terrorist attacks was that of disbelief and/or surprise (Step, Finuace, & Horvath, Chap. 19), followed by a string of physical symptoms, for example, crying, nervousness, and feeling dazed—all reported by more than half of one sample (Greenberg et al., Chap. 1). In Seeger et al.'s nonrandom sample, the emotions were even more pervasive (e.g., more than two thirds expressed sorrow, sadness, confusion, and anger). Additionally, more than half said they were frightened. The Scripps national surveys reported that 56% felt less safe (Stempel & Hargrove, Chap. 2), and this was most apparent among women and younger people. What frightened them? They were worried about flying in a commercial airplane, about the possibility of another major attack, and worried that the activities would affect them personally (Greenberg et al., Chap. 1). Nationally, 30% thought it very or somewhat likely they personally would be the victim of a terrorist attack (Stempel & Hargrove, Chap. 2). Again, these feelings were most manifest in women and younger respondents.

THE CONTENT OF 9/11

Part II contained analyses of both news and non-news content concerning 9/11. The content analysis by Mogensen et al. (Chap. 9) reified what we all saw on television. The first 8 hours (from 8:48 a.m. to 5 p.m. EST) of network television news coverage focused first on the World Trade Center (29%), second on the president and government operations (18%), and third on terrorism (10%). Sharp discrepancies were identified among the networks (e.g., 25% of the Fox news topics were on the presidency and government as compared with 9% on NBC). But there is no specific evidence as to why these differences occur. From those same data, however, it is apparent that the traditional networks (ABC, CBS, and NBC) presented more "overviews," than CNN or Fox.

In the first 8 hours of coverage, three of every four stories were factual and one in five were analytical. This was not a time frame in which the stories were offering consolation or guidance to the viewers. Additionally, less than half the stories (42%) had identifiable sources. Sources most relied on were government officials (18%) and witnesses/observers at the sites of the terrorist attacks. No other single source was found in as many as 5% of the stories in the first 8 hours.

This content analysis also examined the news coverage "frame," in which the frame was identified through the "angle" or story focus. The three primary frames identified were those of the disaster (44%), political considerations (22%), and a criminal frame (12%).

Key issues, defined as the main focus of the problems, questions, or disputes discussed in the coverage, were an important component of the analysis. Description of the incidents and discussion of the severity of the disaster topped the key issue list (18% each), followed by terrorism, the reaction of the U.S. government, and safety concerns—all ranging from 13%–15%, with no other key issues at 10% or higher. The similarity of these percentages across five topics reflects the great variability among the networks (e.g. 13% of the CBS key issues were descriptions of the incidents, compared with 27% at NBC). The origin of these differences is not known.

In contrast to the immediacy of this 8-hour analysis, Dooley and Corman (Chap. 10) examined 66 days (September 11 to November 15) of Reuters news releases. Using several sophisticated computer-analytic and statistical techniques, they identified six themes that they claim captured the major events of the 2-month period. Additionally, they plotted the way these themes changed over time as an indication of their relative influence.

The *WTC attack* theme is initially a major influence and steadily decays across the time period studied. The *economic impact* of the events had an early influence in response to foreign markets, then remained small until there were further influences associated with the anthrax attacks. *Airport security* also had immediate influence, which fell until new airport initiatives were introduced, then fell again until those new initiatives were put in place. The nation's *military response* was of little influence until the U.S. decision to wage its war on terrorism. It remained fairly strong with another major spike in influence when the first major town in Afghanistan fell. The *political response* was influential for a relatively brief period, first when world leaders reacted to the attacks, and more so when Middle East leaders responded to the potential of U.S. retaliation. Finally, the *anthrax* theme did not exist until the 28th day when the Florida anthrax case became known, and it increased linearly until the death of two postal workers, after which it steadily decreased in importance.

The researchers then proposed and tested a stimulus-response model across the themes and periodic changes in the relative influence of these themes. That model suggested that a terrorist event (WTC attack, anthrax) led to an institutional response (military, political, air security) and sense-making about the economic impact on society.

These studies support the need for over-time analyses of news content. The variation over time—be it 8 hours or 66 days—in both studies and among networks in the former study suggest that more static studies are likely to be less generalizable.

Part II also contained several analyses of non-news content concerning the attacks. One of these studies focused on the depiction of the terrorists in cartoons. Hart and Hassencahl (Chap. 11) analyzed portrayals of the "enemy" (i.e., bin Laden, al-Qaida, or the Taliban) in a sample of editorial cartoons from a group of newspapers between September 11 and October 8. They found that 23% of these cartoons portrayed the enemy and the vast majority (91%) did so in a dehumanizing manner. The most common types of dehumanization were enemy-as-animal (e.g., rat, reptile) and enemy-as-aggressor (e.g., carrying weapons). The authors argued that it is important to study dehumanization metaphors because they may cause readers to support the killing of the enemies.

Another analysis focused on the terrorists' manipulation of the news media. Debatin (Chap. 13) argued that the terrorists planned their attacks to receive full media attention by using several strategies. These included (a) the timing of the attacks, as they occurred when most of the world was awake; (b) the aesthetics of the event, which made for a shocking visual image; (c) the redundancy in news coverage, as the media showed the horrific images of the attacks repeatedly during the first hours after they occurred, while providing little background information; and (d) mystification and glorification of the event, as the attack was a surprise and little was known about the terrorists and their motives. Debatin argued that these circumstances led to an environment where the media disseminated information that more closely represented propaganda than thoughtful journalism, and where criticism of the government was considered unpatriotic and intolerable.

Finally, Pompper (Chap. 12) looked at displays of patriotism in Tallahassee, Florida, following the events of 9/11. She found that patriotism existed at three levels: in personal adornment (e.g., pins, ribbons, patriotic clothing), in the home (e.g., flags, posters, signs, banners), and in transit (e.g., bumper stickers). Pompper argued that in recent years, Americans' desire for privacy has precluded their participation in community functions and patriotic events. However, people's renewed interest in displaying patriotism after 9/11 reflected a blurring of private and public space, as individuals came forward to express support for their country.

Taken together, the findings of these analyses of non-news content suggest that expressions of crisis events are not confined to news media, but extend to cartoons and other forms of content. It is important to determine whether these types of portrayals, as well as news portrayals, impact the public's perceptions and attitudes toward crisis events.

RESPONSES TO 9/11

Part III dealt with the public's responses to news of the terrorist attacks. Although a variety of research approaches were used to assess these responses, several similar findings emerged. The first common finding concerned the impact of media exposure to the events on emotional responses. Among undergraduates (Hoffner, Fujioka, Ibrahim, & Ye, Chap. 17), children between the ages of 5 and 17 (Smith, Moyer, Boyson, & Pieper, Chap. 15), and national samples (Snyder & Park, Chap. 14), there was a significant and positive relationship between televised exposure to the events and emotional upset. For example, Hoffner et al. found that those respondents who learned about the events from television reported being more upset about the events. Similarly, those children with more exposure to television news in Smith et al.'s sample were more concerned about their personal safety and flying, according to parents' reports. And, in Snyder and Park's analysis of 30 national opinion polls, they found that media exposure positively predicted posttraumatic stress disorder (PTSD). In particular, exposure to graphic footage of the attacks as well as to information concerning how to take safety precautions was positively related to stress reactions.

Another study measured the amount of interpersonal communication behavior in addition to amount of mass media use in the first two days after 9/11 and found the two were not correlated with each other (Greenberg et al., Chap. 1). Indices of these two modes of communication then were related to the respondents' expressed worries and to their physiological reactions to news of the terrorist attacks. Higher levels of mass media use and interpersonal contacts were related to higher incidence of nervousness, tension, and so on. Higher levels of interpersonal contacts also were related to more intense worries. However, in an online survey, Brown, Bocarnea, and Basil (Chap. 18) found no differences in grief, fear, and sympathy between those respondents who first learned about the events from television and those who learned from interpersonal sources. These findings, taken together, suggest that it was an accumulation of media exposure, as opposed to an initial media experience, that led to stronger emotional responses.

A second common element dealt with gender differences in response to the attacks. Snyder and Park, Hoffner et al., and Smith et al. found that the females reported more fear than the males in their samples. Snyder and Park also reported that women were more likely than men to have nightmares. Further, Baukus and Strohm

(Chap. 20) found that compared with female undergraduates, male undergraduates were more supportive of the use of force to resolve conflicts and were more likely to disagree that the media should report all war-related events. Women also wished they had more time to watch the news coverage, whereas men reported already understanding the war.

A third common finding concerned how individuals coped with the news of the attacks. In their study of undergraduates' responses to 9/11, Hoffner et al. found that those respondents with stronger emotional responses engaged in more interpersonal news diffusion. And, the method used most often to cope with the events was news media exposure, followed by discussion with others.

Other coping mechanisms also were reported. The most common mechanisms were by talking with others and by praying, among different segments of the population (Greenberg et al., Chap. 1). Did the media help people cope? Yes and no from the Scripps studies (Stempel & Hargrove, Chap. 2). One third said they helped them cope, one third said they made them feel worse, and the remainder said they had no effect. More interesting, the men fell more so on the no effect side, and the women split between the media helping them cope and making them feel worse.

News about uncontrollable threatening events, in this case the terrorist attacks, provided the basis for Spirek et al. to study two psychological coping strategies by comparing media diaries of September 10 with September 12. Their blunters prefer to cope by distracting themselves, and they did so by increasing their entertainment viewing. Although the blunters failed to decrease their news viewing, as expected, it would have been difficult for them to do much less than they had done on 9/10. Their monitors prefer to cope by obtaining as much available information as possible, and they did so by increasing their news viewing and decreasing their entertainment viewing. Individual difference variables may be necessary to better explain media exposure differences or what might appear initially to be nondifferences.

A fourth pattern of findings regarded civic action in response to the events of September 11. The 6- to 11-year-old children in Royer and Schmitt's (Chap. 16) sample reported wanting to help others by "stopping the bad guys," "saving the world," or by donating money to those who were impacted by the attacks. Step et al. (Chap. 19) found that the most common reaction of those who identified through television with individuals affected by the tragedy was to help others (e.g., give blood, donate money). Going further, Kim, Ball-Rokeach, Cohen, and Jung (Chap. 21) investigated factors that predicted participation in civic actions. They found that exposure to mainstream media, involvement in community organizations, and talking with neighbors all positively predicted Los Angeles residents' participation in civic activities.

A fifth common finding regarded how reactions changed over time. Both nationally (Snyder & Park, Chap. 14) and internationally (a random sample of German residents; Noelle-Neumann, Chap. 22), individuals' fears about the future diminished as time passed. However, Snyder and Park reported that feelings of increased personal vulnerability, in particular, persisted.

Finally, patriotic responses to the attacks as well as increased interest in and support of one's country also were reported. German residents expressed more interest in domestic and foreign policy, were more supportive of bolstering the German army to assist NATO, and felt more patriotic toward their country after the attacks (Noelle Neumann, Chap. 22). In the United States, children reported how proud they were of their country, and boys in particular named figures such as the president, policemen, and firefighters as their heroes (Royer & Schmitt, Chap. 16). Furthermore, undergraduate women were less likely to question media credibility and bias, compared with media reporting during the Gulf War (Baukus & Strohm, Chap. 20).

In addition to these common themes across the studies, unique findings were reported as well, among children, undergraduates, and both national and international samples of adults. Beginning with children, Smith et al. (Chap. 15) surveyed parents about their 5- to 17-year-old children's fear responses. They found that both news exposure to the 9/11 attacks and fear increased with age. The most frequently reported manifestation of fear was behavioral upset (e.g., nightmares, anxiety attacks).

Royer and Schmitt also found that television news exposure increased with age among their 6- to 11-year-olds. Furthermore, they looked at the extent to which children turned to adults to try to make sense of the events. Of the children who knew about the terrorist attacks (94%), all of the 9- to 11-year-olds and half of the 6- to 8-year-olds reported talking to adults about the events sometimes or a lot.

Also using undergraduate respondents, Step et al. assessed co-viewing, finding that nearly three fourths of their sample watched the television coverage with at least one other person. Individuals' reasons for co-viewing included proximity (e.g., watching together because they were home with family), comfort (e.g., watching together to share the experience with someone else), and sensemaking (e.g., watching together to discuss the events).

Moving to broader populations, Brown et al. (Chap. 18) found that television exposure was positively associated with both emotional (i.e., feelings of fear and sympathy), and informational (i.e., knowledge about the attacks) outcomes among an online sample of U.S. respondents. Exposure to TV news also was positively associated with attributing blame to Islamic radicals.

Seeger and his colleagues offered a linkage between the emotions and the information needs of their respondents. Sadness for example was positively correlated with wanting information about who might be affected and about the larger implications of these events. The amount of confusion felt was positively related to wanting reassuring information from political leaders. Anger was associated with information needs about the rescue operations, who might be affected and political reassurances.

In their analysis of national public opinion polls, Snyder and Park (Chap. 14) found that PTSD, as diagnosed by experiencing intense fear, re-experiencing the event, psychic numbing, arousal, depression, and dysfunction, was high: 6% to 7% of the U.S. population experienced these symptoms after the attacks. As a comparison, one estimate of lifetime prevalence of PTSD is 1% of the population (Helzer, Robins, & McEvoy, 1987). Therefore, reactions to 9/11 were stronger than mental health experts would have predicted. Snyder and Park also reported that of all media, television exposure was the most important predictor of stress on 9/11 and 2 months later, as well as PTSD severity.

Finally, in Noelle-Neumann's (Chap. 22) report of German public opinion polls, she found that the majority of respondents did not believe that life would go on as usual for Europe or America. Indeed, nearly two thirds of the respondents believed that Europe would become involved in the U.S.–Afghanistan conflict. In addition to worry about international conflicts, the German people also reported concern about potential conflict with the Muslim immigrants living in Germany. Hence, respondents were supportive of increased security measures within Germany, including the investigation of foreigners wanting to reside in Germany, more stringent regulation of banks, and unhindered data exchange between security and other public authorities. U.S. leaders in the post 9/11 era have sought parallel measures.

DISCUSSION

One motive in assembling this collection of research and scholarship was to provide a chronicle of strong academic responses to a unique and horrible event. The horror attribute continues to ring true.

However, as we wrote this concluding chapter in May 2002, the week's news announcements from President Bush, Vice-President Cheney, and the head of homeland security all strongly warned that thinking the attack would remain unique in U.S. history would be a serious error in judgment. As citizens, we must prepare ourselves for attacks that may be suicidal, nuclear, and/or biological. As citizens whose concerns about the possibilities of recurring terrorism declined sharply in the months after 9/11, our worry index may be undergoing marked increases with each new colored alert or alarm. Do public opinion polls show worry spurts and do stock market closings show economic dips with each vague pronouncement? How have (and will) our daily lives change in response to actual and potential threats?

Researchers can and should plan ahead. If some believe it ghoulish to prepare for research about disasters, others consider it foolish not to do so. The special skills of communication and media scholars, as well as media professionals, can be brought to focus on a variety of issues, little discussed in this volume. First, how does one best prepare and inform the public about pending security issues and threats of additional attacks? How graphic should the presentation be for terrorist incidents, given the general reluctance of news agencies to present visuals of individuals jumping from the WTC towers? Second, the evidence in this volume is strong that extended media exposure is related to a variety of negative symptomatic outcomes, rather than consoling responses. The origin of that relationship is examined separately in this discussion. Third, given evidence as to how people attempt to cope with such news, can appropriate coping mechanisms or strategies be established in advance that will reduce or contain stress? How different are these to be for children, youth, and adults? What will principals and parents do the next time? Fourth, what can social researchers do to upgrade their preparation, when (and not if, Cheney has avowed) the next serious terrorist attack occurs?

This volume then provides benchmark data, perhaps, rather than unique evidence, if our leaders correctly predict America's near future. Undoubtedly, other studies, not yet made available or known to us, will emerge and will be helpful. Most empirical studies here were of the firehouse variety, packaged over a week or a weekend. Some, as at the University of Southern California, were able to take advantage of ongoing field activities to re-contact their respondents. Others, as at the Pew Center, had baseline estimates of Internet activity against which they could compare Internet behavior on and after 9/11. Preparation for subsequent research might begin now to consider periodic assessments of public concerns about terrorism, children's general levels of fear, normative news media exposure, and the extensiveness and makeup of social communication networks. Additionally, we know too little about individual needs for closure in assigning blame and individual propensities to turn to or turn away from unpleasant news. All these would be instrumental should a next round of research be forthcoming. The point of course is to be as prepared as possible, both as citizens and as researchers.

Another research intrigue is the role of the media and interpersonal communication in assuaging fear and/or consoling grief. Certainly, there was some expectation in several studies reported in this volume that, over time, the media would function to alleviate or ease viewers' concerns. A similar role was perceived for the utilization of our social networks as well. The data do not appear supportive of those expectations. Generally, the findings reflected a positive or null relationship of media experiences with negative physical symptoms and degree of concern. Social communication also was associated more often with stronger worries or concerns and negative symptoms.

Three possible reasons for these outcomes are offered here. First, there is the problem of asking about both media exposure (or talking with others) concurrently with asking about worries and physical reactions to the attacks. This negates the ability to establish an appropriate time sequence. Surely, it is as reasonable to argue that those who were most concerned sought out more media and/or sought out more others with whom to share their concerns, as it is to argue that media-seeking or people-seeking induced stronger concerns.

Second, the issue of time in which such outcomes might occur has not been dealt with thoroughly. For example, consider the way in which Dooley and Corman (Chap. 10) mapped news emphases over 66 days, identifying news surges and their decrements. One anticipates that some individual responses, such as anxiety symptoms and expressed worries, may be relatively flexible. There might be a sharp increase as an immediate response to distressing news, then a waning as calmer news prevails, and new peaks and valleys in reaction to further developments (e.g., the anthrax issue). Thus, if responses are measured at different times or news epochs, it is reasonable to expect that in some of those times, the relationship between media exposure and anxieties will differ than if measured at other times.

We choose to argue more strongly for the third possibility, although it is in part inherent in what we have already said. To focus on amount of media exposure or frequency of interpersonal discussions without regard to the specific content of those experiences ignores much of what we think we know about communication effects. Surely, what is being said is at least as important, and generally more important, than how often it is said. If the media are telling me that I should continue to be wary because of the likelihood of additional acts of terrorism, then that message is unlikely to dispel my concerns. If the people I talk with are expressing concerns at least as severe as my own, then that message also is unlikely to console me. In none of the studies reported in this volume do the message content valence and content emphasis, or reports of them, appear to be examined. A triangulated research opportunity exists in which the content of the media can be analyzed independently, then compared to users' perceptions of that content, and both crossed with pre- and postexposure attitudes, worries and physiological reactions.

Another aspect of anxiety in the context of seemingly uncontrollable events is that of seeking closure. Closure may be obtained in part from providing a target to blame. At the time of the assassinations of John and Robert Kennedy, the early arrest of their assassins brought some measure of closure. At the time of the Oklahoma City bombing, blame was initially misdirected at Arab sources, but served the same purpose until the correct perpetrator was jailed. For 9/11, the speed with which the American public accepted Osama bin Laden as the primary villain was astonishing. If asked who bin Laden was on September 10, perhaps 2% might have been correct; by September 13, two thirds had learned his name and blamed him for the terrible deeds. Thus, the media have a special responsibility in assigning blame because we have a strong need to blame some entity, and are perhaps too willing to accept the first available and identified target.

What is not yet tapped by the available research is the extent to which we then generalize from the specific villain for 9/11 to all Islamic followers, to all Arabs, and so on. In other words, when the villain is a minority race or minority religion, is the majority of America more willing to assume guilt rather than innocence, and to extend that guilt to others who "look like him"? What responsibility do the media have to forestall such generalities and to differentiate what might appear superficially to be alike?

Complete closure comes not with identifying the enemy, but with dispatching the enemy. Will it be sufficient if bin Laden is dealt with, or does the magnitude of the deed require a greater retribution? What role do the media have in increasing or diminishing the call to arms and the call for vengeance?

One issue of interest to several of the researchers in this volume was the Internet's role during a crisis event. Previous diffusion studies have shown the dominance of television during major events, but with Internet access at 64% nationally at the time of the attacks, we wondered whether Americans would turn to it instead of television for information. However, the studies suggest that the Internet played a supplementary role to television during the 9/11 attacks. Why was this the case? The first reason may be technological limitations. At the time of the attacks the Internet had limited video capacities. Because the attacks were a highly visual event, television was superior in conveying information about them. Furthermore, many Web sites were not prepared to handle the massive number of users that attempted to log on during 9/11. Therefore, individuals may have tried to access the Internet for information, but were forced to turn to television when they were not able to log on to a Web site. It seems possible that as video technology and high-speed Internet access become more widespread, and as Web sites become able to handle greater numbers of users, the internet will have the potential to become a primary source of information in times of crisis.

Second, because the Internet is a relatively new medium, it seems likely that individuals may find television more credible, reliable, and even more comforting. Television news is an established format; audiences believe that the information comes from a credible source. In contrast, there is less certainty about the credibility of online information sources. Moreover, on television news, viewers can identify with familiar and trusted faces. Viewers have a history with news anchors and feel safe watching them in times of crisis. At present, the Internet does not have an equivalent counterpart for its users.

However, the Internet allows users to access a greater variety of information and to have more control over what news they receive. Whereas television news is a passive media experience, individuals can actively search for multiple sources of information on the Internet. Furthermore, in addition to getting news about the 9/11 attacks, they can search for background information, for example about Islam, the Taliban, or Afghanistan, to help make better sense of the events. These features may make the Internet an increasingly popular information source for future crises.

Third, situational factors also impact the choice of a medium to get information. If a crisis event occurs during working hours, individuals may have an easier time accessing the Internet than television. In contrast, if an event occurs in the morning, evening, or weekend hours, individuals are more likely to be at home, with easy access to television.

We also were struck by the differences in findings between the two content analyses of news. Mogensen et al.'s (Chap. 9) study showed television's initial responses to the attacks. During the first 8 hours of news coverage, they found stories that were primarily factual rather than analytical in nature and did not include identifiable sources. In contrast, the Dooley and Corman analysis covered 66 days of news wire articles and showed that after reporting initial information about the attacks, the focus of the news shifted to institutional responses as well as sense-making of the events. These differences suggest that content analyses of news events would be more meaningful if they spanned longer time periods. Taking into account the full range of news people have received over time is important when studying the impacts of these messages on audiences. Therefore, it also would be useful to analyze and compare concurrently a broader range of news media outlets—television, newspapers, and the Internet. A more complete mapping of the available information to which individuals are being exposed would be a superior approach. Related content forms (e.g., editorials, photographs, opinion columns) also are fair game for such analyses.

At the same time, the examinations of non-news content suggest interesting issues for future researchers. These studies of cartoon portrayals and displays of patriotism show that messages concerning crisis events can be found in many forms besides traditional news stories. Consider the various sources of information and commentary regarding the 9/11 attacks, ranging from public affairs programming to comedic portrayals, such as editorial cartoons or even comedians' monologues. What are the impacts of such portrayals? They are not created with the journalistic objectives that guide traditional news, yet it is likely that individuals use them to form impressions about the 9/11 attacks. For example, how do humorous portrayals of Osama bin Laden impact Americans' attitudes toward him? Do individuals find non-news portrayals of the events to be credible? By merging qualitative and quantitative approaches to studying these portrayals, we may develop a richer understanding of both the meaning of these messages and their effects.

References

ABC News.com. (2001). On children: Questions and answers. Retrieved October 30th, 2001 from http://moreabcnews.go.com/sections/living/dailynews/wtc.children.

Adams, J., Mullen, J., & Wilson, H. M. (1969). Diffusion of a "minor" foreign affairs news event. *Journalism Quarterly, 46,* 545–551.

Alexander, Y., & Latter, R. (Eds.). (1990). *Terrorism and the media. Dilemmas for government, journalists & the public.* Washington, DC: Brassey's Inc.

American Association of Editorial Cartoonists (2002, March 4). E-mail correspondence.

American Psychiatric Association. (1994). *Diagnostic and statistical manual of mental disorders* (4th ed.). Washington, DC: Author.

Anderson, B. (1991). *Imagined communities.* New York: Verso.

Anderson, D. R., Collins, P. A., Schmitt, K. L., & Smith-Jacobvitz, R. (1996). Stressful life events and television viewing. *Communication Research, 23,* 243–260.

Anthonisse, J. M. (1971, October). *The rush in a directed graph.* Amsterdam: Stichting Mathematisch Centrum.

Astor, D. (2002, February 4). A post-9/11 review of editorial cartooning. *Editor & Publisher, 135*(5), 31.

Babrow, A. (1990). Audience motivation, viewing context, media content, and form: The interactional emergence of soap opera entertainment. *Communication Studies, 41,* 343-361.

Baker, M., & O'Neill, A. (1993). *Stress and coping with disaster.* A handbook compiled for extension professionals following the Midwest flood of 1993. Jefferson City: State of Missouri.

Ball-Rokeach, S. J. (1985). The origins of individual media system dependency: A sociological framework. *Communication Research, 12,* 485-510.

Ball-Rokeach, S. J. (1998). A theory of media power and a theory of media use: Different stories, questions, and ways of thinking. *Mass Communication and Society, 1*(1/2), 5-40.

Ball-Rokeach, S. J., & DeFleur, M. L. (1976). A dependency model of mass-media effects. *Communication Research, 3*, 3–21.

Ball-Rokeach, S. J., Kim, Y., & Matei, S. (2001). Storytelling neighborhood: Paths to belonging in diverse urban environments. *Communication Research, 28*(4), 392–428.

Ball-Rokeach, S. J., Rokeach, M., & Grube, J. W. (1984). *The great American value test: Influencing behavior and belief through television.* New York: The Free Press.

Bandura, A. (1998). Mechanisms of moral disengagement. In W. Reich (Ed.), *Origins of terrorism: Psychologies, ideologies, and theologies, states of mind* (pp. 161–191). Washington, DC: Woodrow Wilson Center Press.

Banta, T. J. (1964). The Kennedy assassination: Early thoughts and emotions. *Public Opinion Quarterly, 28*, 216–232.

Bartels, L. M. (2000). Partisanship and voting behavior, 1952-1996. *American Journal of Political Science, 44*, 35-50.

Baruch, R. (1989, December 12). Importance of television (Washington, DC Metropolitan Cable Club Luncheon). C-SPAN Video Cassette Recording: P.120; Program: 87-1-12-12-1025; Tape 87-1-12-12-1000. West Lafayette, IN: Purdue University C-SPAN Archives.

Basil, M. D., & Brown, W. J. (1994). Interpersonal communication in news diffusion: A study of "Magic" Johnson's announcement. *Journalism Quarterly, 71*, 305-320.

Batson, C. D., Fultz, J., & Schoenrade, P. A. (1987). Distress and empathy: Two qualitatively distinct vicarious emotions with different motivational consequences. *Journal of Personality, 55*, 21–39.

Beaver, B. R. (1997). The role of emotion in children's selection of strategies for coping with daily stresses. *Merrill-Palmer Quarterly, 43*, 129–147.

Benoit, W. L., Kluykovski, A. A., McHale, J. P., & Airne, D. (2001). A fantasy theme analysis of political cartoons on the Clinton-Lewinsky-Starr affair. *Critical Studies in Mass Communication, 18*(4), 377–394.

Bentler, P. M. (1995). *EQS: Structural equations program manual.* Encino, CA: Multivariate Software.

Berson, I. R., & Berson, M. J. (2001). Helping children cope. *Social Education, 65*(6), 385–387.

Beutel, Ann M., & Marini, M. M. (1995). Gender and values. *American Sociological Review, 60*(3), 436–448.

Billings, R. S., Thomas W. M., & Schaalman, M. L. (1980). A model of crisis perception: A theoretical and empirical analysis. *Administrative Science Quarterly, 25*, 300–316.

Bird, S. E. (2002). It makes sense to us: Cultural identity in local legends of place. *Journal of Contemporary Ethnography, 31*(4).

Blendon, R. J., & Benson, J. M. (2001). Past to future. *The Public Perspective, 12*(6), 34.

Blumenberg, H. (1997). *Shipwreck with spectator: Paradigm of a metaphor for existence* (S. Rendall Trans.). Cambridge, MA: MIT Press. (Original work published 1979 as *Schiffbruch mit Zuschauer: Paradigma einer Daseinsmetapher*. Frankfurt: Suhrkamp)

Bocarnea, M. C. (2001). Mediated effects of celebrities: Cognitive and affective paths of processing information about Princess Diana's death. Unpublished doctoral dissertation, Regent University, Virginia Beach, VA.

Bodnar, J. (1992). *Remaking America: Public memory, commemoration, and patriotism in the twentieth century*. Princeton, NJ: Princeton University Press.

Bormann, E. G., Koester, J., & Bennett, J. (1978). Political cartoons and salient rhetorical fantasies: An empirical analysis of the '76 pres-idential campaign. *Communication Monographs, 48*(3), 317–329.

Boster, F. J., & Mongeau, P. (1984). Fear-arousing persuasive messages. In R. N. Bostrom (Ed.), *Communication Yearbook* (Vol. 8, pp. 330–375). Beverly Hills: Sage.

Bradac, J. J. (1989). Message effects in communication science. *Sage Annual Reviews of Communication Research, 17*, 7–9.

Brody, L. R., & Hall, J. A. (2000). Gender, emotion, and expression. In M. Lewis & J. M. Haviland-Jones (Eds.), *Handbook of emotions* (2nd ed., pp. 338–349). New York: Guilford Press.

Brookings/Harvard Forum. (2001, November 28). *What the public thinks of news coverage since Sept. 11*. The Brookings Institution: Washington, DC.

Brosius, B., & Holtz-Bacha, C. (1999). *The German yearbook of communication*. Cresskill, NJ: Hampton Press.

Brown, M. H., Skeen, P., & Osborn, D. K. (1979). Young children's perceptions of the reality of television. *Contemporary Education, 50*, 129–133.

Brown, W. J., Basil, M. D., & Bocarnea, M. C. (1998). *Involvement with an international celebrity: Public responses to the death of Princess Diana*. Paper presented at the annual meeting of the International Communication Association, Jerusalem.

Brown, W. J., Bocarnea, M. C., & Basil, M. D. (2001). *Public responses to the terrorist attacks on the U.S.* Paper presented at the annual conference of the National Communication Association, Atlanta, GA.

Brown, W. J., Duane, J. J., & Fraser, B. P. (1997). Media coverage and public opinion of the O.J. Simpson trial: Implications for the criminal justice system. *Communication Law and Policy, 2*, 261–287.

Bruner, E. M. (Ed.). (1984). *Text, play, and story: The construction and reconstruction of self and society* (pp. 1–16). Prospect Heights, IL: Waveland Press.

Burke, A., Heuer, F., & Reisberg, D. (1992). Remembering emotional events. *Memory & Cognition, 20*, 277–290.

Burke, E. (1901). On the sublime and beautiful. In *On taste. On the sublime and beautiful. Reflections on the French revolution. A letter to the noble lord* (pp. 29–148). New York: Collier. (Original work published 1756–57 as *A philosophical inquiry into the origin of our ideas of the sublime and the beautiful with several other addtions*)

Burleson, B. R. (1994). Comforting messages: Significance, approaches, and effects. In B. R. Burleson, T. L. Albrecht, & I. G. Sarason (Eds.), *Communication of social support: Messages, interactions relationships, and community* (pp. 3–28). Thousand Oaks, CA: Sage.

Bush, G. W. (2001a, October 7). Presidential address to the nation. [On-Line]. Available: http://www.whitehouse.gov/news/releases /2001/10/20011007-8.html.

Bush, G. W. (2001b, September 16). Remarks by the President upon arrival. [On-Line].

Cable Network News. (2001). Children need reassurance in face of tragedy. Retrieved September 13th, 2001, from http://fyi.cnn.com/ 2001/fyi/teachers.ednews/09/12/children.tragedy/index.html.

Cagle, D. (2001, September & October). Dayrl Cagle's Professional Cartoonist Index. [On-Line]. Available: http://cagle.slate.msn .com.

Cantor, J. (1998). *"Mommy, I'm scared": How TV and movies frighten children and what we can do to protect them.* San Diego: Harcourt Brace.

Cantor, J., Mares, M.-L., & Oliver, M. B. (1993). Parents' and children's emotional reactions to TV coverage of the Gulf War. In B. S. Greenberg & W. Gantz (Eds.), *Desert Storm and the mass media* (pp. 325–340). Cresskill, NJ: Hampton Press.

Cantor, J., & Reilly, S. (1982). Adolescents' fright reactions to television and films. *Journal of Communication, 46,* 139–152.

Cantor, J., & Sparks, G. G. (1984). Children's fear responses to mass media: Testing some Piagetian predictions. *Journal of Communication, 34*(2), 90–103.

Cantor, J., Wilson, B. J., & Hoffner, C. (1986). Emotional responses to a televised nuclear holocaust film. *Communication Research, 13,* 257–277.

Cappella, J. N., & Jamieson, K. H. (1997). *Spiral of cynicism: The press and the public good.* New York: Oxford University Press.

Castle, K., Beasley, L., & Skinner, L. (1996). Children of the heartland. *Childhood Education, 72,* 226–231.

CBS (2002). *Inside ground zero.* Available at: http://www.cbs.com/ primetime/9_11/.

Center for Gender Equality. (2002). Women are worried about terrorism— and personal finances. *Research Alert, 20*(1), 4.

Chilton, P. & Lakoff, G. (1995). Foreign policy by metaphor. In C. Schaffner & A. L. Wenden (Eds.), *Language and peace* (pp. 37–59). Amsterdam, The Netherlands: Harwood Academic.

Cocke, B., & McGarvey, K. (2001). *Connecting Californians, finding the art of community change: An inquiry into the role of story in strengthening communities.* San Francisco: The James Irvine Foundation.

Conners, J. L. (1998). Hussein as enemy: The Persian Gulf War in political cartoons. *Harvard International Journal of Press/Politics, 3*(3), 96–114.

Connerton, P. (1989). *How societies remember.* New York: Cambridge University Press.

Corman, S., Kuhn, T., McPhee, R., & Dooley, K. (2002). Studying complex discursive systems: Centering resonance analysis of organizational communication. *Human Communication Research, 28*(2), 157–206.

Coser, L. (1956). *The functions of social conflict*. New York: The Free Press.

Clymer, A. (1991, January 22). Poll finds deep backing while optimism fades. *The New York Times*.

Current Population Survey, (2000, March). (machine-readable data file) conducted by the Bureau of the Census for the Bureau of Labor Statistics. Washington, DC: Bureau of the Census (producer and distributor).

Daten zur Mediensituation in Deutschland. (2001). *Media Perspektiven*. Basisdaten.

Davis, M. (1992). *City of quartz: Excavating the future in Los Angeles*. New York: Vintage Books.

Dayan, D., & Katz, E. (1992). *Media events*. Cambridge, MA: Harvard University Press.

DeFleur, M. L. (1987). The growth and decline of research on the diffu-sion of news, 1945–1985. *Communication Research, 14*, 109–130.

Deledalle-Rhodes, J. (1997). Semiotics and ethics: The image of semiotics and semiotics of image. In W. Nöth (Ed.), *Semiotics of the media. State of the art, projects, and perspectives* (pp. 111–119). Berlin/New York: Mouton de Gruyter.

Dennis, E. E., Stebenne, D., Pavlik, J., Thalhimer, M., LaMay, C., Smillie, D., FitzSimon, M., Gazsi, S., & Rachlin, S. (1991). *The media at war: The press and the Persian Gulf conflict*. New York: Gannett Foundation.

DeSousa, M. A. (1984). Symbolic action and pretended insight: The Ayatollah Khomeini in U.S. editorial cartoons. In M. J. Medhurst & T. W. Benson (Eds.), *Rhetorical dimensions in media: A critical casebook* (pp. 204–230). Dubuque, IA: Kendall/Hunt.

DeSousa, M. A., & Medhurst, M. J. (1982). The editorial cartoon as visual rhetoric: Rethinking Boss Tweed. *Journal of Visual, Verbal Languaging, 2*(2), 43–52.

Deutschmann, P., & Danielson, W. (1960). Diffusion of knowledge of the major news story. *Journalism Quarterly, 37*, 345–355.

Dietz, P. (2002). The media and weapons of mass hysteria. Facsnet. Retrieved February 28, 2002, from http://www.facsnet.org/issues/specials/terrorism/dietz.php3.

Dillard, J. P., Kinney, T. A., & Cruz, M. G. (1996). Influence, appraisals, and emotions in close relationships. *Communication Monographs, 63*, 105–130.

Dillard, J. P., Plotnick, C. A., Godbold, L. C., Friemuth, V. S., & Edgar, T. (1996). The multiple affective outcomes of AIDS PSAs: Fear appeals do more than scare people. *Communication Research, 23*, 44–72.

Dooley, K., & Van de Ven, A. (1999), Explaining complex organization dynamics. *Organization Science, 10*(3), 358–372.

Dorr, A. (1983). No shortcuts to judging reality. In J. Bryant & D. R. Anderson (Eds.), *Chidren's understanding of television* (pp. 199–220). New York: Academic Press.

Duncan, J., & Ley, D. (1993). Introduction: Representing the place of culture. In J. Duncan & D. Ley (Eds.), *Place / culture / representation* (pp. 1–21). New York: Routledge.

Eckenrode, J. (Ed.). (1991). *The social context of coping*. New York: Plenum Press.

Edelman, M. (1971). *Politics as symbolic action: Mass arousal and quiescence*. Chicago: Markham.

Eimeren, V. B., & Ridder, C. (2001). Trends in der Nutzung und Bewertung von Medien 1970-2000. *Media Perspektiven* 11/2001, 538–553.

Elias, N. (1992). *Time: An essay*. Cambridge, MA: Blackwell.

Entman, R. M. (1991). Framing U. S. coverage of international news: Contras in narratives of the KAL and Iran air incidents. *Journal of Communication, 41*, 62–7.

Erikson, E. H. (1980). *Identity and the life cycle*. New York: Norton.

Featherstone, M. (1993). Global and local cultures. In J. Bird, B. Curtis, T. Putnam, G. Robertson, & L. Tickner (Eds.), *Mapping the futures: Local cultures, global change* (pp. 169-187). New York: Routledge.

Fedler, F., Bender, J. R., Davenport, L., & Kostyu, P. E. (1997). *Reporting for the media*. New York: Harcourt Brace College.

Fensch, T. (1990). *Associated Press coverage of a major disaster: The crash of Delta flight 1141*. Hillsdale, NJ: Erlbaum.

Finkel, K. (2001, September 12). *September 12 pages left a lasting impression*. American Press Institute (americanpressinstitute. com).

Finucane, M. O., & Horvath, C. W. (2000). Lazy leisure: A qualitative investigation of the relational uses of television in marriage. *Communication Quarterly, 48*, 311-321.

Fisher, S. (1986). *Stress & strategy*. Hillsdale, NJ: Erlbaum.

Foa, E. B., Cashman, L., Jaycox, L., & Perry, K. (1997). The validation of a self-report measure of posttraumatic stress disorder: The Post-traumatic Diagnostic Scale. *Psychological Assessment, 9*, 445-451.

Forsa. (2001). Survey: TV-Berichterstattung ueber die Terroranschlaege in den USA. Unpublished research report.

Frake, C. (1996). Pleasant places, past times and sheltered identity in rural East Anglia. In S. Feld & K. H. Basso (Eds.), *Senses of place* (pp. 229-258). Santa Fe, NM: School of American Research Press.

Fraser, M. (1973). *Children in conflict*. Harmondsworth: Penguin.

Freeman, L. C. (1979), Centrality in social networks: Conceptual clarification. *Social Networks, 1*, 215-239.

Frijda, N. H. (1993). The place of appraisal in emotion. *Cognition & Emotion, 7*, 357-387.

Frijda, N. H., Kuipers, P., & ter Schure, E. (1989). Relations among emotion, appraisal, and emotional action readiness. *Journal of Personality & Social Psychology, 57*, 212-228.

Fullerton, C. S., & Ursano, R. J. (1997). *Posttraumatic stress disorder: Acute and long-term responses to trauma and disaster*. Washington, DC: American Psychiatric Press.

Galea, S., Ahern, J., Resnick, H., Kilpatrick, D., Bucuvalas, M., Gold, J., & Vlahov, D. (2002). Psychological sequelae of the September 11 terrorist attacks in New York City. *New England Journal of Medicine, 346*, 982-987.

Gallup News Services. (2001). Personal impact on American's lives. Retrieved September 26, 2001 from http://www.gallup.com/Poll/releases/pr010914e.asp.

Galtung, J., & Ruge, M. H. (1965). The structure of foreign news. *Journal of Peace Research 2*, 64–91.

Gans, H. J. (1979). *Deciding what's news: A study of CBS Evening News, NBS Nightly News, Newsweek and Time.* New York: Vintage Books.

Gantz, W. (1983). The diffusion of news about the attempted Reagan assassination. *Journal of Communication, 33*, 56-66.

Gantz, W., & Greenberg, B. (1993). Patterns of diffusion and information seeking. In B. Greenberg & W. Gantz (Eds.), *Desert storm and the mass media* (pp. 166-181). Cresskill, NJ: Hampton Press.

Gantz, W., & Trenholm, S. (1979). Why people pass on news: Motivations for diffusion. *Journalism Quarterly, 56*(2), 365–370.

Gantz, W., Trenholm, S., & Pittman, M. (1976). The impact of salience and altruism on diffusion of news. *Journalism Quarterly, 53*, 727-732.

Geertz, C. (1996). Afterward. In S. Feld & K. H. Basso (Eds.), *Senses of place* (pp. 259-262). Santa Fe, NM: School of American Research Press.

Gilligan, C. (1982). *In a different voice.* Cambridge, MA: Harvard University Press.

Gilligan, C. (1993). *In a different voice.* Cambridge, MA: Harvard University Press.

Gilligan, C., Ward, J., & Taylor, J. (1988). *Mapping the moral domain.* Cambridge, MA: Harvard University Press.

Gillis, J. R. (1994). Memory and identity: The history of a relationship. In J. R. Gillis (Ed.), *Commemorations: The politics of national identity* (pp. 3-24). Princeton, NJ: Princeton University Press.

Glaser, B., & Strauss, A. (1967). *The discovery of grounded theory: Strategies for qualitative research.* Chicago: Aldine.

Gouran, D. S. (1982). *Making decisions in groups.* Glenview, IL: Scott, Foresman.

Gouran, D. S., Hirokawa, R. Y., & Martz, A .E. (1986). A critical analysis of factors related to decisional processes involved in the Challenger disaster. *Central States Speech Journal, 37*(3), 119–135.

Government Web sites see traffic after attacks. (200, September 21). Educause. Available online at http//:www.educause.edu.

Graber, D. A. (1980). *Mass media and American politics.* Washington, DC: Congressional Quarterly Press.

Graber, D. A. (1996). Say it with pictures. *Annals of the American Academy of Political & Social Science, 546*, 85–96.

Grassi, E. (1980). *Rhetoric as philosophy: The humanist tradition.* (J. M. Krois & A. Azodi, Trans.). University Park: Pennsylvania State University Press.

Green, B. L. (1996). Traumatic stress and disaster: Mental health effects and factors influencing adaptation. In F. L. Mak & C. C. Nadelson (Eds.), *International review of psychiatry* (Vol. 2, pp. 177–210). Washington, DC: American Psychiatric Press.

Green, B. L., Korol, M., Grace, M. C., Vary, M. G., Leonard, A. C., Gleser, G. C., & Smitson-Cohen, S. (1991). Children and disaster: Age, gender, and parental effects on PTSD symptoms. *Journal of the American Academy of Child and Adolescent Psychiatry, 30*, 945–951.

Greenberg, B. S. (1964a). Diffusion of news of the Kennedy assassination. *Public Opinion Quarterly, 28,* 225–232.

Greenberg, B. S. (1964b). Person-to-person communication in the diffusion of news events. *Journalism Quarterly, 41,* 489–494.

Greenberg, B. S., Brinton, J., & Farr, R. (1965). Diffusion of news about an anticipated major news event. *Journal of Broadcasting, 9*(2), 129–142.

Greenberg, B. S., Cohen, E., & Li, H. (1993). How the U.S. found out about the war. In B. Greenberg & W. Gantz (Eds.), *Desert storm and the mass media* (pp. 145–152). Cresskill, NJ: Hampton Press.

Greenberg, B. S., & Gantz, W. (Eds.). (1993). *Desert storm and the mass media.* Cresskill, NJ: Hampton Press.

Greenberg, B. S., Gantz, W., & Brand, J. (in press). Community embeddedness and the diffusion of local news. In B. Dervin, S. Chafee, & L. Foreman-Wernet (Eds.), *Communication, a different kind of horse race.* Cresskill, NJ: Hampton Press.

Greenberg, B. S., & Parker, E. (Eds.). (1965). *The Kennedy assassination and the American public: Social communication in crisis.* Stanford: Stanford University Press.

Grimes, T., & Meadowcroft, J. (1995). Attention to television and some methods for its measurement. *Communication Yearbook* (Vol. 18, pp. 133–161). Thousand Oaks, CA: Sage.

Gumpert, G., & Drucker, S. J. (1998). The mediated home in the global village. *Communication Research, 25*(4), 422–438.

Hall, S. (1997). Introduction. In S. Hall (Ed.), *Representation: Cultural representations and signifying practices* (pp. 1–11). Thousand Oaks, CA: Sage.

Hallman, W. K., & Wandersman, A. (1992). Attribution of responsibility and individual and collective coping with environmental threats. *Journal of Social Issues, 48*(4), 101–118.

Halliday, F. (1999). Manipulation and limits: Media coverage of the Gulf War, 1990-91. In T. Allen & J. Seaton (Eds.), *The media conflict: War reporting and representations of ethnic violence* (pp. 127–146). London: Zed Books.

Harvey, D. (1993). From space to place and back again: Reflections on the condition of postmodernity. In J. Bird, B. Curtis, T. Putnam, G. Robertson, & L. Tickner (Eds.), *Mapping the futures: Local cultures, global change* (pp. 3-29). New York: Routledge.

Hatfield, E., Cacioppo, J., & Rapson, R. (1994). *Emotional contagion.* New York: Cambridge University Press.

Haudhuri, A., & Buck, R. (1995). Media differences in rational and emotional responses to advertising. *Journal of Broadcasting and Electronic Media, 39,* 109-125.

Heeter, C., & Greenberg, B. S. (1988). *Cableviewing.* Norwood, NJ: Ablex.

Helzer, J. E., Robins, L. N., & McEvoy, L. (1987, December 24). Post-traumatic stress disorder in the general population: Findings of the epidemiologic catchment area survey. *New England Journal of Medicine, 317,* 1630–1634.

Henaff, M., & Strong, T. B. (Eds.). (2001). *Public space and democracy*. Minneapolis: University of Minnesota Press.

Hermann, C. F. (1963). Some consequences of crisis which limit the via-bility of organizations. *Administrative Science Quarterly, 8,* 61–82.

Hermon, S. J. (1990). The police, the media, and the reporting of terrorism. In Y. Alexander & R. Latter (Eds.), *Terrorism and the media. Dilemmas for government, journalists & the public* (pp. 37–41). Washington: Brassey's Inc.

Hickey, H. (2001). The election night that never ended. *Columbia Journalism Review, 40*(4), 128–129.

Hill, R. J., & Bonjean, C. M. (1964). News diffusion: A test of the regulatory hypothesis. *Journalism Quarterly, 41,* 336–342.

Hirschbury, P. L., Dillman, D. A., & Ball-Rokeach, S. J. (1986). Media system dependency theory: Responses to Mt. St. Helens. In S. J. Ball-Rokeach & M. G. Cantor (Eds.), *Media, audience, and social structure* (pp. 117–126). Beverly Hills, CA: Sage.

Hobsbawm, E. (1983). Introduction: Inventing traditions. In E. Hobsbawm & T. Ranger (Eds.), *The invention of tradition* (pp. 1–14). New York: Cambridge University Press.

Hoffner, C. (1995). Adolescents' coping with frightening mass media. *Communication Research, 22*(3), 325–346.

Hoffner, C. (1997). Children's emotional reactions to a scary film: The role of prior outcome information and coping style. *Human Communication Research, 23*(3), 323–341.

Hoffner, C., & Haefner, M. J. (1993a). Children's affective responses to news coverage of the war. In B. S. Greenberg & W. Gantz (Eds.), *Desert storm and the mass media* (pp. 364–380). Cresskill, NJ: Hampton Press.

Hoffner, C., & Haefner, M. J. (1993b). Children's strategies for coping with news coverage of the Gulf War. *Communication Research Reports, 10,* 171–180.

Hoffner, C., & Haefner, M. J. (1994). Children's news interest during the Gulf War: The role of negative affect. *Journal of Broadcasting & Electronic Media, 38,* 193–204.

Holzapfel, S. (2002). Kompetenz war gefragt. Online-Journalismus. *Message 3*(1), 48–49.

Horn, J. L., & Trickett, P. K. (1998). Community violence and child development: A review of research. In P. K. Trickett & C. J. Schellenbach (Eds.), *Violence against children in the family and the community*. Washington, DC: APA.

Hutchinson, T. H. (1948). *Here is television, your window on the world*. New York: Hastings House.

Ice, R. (1991). Corporate publics and rhetorical strategies. *Management Communication Quarterly, 4,* 341–362.

Irwin-Zarecka, I. (1994). *Frames of remembrance: The dynamics of collective memory*. New Brunswick, NJ: Transaction Publishers.

Ivie, R. L. (1980). Images of savagery in American justification for war. *Communication Monographs, 47,* 279–291.

Ivie, R. L. (1984). Speaking "common sense" about the Soviet threat: Reagan's rhetorical stance. *The Western Journal of Speech Communication, 48*, 39–50.

Ivie, R. L. (1996). Tragic fear and the rhetorical presidency: Combating evil in the Persian Gulf. In M. J. Medhurst (Ed.), *Beyond the rhetorical presidency* (pp. 153-178). College Station: Texas A&M University Press.

Izard, C. E. (1991). *The psychology of emotions.* New York: Plenum Press.

Javaratne, T. E., Flanagan, C., & Anderman, E. (1996). Predicting college student attitudes toward the Persian Gulf War: The role of gender and television exposure. *Peace & Conflict: Journal of Peace Psychology, 2*, 151-171.

Jennings, J., Geis, F.L., & Brown, V. (1980). Influence of television commercials on women's self confidence and independent judgement. *Journal of Personality and Social Psychology, 38*, 203-210.

Jersey, B., & Friedman, J. (Producers and Directors). (1987). Faces of the enemy [Film]. Berkeley, CA: Quest Productions.

Jewitt, C., & Oyama, R. (2001). Visual meaning: A social semiotic approach. In, Th. v. Leeuwen & C. Jewitt (Eds.). *Handbook of visual analysis* (pp. 134–156). London: Sage.

Johnstone, B. (1990). *Stories, community, and place: Narratives from middle America.* Bloomington: Indiana University Press.

Jöreskog, K. G., & Sörbom, D. (1989). *LISREL 7: A guide to the program and applications* (2nd ed.). Chicago: SPSS.

Jun, S. H., & Dayan, D. (1986). An interactive media event: South Korea's televised "family reunion." *Journal of Communication, 36*, 73–82.

Kammen, M. (1991). *Mystic chords of memory: The transformation of tradition in American culture.* New York: Alfred A. Knopf.

Kant, I. (1961). *Critique of judgement* (J.H. Bernard, Trans.). New York: Hafner. (Original work published 1790 as *Kritk der Urteilskraft*. Berlin: Lagarde & Friedrich)

Katz, E. (1980). Media events: The sense of occasion. *Studies in Visual Anthropology, 6*, 84–89.

Katz, E., Blumler, J. G., & Gurevitch, M. (1974). Utilization of mass communication by the individual. In J. G. Blumler & E. Katz (Eds.), *The uses of mass communications: Current perspectives on gratifications research* (pp. 19–32). Beverly Hills: Sage.

Katz, E., & Lazarsfeld, P. E. (1955). *Personal influence: The part played by people in the flow of mass communications.* Glencoe, IL: The Free Press.

Keane, T. J. (1998). Psychological and behavioral treatments of post-traumatic stress disorder. In P. E. Nathan & J. M. Gorman (Eds.), *A guide to treatments that work* (pp. 398-407). New York: Oxford University Press.

Keefer, B. (March 1, 2002). Quieting the homefront: Republicans equate mild war criticism with "aid and comfort to our enemies." In Salon.com. Retrieved on March 17, 2002, from http://salon.com /politics/col/ spinsanity/2002/03/01/lott/index.html.

Keen, S. (1984, February). Faces of the enemy. *Esquire, 101*, 67–72.

Keen, S. (1986). *Faces of the enemy: Reflections of the hostile imagination.* New York: Harper & Row.

Keen, S. (1991). *Faces of the enemy: Reflections of the hostile imagination* (2nd ed.). New York: HarperCollins.

Keen, S. (2001). The new face of the enemy. In Beliefnet (Ed.), *From the ashes: A spiritual response to the attack on America* (pp. 122–125). Emmaus, PA: Rodale.

Kiesler, S., & Kraut, R. (1999). Internet use and ties that bind. *American Psychologist, 54*(9), 783.

Kim, Y., Ball-Rokeach, S., Jung, J., & Loges, W. E. (2002, July). *Ethnicity, place, and communication technology: Geo-ethnic effect on multi-dimensional internet connectedness in urban communities.* Paper presented at the annual conference of the International Communication Association, Seoul, Korea.

Klingman, A. (2001). Israeli children's reactions to the assassination of the prime minister. *Death Studies, 25*(1), 33–50.

Kosterman, R., & Feshbach, S. (1989). Toward a measure of patriotic and nationalistic attitudes. *Political Psychology, 10*, 257–274.

Kubey, R. W., & Peluso, T. (1990). Emotional response as a cause of interpersonal news diffusion: The case of the space shuttle tragedy. *Journal of Broadcasting and Electronic Media, 34*, 69–76.

Kurtz, H. (2001, September 14). Television's endless disaster. *washingtonpost.com*. Retrieved June 8, 2002, from http://www.washingtonpost.com/wp-dyn/articles/A30086-2001Sep14.html.

Kushner, H.W. (1998). *Terrorism in America. A structured approach to understanding the terrorist threat.* Springfield, IL: Charles C. Thomas.

Lakoff, G. (1991). Metaphor and war: The metaphor system used to justify war in the Gulf. *Peace Research, 23*(2/3), 25–32.

Lakoff, G. (2001, September 16). Metaphor of terror. [On-Line]. Available: http://www.press.uchicago.edu/News/911lakoff.html.

Lakoff, G., & Johnson, M. (1980). *Metaphors we live by.* Chicago: University of Chicago Press.

Lang, A. (2000). The limited capacity model of mediated message processing. *Journal of Communication, 50*, 46–70.

Lang, A., Newhagen, J., & Reeves, B. (1996). Negative video as structure: Emotion, attention, capacity, and memory. *Journal of Broadcasting and Electronic Media, 40*, 460–477.

Lansch, M. (1981). Ling und Rechts in Wahrnehmung von Bildfolgen. In G. Bentele (Ed.), *Semiotik und massenmedien* (pp. 321–340). Müchen: Ölschläger.

Laqueur, W. (1999). *The new terrorism. Fanaticism and the arms of mass destruction.* New York & Oxford: Oxford University Press.

Larsen, O. N., & Hill, R. J. (1954). Mass media and interpersonal communication in the diffusion of a news event. *American Sociological Review, 19*, 426–433.

Lasswell, H. (1948). The structure and function of communication in society. In L. Bryson (Ed.), *The communication of ideas* (pp. 37–51). New York: Harper.

Laux, L., & Weber, H. (1991). Presentation of self in coping with anger and anxiety: An intentional approach. *Anxiety Research, 3*, 233–255.

Lazarus, R. S. (1991). *Emotion and adaptation*. New York: Oxford University Press.

Lazarus, R. S. (1999). *Stress and emotion: A new synthesis*. New York: Springer.

Lazarus, R. S., & Folkman, S. (1984). *Stress, appraisal, and coping*. New York: Springer.

Lecoeuche, R., Robertson, D., Barry, C., & Mellish, C. (2000). Evaluating focus theories for dialogue management. *International Journal of Human-Computer Studies, 52*, 23–76.

LeGoff, J. (1992). *History and memory*. New York: Columbia University Press.

Lemish, D. (1985). Soap opera viewing in college: A naturalistic inquiry. *Journal of Broadcasting & Electronic Media, 29*, 275–293.

Leventhal, H. (1984). A perceptual motor theory of emotion. In K. R. Scherer & P. Ekman (Eds.), *Approaches to emotion* (pp. 271–292). Hillsdale, NJ: Erlbaum.

Levi-Strauss, C. (1964). *The raw and the cooked*. New York: Harper & Row.

Lippard, L. R. (1997). *The lure of the local: Senses of place in a multi-centered society*. New York: The New Press.

Loges, W. E. (1994). Canaries in the coal mine: Perceptions of threat and media system dependency relations. *Communication Research, 21*(1), 5–23.

Lombard, M. (1995). Direct responses to people on the screen: Television and personal space. *Communication Research, 22*, 288–324.

Lonigan, C. J., Shannon, M. P., Taylor, C. M., Finch, A. J., & Sallee, F. R. (1994). Children exposed to disaster: II. Risk factors for the development of post-traumatic symptomatology. *Journal of the American Academy for Child and Adolescent Psychiatry, 33*, 94–105.

Luhmann, N. (1984). *Soziale Systemem*. Frankfurt: Suhrkamp.

Lule, J. (1990). Sacrifice and the body on the tarmac: Symbolic significance of U.S. news about a terrorist victim. In Y. Alexander & R. G. Picard (Eds.), *In the camera's eye. News coverage of terrorist events* (pp. 30–45). Washington, DC: Brassey's Inc.

Lull, J. (1980). The social uses of television. *Human Communication Research, 6*, 197-209.

Luminet, O., Bouts, P., Delie, F., Manstead, A. S. R., & Rime, B. (2000). Social sharing of emotion following exposure to a negatively valenced situation. *Cognition and Emotion, 14*, 661–688.

Markus, H., & Nurius, P. (1986). Possible selves. *American Psychologist, 41*, 954–969.

Mayer, M. E., Gudykunst, W. B., Perrill, N. K., & Merrill, B. D. (1990). A comparison of competing models of the news diffusion process. *Western Journal of Speech Communication, 54*, 113–123.

McChesney, R. (1997). *Corporate media and the threat to democracy*. New York: Seven Stories Press.

McGuire, A. J. (1985). Attitudes and attitude change. In G. Lindzey & E. Aronson (Eds.), *The handbook of social psychology: Vol. 2. Special fields and applications* (3rd ed., pp. 233–346). New York: Random House.

McLeod, D. M., Eveland, W. P., Jr., & Signorielli, N. (1994). Conflict and public opinion: Rallying effects of the Persian Gulf War. *Journalism Quarterly, 71*(1), 20–31.

McLeod, D., Perse, E., Signorielli, N., & Courtright, J. A. (1993). Public perceptions and evaluations of the functions of the media in the Persian Gulf War. In B. S. Greenberg & W. Gantz (Eds.), *Desert storm and the mass media* (pp. 197–212). Cresskill, NJ: Hampton Press.

McLeod, D. M., Perse, E. M., Signorielli, N., & Courtright, J. A. (1999). Public hostility toward freedom of expression during international conflicts: A case study of public opinion during the Persian Gulf War. *Free Speech Yearbook, 36*, 104–117.

McMahon, P. (2001, September 19). Civility and politeness bloom from tragedy's ashes. *USA Today*, p. D9.

Mendelsohn, H. (1964). Broadcast vs. personal sources of information in emergent public crises: The presidential assassination. *Journal of Broadcasting, 8*, 147–156.

Merton, R. K. (1968). *Social theory and social structure*. New York: The Free Press.

Meyers, G. C., & Holusha, J. (1986). *When it hits the fan: Managing the nine crises of business*. Boston: Houghton Mifflin.

Meyrowitz, J. (1985). *No sense of place*. London: Oxford University Press.

Miller, D. (1994). Understanding "terrorism": Contrasting audience interpretations of the televised conflict in Ireland. In M. Aldridge & N. Hewitt (Eds.), *Controlling broadcasting. Access policy and practice in North America and Europe* (pp. 69–89). Manchester: Manchester University Press.

Miller, D. C. (1945). A research note on mass communication: How our community heard about the death of President Roosevelt. *American Sociological Review, 10*, 691–694.

Miller, S. M. (1981). Predictability and human stress: Towards a clarification of evidence and theory. In L. Berkowitz (Ed.), *Advances in experimental social psychology* (pp. 204–256). New York: Academic Press.

Miller, S. M. (1987). Monitoring and blunting: Validation of a questionnaire to assess styles of information seeking under threat. *Journal of Personality and Social Psychology, 52*, 345–353.

Miller, S. M. (1990). To see or not to see: Cognitive information styles in the coping process. In M. Rosenbaum (Ed.), *Learned resourcefulness: On coping skills, self-control and adaptive behavior* (pp. 95–126). New York: Springer.

Miller, S. M. (1992a). Individual differences in the coping process: What to know and when to know it. In B. N. Carpenter (Ed.), *Personal coping: Theory, research and application* (pp. 77–91). Westport, CT: Praeger.

Miller, S. M. (1992b). Monitoring and blunting in the face of threat: Implications for adaptation and health. In L. Montada, S. Filipp, & M. J. Lerner (Eds.), *Life crises and experiences of loss in adulthood* (pp. 255–273). Hillsdale, NJ: Erlbaum.

Miller, S. M. (1996). Monitoring and blunting of threatening information: Cognitive interference and facilitation in the coping process. In I. G.

Sarason, G. R. Pierce, & B. R. Sarason (Eds.), *Cognitive interference: Theories, methods, and findings* (pp. 175-190). Hillsdale, NJ: Erlbaum.

Miller, S. M., & Grant, R. P. (1979), The blunting hypothesis: A view of predictability and human stress. In P. Sjoden, S. Bates, & W. S. Dockers, III (Eds.), *Trends in behavior therapy* (pp. 135-151). New York: Academic Press.

Mindak, W. H., & Hursh, G. D. (1965). Television's function on the assassination weekend. In B. S. Greenberg & E. B. Parker (Eds.), *The Kennedy assassination and the American public: Social communication in crisis* (pp. 1310-141). Stanford, CA: Stanford University Press.

Mitroff, I., Pauchant, P., & Shirvistava, P. (1988). Conceptual and empirical issues in the development of a general theory of crisis management. *Technological Forecasting and Social Change, 33,* 83–107.

Monaco, N., & Geier, E. (1987). Developmental level and children's responses to the explosion of the space shuttle Challenger. *Early Childhood Research Quarterly, 2,* 83–95.

Montgomery, D. (1996). *Statistical methods for quality control.* New York, Wiley.

Morland, L. A. (1999). The Oklahoma City bombing: An examination of the relationship between exposure to bomb-related television and posttraumatic stress symptoms following a disaster. Unpublished doctoral dissertation, Pepperdine University, Malibu, CA.

Morrison, D. E. (1992). *Television and the Gulf War.* London: John Libbey.

MSNBC (2002, February 2). 54 percent of U.S. now online. Retrieved March 1, 2002, from http://www.nua.ie/surveys/?f=VS&art _id=905357626 &rel=true.

Mueller, J. E. (1970). Presidential popularity from Truman to Johnson. *American Political Science Review, 64,* 18–34.

Muris, P., Merckelbach, H., Gadet, B., & Moulaert, V. (2000). Fears, worries, and scary dreams in 4- to 12-year-old children: Their content, developmental pattern, and origins. *Journal of Clinical Child Psychology, 29*(1), 43–52.

Muris, P., Steerneman, P., Merkelbach, H., & Meesters, C. (1996). Shorter communications: The role of parental fearfulness and modeling in children's fear. *Behavior, Research, and Theory, 14,* 265–268.

Murphy, L. B., & Moriarty, A. E. (1976). *Vulnerability, coping, and growth from infancy to adolescence.* New Haven, CT: Yale University Press.

Murphy, S. (1984). After Mount St. Helen's: Disaster stress research. *Journal of Psychosocial Nursing and Mental Health Services, 22*(7), 9–18.

Nabi, R. (1999). A cognitive-functional model for the effects of discrete negative emotions on information processing, attitude change, and recall. *Communication Theory, 9,* 292–320.

Nader, K. O., Pynoos, R. S., Fairbanks, L. A., Al-Ajeel, M., & Al-Asfour, A. (1993). A preliminary study of PTSD and grief among the children of Kuwait following the Gulf crisis. *British Journal of Clinical Psychology, 32,* 407–416.

Nathanson, A. I. (2001). Parent and child perspectives on the presence and meaning of parental television mediation. *Journal of Broadcasting & Electronic Media, 45*, 201–220.

Neal, A. G. (1998). *National trauma & collective memory: Major events in the American century.* New York: M. E. Sharpe.

Newhagen, J. E. (1998). TV news images that induce anger, fear, and disgust: Effects on approach-avoidance and memory. *Journal of Broadcasting and Electronic Media, 42*, 265–276.

Nora, P. (1996). *Realms of memory: The construction of the French past* (Vols. 1–3). New York: Columbia University Press.

Norton, A. (2001). Writing property and power. In M. Henaff & T. B. Strong (Eds.), *Public space and democracy* (pp. 189-200). Minneapolis: University of Minnesota Press.

Nyhan, B. (March 5, 2002). Bully brigade. Limbaugh, Novak and Hannity smack down dissenters: Dare to disagree? You're helping the enemy! In Salon.com. Retrieved on March 17, 2002, frmo http://salon.com/politics/col/spinsanity/2002/03/05/dissent/ index.html.

Ochman, J. M. (1996). The effects of nongender-role stereotyped, same-sex role models in storybooks on the self-esteem of children in grade three. *Sex Roles, 35*, 711–735.

O'Keefe, M. T., & Kissel, B. C. (1971). Visual impact: An added dimension in the study of news diffusion. *Journalism Quarterly, 48*, 298–303.

Owen, P. R. (1998). Fears of Hispanic and Anglo children: Real-world fears in the 1990's. *Hispanic Journal of Behavioral Sciences, 20*, 483–491.

Oyserman, D., & Markus, H. R. (1990). Possible selves and delinquency. *Journal of Personality and Social Psychology, 59*, 112–125.

Paris, S. G., & Upton, L. R. (1976). Children's memory for inferential relationships in prose. *Child Development, 47*, 660–668.

Parish, T. S., Bryant, W. T., & Prawat, R. S. (1977). Reversing effects of sexism in elementary school girls through counter conditioning. *Journal of Instructional Psychology, 4*, 11–16.

Pauchant, T. C., & Mitroff, I. I. (1992). *Transforming the crisis-prone organization.* San Francisco: Jossey-Bass.

Paxton, P. (1999). Is social capital declining in the United States? A multiple indicator assessment. *American Journal of Sociology, 108*, 88–127.

Peled, T., & Katz, E. (1974). Media functions in wartime: The Israel home front in October 1973. In J. G. Blumler & E. Katz (Eds.), *The uses of mass communication: Current perspectives on gratifications research* (pp. 49–69). Beverly Hills: Sage.

Peltu, M., (1985). The role of communication media. In H. Otway & M. Peltu (Eds.), *Regulating industrial risks: Science, hazards and public protection* (pp. 128–148). London: Butterworths.

Perrow, C. (1984). *Normal accidents.* New York: Basic Books.

Perry, S. (1983). Rhetorical funtions of the infestation metaphor in Hitler's rhetoric. *Central States Speech Journal, 34*, 229–235.

Perse, E. M. (1990). Involvement with local television news: Cognitive and emotional dimensions. *Human Communication Research, 16*, 556–581.

Perse, E. M. (2001). *Media effects and society.* Mahwah, NJ: Erlbaum.

Perse, E. M., & Courtright, J. A. (1993). Normative images of communication media: Mass and interpersonal channels in the new media environment. *Human Communication Research, 19*, 485–503.

Pettey, G. R., Perloff, R. M., Neuendorf, K. A., & Pollick, B. (1986). Feeling and learning about a critical event: The shuttle explodes. *Central States Speech Journal, 37*(3) 166–179.

Pew Research Center. (2001a). Attack at home draws more interest than war abroad. www.peoplepress.org, October 22, 2001.

Pew Research Center (2001b). Terror coverage boosts news media's image. <http://www.people-presss.org/reports/display.php3? reportID=143, November 28, 2001

Pew Research Center. (2002, February 23). American psyche reeling from terror attacks. <http://www.people-press.org/reports/display.php3?reportID=3.html> February 28, 2002.

Pfefferbaum, B., Nixon, S. J., Krug, R. S., Tivis, R., Moore, V., Brown, J., Pynoos, R., Foy, D., & Gurwitch, R. (1999). Clinical needs assessment of middle and high school students following the 1995 Oklahoma City bombing. *American Journal of Psychiatry, 156*, 1069–1074.

Pfefferbaum, B., Seale, T. W., McDonald, N. B., Brandt, E. N., Rainwater, S. M., Maynard, B. T., Meierhoefer, B., & Miller, P. D. (2000). Posttraumatic stress two years after the Okalahoma City bombing in youths geographically distant from the explosion. *Psychiatry, 63*, 358–370.

Poole, M., Van de Ven, A., Dooley, K., & Holmes, M. (2000). *Organizational change and innovation process: Theory and methods for research.* New York: Oxford University Press.

Prost, A., & Vincent, G. (Eds.). (1991). *A history of private life: Riddles of identity in modern times.* Cambridge, MA: Belknap Press.

Putnam, R. D. (1995). Tuning in, tuning out: The strange disappearance of social capital in America. *PS: Political Science & Politics, 284*, 664–683.

Putnam, R. D. (2000). *Bowling alone: The collapse and revival of American community.* New York: Simon & Schuster.

Putnam, R. D. (2002, February 11). Bowling together. *The American Prospect, 13*(3), 20–22.

Pynoos, R. S., Frederick, C., Nader, K., Arroyo, W., Steinberg, A., Eth, S., Nunez, F., & Fairbanks, L. (1987). Life threat and posttramatic stress in school-age children. *Archives of General Psychiatry, 44*, 1057–1063.

Quarantelli, E. I. (1988). Disaster crisis management: A summary of research findings. *Journal of Management Studies, 25*, 273–385.

Quarles, R. L., Jeffres, L. W., Sanchez-Ilundian C., & Neuwirth, K. (1983). News diffusion of assassination attempts on President Reagan and Pope John II. *Journal of Broadcasting, 27*(4) 387–394.

Raphael, B. (1986). *When disaster strikes.* New York: Basic Books.

Ray, S. (1999). *Strategic communication in crisis management.* Westport, CT: Quorum.

Reardon, K. K., & Rogers, E. M. (1988). Interpersonal versus mass media communication: A false dichotomy. *Human Communication Research, 15*, 284–303.

Resnick, H. S., Kilpatrick, D. G., Dansky, B. S., Saunders, B. E., & Best, C. L. (1993). Prevalence of civilian trauma and posttraumatic stress disorder in a representative national survey of women. *Journal of Consulting and Clinical Psychology, 61*, 984–991.

Reuters. (2001). http://about.reuters.com/investormedia/ company_info/index.asp.

Richardson, L. (1990). Narrative and sociology. *Journal of Contemporary Ethnography, 19*, 116–135.

Ridder, C. et al. (2001). Daten zur Mediensituation in Deutschland 2001. *Media Perspektiven.* Basidaten.

Riffe, D., Lacy, S., & Fico, F. (1998). *Analyzing media messages: Using quantitative content analysis in research.* Mahwah, NJ: Erlbaum.

Riffe, D., & Stovall, J. G. (1989). Diffusion of news of the shuttle disaster: What role for emotional response? *Journalism Quarterly, 66*, 551–560.

Rime, B., Finkenauer, C., Luminet, O., Zech, E., & Philippot, P. (1998). Social sharing of emotion: New evidence and new questions. *European Review of Social Psychology, 9*, 145–189.

Roeser, J., & Schaefer, G. (2001). Wahrnehmung von Politikberichter stattung. Unpublished interim report, University of Bochum.

Rogers, E. M. (2000). Reflections on news event diffusion research. *Journalism and Mass Communication Quarterly, 77*(3), 561–576.

Roper Center for Public Opinion Research. (2002). Posttraumatic stress two years after the Oklahoma City bombing in youths geographically distant from the explosion. *Psychiatry, 63*, 358–370.

Roseman, I. J., & Smith, C. A. (2001). Appraisal theory: Overview, assumptions, varieties, controversies. In K. R. Scherer, A. Schorr, & T. Johnstone (Eds.), *Appraisal processes in emotion: Theory, methods, research* (pp. 3–19). New York: Oxford University Press.

Roseman, I. J., Wiest, C., & Swartz, T. S. (1994). Phenomenology, behaviors, and goals differentiate discrete emotions. *Journal of Personality & Social Psychology, 67*, 206–221.

Rosengren, K. E. (1973). News diffusion: An overview. *Journalism Quarterly, 50*, 83–91.

Rosengren, K. E. (1987). The comparative study of news diffusion. *European Journal of Communication, 2*, 227–255.

Ross, D. (Ed.). (2001). Front lines and deadlines: Perspectives on war reporting. *Media Studies Journal, 15*(1). Arlington, VA: The Freedom Forum.

Royer, S. (2001). *Life through the eyes of children in middle childhood* (APA symposium). San Francisco: CA.

Rubin, A. M. (1994). Media uses and effects: A uses and gratifications perspective. In J. Bryant & D. Zillmann (Eds.), *Media effects: Advances in theory and research* (pp. 417–436). Hillsdale, NJ: Erlbaum.

Rubin, A. M., Perse, E. M., & Powell, R. A. (1985). Loneliness, parasocial interaction, and local television news viewing. *Human Communication Research, 12*, 155–180.

Rubin, A. M., & Rubin, R. B. (2001). Interface of personal and mediated communication: Fifteen years later. *The Electronic Journal of Communication, 11*(1).

Rubin, A. M., & Step, M. M. (2000). Impact of motivation, attraction, and parasocial interaction on talk radio listening. *Journal of Broadcasting & Electronic Media, 44*, 635–654.

Rubin, R. B., Perse, E. M., & Barbato, C. A. (1988). Conceptualization and measurement of interpersonal communication motives. *Human Communication Research, 14*, 602–628.

Saarni, C. (1997). Coping with aversive feelings. *Motivation and Emotion, 21*, 45–63.

Sampson, R. J., Raudenbush, S. W., & Earls, F. (1997). Neighborhoods and violent crime: A multilevel study of collective efficacy. *Science, 277*, 918–924.

Schaalman, W. (1965). Communication in crisis. In B. S. Greenberg & E. B. Parker (Eds.), *The Kennedy assassination and the American public: Social communication in crisis* (pp. 1–25). Stanford, CA: Stanford University Press.

Scherer, K. R. (1993). Studying the emotion-antecedent appraisal process: An expert system approach. *Cognition & Emotion, 7*, 325–355.

Scherer, K. R., Schorr, A., & Johnstone, T. (2001). *Appraisal processes in emotion: Theory, methods, research.* New York: Oxford University Press.

Schorr, A. (2001). Appraisal: The evolution of an idea. In K. R. Scherer, A. Schorr, & T. Johnstone (Eds.), *Appraisal processes in emotion: Theory, methods, research* (pp. 20–34). New York: Oxford University Press.

Schuster, M. (2002, January 4). A national survey of stress reactions after the Sept. 11, 2001 terrorist attacks. *Research Alert, 20*, 1, 5.

Schuster, M. A., Stein, B. D., Jaycox, L. H., Collins, R. L., Marshall, G. N., Elliott, M. N., Zhou, A.J., Kanouse, D. E., Morrison, J. L., & Berry, S.H. (2001). A national survey of stress reactions after the September 11, 2001, terrorist attacks. *New England Journal of Medicine, 345*, 1507–1512.

Schwartz, D. A. (1973). How fast does news travel? *Public Opinion Quarterly, 37*, 625–627.

Schwarz, E. D., & Kowalski, J. M. (1991). Malignant memories: PTSD in children and adults after a school shooting. *Journal of the American Academy for Child and Adolescent Psychiatry, 30*, 936–944.

Scott, W. A. (1955). Reliability of content analysis: The case of nominal scale coding. *Public Opinion Quarterly, 19*, 321–325.

Seeger, M. W. (1986). The Challenger tragedy and search for legitimacy. *Central States Speech Journal, 37*, 147–157.

Seeger, M. W., & Bolz, B. (1996). Technological transfer and multinational corporations in the Union Carbide Crisis Bhopal, India. In J. Jaksa & M. Pritchard (Eds.), *Responsible communication: Ethical issues in business, industry, and the professions* (pp. 245–265). Cresskill, NJ: Hampton Press.

Seeger, M. W., Sellnow, T., & Ulmer, R. R. (1998). Communication organization and crisis. In M. E. Roloff (Ed). *Communication Yearbook* (Vol. 21, pp. 221–237). Thousand Oaks, CA: Sage.

Sellnow, T., & Seeger, N. W. (2001). Exploring the boundaries of crisis communication: The case of the 1997 Red River Valley flood. *Communication Studies, 42*(2), 153–167.

Sellnow, T., Seeger, M. W., & Ulmer, R. R. (in press). Chaos theory, informational needs, and natural disasters. *Journal of Applied Communication Research.*

Sellnow, T. L., & Ulmer, R. R. (1995). Ambiguous argument as advocacy in organizational crisis communication. *Argumentation and Advocacy, 31,* 138–150.

Shalev, A. Y. (2000). Measuring outcome in posttraumatic stress disorder. *Journal of Clinical Psychiatry, 61*[supplement 5], 33–39.

Shapiro, R., & Mahajan, H. (1986). Gender differences in policy preferences: A summary of trends from the 1960s to the 1980s. *Public Opinion Quarterly, 50,* 42–61.

Shaver, P., & Klinert, M. (1982). Schachter's theories of affiliation and emotion: Implications of developmental research. *Review of Personality and Social Psychology, 3,* 37–71.

Shore, B. (1996). *Culture in mind: Cognition, culture, and the problem of meaning.* New York: Oxford University Press.

Siegel, R. S. (1965). Television and the reactions of schoolchildren to the assassination. In B. S. Greenberg & E. Parker (Eds.), *The Kennedy assassination and the American public* (pp. 199–219). Stanford, CA: Stanford University Press.

Simons, R. F., Detenber, B. H., Roedema, T. M., & Reiss, J. E. (1999). Emotion processing in three systems: The medium and the message. *Psychophysiology, 37,* 619–627.

Singletary, M. (1994). *Mass communication research: Contemporary methods and applications.* New York: Longman.

Sleek, S. (1998) After the storm, children play out fears. *APA Monitor, 29*(6), 1–3.

Smith, D. W., Christiansen, E. H., Vincent, R., & Hann, N. E. (1999, April). Population effects of the bombing of Oklahoma City. *Journal of the Oklahoma State Medical Association, 92,* 193–198.

Smith, S. L., Suding, P., Boyson, A., Moyer, E., & Pieper, K. M. (2001). *Teachers' perceptions of their students fear responses to September 11th, 2001.* Paper presented at the annual conference of the National Communication Association, Atlanta, GA.

Smith, S. L., & Wilson, B. J. (2000). Children's reactions to a television news story: The impact of video footage and proximity of the crime. *Communication Research, 27,* 641–673.

Smith, S. L., & Wilson, B. J. (2002). Children's comprehension of and fear reactions to television news. *Media Psychology, 4,* 1–26.

Smith, T. (1984). The polls: Gender and attitudes toward violence. *Public Opinion Quarterly, 48,* 384–396.

Snyder, L. B., & Park, C. L. (2002a). *Post-traumatic stress disorder symptoms among U.S. adults after the September 11, 2001 terrorist attacks.* Manuscript in preparation.

Snyder, L. B., & Park, C. L. (2002b, July). *Stress and media exposure to the September 11, 2001 attacks.* Paper presented at the annual meeting of the International Communication Association, Seoul, South Korea.

Solomon, S. D., & Green, B. L. (1992). Mental health effects of natural and human-made disasters. *PTSD Research Quarterly, 3*(1), 1–3.

Sparks, G. G. (1986). Developmental differences in children's reports of fear induced by the mass media. *Child Study Journal, 16,* 55–66.

Sparks, G. G. (1989a). The prevalence and intensity of fright reactions to mass media: Implications of the activation-arousal view. *Communication Quarterly, 37,* 108–117.

Sparks, G. G. (1989b). Understanding emotional reactions to a suspenseful movie: The interaction between forewarning and preferred coping style. *Communication Monographs, 56,* 325–340.

Sparks, G. G., & Spirek, M. M. (1988). Individual differences in coping with stressful mass media: An activation-arousal view. *Human Communication Research,* 195–216.

Sparks, G. G., Spirek, M. M., & Hodgson, K. (1993). Individual differences in arousability: Implications for understanding immediate and lingering emotional reactions to frightening mass media. *Communication Quarterly, 41*(4), 465–476.

Spigel, L. (1992). The suburban home companion: Television and the neighborhood ideal in postwar America. In B. Colomina (Ed.), *Sexuality and space* (pp. 185-217). Princeton, NJ: Princeton Architectural Press.

Spirek, M. M. (1992). The impact of children's coping style on emotional reactions to a frightening movie. Unpublished doctoral dissertation, Purdue University, West Lafayette, IN.

Star, S. L., & Bowker, G. C. (2002). How to infrastructure. In L. A. Lievrouw & S. M. Livingstone (Eds.), *Handbook of new media: Social shaping and consequences of ICTs* (pp. 151–162). Thousand Oaks, CA: Sage.

Steinfatt, T., Gantz, W., Siebold, D., & Miller, L., (1973, December) News diffusion of the George Wallace shooting: The apparent lack of interpersonal communication as an artifact of delayed measurement. *Quarterly Journal of Speech,* 401–411.

Stempel, G. H., III, Hargrove, T., & Bernt, J. P. (2000). Relation of growth of use of the Internet to changes in media use from 1995 to 1999. *Journalism & Mass Communication Quarterly, 77*(1), 71–79.

Step, M. M. (1998). An emotional appraisal model of media involvement, uses and effects (Doctoral dissertation, Kent State University, 1998). *Dissertation Abstracts International, 60,* 15.

Stone, R. A., & Levine, A. G. (1985). Reactions to collective stress: Correlates of active citizen participation at Love Canal. *Prevention in Human Services, 4*(1–2), 153–177.

Strasburger, V., & Wilson, B. J. (2002). *Children, adolescents and the media.* Beverly Hills, CA: Sage.

Talbot, D. (2001, September 29). Democracy held hostage. Salon.com. Retrieved January 1, 2002, from http://www.salon.com/news/feature/2001/09/29/democracy/print.html.

Tamborini, R., & Stiff, J. (1987). Predictors of horror film attendance and appeal: An analysis of audience for frightening films. *Communication Research, 14*, 415–436.

Tamborini, R., Stiff, J., & Zillmann, D. (1987). Preference for graphic horror featuring male verses female victimization. *Human Communication Research, 13*, 529–552.

Tapscott, D. (1998). *Growing up digital: The rise of the net generation.* New York: McGraw-Hill.

Tardy, R. W., & Hale, C. L. (1998). Getting plugged in: A network analysis of health information seeking among stay-at-home moms. *Communication Monographs, 65*, 336–357.

Tassey, J. (1996). Coping with the aftermath of disaster. American Psychological Association. Available: http://helping.apa.org/daily/tassey.html.

Terr, L. C., Bloch D. A., Michel, B. A., Shi, H., Reinhardt, J. A., & Metayer, S. (1997). Children's thinking in the wake of Challenger. *American Journal of Psychiatry, 154*, 744–751.

Terr, L. C., Bloch D. A., Michel, B. A., Shi, H., Reinhardt, J. A., & Metayer, S. (1999). Children's symptoms in the wake of Challenger: A field study of distant-traumatic effects and an outline of related conditions. *American Journal of Psychiatry, 156*, 1536–1544.

Toller, M. (2001). Americans turn to TV in crisis: The impact of 9/11 on current and future viewing levels. *Empower Media Marketing Impact, 3*(5). Available at: http://www.imakenews.com/empower/e_article000045955.cfm.

Tomkins, S. S. (1984). Affect theory. In K. R. Scherer & P. Ekman (Eds.), *Approaches to emotion* (pp. 163–195). Hillsdale, NJ: Erlbaum.

Tuan, Y-F. (1991). Language and the making of place: A narrative-descriptive approach. *Annals of the Association of American Geographers, 81*, 684–696.

Tucker, D. M., & Williamson, P. A. (1984). Asymmetric neural control systems in human self-regulation. *Psychological Review, 91*, 185–216.

Turner, B. (1976). The organizational and interorganizational development of disasters. *Administrative Science Quarterly, 21*, 378–397.

TV Today. (2001, October 12). TV–Berichterstattung über die Terroranschläge auf die USA. *TV Today* 22/2001.

University of Michigan. (2001), October 9). *How America responds, Part 2.* Press release. http:/www.umich.edu/~newsinfo/releases/ Oct01/ r100901b.html.

Uricchio, W. (2001). Television conventions. In *Television Archive.* Retrieved November 27, 2001, from http://tvnews3.television archive.org/ tvarchive/html/article_wu1.html.

van der Voort, T. H. A., van Lil, J. E., & Vooijs, M. W. (1993). Parent and child emotional involvement in the Netherlands. In B. S. Greenberg & W. Gantz (Eds.). *Desert storm and the mass media* (pp. 341–352). Cresskill, NJ: Hampton Press.

Walker, J. L., Jr. (1991). *Mobilizing interest groups in America: Patrons, professions, and social movements.* Ann Arbor: University of Michigan Press.

Warburton, L. A., Fishman, B., & Perry, S. W. (1997). Coping with the possibility of testing HIV-positive. *Personality and Individual Differences, 22*(4), 459–464.

Warren, M. (1998). Community building and political power. *The American Behavioral Scientist, 42*(1), 78–92.

Weber, R. P. (1990). *Basic content analysis.* Thousand Oaks, CA: Sage.

Weick, K. (1988). Enacted sensemaking in a crisis situation. *Journal of Management Studies, 25,* 305–317.

Weick, K. E. (1993). The collapse of sensemaking in organizations: The Mann Gulch disaster. *Administrative Science Quarterly, 38,* 628–652.

Weigel, M. (2001). Terrorism and the sublime. Or why we keep watching. In *Television Archive.* Retrieved November 27, 2001, from http://tvnews3.televisionarchive.org/tvarchive/html/article _mw1.html.

White, E. (2001, September 21). CNN whups butt in cable news race. *Media Life* [online newsletter]. Available: http://www.medialife magazine.com.

Wiebersiek, K. (2002). Run auf die Information. *Message, 3*(1), 44–47.

Wiggins, R. W. (2001). The effects of September 11 on the leading search engine. *First Monday, 7*(10), Available at: http://www.firstmonday.dk/issues/issue6_10/wiggins/.

Wilkens, L., & Patterson, P. (1987). Risk analysis and the construction of news. *Journal of Communication, 37*(3), 80–92.

Wilkinson, P. (1990). Terrorism and propaganda. In Y. Alexander & R. Latter (Eds.), *Terrorism and the media. Dilemmas for government, journalists & the public* (pp. 26–33). Washington, DC: Brassey's Inc.

Williams, M. (1991, February 18). The battle and the sexes. *The Washington Post*, Section C.1.

Wober, M., & Young, B. M. (1993). British children's knowledge of, emotional reactions to, and ways of making sense of the war. In B. S. Greenberg & W. Gantz (Eds.), *Desert Storm and the mass media* (pp. 381–394). Cresskill, NJ: Hampton Press.

Wright, C. R. (1986). *Mass communication: A sociological perspective* (3rd ed.). New York: Random House.

Wright, J. C., Kunkel, D., Pinon, M., & Huston, A. C. (1989). How children reacted to televised coverage of the Space Shuttle disaster. *Journal of Communication, 39*(2), 27–45.

Wyatt, R. O., Katz, E., & Kim, J. (2000). Bridging the spheres: Political and personal conversation in public and private spaces. *Journal of Communication, 50*(1), 71–92.

Young, P., & Jesser, P. (1997). *The media and the military.* New York: St. Martin's Press.

Zillmann, D., & Bryant, J. (1994). Entertainment as media effect. In J. Bryant & D. Zillmann (Eds.), *Media effects: Advances in theory and research* (pp. 437–461). Hillsdale, NJ: Erlbaum.

Zoellner, L. A., Sacks, M. B., & Foa, E. B. (2001). Stability of emotions for traumatic memories in acute and chronic PTSD. *Behavior, Research, and Therapy, 39,* 697–711.

Author Index

Subject Index